LIVES OF SAINTS

BOOK TWO

WITH EXCERPTS FROM THEIR WRITINGS

Selected
and
Illustrated

EDITED BY FATHER LOUIS F. HARTMAN, C.SS.R.

JOHN J. CRAWLEY & CO., INC.

NEW YORK

NIHIL OBSTAT   John P. Lerhinan, C.SS.R.
Censor Deputatus

IMPRIMI POTEST   James T. Connolly, C.SS.R.
Provincial Superior
August 15, 1962
The Assumption of the
Blessed Virgin

† † † †

NIHIL OBSTAT   John A. Goodwine, J.C.D.
Censor Librorum

IMPRIMATUR ✠ Francis Cardinal Spellman
Archbishop of New York
September 8, 1962
The Nativity of the
Blessed Virgin

Contents

CONTENTS

Illustrations

Acknowledgments

For the right to include the copyrighted items in this volume, the publisher is indebted to the following:

Biblioteca Apostolica Vaticana (Reparto Fotografico), Vatican City—Rome, for the autograph letters of Saints Robert Bellarmine and Peter Canisius.

Burns & Oates Ltd., for the selections from Saint John of the Cross' *Ascent of Mount Carmel* as translated by E. Allison Peers in Volume I of *The Complete Works of Saint John of the Cross.*

Charles Scribner's Sons, for the selections from Saint John Chrysostom's *46th Homily on the Gospel according to Saint John* from the translation by the Rev. Philip Schaff in Volume XIV of *The Nicene and Post-Nicene Fathers, First Series;* and for the selections from Saint John Chrysostom's *First Sermon on Eutropius* from the translation by the Rev. W.R.W. Stephens in Volume IX of *The Nicene and Post-Nicene Fathers, First Series.*

D. & J. Sadlier & Co., for the selections from *Revelations of Saint Bridget of Sweden.*

Fathers of the Church, Inc., for the selections from Saint Basil's *Homily on Humility* as translated by Sister M. Monica Wagner, C.S.C. in the volume *Saint Basil—Ascetical Works;* for the selections from the *Letter to the Corinthians by Saint Clement of Rome* as translated by the Rev. Francis X. Glimm in the volume *The Apostolic Fathers;* and for the selections from *On the Trinity* by Saint Hilary of Poitiers as translated by the Rev. Stephen McKenna, C.SS.R., in the volume *Saint Hilary of Poitiers: The Trinity.*

Redemptorist Fathers, for the selections from *The Passion and Death of Jesus Christ* taken from *The Complete Works of Alphonsus de Liguori (The Ascetical Works).*

* * *

Grateful acknowledgment is made to the following organizations for the right to reproduce the illustrations in this volume: American Archives of World Art, Inc., Barton-Cotton, Inc., Camera Clix, The Metropolitan Museum of Art, and Three Lions, Inc.

Introduction

WHO ARE THE saints, and why should we know more about them? The English word "saint" is derived from the Latin word *sanctus,* meaning "holy." In the New Testament this word is used as a snyonym for "Christian." All those who through faith and baptism are united to Christ share in His divine holiness, and therefore are rightly entitled to be spoken of as "the saints" or the holy ones. It is in this sense, too, that all who are in heaven can rightly be called "saints." To honor all these holy souls the Church celebrates the solemn feast of All Saints on the first of November.

Ordinarily, however, this word is now used in the restricted sense as referring to those extremely holy men and women who share in God's holiness to an extraordinary degree. The "saints" in this sense are those men and women who have led such outstandingly holy lives on earth that the fact of their now being in heaven, and indeed in a very high place in heaven, cannot be doubted.

At the end of the *Gloria* at Mass the Church says of Christ, *Quoniam Tu solus sanctus*—"For Thou alone art holy." Creatures can have holiness or sanctity only as a free gift from God; no one can become holy by his own efforts. In honoring the saints, therefore, we are really rendering praise to God for having given such great grace to His creatures.

Yet this honor rightly redounds to the saints, too. God does not force His gifts on anyone; divine grace requires the cooperation of man's free will. The saints, then, are those heroes and heroines of the Faith who fully cooperated with the great graces that God bestowed on them. While we speak of them as having practised all the virtues "to an heroic degree," we should not

forget that they owed everything to God Who assisted them by
His grace from beginning to end. They themselves would be the
first to proclaim this truth, as the Blessed Virgin Mary, the
greatest of all God's saints, says in her Magnificat, "He who is
mighty has done great things for me, and holy is *His* name."

Though all the saints have in common this characteristic of
sharing in God's holiness, they differ among themselves in the
manner in which this divine sanctity is made manifest in their
lives. There are, for instance, the martyrs who showed the divine
sanctity that was in them by laying down their lives for the sake
of Christ. Even if we know no more about a man than that he
was a genuine martyr we can be certain that he is a true saint. As
a matter of fact, nothing is known about many of the early
martyrs except their names. Some of these martyrs had later
"legends" or spurious "acts" written about them, and even
though these stories may be devoid of historical worth they still
have value in telling us of the simple devotion which later generations had for these martyrs.

The Church honors some men and women as saints to whom
this honor may seem at times to us to be given more on account
of the great service that they rendered to the Church than on account of their own personal virtues. Yet it is surely reasonable to
assume that God would not have enabled them to be so useful to
the Church unless the holiness of their personal lives were in
keeping with the mission given them by God.

In the early ages of the Church the saints were generally
recognized and proclaimed as such by what we might call "popular opinion." The faithful knew a saint when they saw one; the
Holy Spirit who abides in the members of Christ's Mystical Body
would keep them from judging wrongly in this matter. However,
during the course of the Middle Ages the Church evolved a more
elaborate process for judging that someone was really a saint.
Within the last few centuries this process has been minutely
regulated by the laws of the Church. Ordinarily the matter now
proceeds as follows.

Some time after the death of one who is widely regarded as having lived a very holy life, the reputation for sanctity which this one enjoys is examined before a local tribunal or "diocesan court," as it is called. If the case is considered worthy of being pursued further, all the evidence from witnesses, written documents, and so forth is gathered together and submitted to a special ecclesiastical court in Rome set up for the purpose of judging such cases. When it is proved to the satisfaction of this court that the one in question has truly practised to an heroic degree the various virtues of a Christian life, that is, the theological virtues of faith, hope, and charity, and the cardinal virtues of prudence, justice, fortitude and temperance, this person is given the title of "Venerable," and the process can then advance to the stage where the Pope "beatifies," that is, declares "blessed" or in heaven, the one whose virtues have been pronounced as heroic.

Moreover, the Church wishes that God Himself should concur in this decision, and therefore before anyone is beatified, it is necessary to prove that at least two unquestionable miracles, usually miraculous cures, have been wrought by God through the intercession of the candidate for beatification. Beatification is sometimes spoken of as "being raised to the altar" because only one who has been beatified may have his statue on a public altar in church and may have a special Mass said in his honor.

While beatification grants only limited honors to one who has led an heroically holy life, canonization gives him the full honors of the Church. To obtain the canonization of one who has been beatified, two new miracles must be proved as wrought through his intercession since the time he was declared "blessed." Only in connection with the beatification and canonization of genuine martyrs does the Church dispense with the need of such miracles. The term "canonization" means literally having one's name added to the "canon" or official "list" of the saints. In canonizing a saint the Church speaks with her infallible authority; hence, the fact that a canonized saint is truly in heaven is just as cer-

tain as any other doctrine which we believe on the authority of
the Church.

The veneration which the Church pays to her saints is not, of
course, worship or adoration in the strict sense. This can be giv-
en only to God. Considered even from a merely natural, human
viewpoint, it is a perfectly good and proper thing for any group
of people to honor its heroes. No one objects to having statues
of certain illustrious citizens in public parks. Why then should
anyone find fault with the Catholic practice of having statues
and pictures of the saints in our churches?

The Church's honor of her saints, however, goes further than
this. Because of the Christian doctrine of the "communion of the
saints," which is clearly taught in the New Testament, we hold
as Catholic faith that it is right and proper, nay, even necessary,
to ask the saints to intercede for us before God's throne in
heaven. In the phrase, "the communion of saints," the word
"saints" is used in its original broad sense as referring to all the
faithful who are in God's grace, whether on earth, in purgatory,
or in heaven. By "communion" we mean that they can share in
each other's merits. Because the great saints, the "saints" in the
limited sense of the word, have a superbundance of merits, they
share these with us and their prayers are more readily answered
by God than are our own poor petitions since we ourselves are
so poor in virtue and merit.

For special reasons connected with their lives on earth, or perhaps for reasons known to God alone, the intercession of certain
saints seems to be more efficacious than that of other saints for
certain particular needs. We thus speak of such-and-such a saint
as being the "patron" of those who have such-and-such a need,
or as the patron of a certain particular class of people. Far from
considering any taint of superstition in such a practice, the
Church in her indulgenced prayers to various individual saints
often stresses this idea. The saints, however, are not only our
intercessors with God; they are also our models in the practice of
the virtues. This is one of the principal reasons why the Church

solemnly canonizes her saints, that is, that she may set them before us as examples which we should follow in our own lives if we, too, wish one day to enjoy their company in heaven.

In this matter, however, it should be noted that it is essentially the spirit and not the letter of the lives of the saints that we should imitate. Our circumstances in life are seldom exactly the same as were those of the saints. Therefore it would often not be possible or even right for us to try to do exactly what this or that saint may have done. Sometimes we hear it said that what such-and-such a saint did is more to be admired than imitated. This is true enough if, by imitation, we mean trying to reproduce in our own lives the precise deeds of such a saint. Take, for instance, the matter of penance and mortification. Many of the saints practised extreme forms of penance, fasting rigorously until they were but skin and bones, sleeping only a few hours at night, torturing their bodies with hairshirts, and so forth. Obviously it is not God's will that ordinary men and women who have different duties to perform in the world should lead such austere lives. Yet the same *spirit* that prompted such heroic deeds of penance in the saints can and should also be ours if we wish to be the followers of our crucified Savior.

This spirit is essentially one of generous sacrifice for love of God. On account of our fallen human nature a certain minimum amount of self-denial is absolutely necessary for all of us, if we wish to remain in God's grace. The words of Christ are as true today as they were when first spoken in Galilee nearly two thousand years ago: "If anyone will be My disciple, let him deny himself, take up his cross and follow Me." Without a love of our own cross for the sake of Him who died on the cross for love of us there can be no true love of God. Sacrifice is the proof of love. The saints were so filled with love for God that they voluntarily imposed on themselves frightening sacrifices, over and above the call of duty, to show in some small measure how little they cared for themselves and how much they loved the all-good and all-holy Lord.

Only in proportion as a man empties himself of self-love can he be filled with God's love, and basically it is the love of God that unites us with Him and lets us share in His infinite holiness. The other virtues are, of course, all necessary, too: humility, purity, patience, and the rest—above all charity and love of our fellow men, but unless these virtues are practiced for the love of God they are of no value in themselves for obtaining eternal bliss.

This is the lesson that the lives of the saints teach us. We humbly beg their intercession to learn it well.

Saint Agatha
Virgin and Martyr

2 5 1

(February 5)

ONE OF THE most famous of the girl martyrs of the early
Church is Saint Agatha. Ever since the time that she gave
her life for Christ during the persecution which the Roman emperor Decius decreed against the Christians in the middle of the
3rd century, she has been venerated throughout the Christian
world. In fact, she can be described as *the* most highly venerated
virgin martyr of Christian antiquity. In the canon of the Roman
Mass her name is mentioned before the Pater Noster together
with six other women who were famous martyrs of the ancient
Church—immediately after the still earlier heroines, Felicitas and
Perpetua, and before Lucy, Agnes, Cecilia, and Anastasia.

Unfortunately we do not possess the true "Acts" or account of
the martyrdom of St. Agatha, as we do for her sister martyrs of
northern Africa, Perpetua and Felicitas. The earliest account of
Agatha's sacrifice for Christ probably does not precede the 6th
century, although it may well contain the essential elements of
historical truth (together with later additions that can best be
described as pious romance). The frightful torments which are
mentioned in her "Acts" may not all have been inflicted on her,
but Christian tradition was not mistaken in believing that most
of these barbarous tortures were inflicted at times on some of the
martyrs, women as well as men, during the Roman persecutions.
It is certain that the place where Agatha suffered her martyr-

dom was Catania, at the foot of the still active volcano of Mt.
Etna in Sicily. However, both Palermo, on the northwest coast
of Sicily, and Catania, (on the eastern coast), contend for the
honor of being her birthplace. Her parents were probably Greek-
speaking, as were many of the inhabitants of Sicily at that time,
since they gave her the lovely name of "Agatha," which means
the "good" girl in Greek.

According to her late "Acts," Quintianus, a Roman official in
Sicily, was captivated by Agatha's beauty and goodness and fell
in love with her. She, however, was firm in her refusal to marry
him. Realizing that her religion was the cause of this refusal,
Quintianus decided that he would make use of the Emperor's
edict against the Christians as a means of obtaining his coveted
goal. He, therefore, ordered Agatha to be arrested as a Christian,
and he himself acted as the judge at her trial.

Quintianus first attempted to break down Agatha's modesty
and purity, hoping that if she lost her virginity, she would be
more willing to renounce her Christian religion and then consent
to marry him. His first sentence against her, therefore, was that
she should be handed over to a certain wicked woman called
Aphrodisia who ran a house of ill fame. However, Agatha prayed
to God for strength to resist all the seductions of Satan, and
Aphrodisia was soon forced to admit to Quintianus that she could
not succeed in getting this Christian girl to consent to impurity.

At the next session of her trial the pagan judge asked Agatha
if she, who was born of noble parents, was not ashamed of belonging to a religion of slaves. "To be God's slave in Christian
lowliness," answered Agatha, "is a far more excellent thing than
all the wealth and pride of kings." Then, when she proceeded to
insult the pagan gods, the judge ordered her face to be slapped
and had her sent to prison. As one going to a festive banquet,
Agatha, praying to God to give her strength in her coming ordeal, went with joy to her dungeon cell.

On the following day, when the Christian virgin still insisted
that she would not renounce her faith, Quintianus ordered her to

be stretched on the rack and tortured. After having her whole body whipped with scourges, she even endured the torment of being burned with lighted torches and torn with iron hooks. The ultimate in cruelty was finally inflicted upon her when the executioners wrenched her breasts away with sharp pinchers.

That night, half-dead in prison, Agatha had a vision of an old man who told her that he was an apostle of Christ and had come to cure her wounds. Four days later Agatha was again subjected to torture, this time being rolled over live coals mixed with broken potsherds. She prayed: "Lord, Thou hast protected me from my infancy and guided me in my girlhood; Thou hast taken from my heart all love of the world and given me strength to triumph over the tortures of the executioners. Now receive my spirit, I pray Thee, for the time has come for Thee to call me from this world to Thy eternal mercy." When she had said this, she fell asleep in the Lord.

As the chief patron of Catania, where she suffered her martyrdom, Agatha is invoked for protection against sudden eruptions from Mount Etna, the great volcano that looms high behind this city. She is also invoked elsewhere against sudden fires. In art, she is traditionally pictured with a large pair of pinchers and a plate upon which are two female breasts. In the Middle Ages the latter item was misunderstood as being two round loaves of bread on a dish, and from this a practice arose of blessing "St. Agatha's bread" on her feastday.

Even though the legendary "Acts" of her martyrdom may be false, there is no doubt about the fact that St. Agatha was one of the great heroines who suffered for Christ in the early centuries of the Church. Before the Pater Noster of the Mass we recall the memory of these holy martyrs and, trusting in God's boundless mercy, we humbly pray that He, not as a Judge of merits but as a Giver of pardon, may grant us some little share in their fellowship and admit us into their company.

St. Albert The Great
Bishop, Doctor of the Church

1 2 8 0
(November 15)

IN THE 13th century, the golden age of Catholic philosophy and theology, it was customary to distinguish one famous "doctor" or teacher from the other famous ones by adding an adjective to his title that would call attention to his most outstanding trait. Thus, Saint Thomas Aquinas, because of his mind that seemed to equal the intellect of an angel, was known as the *doctor angelicus* or "Angelic Doctor"; Saint Bonaventure, whose writings were filled with such ardent love for God that he seemed to be aflame with the fire of the Seraphim, was called the *doctor seraphicus* or "Seraphic Doctor"; and so forth. Yet there was one of these renowned teachers who was such an expert in every branch of learning that he was spoken of as the *doctor universalis* or "Universal Doctor." This was Albert, and because he had such a gigantic intellect, he was more often called simply *Albertus Magnus* or "Albert the Great."

Albert was born around the end of the 12th or the beginning of the 13th century in the castle of Lauingen on the upper Danube, in Swabia (which is now a part, in the south, of western Germany). About the year 1220 his father, the Count of Bollstaedt, sent him to the University of Padua, in northern Italy, which at that time was a renowned center of the liberal arts. Here Albert began the study of the natural sciences for which he never lost his great interest. He would, no doubt, have become merely a worldly-wise scientist had not God other plans for him.

In 1223 he went to hear the sermons of Blessed Jordan of Saxony who was then preaching at Padua. This preacher had succeeded St. Dominic (who died in 1221) as head of the Order of Friars Preachers, or Dominicans, as they are more commonly called. Moved by divine grace, Albert promptly became a Dominican himself. After completing his ecclesiastical studies and being ordained a priest, he taught philosophy and theology in several Dominican colleges, especially at Cologne and Paris. One of his students at these last two places was a young Dominican friar called Thomas Aquinas, who later surpassed his master, not indeed in the extent of his knowledge, but in the depth of penetrating understanding. Not one of the least merits of Albert is that he discovered and developed the sheer genius of Thomas, who became not only the greatest theologian of the Church, but also one of the outstanding philosophers of the world. It was at the University of Paris that Albert received his doctor's, and Thomas his bachelor's degree. When they went back to Cologne, Albert was made regent of the college, and Thomas an assistant professor and prefect of the students.

Besides teaching, Albert was employed in many administrative positions. In 1245 he was made Provincial of the Dominicans in Germany. To defend the Mendicant (or "begging") Orders, such as the Franciscans and Dominicans, against the attacks of William of St. Amour, Albert journeyed to Italy in 1256. After residing in Rome for a few years, he was appointed by the Pope in 1260 to the bishopric of Ratisbon(or, Regensburg, in Bavaria). Although his administration as bishop was most successful, he resigned his see after two years, feeling that he was called to a more humble life, and returned to the Dominican college in Cologne. This remained his headquarters for the rest of his life, but he still made several journeys in the interest of the Church. Thus Pope Urban IV appointed him Papal Legate to preach, in Germany and Bohemia, the Crusade on which St. Louis of France, Albert's good friend, was eventually to lose his life. Despite all these external activities, Albert wrote an astounding number of books on an endless variety of subjects. In the decree of his canonization it is stated that he treated of "astronomy and cosmography, meteorology and climatology, physics and mechanics, architecture and chemistry, minerology and anthropology, zoology and botany." Moreover, he wrote on such practical topics as the arts of weaving, navigation and agriculture. It is true that as a scientist Albert's knowledge was rather primitive when viewed in the light of modern science, but it must be remembered that he and his contemporary, the Franciscan Friar Roger Bacon, were practically the only ones who undertook a serious investigation of these questions between the time of the Greek philosophers of the last centuries before Christ and the scholars of the late Renaissance.

Albert's greatest contribution, however, was in the fields of philosophy and theology. He was one of the leaders in the movement to reintroduce the philosophy of Aristotle into European thought and to show how, when further refined and purified, this light of natural reason could serve to clarify the truths of supernatural revelation. This method of systematizing and explaining the doctrines of Christian faith with the aid of Aristotelian philosophy is an important element of scholastic theology. It was on this foundation laid by Albert that Thomas Aquinas erected his magnificent structure of Catholic thought.

Even in his treatment of the natural sciences, Albert's thinking was always directed toward religious ends to show the harmony between natural and supernatural truths and to reveal the glory of the Lord in His creation. It is not surprising, therefore, that he also devoted himself to writings of a more specific religious nature, such as a treatise on mysticism, which had great influence on the German mystics of the 14th century, along with a commentary on St. Luke's Gospel.

Albert was especially devoted to the Holy Eucharist and composed an admirable treatise on "The Blessed Sacrament of the

Altar." To him Holy Communion was a true and real union not only between Christ and the individual Christian, but also, in and through Christ, between Christians themselves. Hence, Albert coupled his ardent love for God with deep Christian charity for all mankind.

Another characteristic was his tender love for the Mother of Christ. His "Treatise on the Praises of the Blessed Virgin" is deep and comprehensive, but also beautiful and frequently lyrical. He wrote, for instance: "What does Mary bestow on us out of the fullness of her graces? . . . From Mary we receive the price of our redemption, the waters of purification, bread for our soul's nourishment, a remedy for our recovery, the armor for our defense, and the reward of merit." The story is told of him that, when as a young man he was having difficulties with his studies and was thinking of quitting them, he appealed to Mary. She appeared to him and promised him that, if he would persevere in his studies, no one would surpass him in learning. However, she also added, in warning, that his wisdom and knowledge were gifts from God, and he would be deprived of them before his death. When, as an old man, his mental powers began to fail, he knew that death was near. Not long afterwards, on the 15th of November in 1280, his once brilliant spirit left its mortal frame to be united with the infinite Author and Giver of wisdom and knowledge.

From the time of his death Albert the Great was widely regarded as a saint. Yet strange to say, although many Popes, such as Innocent VIII in 1484, Gregory XV in 1622, Urban VIII in 1631, Clement X in 1670, and Pius IX in 1856, spoke of him as "Blessed" and allowed his feast to be liturgically celebrated in many parts of the world, it was not until recently that he formally received even beatification. In 1931 Pope Pius XI rectified this state of affairs by solemnly declaring Albert "a Saint and a Doctor of the Church." This was done, not by the usual ceremony of canonization in the Roman Basilica of St. Peter, but by the seldom used means of a "Decretal Letter."

In this letter of canonization the Pope explains that he was especially led to do this in order that St. Albert the Great might serve as a model for us in this modern age of ours, "which longs so ardently for world peace and which feels so confident that the marvels of scientific inventions will assure it a wonderful future." Albert, said the Holy Father, taught that true peace can only be established on the basis of justice and charity in keeping with the divine laws of the Prince of Peace, and in his own time he did much to foster peace and concord among the rulers and peoples of Christendom. Science also, continued the Pope, is conducive to the peace and prosperity of the world, provided it is always subject to right reason and supernatural revelation. However, in trusting only in itself and ignoring the truths of religion, as is only too often the case in the modern world, science can do immeasurably more harm than good. The abandonment of the God of justice and charity leads but to social injustice, economic hardships, and the vicious rivalry between nations that brings only one worse world war after another; and in which science, in the service of Satan rather than of God, supplies the weapons for the annihilation of mankind.

"In Albert the Great," wrote Pius XI, "there is a marvelous interplay between the rays of human and those of divine knowledge, and these rays shine round about him in resplendent glory. He proves to all that between science and faith, between the true and the good, between knowledge and holiness there is no opposition, but rather the closest union. Thus, just as St. Jerome did from the desert, so also Albert in his wonderful writings cries out with a loud voice and fully demonstrates that genuine science on the one hand and faith, together with a life lived according to faith on the other, can and should flourish simultaneously in man since supernatural faith bestows most efficaciously upon science its completion and perfection."

Saint Aloysius Gonzaga

Confessor

1 5 9 1

(June 21)

THERE IS A common but utterly mistaken notion that Saint Aloysius Gonzaga had something soft and diffident about him. Perhaps this wrong idea is partly due to the name itself with its soft "s"'s, though "Aloysius" is merely the Latin form of "Aluigi," a variant of "Luigi," the Italian for "Louis." More likely this distorted concept of Aloysius is derived from the sentimental pictures of him in which he is portrayed in so overpious a pose (with his head bent sideways at a ridiculous angle, and with a girlish look on his face which artists imagine to be "angelic"), that any red-blooded boy could not help thinking him a "sissy." Yet Aloysius was far from being a weakling, either in body or in spirit. He was as tough as nails. It was, in fact, precisely his iron will (aided of course throughout by divine grace) that brought him to triumph over almost insurmountable obstacles and made him the saint that he is.

Aloysius was born on March 9, 1568, in the castle of Castiglione, which lay a third of the way going south from Brescia to Mantua in Lombardy (northern Italy). Both his father, Ferrante Gonzaga, the Marquis of Castiglione, and his mother, Marta de Tana-Santena, were related to the Ducal House of Mantua as well as to many illustrious prelates. While his mother, who was a devout woman, wished in her heart that her son might become a churchman, his father expected him to be a military man like himself. When only four years old, Aloysius was dressed in tiny soldier's clothing and allowed to roam freely among the armed men of his father's camp. This, of course, delighted the little lad. However, on one occasion he almost managed to get himself accidentally killed, and at another he set off an explosion that made everyone think the castle was being attacked. From the soldiers he also learned some "military language" that simply shocked the ladies of the court. After it was explained to him that a gentleman did not use such words, he was deeply sorry. In fact, later in life he used to reproach himself for these sins of his childhood, though he well knew that because of his ignorance at the time, they were really not sinful.

Aloysius resembled his mother more than his father. From her he also inherited his ability to face facts, calm judgment and intense spirituality. His love for her was very deep, and he could always talk with her more freely than with anyone else. While she probably exercised the greatest influence on his life, he also owed much to his tutor, Pierfrancesco del Turco.

Aloysius was only seven when he had what he called his "conversion." He was now fully conscious of the fact that he had always wished to give himself wholly to God. Much of his time was spent in prayer, though this was still only vocal prayer, the reading of the Psalms and other "devotions" from a prayer book. He was already trying to discipline his body as well as he could in his surroundings. About this time, also, he caught malaria which put an end to his playing soldier. When his father, who had been away at war, returned home, he found that his oldest son, Aloysius, was a changed boy. Yet Ferrante was still delighted with him. If he will not be a soldier, thought the father, at least he has the makings in him of a clever politician, a great statesman. It was not yet time for the boy to tell his father what he really wanted to be—a religious. In fact, it is doubtful whether Aloysius himself clearly realized as yet the special mission in life to which God was calling him.

To understand the virtue and mission of Aloysius it is necessary to remember that he lived in the period of the late Renaissance and to know what this means. The times were unspeakably evil. It is almost a falsehood against ancient paganism to call this age the rebirth of paganism. Murders by poison or the dagger were everyday occurrences. Adultery was widespread and practically taken for granted. If the injured spouse did not laugh it off as a joke, the unfaithful party could always be poisoned or stabbed to death with impunity. Illegitimacy was no bar to the highest social standing and power, and combined with every vulgar form of sensual pleasure was a horrible amount of barbarous cruelty.

Castiglione, as one of the smaller courts, was no doubt less corrupt than were the more sumptuous palaces of Italy, though even here the surroundings were definitely not conducive to sanctity. The nobility at Florence, however, where Aloysius and his younger brother Rodolfo were taken in 1577 on account of the plague in Lombardy, had sunk to a much deeper pit of immorality. This was the Florence, the magnificent capital of Tuscany in the heart of Italy, which a generation or two before had been the home of Michelangelo and Raphael and a score of other famous painters, sculptors, architects, poets, and musicians. Cosimo de' Medici (1519-1574), "Cosimo the Great," had until recently been the ruler of Florence, the Grand Duke of Tuscany, but the artistic glory of Florence was beginning to be a thing of the past. The glittering shell had worn shallow, and only the rotten core remained. Almost insane vices were rampant and even public. Immorality in all its aspects was the chief topic of conversations, writings, and "learned discussions." Amusements and games that used every kind of impure suggestions were daily indulged in. Over the beauty, riches and magnificence there lay the hideous pall of vileness.

It was in the midst of this immorality that Aloysius, who had firmly resolved never to commit a mortal sin, was thrown. Besides the natural repulsion that he felt, his reaction in the pres-

ence of this corruption was twofold. First of all, he had to take
means to defend himself against the immoral contagion that was
spread all around him. As the eldest son of one of the leading
noblemen of Italy, he was considered a very important person
despite being only a boy of ten. He was obliged, therefore, to attend a certain number of the social functions, though he stayed
away from the silly, indecent "games" as much as he could.
While addressed as "Your Magnificence" and fawned upon and
flattered, especially by the girls and women, his hard core of
masculinity rebelled against the absurd and degenerate modes of
his day. Of course, he was called a "woman hater." At this time,
also, he began the habit of keeping his eyes cast down as much
as possible which he continued for the rest of his life. This was
not caused by prudishness. Aloysius could not possibly have
been a prude, considering his surroundings. To avert his glance
from sights that would have been a source of temptation for him
was the only sensible thing he could do. Unfortunately his
habitual modesty of the eyes led his early biographers to make
exaggerated statements which cannot possibly be true. The last
thing that Aloysius wanted to do was to make himself conspicuous by any stupid mannerism. One such falsehood of his overpious biographers is that he never looked at the face of a woman,
not even his mother! Nonsense! There is a painting, made at
Castiglione, of Aloysius and his mother in which he is portrayed
as looking straight into her eyes. He was utterly devoted to his
mother—"our mother and such a mother," as he once wrote in
rebuke to Rodolfo. It was she who had inspired him to lead a
pure life. How could anyone ever imagine that he would have
felt tempted to impurity by looking at *her*!

The other reaction of Aloysius to the corruption in which he
was forced to live at Florence and elsewhere was his desire, perhaps unconsciously at first to make reparation to the all-holy
God for the outrages committed against Him by the innumerable
sins of impurity in that age. By severely disciplining his own innocent body he would make some amends for the sensuality all

around him. This is no doubt one of the motives that led him to lead such an austere life despite the luxury that could have been his. To Christians who believe in the atoning nature of Christ's sufferings, and in the possibility of the members of Christ's Mystical Body uniting their voluntary sacrifices with Him to atone for the sins of the world, the discipline practiced by Aloysius is quite understandable. Yet even others, who regard such rigors as extreme, can at least appreciate Aloysius' actions as a silent protest against the immorality of his contemporaries. God wished him to be an antidote against the poison of an immoral, modern world, not by any preaching or writing, but solely by his shining example.

From Florence the Gonzaga boys were taken by their father to Mantua in northern Italy. Aloysius liked this city no more than he had liked Florence. The court of the Duke of Mantua was almost as corrupt. It was here that he said, "It is better to be God's servant than the whole world's king." He now learned to make mental as well as vocal prayer, to think of God and talk to Him heart to heart.

After three years absence from Castiglione, the two boys were brought back there to their mother, who had earnestly begged to see them again. At this time Saint Charles Borromeo, the Cardinal Archbishop of Milan, who was a distant relative of the Gonzagas, passed through Castiglione on an Apostolic Visitation. He was delighted with Aloysius. When Borromeo learned that the twelve-year-old boy had not yet made his first Holy Communion, he instructed him and was the first to administer the Holy Eucharist to him.

In the following year the Gonzagas went to Spain as one of the princely families in the retinue of Mary of Austria, daughter of the Emperor Charles V, who was on a visit to her brother, Philip II of Spain. Aloysius' calm dignity and gravity found the proud atmosphere of Spain more to his liking than the lush vice of Italy, but life in Madrid was still threatening his determination to serve God in the religious life. It was well nigh impossible for him to pray in secret; curious people and servants were always spying on him. However, he finally found a woodshed where he could speak to God in peace.

At last his mind was fully made up. He decided to become a Jesuit, and once his decision was made nothing could deter him from it. On August 15, 1583, he went to Communion in a Jesuit church and, as he knelt to give thanks before a picture of Our Lady, he distinctly heard an interior voice telling him that this was God's will for him. His confessor agreed, but added that his father's consent was necessary. As was to be expected, when Ferrante Gonzaga heard of it, he let loose like a battery of his siege guns. The Gonzaga name was famous among the nobility of northern Italy since the beginning of the 12th century, and now the heir of this illustrious family had the silly idea of becoming a Jesuit! Ferrante's other sons gave him no hope of worthy descendants. As a matter of fact, Rodolfo, the second-born was a scoundrel who eventually, while under excommunication, fell a victim to an assassin's dagger. This first battle between Aloysius and his father ended in a draw. Neither side would give in.

The next day Aloysius simply went to the Jesuits' house in Madrid and refused to leave, much to the embarrassment of the good Fathers. Ferrante was furious and demanded his return; the determined young man could at least wait till he got back to Italy before taking such a step. The father hoped that, given enough time, he would eventually bring his son around to his way of thinking. Since Aloysius was sure that God's will would be done in the end, he could well afford to bide his time. Though strong-willed, he was too sensible to be stubborn. Perhaps, too, he realized that he had gone too far in trying to force the issue. After all, the Jesuits could not accept him as a novice without his father's consent. Thus Aloysius gave in to his father's demands for the time being.

In the spring of 1584 the Gonzagas returned to Italy. Back at Castiglione the fight between father and son continued. Ferrante, laid up with gout, sent the seventeen-year-old youth on a journey which brought him in touch with various prelates who were related to the Gonzagas. In vain they coaxed and argued; his mind was set and that is all there was to it. At last, sure that the journey had wrought the desired change in Aloysius his father ordered him back home. The meeting between the two was brief but explosive. "Son, what do you propose to do?" "Enter the Society of Jesus." Then the roof went off the castle of Castiglione. Aloysius was told to get out. Promptly he went to one of their houses on the outskirts. Some days later, when Ferrante learned that his son had only gone a mile from the castle, he ordered him back and told him to keep to his room. The footman, peeking through a hole in the door, saw a terrifying scene— Aloysius scourging himself. Poor Ferrante, on hearing of this, had himself carried there. The sight was too much for him. His son's bleeding back made him weep, and he gave in. He wrote, asking Claudius Acquaviva, the General of the Jesuits, to receive his son, "the dearest thing that I possess in this world."

However, there was still some delay. Since the Gonzagas were royal princes, the consent of the emperor had to be obtained. The legal technicalities necessary for Aloysius to abdicate his title of "Marquis" had to be gone through. When told that Rodolfo must be delighted at succeeding to the marquisate, Aloysius replied: "Not half as glad as I am to get rid of it!"

Finally, on November 25, 1585, Aloysius entered the Jesuit novitiate. He now found that his bodily penances were much curtailed. Yet in the practice of humility, obedience and poverty he still had plenty of opportunity for exercising himself in self-denial. "I am a piece of twisted iron," he used to say; "I have entered the religious life to get twisted straight." Most of the second year of his novitiate he spent in the Jesuit house at Naples, but it was back in Rome that he made the profession of his simple vows on November 25, 1587.

Aloysius then continued his studies for the priesthood at the "Roman College" of the Jesuits. He had already made excellent progress in the natural sciences earlier in life, and in Spain had successfully passed the public examinations in philosophy and theology. He now deepened his knowledge of these last two.

It is not only for his moral virtues that Aloysius is proposed as the model of college students. With his brilliant mind and spirit of industry he is a worthy example for every student to follow. In 1589 he was obliged to go up to northern Italy to attend to affairs of his family, since his brother Rodolfo was making a mess of things. On this occasion he had the happiness of seeing his dear mother once more—and for the last time.

Again in Rome, he was now past all the long, tortured years. His soul was filled with God's love and had found peace at last. It would not be long before he would be ordained a priest, and then he could devote all his activity to the Lord's work in the ministry.

However, God had ordained otherwise. In 1591 there was a bad famine in Italy, and this was followed by the plague. Aloysius begged for the starving and worked in the hospitals. He himself was sickly, but he struggled on, fighting his repulsion at the horrors of the plague-stricken and seeking out the worst cases. His superiors became frightened and forbade him this kind of work. Finally he was permitted to work in one hospital where the infected were seldom taken. At least one such patient, however, must have been brought there. Aloysius caught the plague and, on March 3, 1591, had to take to his bed as a patient himself. He wasted away for three months, dying day by day. Joyful at the thought of death, he prayed that it might come soon because he felt "safe now, but might not be so later on."

Three days before his death he said to his Provincial, "We're off, Father Provincial!" "Off! Off where?" "Why, to heaven, of course, if my sins do not stop me." "Listen to the young man," the Provincial murmured; "he talks of going to heaven as we would of going to Frascati." Frascati happened to be the suburb of Rome where the Roman Jesuits had their summer vacation home. Shortly before midnight on June 20, 1591, which in that year was the octave day of Corpus Christi, Aloysius Gonzaga departed for his heavenly home. He was only a little more than twenty-three years old.

During his lifetime as a Jesuit many had thought that Aloysius would some day be one of the greatest teachers or missionaries of the Jesuits, perhaps even their Father General. Yet he had already fulfilled his mission. Long after, St. Therese of Lisieux, "the Little Flower of Jesus," in replying to a nun who had reproved her for desiring an early death, said of the young Jesuit saint: "Look at St. Aloysius. God could have made him live long, to evangelize the nations. But He did not choose to do so, because He destined him for a far more fruitful mission. This young saint did much more good through dying before he was twenty-four than he would otherwise have done if he had lived to eighty. He is doing an apostolic work in heaven."

Aloysius was beatified by Pope Gregory XV in 1621. As early as 1605 the commission appointed by Pope Paul V had declared that he could safely be pronounced a "Saint" as well as merely "Blessed." However, the Society of Jesus twice requested that the canonization of Aloysius be postponed till Ignatius Loyola, Francis Xavier and Francis Borgia had first been canonized. Hence, it was only in 1726 that Benedict XIII bestowed upon him the highest honors of the Church as one of its Saints.

Ferrante Gonzaga, in finally consenting to let his eldest son enter the Jesuit novitiate, had written to the Jesuit General concerning Aloysius: "I am giving into Your Reverence's hands the most precious thing I possess in the world and my chief hope, which I have placed entirely in him, of maintaining and giving glory to my Family." Poor Ferrante, who died a good death in the following year, while Aloysius was in the novitiate, could hardly have guessed in what way the "glory" of his family name would be preserved in the world.

Saint Alphonsus de Liguori

Founder, Bishop and Doctor

1 7 8 7

(August 2)

I n 18th century Europe religion was at a low ebb. The so-called Catholic kings of the time, claiming to rule by divine right, interfered in the government of the Church and crippled its healthy functioning. The leading philosophers of the age were atheists. Many of the would-be leaders in Catholic life were Jansenists, rigorists in morals and formalists in piety, who, by making religion a loveless thing, made the people irreligious. It was an age of artificiality when everything, from the powdered wigs of the men and women to their art and poetry and devotions, was a sham.

Against this moral corruption which was finally to be wiped out in the blood bath of the French Revolution and the Napoleonic wars, God raised up a spiritual hero in the person of Saint Alphonsus de' Liguori who fought strenuously during all the years of his long life to restore true religion as a missionary, a writer, a bishop, and as a founder of religious congregations of men and women to carry on his work.

Alphonsus, the first of eight children, was born on September 27, 1696, at Marianella, a suburb of Naples, where his family had its country home. Two days later he was baptized, and the baptismal register, still extant, lists no less than nine Christian names given to him at the font, beginning with Alfonso, Maria, Antonio,

Giovanni, etc., but he is now usually known in English by the Latin form of his first name, Alphonsus.

In the normal course of events Alphonsus would have been expected to follow his ancestors (who belonged to the lesser nobility) in the service of the state. His father, Don Joseph de' Liguori, was a captain in the royal navy of the Kingdom of Naples. His maternal grandfather was a councillor at the Royal Court of Naples. With such a life in view, Alphonsus received an excellent education from private tutors in all the arts and sciences of his time, not merely in serious studies, but in such accomplishments as painting, poetry and music, and even in such social graces as dancing and fencing. With all his later humility and mortification and sanctity, Alphonsus always remained a cultured gentleman. All of this early education, apart from his youthful skill at dancing and fencing, was to serve him in good stead in his work for the Church and religion. Thus, as a missionary in later life he composed several hymns which are still popular in Italy. What *Silent Night* and *Adeste Fideles* are to Christmas in America, the hymn *Tu Scendi dalle Stelle*—"Thou Comest down from the Stars," is to Christmas in Italy, and both its words and music were written by Saint Alphonsus. His skill at the harpsichord was not forgotten, and years later he would entertain his religious brethren at recreation by playing this quaint forerunner of the piano.

But the early education that was to leave the deepest impression on his later work was his study of the law. Even though he was no doubt a brilliant student, the influence of his noble family must have had something to do with the fact that at the astonishingly early age of sixteen Alphonsus successfully passed the examination and received the degree of Doctor in Canon and Civil Law. When only nineteen years old, he was admitted to the bar and began to practice law, and for eight years he continued as a very successful lawyer.

Yet the parents of Alphonsus had also educated him for higher things. His mother, Donna Anna Cavalieri, was an especially

devout woman. Her sister was a nun, and her brother, Emilio
Cavalieri, was bishop of Troia, a city near Foggia situated about
100 miles northeast of Naples. The bishop, incidentally, proved
a friend in need to Saint Paul of the Cross, the founder of the
Passionists and a contemporary of Saint Alphonsus. Not only his
mother's teaching and good example left a lasting impression on
Alphonsus; his father also, despite his desires for the worldly
success of his eldest son, was instrumental in making a saint of
him. A stern disciplinarian (as a sea captain naturally would be),
Don Joseph saw to it that Alphonsus did not waste time in idle
amusements and, as a devout Christian, he took him with him
each year for the annual religious retreat that both men made together. Twice the father made arrangements for what looked
like a brilliant marriage for his son, but each time Alphonsus
diplomatically avoided the matrimonial ties. Deep in his heart
Alphonsus felt that God was calling him to higher things. He was
almost twenty-seven years old when, in 1723, the crisis of his
life occurred.

In this year Alphonsus was the chief attorney for a Neapolitan nobleman who was engaged in a lawsuit with a wealthy landowner of Tuscany in an affair that involved more than a half
million dollars. Certain of the justice of his case, and convinced
of the force of his arguments, Alphonsus made a brilliant speech,
but he had overlooked or misunderstood one small point of evidence, and he lost his case. Deeply humbled, he cried out: "O
world, I know you now! Courts, you shall see me no more!"

This proved a turning point in his life. Gradually he understood that the humbling defeat had come from God Who wished
to break his pride and wean him from the love of the world.
Not yet certain of what God was asking of him, he gave himself
more and more to prayer and to works of charity. Even as an
active lawyer, he used previously to visit the sick in the hospitals
and bring them bodily and spiritual comfort. He now gave much
more time to this good work as he prayed for light to know God's
will. At several times his father let him know how bitterly dis-

SAINT AGATHA

One of the most highly venerated virgin martyrs of the early Church,
Saint Agatha gave her life for Christ in the middle of the third century.
Her name is mentioned in the Canon of the Mass, and as the chief patroness of Catania in Sicily, Saint Agatha is invoked for protection against
sudden eruptions from volcanic Mt. Etna.

SAINT ALBERT THE GREAT

In the thirteenth century it was customary to distinguish one famous "doctor" of the Church from another by adding an adjective to his name. Thus Saint Albert, because of his gigantic intellect, was called *Albertus Magnus,* or "Albert the Great." As a Dominican, he taught, administered many posts, and wrote an astounding number of books on an endless variety of subjects proving that genuine faith and science can flourish simultaneously.

appointed he was in seeing his eldest son abandoning a promising career and acting like a foolish monk. Each of the two had an iron will, and neither would give in. Then, on August 28 of this year 1723, when Alphonsus refused to accompany his father to a celebration at the royal court, the latter cried out at him in anger: "Leave the house and do what you want!"

Full of sorrow at displeasing his father and worried in conscience at having disobeyed him, Alphonsus sought some relief of soul in his favorite occupation of nursing the sick. This day, while engaged in this lowly task, he suddenly seemed to see a dazzling light about him and to hear a voice say to him: "Leave the world and give yourself to Me." Frightened and perplexed, he began to leave the hospital when the same thing again happened to him. From this Hospital of the Incurables, as it was called, he went right to the little Church of Our Lady of Ransom and, as he prayed before the altar of the Madonna, he beheld the dazzling light and heard the same words for the third time. Like Paul of old on the road to Damascus, he answered: "Lord Jesus, too long have I resisted Thy grace. Do with me what Thou wilt." Taking off his sword belt and sword, the symbols of his nobility, he laid them on Our Lady's altar and promised God that he would renounce his title and rights as eldest son and would give himself wholly to God's service.

For two months Alphonsus suffered persecution from his father, but in the end this basically good man had to give in. Cardinal Pignatelli, archbishop of Naples, accepted Alphonsus as a cleric of his diocese, and on October 23, 1723, gave him the official clerical garb—a black cassock with white linen collar and a black cincture which was then the ordinary dress of the secular clergy of Naples and which, with the addition of a fifteen decade rosary hung on the cincture, was to become the religious habit of the Redemptorists, the order which the saint was eventually to found.

Alphonsus now devoted himself with his usual energy to the theological studies necessary for the priesthood, though even

now he took a certain active part in the ministry by visiting and
taking spiritual care of the prisoners of Naples. While still only
in Minor Orders, he joined a group of secular priests who gave
missions and he acted as catechist on these missions. He was ordained subdeacon on September 22, 1725, and deacon on April
26, 1726. With the reception of the diaconate, Alphonsus began
his career as a preacher, for the archbishop of Naples then gave
him permission to preach in all the churches of his diocese. His
first sermon, on the occasion of the Forty Hours Devotion, was
on the love of Christ in the Holy Eucharist, one of his favorite
topics throughout life. The eloquence he had acquired as a lawyer he now used in pleading God's cause, and the fame of Don
Alfonso as a preacher soon resounded in all Naples.

On December 21, 1726, when he was thirty years old, Alphonsus was ordained to the priesthood, and now, as a full-
fledged member of his group of secular priests, the Congregation
of Apostolic Missions, he devoted himself entirely to preaching
and hearing confessions in the various churches of Naples and
vicinity. There were enough priests who could deliver learned
and flowery sermons in the artificial eloquence of the day; Alphonsus addressed himself primarily to the poor, simple, ignorant people, his "most abandoned souls," as he used to call them
—and he spoke their language, simple, plain talk that moved
them to repentance and love of God.

For the first few years of his priestly life Alphonsus continued
to reside regularly in his father's house. Don Joseph was now
resigned to his son's vocation and in fact began to take some
pride in the young missionary's success. But in 1729 Alphonsus
accepted the offer to become chaplain at the so-called "Chinese
College," a seminary which Father Matthew Ripa, who had
spent many years as a missionary in China, had recently founded for prospective missionaries for the Orient. Alphonsus himself was much attracted by the idea of going on the foreign missions, but it was God's will that his China should lie no farther
afield than the towns and villages of the Kingdom of Naples.

Meanwhile he resided at the Chinese College and had charge of the attached chapel, which was open to the public. In his little room at this institution he could now give himself to more bodily penance than he could in his father's house, and he always felt the need of atoning for his own sins, slight though they were, and for the sins of the people to whom he preached, by voluntarily sharing in the physical pains of his scourged and crucified Savior.

While living at this institution, Alphonsus met Father Thomas Falcoia, a saintly priest who was destined to play an important part in St. Alphonsus' founding of the Redemptoristine Nuns and the Redemptorist Fathers and Brothers. Father Falcoia, who was then just twice the age of Alphonsus, sixty-six to thirty-three, now became his spiritual director, and he told him of certain visions he had had years before in Rome concerning the founding of a religious order of priests who would imitate Christ's virtues and His work of preaching to the abandoned people. Falcoia had been spiritual director of a recently founded convent of nuns at Scala, on the cliff above Amalfi, south of Naples, and here a certain nun, Sister Maria Celeste had also had visions from Christ on the same lines. In 1730, when Falcoia was made bishop of Castellamare, not far from Scala, he asked Alphonsus to preach a retreat to these nuns. Alphonsus studied the report of the visions of this Sister and became convinced they were from God. He also revised the Rule which she had received in her visions and, having induced a few objecting members of her community to accept it, he witnessed on the feast of the Transfiguration, August 6, 1731, the establishment of the convent of the Redemptoristines, a religious order of cloistered nuns now established in several countries, including the United States, whose special object is to pray and offer the sacrifices of their penitential lives for God's blessings on missionaries preaching to the most abandoned souls.

A few months later Sister Maria Celeste had a vision in which Christ ordered her to tell Alphonsus that he was to found a religious order of priests and brothers who, while striving to imitate the virtues of Christ, would preach the gospel to the abandoned country folk of the Kingdom of Naples as the Savior had preached the word of God to the people of Galilee, who were scattered like sheep that had no shepherd.

Alphonsus dreaded the idea. He was already under obligations in Naples to the group of secular priests to which he belonged; he had no immediate prospects of members for his new institute; and in his humility he preferred to be an obedient subject of others rather than a superior over them. For a whole year he thought and prayed over the project, and especially he took counsel with his spiritual director, Bishop Falcoia. The latter, of course, was enthusiastically in favor of the plan, and he encouraged and urged Alphonsus to undertake the task. Some years later, when the new religious order of missionaries was an accomplished fact, Alphonsus wrote to Sister Maria Celeste: "My Sister, know once and for all that I did not enter the institute to be its head and director or to take precedence in anything, as you suggest. . . . I have come here solely, yes, solely, to obey God, and I hope never to leave it, no matter what pressure may be brought to bear on me. . . . But understand that in this I am not following your revelations, as I wrote you in the beginning, but I follow only the safe and ordinary path of holy obedience to my spiritual fathers, where, as Jesus Christ has promised us, we are sure to know the will of God—a thing He has not promised to any revelation in the world, as all the masters of the spiritual life tell us."

Finally, on November 9, the feast of the Dedication of the Basilica of the Most Holy Savior in Rome (St. John Lateran), in the year 1732 Alphonsus with seven companions inaugurated at Scala the new institute. At first it was called "the Congregation of the Most Holy Savior," but, because there was already a religious order in the Church called "the Canons of the Most Holy Savior," in 1749, when the institute founded by St. Alphonsus received papal approbation, its title was changed to "the

Congregation of the Most Holy Redeemer," and its members have ever since been commonly known as "Redemptorists."

The congregation had plenty of troubles in its early years. Within the first few months serious dissensions developed among the members over the question of authority and over the type of Rule to be adopted. While all wished Alphonsus to be the superior, most of his companions objected to the influence that Falcoia, as his director, had on him. The Rule which had been revealed to Sister Maria Celeste was merely a general exhortation. On various particular points, particularly on the matter of religious poverty, opinions among the members differed widely. Gradually one member after another left Alphonsus till by April 1733 he found himself alone with one faithful lay brother, Vito Curtius.

But God was merely testing the virtue of His holy servant through these severe trials. Soon new postulants came and accepted the Rule as drawn up by Alphonsus. Though the original foundation at Scala was found impractical and had to be abandoned in 1738, by 1746 the Redemptorists had four flourishing foundations — at Nocera de' Pagani, Ciorani, Iliceto, and Caposele — all in the mountains southeast of Naples. Pope Benedict XIV approved of the Rule of the Redemptorists in 1749 and that of the Redemptoristines in 1750.

Because of all his later activity, it is sometimes forgotten that St. Alphonsus was first and foremost a missionary and that his principal occupation from 1726 to 1752 was the preaching of missions. Most of the year he and his fellow Redemptorists went from one parish to another throughout the Kingdom of Naples, instructing the forsaken people, reminding them of the basic eternal truths of salvation, hearing their confessions, and exhorting them to lives of virtue and holiness. A special feature of St. Alphonsus' method of giving missions was the return within a year to the place where a mission had been given and on this "renewal of the mission," as it was called, preaching to the people the way of the "devout life" of prayer and the frequentation of the sacraments. The substance of St. Alphonsus' simple, yet deeply moving sermons can best be seen in his numerous books.

After 1752, when Alphonsus was fifty-six years old, various bodily ailments curtailed his activities on the missions. But he who had taken a vow never to lose a moment of time now occupied himself largely with writing and publishing religious books. This work he kept up till he was nearly ninety years old, so that by his death he had over a hundred publications to his credit, many of them, it is true, not much more than pamphlets, but several of them quite substantial volumes. Of these, sixty-four can be classified as ascetical or religious works, while thirty-one are in the field of moral theology, and fifteen in that of dogmatic theology. One of his earliest publications, the "Visits to the Blessed Sacrament and to the Blessed Virgin," is still one of his most popular ones. Other well-known books of St. Alphonsus are the "Glories of Mary," "The True Spouse of Jesus Christ," and "The Great Means of Prayer."

In all these religious books St. Alphonsus shines forth as a man of prayer. The form of prayerful meditation which he always practiced himself and which he taught to others by the spoken and the written word consists in a brief consideration of some aspect of the mysteries of our Redemption followed by a few words addressed to God or to Christ or His blessed Mother and filled with feelings of love, contrition and other sentiments of devotion. Alphonsus' prayer is essentially *affective,* not a mere exercise of the mind, but a true lifting up of the heart to God. Though he himself reached the sublimest heights of mystical contemplation and was often rapt in ecstacy, he preferred the simplest form of prayer that is essentially nothing more than talking heart to heart with God on any matter that concerns Him and our relation to Him. The saint's favorite devotions were to the Infant Jesus, to Christ in His holy Passion, to the Blessed Eucharist, and to the Blessed Mother.

In his dogmatic works St. Alphonsus was chiefly concerned with defending the truths of the Catholic faith, particularly the rights of the pope as head of the Church. But his fame as a theologian rests primarily on his work in moral theology. In fact, he can rightly be called the "father" of moral theology, for up to his time it had been but a secondary branch of theology in general and it was he more than anyone else who made it a separate ecclesiastical science, independent in its own right. It was his work as a moral and dogmatic theologian which won him the title of "Doctor" of the Church—still the most recent in life, though not the most recent in receiving this title which the Church has now bestowed on thirty of its saints. Besides the many shorter works which Alphonsus published on moral questions, his great masterpiece is called simply "Moral Theology." During his own lifetime it went through nine editions. His legally trained mind is evidenced in every page of this voluminous work. A jurist is accustomed to weigh all the evidence and have a high regard for precedents before forming an opinion of his own on a legal point. In his "Moral Theology" St. Alphonsus has assembled no less than seventy-thousand quotations from the Fathers of the Church and the older theologians. In his interpretation of the moral law he follows a middle course, avoiding the extreme of rigorism as well as the extreme of overlaxity. With lesser men the legalistic mentality can lead to a devotion for the mere letter of the law, the "letter that kills," against the "spirit that gives life"—an attitude so vigorously condemned in the New Testament. But a saint like Alphonsus, who was always led by the Holy Spirit of God, never let the darkness of legal Phariseeism extinguish the light of Christ's moral teachings in the Gospel that gives Christians the glorious liberty of the children of God. The Holy See, therefore, in a decree dated July 22, 1831, declared that priests could follow any opinion of St. Alphonsus in moral questions without weighing for themselves the reasons on which it is based.

Such a shining light in the Church could not long remain hidden. In 1747 King Charles of Naples wished to have Alphonsus made archbishop of Palermo in Sicily, this island belonging at

the time to the Kingdom of Naples. Only by the most earnest
entreaties was the saint able to avoid this honor. In 1762, however, when Alphonsus was sixty-five years old, the appointment
to the bishopric of Sant' Agata de' Goti (St. Agatha of the
Goths), a small diocese northeast of Naples, came to him directly from the pope with strict orders to accept the office, and Alphonsus had no choice but to obey.

After his consecration in Rome on June 20 of that year, the
only time in his whole life that he left the Kingdom of Naples,
Alphonsus at once began to restore the spiritual life of his little
see, which had fallen on evil days. He had missions preached in
every parish of his diocese, and his own canonical visitations to
his churches were short but veritable missions. In the disastrous
famine that overwhelmed southern Italy in 1764 Alphonsus sold
practically all of his episcopal furniture to buy food for the poor
of his diocese. When the starving people of Sant' Agata started
a riot and threatened to kill the mayor for withholding food from
them, Alphonsus quieted them by offering his own life in place
of the mayor's. For thirteen years this holy bishop labored un-
remittingly in banishing scandals from his territory, in instructing the people, in reorganizing his seminary, in reforming his
convents, and in filling his clergy with a spirit of zeal and devotion. Yet despite all this he was forever begging the pope to accept his resignation because he was too old and ill to do any
good for the diocese! Actually, during most of his episcopacy he
was suffering from various bodily ailments. But as if all his
prodigious work as a bishop were not enough, during these years
he continued to write book after book for his publishers, and he
still took a lively interest in the affairs of his Redemptorist Congregation, of which he remained the Superior General, though he
had appointed a vicar for its ordinary administration.

In May, 1768, Alphonsus suffered a bad attack of rheumatic
fever that kept him bedridden till June, 1769. After that he
managed to get around with difficulty, and he went back to his
work, especially of writing, as far as he was able. But he remain-

ed paralyzed for the rest of his life. The paralysis especially affected his neck and kept his head bent so far down that a sore developed on his chest from the pressure of his chin. He could only drink at meals through a tube and had to say Mass, with proper dispensation, seated in a chair, which was tilted back when he drank the Precious Blood. Modern pictures of the saint usually show him with head more or less bent forward.

It was near the end of his episcopacy that there occurred one of the strangest miracles in the life of this saint of whom many miracles were reported. In 1774 from the middle of the morning of September 21 to midmorning of the following day Alphonsus fell into a seemingly lifeless trance, that greatly frightened his household. On awakening from this long deep slumber, he said to those around him, "I have been assisting the pope, who has just died." A few days later word arrived that it was on the morning of that September 22 that Pope Clement XIV, the much harassed pontiff who had been forced by the political powers to suppress the Jesuits, had passed to a better life. This miracle of St. Alphonsus is often spoken of as one of bilocation, but it should more properly be called one of clairvoyance trance.

Finally, in the spring of 1775, when Alphonsus was eighty years old, the new pope, Pius VI, acceded to the repeated requests of the saint to relieve him of the burden of his bishopric. Alphonsus thereupon returned to Pagani, to pass the last years of his life among his beloved Redemptorist brethren. Thirteen years before he had left there in poverty; he had always lived in poverty as a bishop, and he now returned as poor as he had left. Whatever money he made on his books he gave away in charity. He had thought that he was returning home merely to prepare for death. But death was still a good dozen years away, and all these last years were passed, not only in constant bodily pain, but in such sorrows and afflictions as God sends only to His dearly loved saints.

It should not be forgotten that St. Alphonsus founded and developed his religious order at the very time when the Jesuits were being suppressed in one country after another and finally by the Church itself. In 1767 they were suppressed in the Kingdom of Naples, and from then on the Redemptorists were looked upon by the government as merely Jesuits in disguise and were harassed in various ways. When Alphonsus resigned his bishopric and returned to Pagani, the headquarters of the Redemptorists, his religious order had four houses in the Papal States as well as five in the Kingdom of Naples. Fearing the worst for his Neapolitan houses, he hoped that the future of the Redemptorists would be secure in the Papal States. This indeed is what happened, but not in the way he expected.

To save the Neapolitan houses from being suppressed by the government, the Vicar General of the Redemptorists, Father Villani, in 1779, agreed to a revised form of their Rule, called the "Regolamento," which established them as secular priests living in community without vows and thus changed completely the Rule as approved by Pope Benedict XIV. Father Villani told the holy founder nothing of the true nature of this "Regolamento" when he asked him to sign it. Alphonsus was now eighty-five years old, crippled, deaf, and nearly blind. Trusting in his friend's word that his signature would be for the good of the Redemptorists, Alphonsus signed the document which almost destroyed the institute he had labored so hard to propagate.

When word of the "Regolamento" reached Rome, the pope declared all of the houses of the Redemptorists in the Kingdom of Naples to be outside the Congregation of the Most Holy Redeemer which the Holy See had approved, and all of their members, including Alphonsus himself, to be no longer Redemptorists! The heart of the old saint was broken, but he bowed in obedience to the pope and offered up the sacrifice for the good of his beloved Congregation. By a strange irony, the very same pontiff, Pope Pius VI, who cut off Saint Alphonsus from the Congregation he had founded and let him die outside of it, was later to give him the title of "Venerable" in preparation for his beatification.

It was only after the saint's death that the Neapolitan government, in 1793, allowed the Redemptorist houses in the Kingdom of Naples to observe the original Rule, and thus become once more united with the Redemptorists in the Papal States. Before the saint died in 1787 the first non-Italian, Saint Clement Mary Hofbauer, had become a Redemptorist in the Papal States, and in 1785 founded the first Redemptorist house north of the Alps. Though Saint Clement himself was to spend his whole life in a hopeless fight against anti-clerical governments of Europe, his disciples after his death quickly spread the Congregation of the Most Holy Redeemer throughout Europe and America.

Alphonsus was beatified by Pope Pius VII in 1816, canonized by Pope Gregory XVI in 1839, and declared a Doctor of the Church by Pope Pius IX in 1871. In 1953 Pope Pius XII made St. Alphonsus the heavenly patron of moral theologians, and of all priests engaged in hearing confessions.

Selections from

THE PASSION AND THE DEATH
OF JESUS CHRIST

by Saint Alphonsus Liguori

Jesus chose to suffer so much for us, in order that we may understand the great love He has for us.

"Two things," says Cicero, "make us know a lover—that he does good to his beloved, and that he suffers torments for him; and this last is the greatest sign of true love." God has indeed already shown His love to man by many benefits bestowed upon him; but His love would not have been satisfied by only doing good to man, as says St. Peter Chrysologus, if He had not found the means to prove to him how much He loved him by also suffering and dying for him, as He did by taking upon him human flesh: "But He held it to be little if He showed His love with-

out suffering;" and what greater means could God have discovered to prove to us the immense love which He bears us than
by making Himself man and suffering for us? "In no other way
could the love of God towards us be shown," writes St. Gregory
Nazianzen.

My beloved Jesus, how much hast Thou labored to show
me Thy love, and to make me enamoured of Thy goodness!
Great indeed, then, would be the injury I should do Thee if I
were to love Thee but little, or to love anything else but Thee.

Ah, when He showed Himself to us, a God wounded, crucified, and dying, did He not indeed (says Cornelius a Lapide)
give us the greatest proof of the love that He bears us? "God
showed His utmost love on the cross." And before Him St.
Bernard said that Jesus, in His Passion, showed us that His
love towards us could not be greater than it was: "In the shame
of the Passion is shown the greatest and incomparable love."
The Apostle writes that when Jesus Christ chose to die for our
salvation, then appeared how far the love of God extended towards us miserable creatures: *The goodness and kindess of God
our Saviour appeared.*

O my most loving Saviour! I feel indeed that all Thy
wounds speak to me of the love that Thou bearest me. And who
that had so many proofs of Thy love could resist loving Thee
in return? St. Teresa was indeed right, O most amiable Jesus,
when she said that he who loves Thee not gives a proof that he
does not know Thee.

Jesus Christ could easily have obtained for us salvation
without suffering, and in leading a life of ease and delight: but
no, St. Paul says, *having joy set before Him, He endured the
cross.* He refused the riches, the delights, the honors of
the world, and chose for Himself a life of poverty, and death
·full of suffering and ignominy. And wherefore? Would it not
have sufficed for Him to have offered to His eternal Father one
single prayer for the pardon of man? for this prayer, being of
infinite value, would have been sufficient to save the world, and
infinite worlds besides. Why, then, did He choose for Himself so
much suffering, and a death so cruel, that an author has said
very truly, that through mere pain the soul of Jesus separated

itself from His body? To what purpose so much cost in order to save man? St. John Chrysostom answers, a single prayer of Jesus would have indeed sufficed to redeem us; but it was not sufficient to show us the love that our God has borne us: "That which sufficed to redeem us was not sufficient for love." And St. Thomas confirms this when he says, "Christ, in suffering from love, offered to God more than the expiation of the offence of the human race demanded." Because Jesus loved us so much, He desired to be loved very much by us; and therefore He did everything He could, even unto suffering for us, in order to conciliate our love, and to show that there was nothing more that He could do to make us love Him: "He endured much weariness," says St. Bernard, "that He might bind man to love Him much."

And what greater proof of love, says our Saviour Himself, can a friend show towards the person he loves than to give his life for his sake? *Greater love than this no man hath, that a man lay down his life for his friends.* But Thou, O most loving Jesus, says St. Bernard, hast done more than this, since Thou hast given Thy life for us, who were not Thy friends, but Thy enemies, and rebels against Thee: "Thou hast a greater charity, Lord, in giving Thy life for Thy enemies." And this is what the Apostle observes when he writes, *He commendeth His charity towards us, because when as yet we were sinners, according to the time Christ died for us.*

Thou wouldst then die for me, Thy enemy, O my Jesus; and yet can I resist so much love? Behold, here I am; since Thou dost anxiously desire that I should love Thee, I will drive away every other love from my breast, and will love Thee alone.

St. John Chrysostom says that the principal end Jesus had in His Passion was to discover to us His love, and thus to draw our hearts to Himself by the remembrance of the pains that He has endured for us: "This was the principal cause of the Passion of our Lord; he wished it to be known how great was the love of God for man,—of God, who would rather be loved than feared." St. Thomas adds that we may, through the Passion of Jesus, know the greatness of the love that God bears to man: "By this man understands the greatness of the love of God to man." And St. John had said before, In this we have known the charity of God, because He hath laid down His life for us.

O my Jesus, Immaculate Lamb sacrificed on the cross for me! let not all that Thou hast suffered for me be lost, but accomplish in me the object of Thy great sufferings! Oh, bind me entirely with the sweet chains of Thy love, in order that I may not leave Thee, and that I may nevermore be separated from Thee: "Most sweet Jesus, suffer me not to be separated from Thee; suffer me not to be separated from Thee."

St. Luke relates that Moses and Elias on Mount Tabor, speaking of the Passion of Jesus Christ, called it an excess: *And they spoke of His excess that He should accomplish in Jerusalem.* "Yes," says St. Bonaventure, and rightly was the Passion of Jesus called an excess; for "it was an excess of suffering and an excess of love." And a devout author adds, "What more could He suffer that He has not endured? The excess of his love reached the highest point." Yes, indeed; for the divine law imposes on men no other obligation than that of loving their neighbors as themselves; but Jesus has loved man more than Himself: "He loved these more than Himself," says St. Cyril.

Thou didst, then, O my beloved Redeemer,—I will say to Thee with St. Augustine,—love me more than Thyself, since to save me Thou wouldst lose Thy divine life,—a life infinitely more precious than the lives of all men and angels put together. Thou didst love me more than Thyself, because Thou wert willing to die for me.

O infinite God! exclaims the Abbot Guerric, Thou hast for the love of men (if it is lawful to say so) become prodigal of Thyself. "Yes, indeed," he adds, "since Thou hast not been satisfied with bestowing Thy gifts, but Thou hast also given Thyself to recover lost man." O prodigy, O excess of love, worthy only of infinite goodness!

"And who," says St. Thomas of Villanova, "will ever be able, Lord, to understand even in the slightest degree the immensity of Thy love in having loved us miserable worms so much that Thou didst choose to die, even upon a cross, for us?" "Oh, how this love," continues the same saint, "exceeds all measure, all understanding!"

It is a pleasing thing to see a person beloved by some great man, and more so if the latter has the power of raising him to some great fortune; but how much more sweet and pleasing must it be to us to see ourselves beloved by God, who can raise us up to an eternity of happiness? Under the old law men might have doubted whether God loved them with a tender love; but after having seen Him shed His blood on an infamous gibbet and die for us, how can we doubt His loving us with infinite tenderness and affection? O my soul, behold now thy Jesus, hanging from the cross all covered with wounds! behold how, by these wounds, He proves to thee the love of His enamoured heart: "The secrets of His heart are revealed through the wounds of His body," says St. Bernard.

My dearest Jesus, it does indeed afflict me to see Thee dying with so dreadful sufferings upon an ignominious tree; but at the same time I am greatly consoled and inflamed with love for Thee, when I see by means of these wounds the love that Thou bearest me. O heavenly seraphs, what do you think of the love of my God, *who loved me and delivered Himself for me?*"

St. Paul says that when the Gentiles heard it preached that Jesus was crucified for the love of men, they thought it such nonsense that they could not believe it. *But we preach Christ crucified, unto the Jews, indeed, a stumblingblock, and unto the Gentiles foolishness.* And how is it possible, said they, to believe that an omnipotent God, who wants nothing in order to be perfectly happy as He is, would choose to become man and die on a cross to save men? This would be the same, said they, as to believe that a God had become mad for love of men: *But unto the Gentiles foolishness.* And thus they refused to believe it. But faith teaches us that Jesus has really undertaken and accomplished this great work of redemption which the Gentiles esteemed and called folly. "We have seen," says St. Laurence Justinian, "Eternal Wisdom, the only-begotten of God, become as it were a fool through the excessive love He bears man." Yes, adds Cardinal Hugo, for it seemed nothing but a folly that a God should choose to die for men: "It seemed a folly that God should die for the salvation of men."

The Blessed Giacopone, who in this world had been a man of letters, and afterwards became a Franciscan, seemed to have become mad through the love that he bore to Jesus Christ. One day Jesus appeared to him and said, Giacopone, why do you commit these follies? "Why," he answered, "because Thou has taught them me. If I am mad," said he, "Thou hast been more mad than I, in that Thou hast died for me. I am a fool, for Thou hast been a greater fool,"

Thus, also, St. Mary Magdalen of Pazzi, being in an ecstasy, exclaimed, "O God of love! O God of love! The love that Thou bearest to creatures, O my Jesus, is too great indeed." And one day, when quite enraptured, she took an image of the Crucified, and began running about the monastery, crying, "O Love! Love! I shall never rest, my God, from calling Thee Love." Then turning to the religious, she said, "Do you not know, my dear sisters, that Jesus Christ is nothing but love? He is even mad with love, and I will go on saying it continually." And she added that she wished she could be heard by the whole universe when she called Jesus "Love," in order that the love of Jesus might be known and loved by all. She sometimes even began to ring the bell, in order that all the people in the world should come (as she desired, if it had been possible) to love her Jesus.

Yes, my sweetest Redeemer, permit me to say so, this Thy spouse was indeed right when she called Thee mad with love. And does it not indeed seem a folly that Thou shouldst choose to die for love of me, for so ungrateful a worm as I am, and whose offences Thou didst foresee, as well as the infidelities of which I should be guilty? But if Thou, my God, art thus become mad, as it were, for the love of me, how is it that I do not become mad for the love of a God? When I have seen Thee crucified and dead for me, how is it that I can think of any other than Thee? Yes, O my Lord, my sovereign good, more worthy of love than every other good, I love Thee more than myself. I promise for the future to love none other but Thee, and to think constantly on the love Thou hast shown me by dying in the midst of so many sufferings for me . . . . Amen.

SAINT ALPHONSUS DE LIGUORI

Against the moral corruption and atheism of the eighteenth century, God raised up a spiritual hero in the person of Saint Alphonsus who fought strenuously through all the years of his long life to restore true religion. He served as missionary, writer, bishop, and as founder of religious congregations to carry on his work. Today, the Saint is honored as the patron of moral theologians and of all priests hearing confessions.

SAINT ALOYSIUS GONZAGA

Born of the Italian royalty, Aloysius was only seven when he experienced his "conversion." He took an early vow of perpetual chastity, and at seventeen entered the Jesuit novitiate. For the remaining six years of his life, he lived the exemplary life; he died in 1591 attending the plague-stricken victims of Italy. The artist has symbolized the Saint's royal lineage with the crown; his purity in the lilies.

Saint Andrew

Apostle

First Century

(*November 30*)

RELATIVELY MORE is known from the New Testament about Saint Andrew than about most of the other twelve Apostles. Although he was born in Bethsaida of Galilee (John 1, 44), (at the northern end of the Lake of Genesareth where Aramaic was the common language at the time), his Jewish parents gave him the Greek name of Andreas, which means "manly." When Jesus began His public ministry, Andrew was living with his brother Simon Peter at Capharnaum (Mark 1,29), the important town on the western shore of the Lake of Genesareth where the two of them earned their livelihood as fishermen. They were business partners, along with another pair of brothers, James and John, the sons of Zebedee (Luke 5,10). Before they met Jesus, Andrew and John were disciples of John the Baptist, but when the latter pointed Jesus out to them as "the lamb of God," they became disciples of Jesus. It was, in fact, due to Andrew that his brother Simon Peter also became one of Jesus' disciples (John 1, 35-42).

When these four fishermen of Galilee witnessed the miracle of the great draught of fish which they caught at Jesus' word (Luke 5, 1-11), they abandoned their boats and nets and followed Him on His missionary journeys, thus becoming the inner core of His special twelve Apostles. In all four official lists that we have of

the Apostles, Simon Peter is named first. In the lists of Matthew
(10, 2-4) and Luke (6, 13-16) his brother Andrew is named
immediately after him, but in those of Mark (3, 14-19) and
Acts (1-3), Andrew's name comes after the names of the two
sons of Zebedee (James and John).

On the occasion when Jesus miraculously fed five thousand
persons, it was Andrew who said to Him, "There is a young boy
here who has five barley loaves and two fishes; but what are
these among so many?" even though it was to the Apostle Philip
that Jesus had directed His question: "Whence shall we buy
bread that these may eat?" (John 6, 5-9).

On another occasion, Andrew likewise acted jointly with Philip.
"Now there were certain Gentiles among those who had gone up
to worship on the feast. These therefore approached Philip, who
was from Bethsaida of Galilee, and asked him, saying, 'Sir, we
wish to see Jesus,' Philip came and told Andrew; again, Andrew
and Philip spoke to Jesus" (John 12, 20-22). It is worthy of note
that these are the only two Apostles who had Greek names;
Philip's name in Greek, *Philippos*, means "horse-lover." Perhaps
these two spoke Greek better than any of the other twelve
Apostles.

Andrew is not mentioned elsewhere in the New Testament.
According to later tradition, his missionary work after Christ's
ascension into heaven was mostly in certain regions which are
now part of southern Russia and the Balkans. He is said to have
suffered martyrdom by being bound to an X-shaped cross from
which he preached to the people for two days. The site of his
death and burial is given as Patras, a city near the western end
of the Gulf of Corinth in Greece. In 356, his relics were taken
from here to Constantinople, and in 1210 the Crusaders removed
them to Amalfi, near Salerno, on the coast of Italy south of
Naples.

Not only Russia, where Andrew is believed to have brought
the faith of Christ, but also Scotland venerates this Apostle as a
national patron. An interesting legend connects him with Scot-

land. According to this account a certain St. Regulus (who lived in Patras where St. Andrew was buried) received a command from an angel to bring a part of the Apostle's relics to a distant place that would be indicated to him. Regulus sailed with the relics in a northwesterly direction "towards the ends of the earth," until he landed at a place on the eastern shore of Scotland which is now called St. Andrews. Here he built a chapel to house the relics, and from here he proceeded to convert the native heathens to Christianity. The ancient Scottish town of St. Andrews may now be more famous for its renowned golf course than for its holy relics of the Apostle, but the X-shaped cross of St. Andrew is still the national emblem of Scotland. With the crosses of St. George of England and St. Patrick of Ireland, it forms a conspicuous part of the Union Jack, the flag of the United Kingdoms.

St. Andrew, the fisherman of the Sea of Galilee, is naturally enough the patron of fishermen. He is also the patron of old maids, apparently because his feast (on the 30th of November) occurs at the very end of the liturgical year of the Church which begins with the first Sunday of Advent and should, therefore, remind the elderly maiden ladies that it is never too late to hope for a husband. It is more difficult to see why St. Andrew is invoked especially by those who suffer from gout or sore throat.

At Mass, in the prayer that follows the Pater Noster, we beg God "to grant us peace in our days" through the intercession of the Blessed Virgin Mary together with that of "Peter and Paul and Andrew." The insertion of Andrew's name here, after the names of the two Princes of the Apostles, is commonly attributed to St. Gregory the Great (end of the 6th century) who had a great devotion to this holy Apostle, but it may well be of still older origin.

Saint Andrew Avellino
Confessor
1 6 0 8
(November 10)

S OME OF GOD'S saints have done such heroic deeds of charity for their fellowmen that their names are well known even to those who have no understanding of their true supernatural sanctity. Other saints, on the contrary, whose lives were spent almost entirely in doing spiritual good for mankind are known only to those who have eyes of faith to see true worth as it is in God's sight. Among the latter class of saints is Saint Andrew Avellino whose long life was spent as a zealous priest laboring for the salvation of souls.

This saint received his name of Andrew only when he became a religious. He was known in his early life by his baptismal name of Lancelot. He was born in 1521, in the small town of Castronuovo (in the region of southern Italy known as Lucania or the Basilicata) which at that time was part of the Kingdom of Naples. After elementary schooling in his home town, he went to Venice for higher studies in the humanities and philosophy. Later, at Naples, he studied civil and canon law as well as theology, and here at the age of twenty-six he was ordained a priest. Having received the doctorate in both laws, he spent the first few years of his priesthood as a lawyer in the ecclesiastical court of Naples. He might have continued for the rest of his life merely as a good but ordinary ecclesiastic were it not for what his biographers call his "conversion."

568

The turning point in his life, however, can hardly be called a "conversion" in any strict sense, for Don Lancelotto Avellino was really never anything but a devout and virtuous man. Even as a boy his piety was outstanding, and as a college student at Venice he gave good proof of his love of chastity. Here some young ladies found his handsome looks and courteous manners so attractive that, as his biographers affirm, he was obliged on several occasions to use violence to free himself from their importunities. The occasion for his "conversion" was a lie which he uttered in the heat of an argument to further the cause of a client of his in court. Shortly thereafter, when he happened to read the words of Scripture, "A lying mouth slays the soul" (Wis 1,11), he was filled with such remorse that he resolved to give up the practice of law forever. Not that he would have claimed that to be a successful lawyer one must necessarily be a good liar; he had too high a regard for his profession to say that. A deeper motive led to hs decision. For him the practice of even canon law was not the ideal work of a priest. It savored too much of worldly wisdom and it brought too many distractions of spirit. Henceforth he would devote himself entirely to the priestly ministry in the salvation of souls.

Cardinal Scipio Ribiba, the archbishop of Naples, noticed the zeal of Don Lancelotto and gave him the difficult task of trying to reform a convent of nuns at Baiano near Naples. The laxity and lack of religious discipline shown by these supposedly cloistered women had become a public scandal. Through his ardent urgings and the example of his own austere life, he had some initial success in this delicate undertaking. However, when he endeavored to prevent certain men from entering the convent and holding clandestine meetings with some of its inmates, these libertines decided to get rid of the zealous young priest. Though foiled in their first attempt to waylay him, they caught him in their second assault. He fell badly wounded beneath their stilettos with three ugly gashes on his face. The assailants were later apprehended, but Don Lancelotto pardoned them and ask-

ed the civil authorities not to prosecute them. This same generous spirit of clemency was exhibited on another occasion when
his nephew was killed in a brawl. Those were indeed disorderly
times, and the hot tempers of the Neapolitans could erupt as
violently as their Vesuvius.

While recuperating from his wounds in the monastery of the
Theatine Fathers at Naples, Don Lancelotto got to know and
love these zealous religious. Longing for a more perfect life than
was possible for him as a secular priest, he asked to be admitted
as one of their members. In 1556, at the age of thirty-five, he
received the Theatine habit and took the name of Andrew in
honor of the holy apostle who was renowned for his love of the
cross.

In the 16th and 17th centuries the Theatines were one of the
great religious orders in the Church, but with the suppression of
the orders by the governments of Europe in the 18th and 19th
centuries they were greatly reduced in numbers and are hardly
known in America, except in Colorado, where they have a few
foundations. Their official name is "Clerics Regular," but they
are more commonly known as "Theatines" from the place where
they were founded, Theate in Latin (Chieti in Italian), in the
region called the Abruzzi on the Adriatic east of Rome. They had
been founded by St. Cajetan in 1524, a little more than thirty
years before Andrew Avellino joined them. One of Cajetan's first
companions was John Peter Carafa who later became Pope Paul
IV. The date of the founding of the Theatines should be noted.
It was just at the time when Martin Luther was beginning his
revolt against the Church. Cajetan founded his religious congregation primarily for a reformation of the Church, but a reformation achieved within the Church, not against it. There was need,
as he well knew, to throw out a good deal of dirty bath water,
but the baby itself should not be thrown away with it. Cajetan's
Clerics Regulars formed a new sort of religious order, the first of
its kind in the Church, differing from the older monastic and
mendicant orders by giving its members more opportunity to en-

gage in the active ministry, in education, in foreign missions, and in other needs of the Church in the modern world. All later orders of Clerics Regulars, such as the Jesuits, Barnabites, Somaschi and several others have been modelled upon the order of the Theatines.

After his profession as a Theatine, Andrew Avellino threw himself with tremendous energy into the work of his order. In the towns and villages of the Neopolitan Campagna he preached missions and retreats, bringing new spiritual life not only to the laity, but also to priests and religious. For the first fourteen years of his life as a Theatine the monastery of his order at St. Paul's in Naples was his headquarters. His outstanding goodness, fervor and exactness in the observance of the rules caused him soon to be made master of novices, an office which he held for ten years. Thereafter he was elected superior of his community at Naples. The fame of Andrew Avellino as a restorer of good morals among the clergy reached the ears of several of the Italian bishops who were anxious for a true Catholic reformation in their doceses. Among these was St. Charles Borromeo, cardinal archbishop of Milan, who, in 1570, induced the Father General of the Theatines to send Andrew to his diocese. Here the latter, who became the close associate and counsellor of the archbishop in his work of reform, founded a new house of his order.

Likewise in northern Italy he established a monastery of the Theatines at Piacenza in the neighboring Duchy of Parma. Here his preaching converted so many noble ladies and led so many of the young women to the convent that some disgruntled men complained to the Duke of Parma that Andrew Avellino was turning their city upside down. The Duke summoned Andrew to appear before him and answer the charges. Andrew not only fully satisfied the Duke, but he made such an impression on the Duchess that she asked the saint to become her spiritual director.

It was largely due to the zeal of such fervent preachers as St. Andrew Avellino and his fellow Theatines in the second half of the 16th century that Italy remained true to the Catholic faith. Protestantism had begun to make some inroads here, especially in the north of Italy. The decrees of the Council of Trent which were aimed at genuine reformation to counteract the false reformation of Luther, Calvin, Zwingli and their ilk, were all well and good in themselves, but without zealous preachers to induce the clergy and laity to observe these decrees they would have remained a dead letter.

The copious fruit of St. Andrew Avellino's activity in the ministry was borne by the seed of true sanctity deeply planted in his soul. Not satisfied with the ordinary vows of a religious, he had also taken at his profession a vow always to deny his own will along with another vow to strive for ever greater spiritual perfection. In actual practice he lived as if he had also taken a vow never to lose a moment of time. He allowed himself but the minimum of required sleep. When not engaged in preaching and hearing confessions, he spent his time in prayer and study and the writing of spiritual books. Better known, however, than his own ascetical works is the *Spiritual Combat,* a book written by a disciple of his, Father Laurence Scupoli, which for several generations formed a good part of the ascetical fare of the pious laity as well as of members of religious congregations.

Even during his life St. Andrew Avellino was approved by God through the evidence of many miracles. It is said that on certain occasions when he was reciting the Divine Office, or praying to the Blessed Virgin Mary to whom he was always tenderly devoted, the sound of angels singing about him was heard by the bystanders. To reward the self-sacrificing love of St. Andrew for his fellowmen God helped him at times through miraculous means in the exercise of his works of charity. Once when he had gone out at night in a raging storm to hear the confession of a sick man the wind and rain put out his torch. The laymen who accompanied him did not know how they could possibly continue on through the darkness and the downpour. To their surprise they beheld around the saint a marvelous brightness that shed more than enough light on the road for them to find their way and, to their utter amazement, they found on arriving at his home that both he and they were perfectly dry despite their long walk in the drenching rain.

St. Andrew himself told another strange story which, though it did not involve a miracle in his own regard, is worth retelling here. A certain man once rushed to him in terror and remorse to confess what he had done. This poor sinner, more of a heretic than a Catholic, had boasted that he did not believe in the real presence of Christ in the Blessed Eucharist. To prove his point he had the audacity to receive Holy Communion sacrilegiously. Instead of swallowing the sacred Host, he spit it out as soon as possible in his handkerchief which he then put in his pocket. On returning home he took out the handkerchief and to his horror found it dripping with blood.

After St. Andrew's long years in untiring service of the Lord, Pope Gregory XIV offered to make him a bishop in 1590, but the humble saint begged to be allowed to continue his work as an ordinary priest and simple member of his religious order until his death. Death was still long in coming for him. When it did finally come, its arrival was dramatically sudden. For ordinary mortals a sudden death can often be a spiritual calamity, for it may find them unprepared to meet their God. St. Andrew however, was always ready for the coming of his Lord. On November 10, 1608, in his eighty-eighth year, he went as usual to celebrate holy Mass. Scarcely had he said its opening words, "I will go to the altar of God," when a stroke of apoplexy laid him low. A few hours later, after receiving the last sacraments of the Church, he calmly breathed his last. His body was laid to rest in the crypt of the Theatine Church of St. Paul in Naples where he had faithfully served the Lord for so many years.

It is said that the strange miracle known as the "liquefaction of blood," an unexplained phenonmenon connected particularly with Neopolitan saints, occurred for some years in connection with the blood of St. Andrew Avellino. When his body was laid out for burial it was visited by thousands of people. Many of these snipped off locks of his hair for relics and, in their clumsiness, they accidentally cut his skin. Marvellous to say, blood continued to flow for several hours from these cuts in his flesh, just as if his body were still alive. Physicians who came to investigate the phenomenon made more cuts in his flesh, and for a day or two new blood continued to flow from these cuts. Four days later, this blood, which was kept in a little bottle, seemed to be bubbling. Eventually the blood dried up, but it was claimed that for a certain number of years (on the anniversary of the saint's death), when the dried blood in the bottle was brought near his sacred remains, it appeared to become liquid. However, Monsignor Pamphili, who later became Pope Innocent X, testified in the process for the canonization of Andrew Avellino that for several years he had had a vial of the solidified blood in his care and that he had never observed any liquifaction in it on any occasion. The evidence, therefore, of a miracle in connection with Andrew's blood was judged inadequate and not accepted as valid in the process of canonization.

There was no need though, for such bizarre miracles to show God's approval of Andrew Avellino's heroic sanctity. Ample proof of this was given by several unquestionable miracles, cures wrought through the saint's intercession which could not be explained as happening by any known natural means. Thus, in 1624, only sixteen years after his death, Andrew Avellino was beatified by Pope Urban VIII, and in 1712 he was canonized by Pope Clement XI. St. Andrew Avellino, whose body still reposes in the beautiful Church of St. Paul in downtown Naples, is one of the principal patrons of this city. Throughout the world he is invoked against apoplexy and every form of sudden, and unprovided for, death.

Saint Apollonia
Virgin and Martyr
2 4 9
(February 9)

ONE OF THE best sources of exact information on the Christian martyrs of the Roman persecutions is the Church historian Eusebius (c. 260-340), bishop of Caesarea in Palestine. In his *Ecclesiastical History* (vi. 41) he quotes from a letter in which Saint Dionysius, archbishop of Alexandria in Egypt (writing to Fabius, archbishop of Antioch in Syria) gives a long account of the martyrs who gave their lives for Christ at Alexandria during his episcopate there in the middle of the 3rd century.

In the last year of the reign of the Roman emperor Philip (244-249), and therefore a whole year before the next emperor, Decius, issued his edict of bloody persecutions against the Christians, the populace of Alexandria was roused to violence against the Church by a second-rate pagan poet. The latter stirred up the mob by telling them that the Christians were the enemies of their ancient culture, religion and prosperity. The first victims of the pagan fury were a venerable old man called Metrius, who was beaten, tortured and stoned to death, and a certain woman named Quinta, who, when she resisted the efforts made to force her to participate in pagan worship, was dragged by the feet through the streets of the city, cruelly scourged, and finally stoned to death.

The third victim of this mob violence (which later claimed many more martyrs) was St. Apollonia, a highly respected Christian lady whom Dionysius calls in Greek a *parthenos presbytis*.

This is usually translated as "an elderly virgin," but some scholars take it to mean "a virgin presbyter," that is, merely "a deaconess," with no reference to her age. When the mob seized and bound her, they tried to force her to repeat certain words which they used in their pagan worship. As she persisted in her refusal to say these words which she rightly considered as blasphemous against God, they beat her so savagely in the face that they knocked out all her teeth. Then they threatened to throw her into a big bonfire which they enkindled in front of her in the street, unless she denounced her Christian religion. Giving them the impression that she was weakening in her resolve, she asked to be freed from her bonds. Scarcely was she thus released than she ran of her own accord into the flames and was burned to death. Probably she wished thereby to show the pagans that she was gladly sacrificing her life for Christ.

St. Augustine, however, in treating of the question of suicide in his *City of God* (1, 26), is at pains to defend the morality of her action. While admitting that the Church honors as true saints those martyrs who, like St. Apollonia, hastened their own death for Christ, he seems to feel that, objectively, their deeds cannot be justified. Subjectively, though, since they thought they were acting under an inspiration from God, they were free from all guilt in taking their own lives. On the other hand, St. Dionysius, in telling how Apollonia suffered for the faith, does not give the slightest indication of thinking that there was anything at all wrong in the fact that she did not wait until the pagans had thrown her into the flame. Moreover, not only at Alexandria, but especially at Rome, where a church was built in her honor, did she receive the veneration granted only to genuine saints of God.

As one of her tortures consisted in having all of her teeth knocked out, St. Apollonia is invoked particularly by those who suffer from toothache, and she is the special patron of dentists. She is often represented in art as carrying a palm branch, the symbol of victory for all holy martyrs.

Saint Barbara
Virgin and Martyr

c. Third Century
(December 4)

THERE MUST HAVE been a real Saint Barbara; God would not have allowed so much devotion to be paid to a nonentity. The name "Barbara" itself, which means "foreign woman," was commonly given by the Greeks and Romans to their slave girls, and among the thousands of martyrs of the early centuries there would no doubt have been more than one maiden by this name who gave her life for Christ.

However, the fact remains that we know almost nothing of this real Saint Barbara. Not the slightest mention is made of any saint by this name until the seventh century when an exciting "Life of Saint Barbara" appeared. This was written originally in Greek, but it was soon translated into Latin and Syriac and then into many other later languages of Europe. During the Middle Ages Saint Barbara was one of the most popular saints, and she has still retained much of her popularity. Since at least the ninth century, her feast appears in the calendar of the Church as celebrated on the 4th of December.

According to the variant forms of her legend, Barbara suffered martyrdom during the reign of either Maximin (235-238), or Maximian (286-305). The site of her martyrdom is placed in so many different cities that it is impossible to decide where the original legend put it.

Barbara's father, says the story, was a rich pagan named Dioscorus. To hide her great beauty from men until the proper husband could be found for her, Dioscorus kept his daughter locked up in a high fortress tower. He did, indeed, introduce several handsome princes to her, but she rejected all of them.

Before leaving on a long journey, Dioscorus arranged to have a Roman bath, that is, a sort of enclosed swimming pool, built for his daughter. When Barbara saw that her father's plans called for only two windows in this room, she had the builders put three, instead of two windows in it. On his return home, Dioscorus was surprised to see the additional third window in the new room, and he asked his daughter about it. She told him that she had made the builders put three windows in the room in honor of the Most Blessed Trinity, the source of all the physical and spiritual light in the world, and she added that in this bathing pool she had been baptized a Christian.

Dioscorus was so enraged at this that he almost killed her then and there. Thinking, however, that he might induce her to renounce Christianity, he brought her to the pagan judge. On the way to her martyrdom Barbara prayed: "Lord Jesus Christ, who hast formed heaven and earth, I beg Thee to give me Thy grace and hear my prayer for those who are mindful of Thy name and Thy Passion. Grant that Thou wilt not remember their sins, for Thou knowest our fraility." When the flatteries, arguments and threats of the judge failed to make Barbara give up her Christian faith, he ordered her scourged and cruelly tortured in other ways. Her brutal father not only remained unmoved as he looked on these torments of his daughter, but when sentence of death was finally passed, he requested and was granted permission to carry it out himself. He drew his sword and struck off her head. On the same occasion, Barbara's servant girl, Juliana (who was also a Christian and had taught her mistress the Christian faith), likewise gained the crown of martyrdom.

When Dioscorus was returning home from this gruesome scene, a bolt of lightning suddenly struck and killed him.

The story of St. Barbara, as told in Caxton's Golden Legend, ends with the words: "A nobleman called Valentine buried the bodies of these two martyrs and laid them in a little town in which many miracles were showed in praise and glory of God Almighty."

Saint Barbara is one of the so-called "Fourteen Holy Helpers." She is invoked for protection against fire and especially, because of her dying prayer, for the grace of receiving the Last Sacraments worthily before death. As a result of the changes she made in her father's building plans, she is one of the patrons of architects, and in art she is usually represented as holding a small tower in her arms. On account of the bolt of lightning that killed her father, she is also patron of miners who blast away the underground rock, and particularly the patron of artillery soldiers whose weapons are similar to the lightning that punished her wicked father.

Saint Bartholomew

Apostle

First Century

(August 24)

I N ARAMAIC THE word *bar*, meaning "son," was used with the name of a man's father to form a sort of "family" name for him. Thus, before the Prince of the Apostles was given the name of "Peter," meaning "the Rock," by our Lord, his full name was Simon Bar-Jona, that is, Simon son of Jonas. The name "Bartholomew," therefore, is really the "last," or family name, of the Apostle Saint Bartholomew. It means "son of Tolmai."

There is good reason to believe that Bartholomew's "first" or proper name was "Nathanael," which means "God has given (us a son)." In the 21st chapter of St. John's Gospel, where the story is told of how Christ appeared after His Resurrection to several of His Apostles while they were fishing on the Sea of Tiberias, Nathanael is mentioned (in the 2nd verse) after Peter and Thomas (but before the sons of Zebedee (James and John)) in such a way that it seems practically certain that he was one of the twelve Apostles. Yet outside of the Gospel of St. John, Nathanael is not mentioned in the New Testament. If, as seems quite certain, he was one of the Apostles, he must be mentioned under some other name in the official lists of the Apostles that are given in the other three Gospels, and in the Acts of the Apostles. Now, the Apostle who is mentioned in this list only by his family name of Bartholomew is the most likely candidate for being identified

SAINTS ANDREW, JOHN THE BAPTIST, JOHN THE EVANGELIST, MARY MAGDALENE and MICHAEL THE ARCHANGEL (*Courtesy of the Metropolitan Museum of Art, Bequest of George Blumenthal,* 1941)

This Spanish (Castilian) altarpiece of the fifteenth century highlights the Pieta, and features the Madonna and Child, Saint Andrew (upper right); John the Baptist (lower right); Saint Michael the Archangel (upper left), and Saint Peter (lower left).

SAINT APOLLONIA

A Christian martyr of the third century at Alexandria, Apollonia was the
victim of pagan mob violence. As one of her tortures resulted in the loss
of her teeth, she has become the patron saint of dentists, and is particularly invoked by those suffering toothache. She is often represented in art
as depicted here—carrying a palm branch, the symbol of victory for all
the Church's holy martyrs.

with Nathanael. This is confirmed by the fact that in Saint John's Gospel (1,48), Nathanael is spoken of in close connection with Philip (it was Philip who introduced him to Jesus); while in the first three Gospels (which list the twelve Apostles in the form of six pairs), the third pair (after Peter and Andrew, James and John) is always "Philip and Bartholomew" (Matt. 10,3; Mark 3,18; Luke 6,14).

Since we are thus justified in identifying Bartholomew with Nathanael, we can learn more about the former by reading what is said of the latter. Saint John tells us in his Gospel (1,45-49) how Nathanael came to be a follower of Christ. After Philip had come to believe in Jesus as the promised Messiah, he told his friend Nathanael about Him, but when Nathanael heard that this Messiah came from the little town of Nazareth, he found it hard to believe. "Can anything good come from Nazareth?" he asked. Nevertheless, at Philip's urging, Nathanael went to see Jesus. Our Lord's first words to Nathanael were: "Behold a true Israelite in whom there is no guile!" This is certainly a magnificent tribute from Christ, who can read the hearts and minds of men. Nathanael was surprised at this praise, and he asked Jesus how He knew him. In answer, Jesus said to him, "Before Philip called thee, when thou wast under the fig tree, I saw thee." What these rather cryptic words mean is hard to say. Apparently they refer to Christ's supernatural knowledge of some crisis that was going on at that time in Nathanael's mind, for the latter's response is a full act of faith in this supernatural mind reader: "Thou art the Son of God, Thou art the King of Israel."

We also learn from Saint John's Gospel (21,2), that Nathanael's home town was Cana of Galilee. This is the same Cana of Galalee where Jesus changed water into wine at the wedding feast, His first public miracle (John 2,1-11). Was Nathanael in some way connected with the wedding, perhaps even as the bridegroom? Possibly, but there is no way of knowing for certain.

Later traditions concerning the countries where St. Nathanael-Bartholomew preached the gospel after Christ's ascension into

heaven are rather conflicting and uncertain. According to one tradition, he preached the glad tidings of Christian salvation in
"India." However, ancient writers often used the word "India"
to designate what we would now call southern Arabia. It is not
improbable that the Saint could have evangelized this part of the
world, for even at the time of Christ there were probably Jewish
settlers in Yemen or southern Arabia, and the Apostles had
received the commission from their divine Master to preach His
gospel in every place where there were Jews.

According to another tradition Saint Bartholomew preached the
gospel of Christ in Armenia. This tradition also cannot be called
improbable. The ancient kingdom of Armenia (just northeast of
Asia Minor) bordered on the Roman empire and might, therefore,
have first heard of the gospel at a very early date. This tradition
says that Saint Bartholomew suffered martyrdom in the city of
Albanopolis (modern Derbent, on the western shore of the Cas-
pian Sea) in what was then part of the Kingdom of Armenia, but
is now part of Russia. Bartholomew is said to have been first
flayed alive and then beheaded by order of an Armenian king
called Astyages. Because of his flaying, he is often represented in
art as holding a knife in his hand. The Armenians venerate him
as their national patron.

The relics of Saint Bartholomew are believed to have been
brought, after much journeying, to Benevento in southern Italy.
From there, a part of them were brought to Rome where they are
venerated in the church of St. Bartholomew on the Island of the
Tiber.

Saint Basil the Great
Bishop and Doctor

3 7 9

(June 14)

EVEN IN HIS own lifetime St. Basil of Caesarea in Cappadocia was known as "the Great"—an epithet which he well merited. After St. Athanasius of Alexandria (who died in 373), Basil was the principal defender in the East of orthodox Christianity as defined by the Council of Nicea. He also left his mark for all times on the history of Christian monasticism as well as on the Liturgy of the Eastern Church.

There were several cities in the Roman empire which, named after the "Caesar" or emperor, were called "Caesarea." The particular city by this name in which Basil was born towards the end of the year 329, and of which he was later to become its most illustrious bishop, was situated in that region of Eastern Asia Minor (now Turkey) which was then known as Cappadocia. His ancestors, however, who were of old Christian stock, came orginally from the region to the northwest known as Pontus. Here one of his great-grandfathers had died as a martyr for the Faith. It was mainly on account of the persecution which the Roman emperor Maximinus Galerius had launched against the Christians that Basil's family had migrated from Pontus into Cappadocia in the year 311.

Basil belongs quite literally to a family of saints. His grandmother is venerated by the Church as Saint Macrina the Elder, his parents as Saint Basil the Elder and Saint Emmelia. His brother was Saint Gregory, the famous bishop of Nyssa, while his sister was the holy abbess, Saint Macrina the Younger. Basil the Elder, a prominent Christian lawyer of Pontus and Cappadocia, who had suffered exile and impoverishment for the Faith, died while his namesake son was still young. The boy's mother, who had given her husband ten children, saw to it that the boy was well reared in her model Christian home. Basil the Great also speaks of the debt of gratitude that he owed to his grandmother, Saint Macrina the Elder, for his early lessons in Christianity.

After completing his elementary schooling in his native city of Caesarea, Basil first went for higher studies to the capital of the empire, Constantinople, where the renowned rhetorician, Libanius, was his teacher. Though Libanius alway remained a pagan and was, in fact, quite hostile to Christianity, he retained a warm friendship and a high regard for his brilliant pupil from Caesarea.

Having finished his literary studies at Constantinople, Basil went to the ancient university city of Athens for the study of philosophy and the related sciences. During his years here, 352 to 355, one of his fellow students was Julian, who was later to become emperor and win for himself the unenviable title of "the Apostate" or account of his relapse from Christianity into paganism. It is doubtful, however, whether there was ever any personal friendship between Basil, the pious son of a provincial lawyer of Cappadocia, and Julian the royal heir of the imperial house. On the contrary, Basil's intimate friend at Athens was his fellow Cappadiocian, Gregory, who was later to become bishop of Nazianzus. Both of them were serious students and they exercised a healthy influence on each other. Together with Basil's brother Gregory, who was later consecrated bishop of Nyssa, these "three Cappadocians," as they are called, were eventually to be numbered among the Doctors of the Church. All three of them followed the example of the learned Father of the third century, Clement of Alexandria, in taking all that was good in ancient pagan education — its philosophy and science, its literature and culture — and developing it into a new whole with the Christian faith.

Although Basil belonged to a very pious Christian family he did not receive the sacrament of baptism until he was a mature man. Thus it was only on his return from Athens to Caesarea in 356, when he was about twenty-six years old, that he was baptized by Dianius, bishop of his native city. Basil considered this a genuine turning point in his life, his "conversion," as he called it, in a special sense of the word. He now felt that his early life, though innocent enough in itself, was mere worldliness. Henceforth he would devote his life solely to God.

For this purpose he first set out on a journey of two years (357-358) to visit the various "deserts" or solitary sites in Asia Minor, Mesopotamia, Syria, Palestine, and Egypt, where holy men lived as hermits, spending their lives far from the distractions of the world in prayer and penance. Saint Anthony of Egypt had already given to many of these groups of hermits a loosely knit form of community or "coenobitic" life. While Basil was full of admiration for the exemplary lives of these hermits, his practical sense told him that it would be more profitable, not only for the monks themselves, but also for their fellow Christians, if the hermits of any given group would join their cells together so as to form one "laura" or monastery. Thus, while they continued to live lives of self-denial and contemplation, they would also have the spiritual advantage of practicing more perfect obedience to an abbot who had greater authority in the guidance and government of his monks and, at the same time, their manual labor on the field and their intellectual work in the library and classroom would bear more beneficial fruits for their fellow-men.

Therefore, on his return to Asia Minor in 359, Basil, together with his friend Gregory, established the first monastery of this kind. His mother, Emmelia, and his sister, Macrina, had already founded a sort of convent for nuns at their ancestral property on the bank of the River Iris in Pontus. On the opposite shore of this stream Basil then set up his monastery for monks who wished to live in common under one abbot or superior. Other holy men soon joined the two Cappadocians, and in a few years several monasteries of this nature were founded in the neighboring regions of Asia Minor. For the benefit of these monks Saint Basil wrote a number of ascetical works such as his "Little Rule," his "Great Rule," and his "Moralia." These "Rules" of Saint Basil do not consist of a series of exact precepts such as are considered the proper constituent elements of a "Rule" for a religious community; they are rather more or less of the nature of general exhortations. Yet these exhortations really form the basis of what is now known as the Basilian Rule upon which all the monasteries of Eastern Christianity are based. Saint Basil the Great is, therefore, rightly entitled to be called "the Father of Eastern Monasticism," just as Saint Benedict of Nursia is known as "the Father of Western Monasticism." In fact, the "Rules" written by Saint Basil had no small influence on the Rule which Saint Benedict (480-543) drew up for his monks of the West. Besides, not only in the East, but also in the Western Church the religious order of Basilian monks is still flourishing. At least indirectly, therefore, that element of present-day Catholicism known as "the Religious Life," with its innumerable orders and congregations of religious men and women who live a community life under the three vows of poverty, chastity and obedience, is in no small measure the result of the genius of this great Cappadocian.

It was largely because of the religious controversies of his time that Saint Basil was forced to leave the peace of his monastery to defend the orthodox faith of Christianity against the heresy of Arianism. The Arians, in asserting that Jesus Christ was not the Son of God in the strict sense, equal to the eternal Father in all things, denied the teaching of the Church as formulated in the Nicene Creed regarding both the Blessed Trinity and the Incarnation. For the purpose of preaching in defense of the orthodox faith against the attacks of the Arian heretics, Basil consented to be ordained a priest in the year 363 by his good friend, Bishop Eusebius of Caesarea. During the following years,

therefore, he remained in this city, acting as a bulwark of orthodoxy by his preaching and writing. Since he had really been for
a long time the power behind the episcopal throne, when Eusebius
died in 370, Basil was chosen to succeed him as bishop of Caesarea.

For the next eight and a half years Basil continued his heroic
labors for the spiritual and temporal welfare of his flock. Although the extent of his work in reforming the sacred Liturgy is
difficult to determine, his influence here must have been considerable otherwise the Eastern Church would not have called
one of the forms in which the Sacrifice of the Mass is celebrated
in the East "the Liturgy of Saint Basil." Still keeping to his monastic life of poverty even as archbishop, Basil devoted all the
income of his see to the good of his people. Besides several
churches which he erected, he also founded an immense charitable
institution, later known as the Basiliade, which included a hospital for the sick poor, a hospice for the strangers and the homeless, an asylum for the orphans, and a school for the young.

Despite his very active life, Saint Basil found time during these
years for a surprisingly large amount of writing. In addition to
his ascetical and dogmatic works, some three hundred and sixty
of his letters, nine of his homilies on the creation of the world,
nine more on the Psalms, and twenty-four other sermons on various religious subjects have come down to us. In the history of
dogmatic theology Saint Basil the Gretat is of prime importance
because of his clear exposition of the Catholic doctrine on the
Blessed Trinity and the Incarnation. It is especially here that
the fruit of his early studies in philosophy can best be seen.

Basil's controversies with the Arians, however, were not confined to merely preaching and writing. He literally had to bear
the brunt of a physical struggle. The Arian emperor Valens did all
he could to force Basil to subscribe to the heretical tenets of
Arianism, even going so far as to send Modestus, the imperial
"prefect" or chief of police, to intimidate him with threats of torture and exile. Basil replied that the threats of banishment meant

nothing to him since he was already an exile from heaven and no place on earth was really his home. Nor did he fear the tortures with which Modestus threatened him for he was, as he said, already suffering much from a chest ailment and with the first few lashes of the scourge he would leave this world to be with Christ — a thing he ardently longed for.

Actually the great Cappadocian had already spent the last year of his life in Christ's cause. Worn out by his many labors and infirmities, Basil breathed his last on January 1, 379. The Eastern Church celebrates his feast on this very day, the first of January, besides having another special feast on the thirtieth of January in honor of "the Three Cappadocians": Saint Basil the Great, his brother Saint Gregory of Nyssa, and their friend Saint Gregory of Nazianzus.

From St. Basil's Homily on Humility (*Homily 20*)

Would that man had abided in the glory which he possessed with God — he would have genuine instead of fictitious dignity. For he would be ennobled by the power of God, illumined with divine wisdom, and made joyful in the possession of eternal life and its blessings. But, because he ceased to desire divine glory in expectation of a better prize, and strove for the unattainable, he lost the good which it was in his power to possess. The surest salvation for him, the remedy of his ills, and the means of restoration to his original state is in practicing humility and not pretending that he may lay claim to any glory through his own efforts but seeking it from God. Thus will he make amends for his error, thus will he be cured of his malady, thus will he return to the observance of the holy precept which he has abandoned. For the Devil, having caused man's ruin by holding out to him the hope of false glory, ceases not to tempt him still by the same allurements and he devises innumerable schemes to this end. For instance, he represents a large fortune to him as a great good, so that man will regard it as a cause for boasting and expend great effort to obtain it. Wealth, however, leads not to glory but to great peril. To build a fortune is to lay the foundation for avarice, and the acquisition of money bears no relation to excellence of character. Rather, it blinds a man to no purpose, arouses vain conceit, and produces in his soul an effect something like an inflamed swelling. Now, a tumor combined with inflammation is neither healthful nor beneficial to the body, but unwholesome, injurious, a source of danger, and a cause of death. Such an effect does pride engender in the soul . . . .

Why, then, pray, do you glory in your goods as if they were your own instead of giving thanks to the Giver for His Gifts? 'For what hast thou that thou hast not received? And if thou has received, why dost thou glory as if thou hadst not received it?' You have not known God by reason of your justice, but God has known you by reason of His goodness. 'After that you have known God,' says the Apostle, 'or rather are known by God.' You did not apprehend Christ because of your virtue, but Christ apprehended you by His coming. 'I follow after,' says the Apostle, 'if I also may comprehend wherein I am also apprehended by Christ.' 'You have not chosen me,' says the Lord, 'but I have chosen you.' Yet you, because honor is accorded you, exalt yourself and find an occasion for pride in the mercy that is granted you. Know yourself, at length, for what you are — Adam expelled from paradise, Saul abandoned by the Spirit of God, Israel cut off from the sacred root. 'But thou standest by faith,' says the Apostle 'be not high-minded but fear.' Judgment will be in accordance with grace, and the Judge will make examination of how you have used the graces bestowed upon you. If you do not understand that you have received grace and by an excess of stupidity ascribe to yourself the success which is a gift of grace, you will fare no better than St. Peter. Indeed, you will not be able to surpass in love for the Lord him who loved Him so ardently that he desired to die for Him. Yet, because he spoke boastfully, saying: 'Although all shall be scandalized in thee, I will never be scandalized,' he fell a victim to human cowardice and committed the act of denial, gaining prudence and caution through his fall. Moreover, he learned by discovering his own weakness to be indulgent to the weak. And clearly did he come to understand that, just as he had been lifted up by the helping Hand of Christ when he was sinking into the sea, so, when he was in mortal danger from the billow of scandal because of his incredulity, he was protected by the power of Christ who had foretold to him what was to be, saying: 'Simon, Simon, behold Satan hath desired that he may sift you as wheat; but I have prayed for thee that thy faith fail not; and thou, being once converted, confirm thy brethren.' Peter, thus reproved, was deservedly given aid, for he had learned how to put away his pride and show forebearance toward the weak. Again, that stern Pharisee, who in his overweening pride not only boasted of himself but also discredited the publican in the presence of God, made his justice void by being guilty of pride. The publican went down justified in preference to him because he had given glory to God, the Holy One, and did not dare to lift his eyes, but sought only to win mercy, accusing himself by his posture, by striking his breast, and by entertaining no other motive except propitiation. Be on your guard, therefore, and bear in mind this example of grievous loss sustained through arrogance. The one guilty of insolent behavior suffered the loss of his justice and forfeited his reward by his bold self-reliance. He was rendered inferior to a humble man and a sinner because in his self-exaltation he did not await the judgment of God, but pronounced it for himself. Never place yourself above anyone, not even great sinners. Humility often saves a sinner who has committed many grievous transgressions. Do not, then, justify yourself as regards another and never condemn yourself on the verdict of God by justifying yourself on the basis of your own. 'I judge not my own self,' says Paul, 'for I am not conscious to myself of anything, yet I am not hereby justified; but he that judgeth me is the Lord.' . . .

But how shall we, casting off the deadly weight of pride, descend to saving humility? If such an aim governed our conduct under all circumstances, we should not overlook the least detail on the ground that we would suffer no harm therefrom. The soul comes to take on a resemblance to its preoccupations and it is stamped and molded to the form of its activities. Let your aspect, your garb, your manner of walking and sitting, your diet, bed, house and its furnishings reflect a customary thrift. Your manner of speaking and singing, your conversation with your neighbor, also, should aim at modesty rather than pretentiousness. Do not strive, I beg you, for artificial embellishment in speech, for cloying sweetness in song, or for a sonorous and high-flown style in conversation. In all your actions, be free from pomposity. Be obliging to your friends, gentle toward your slaves, forebearing with the forward, benign to the lowly, a source of comfort to the afflicted, a friend to the distressed, a condemnor of no one. Be pleasant in your address, genial in your response, courteous, accessible to all. Speak not in your own praise, nor contrive that others do so. Do not listen to indecent talk, and conceal insofar as you can your own superior gifts. On the other hand, where sin is concerned, be your own accuser, and do not wait for others to make the accusation. Thus, you will be like a just man who accuses himself in the first speech made in court, or like Job who was not deterred by the crowd of people in the city from declaring his personal guilt before all. Be not rash in rebuking, nor quick to do so. Do not make accusations while your passions are aroused (for such action savors of wilfulness), not condemn anyone in matters of slight consequence as if you yourself were perfectly just. Receive those who have fallen away and give them spiritual instruction, 'considering thyself also lest thou be tempted,' as the Apostle advises. Take as much care not to be glorified among men as others do to obtain this glory, as you remember the words of Christ, that one forfeits a reward from God by voluntarily seeking renown from men or do good to be seen by men. 'They have received their reward,' He says. Do not cheat yourself by desiring to be seen by men, for God is the great Witness. Strive for glory with God, for His is a glorious recompense. . . . To sum up, strive after humility as becomes a lover of this virtue. Love it and it will glorify you . . . . Amen.

Saint Bernardine of Siena

Confessor

1 4 4 4

(May 20)

THE COMMON CHRISTIAN symbol, IHS, is happily no longer explained to children as standing for the English words, "I Have Suffered"; after all, it is used by very many people who do not speak English. Most informed Catholics now know that this symbol, IHS, is our Lord's monogram and consists of the first three letters of the Holy Name of Jesus as written in Greek: IHSOUS. But there are probably few people who know that the widespread custom of using this symbol as a public profession of our Christian faith in Jesus is due above all to Saint Bernardine of Siena, one of the brightest lights of the Franciscan order and one of the greatest preachers and missionaries that Italy has ever known.

It was in the year 1380 that Siena gave back to God its precious treasure, the famous mystic, St. Catherine of Siena. Only a few months later in the same year there was born another saint who was destined by God to bring new glory on the name of this ancient city of Tuscany — St. Bernardine of Siena.

St. Bernardine's birthday in 1380 coincided with the birthday of the Blessed Virgin Mary, the 8th of September. This feast of Mary's Nativity was a memorable one in the life of St. Bernardine, for it was on the 8th of September in the year 1402 that he received the holy habit of St. Francis of Assisi; on the same day one year later he took his vows as a Franciscan; and on the selfsame day in the following year he was ordained to the priesthood.

Although Bernardine's name is always connected with that of Siena, where he grew up as a youth and which he always loved as his "home town," he was not born here, but at Massa Marittima, a Tuscan city situated approximately fifty miles to the southwest of Siena. St. Bernardine's father, Dino Tollo, the mayor of Massa Marittima, was a member of one of Siena's most noble families, the Albizeschi. Bernardine's mother, Nera, was also of noble descent, a daughter of the house of the Avveduti.

Bernardine was only three years old when his young mother died, and three years later his father followed her in death. The young boy was left in the care of his mother's sister, Diana, a widow, who brought him up as her own son. Like his parents, this good lady had a great devotion to the Blessed Mother of God, and all of them had a part in instilling into the heart of the boy that intense love for Our Lady which grew with his years. His aunt Diana also taught him to use care in the choice of his companions and to keep himself chaste and pure.

This devoted aunt, however, died when Bernardine was eleven years old, and his relatives then took him from Massa Marittima to Siena, the ancestral home of his family. Here another uncle and aunt, Christopher and Pia, received him into their home and, having no children of their own, treated him as if he were their own son. Aunt Pia often used to take the boy with her to Mass and, on his return home from church, he would repeat to the other children the sermon he had heard — a foreboding of the career which would make his name a household word all over Italy. This aunt of his, as she continued to foster in him a love for Mary, taught him to say the Little Office of the Blessed Virgin Mary.

At Siena Bernardine attended the recently opened school of John of Spoleto, where he was taught Latin grammar, rhetoric, and the humanities. He was a serious student and made excellent progress in his studies. Bernardine became greatly devoted to John and stayed with him as much as he could, while the teacher in turn dearly loved his brilliant pupil. This was the period of the *Risorgimento* ("new rising") or early Italian Renaissance, and Bernardine was a child of his age. There was never anything of the fanatic about him. Saint though he was, he appreciated all that was good in the "new learning," and counted among his friends in later life the leading scholars and artists of his time. In his later position as Vicar General of the Observant Franciscans he encouraged study and learning among his Friars. Tuscany of the Fifteenth Century, the famous *Quattro Cento* or "Four Hundreds," as the Italians call it, produced an amazing number of geniuses in the arts; in Bernardine it produced a genius in the art of preaching as well as in sanctity.

After finishing his schooling with John of Spoleto, Bernardine studied canon and civil law at Siena, though it seems that he did not go on to receive the doctorate in this field. His heart was rather in the study of Sacred Scripture, which he pursued with joy during these years.

Several stories are told of Bernardine's youth at Siena which show that he combined an ardent love of virtue with that wholesome exuberance and joy in life which is typically Tuscan. On one occasion he was accosted by a man who used such vile language that Bernardine, without a moment's hesitation, let him have a hard punch in the jaw that set him flying. Since the youth's handsome appearance and charming personality made him quite attractive to the young ladies, one of these once went so far as to. use her feminine wiles in an effort to seduce him. Bernardine got rid of her as quickly as he had sent his male tormentor packing, though presumably not by such violent means.

If he ever had a "lady friend," it was his cousin Tobia, the daughter of his aunt Diana. The two were indeed much devoted to each other, but not, of course, in the ordinary sense as "lovers." Tobia was more than thirty years his senior and was more like a mother than even like an older sister to the teen-age youth. A very devout woman and a member of the Third Order of St. Francis, she made her home the center of various charitable works for the poor, the sick, the pilgrims and the prisoners.

With all his religious zeal and piety, Bernardine was quite a normal young man and not above teasing his cousin Tobia. Once he confided to her that he was in love with a most beautiful lady and that he went to visit her every day; some day, he added, he would leave his cousin forever for the sake of this lady. Tobia at first thought he was joking. But noticing that he was indeed absent for a good part of each day, she began to fear that he might perhaps have fallen a victim to the wiles of some good-for-nothing girl. So one day she secretly followed him as he left her house, and then she found out who his "lady friend" really was: there he was, kneeling for a long time in church before an image of the Mother of God.

In his late teens Bernardine joined the Confraternity of Our Lady, a group of pious men attached to the large hospital in Siena that was called the Ospitale di Santa Maria della Scala. These men were also known as the "Disciplinati" from their custom of using the discipline or scourge on themselves as a means of penance. Though Bernardine faithfully adhered to their austere life of fasting and mortification, he was always most cheerful and friendly and never gave the least sign of leading an ascetical life.

In the year 1400 a dreadful pestilence struck the city, and the hospital was filled to overflowing with the victims of this plague. With his usual spirit of generosity Bernardine offered his full-time services to the head of the hospital. Though only twenty years old, he was already proving himself a born leader. Earnestly appealing to the members of his Confraternity and to others among his friends, he won their help in this good cause. The head of the hospital was so pleased with this welcome assistance that he turned over to Bernardine the full charge of his institution. For over four months the young man labored night and day in the care of the plague-stricken who crowded into the

hospital. But then, as the pentilence abated, he himself was laid
low by it, and for four months was seriously ill. On finally recovering his health and vigor, he took over the nursing care of an
aged aunt, who, as she now drew near her ninetieth year, was
blind, deaf and ill, and he attended her till she died about a year
later. This aunt rewarded him for his generous service by teaching
him the devotion to the Holy Name of Jesus, a practice which
was to play an important role in his later life.

At last free from his obligations to his relatives, Bernardine,
now twenty-two years old, resolved to devote the rest of his life
to the service of God as a member of a religious order. Retiring to
an isolated house in the suburbs, he spent several months in
prayer and the practice of rigorous austerities, in order to learn
more clearly what God wished him to do. Two religious orders
were especially appealing to him: that of St. Dominic's Order of
Preachers, and that of St. Francis' Friars Minor (literally, "Little
Brothers"). Finally enlightened in a vision, he decided to join
the Friars Minor. He was graciously received by Father John
Ristori, superior of the monastery of San Francesco in Siena, who
gave him the habit of St. Francis on September 8, 1402.

After two months, however, Bernardine found that this monastery in the heart of Siena was too distracting for his liking. He
therefore asked and was given permission to finish his novitiate
at the small monastery of the Friars of the Observance, who lived
a more austere life, in a place called Colombaio, a short distance
from the city. This monastery, which had been founded by St.
Francis himself, always remained Bernardine's favorite place of
retreat, where he could commune in quiet intercourse with his
beloved Lord.

One year after Bernardine had taken his vows as a Franciscan,
he was ordained to the priesthood and at once began, though
at first in a quiet, simple way, his active work for the salvation
of souls. A year later, that is, in 1405, the new Superior General
of the order, Father Antonio Piretto, hearing of the zeal of the
holy young friar, and of his ability in preaching, appointed him

SAINT BARTHOLOMEW   Michelangelo

From the Gospel of St. John we are justified in identifying Bartholomew
with Nathanael. One of the twelve Apostles, Bartholomew's home town was
Cana of Galilee wherein Our Lord changed water into wine. Martyred in
Armenia, the Saint is venerated by the Armenians as their national patron.
Here he is depicted from Michelangelo's "Last Judgment," probably the
world's most famous painting.

SAINT BARBARA   Van Eyck

This Saint suffered martyrdom following her revelation that she had been
baptized a Christian during the reign of either Maximin, or Maximian, in
the third century. As one of the "Fourteen Holy Helpers," Barbara is invoked for the grace of receiving the Last Sacrament. In this reproduction
of Van Eyck's painting, she is portrayed before the fortress in which her
pagan father kept her imprisoned.

to the office of public preacher. At first Bernardine felt handi-
capped by a somewhat weak and raucous voice. But in answer to
his prayers God soon gave him such a strong, ringing voice that
he could easily be heard by everyone in the vast gatherings
which eventually came to his sermons. Even in this early period
of his missionary life there were times when people came from
far and wide to listen to his stirring preaching. On one such
occasion so large was the number of people who assembled to hear
him that the church could not contain them. Bernardine therefore
preached to them in the open air, using a tree for a pulpit. An
ancient painting has perpetuated this scene, showing, at the place
where the sermon was delivered, the small church and hermitage
of St. Onofrio on the hill of Capriola, about a mile from Siena.
This hermitage had been the property of the Hospital of Santa
Maria della Scala. When Bernardine expressed a desire of having
it as a place where he and his companions could live in the strict
observance of the Franciscan rule in the same way as he had
lived in the Colombaio monastery, the head of the hospital, remembering the saint's services during the plague, gladly ceded
the place to him and his companions.

Italy in the period of the early Renaissance presented a strange
mixture of Christianity and paganism. The upper classes, when
not reveling in their new-found luxury, were engaged in the
bloody warfare of their poltical factions. The ordinary people
were often sunk in practices of barbarity, sensuality and magic.
Sorcery and charms seems almost as important to them as the
holy rites of the church. Gambling was widespread, and the shows
and amusements were generally far from edifying. Holy Mass
and the sacraments were in danger of becoming meaningless
ceremonies for the ignorant people.

Bernardine longed to do something towards reforming the
morals of the people and bringing them back to God. But in
his humility he felt himself entirely unequal to the task. Then
the great Dominican preacher and missionary, St. Vincent Ferrer,
came into northern Italy, and the young Franciscan of Siena

went to hear him preach. The two met at Alessandria, inland from Genoa. Vincent received Bernardine most kindly and quickly recognized his worth. The next day the humble Franciscan was astounded to hear the famous Dominican preacher say during his sermon that there was a young Friar Minor in his audience who would be his successor in evangelizing Italy and whose fame as a preacher would surpass his own.

Yet ten years were to pass before this prophecy of St. Vincent Ferrer proved to be true. During these years Bernardine apparently lived at Capriola and limited his zeal to Siena and the immediate vicinity. In 1418, however, he was invited to the important city of Milan in northern Italy, to preach the series of Lenten sermons there. As is still the custom in Italy, the Lenten preacher gave a long sermon every day during the holy season of penance. Bernardine's series of sermons at Milan began in a very strange way. In the course of his first sermon, on Ash Wednesday, he suddenly stopped short and excused himself for not being able to continue at present. When asked that day by his friends about this, he said that in the pulpit he had suddenly seen a vision of the soul of his dear cousin Tobia going to heaven. A few days later news reached Milan that Bernardine's cousin Tobia had indeed died at the very hour when he interrupted his sermon. Word of this remarkable vision spread throughout the city, and the people began saying that their Lenten preacher was a saint. Bernardine's humility was too deep and genuine to let this move him to any feelings of vanity, but he did rejoice to see the good effect that it had on the people. Larger and larger crowds flocked to hear his sermons. Innumerable penitents went to confession and reformed their lives.

The same thing now happened in one city after another where Bernardine was invited to preach. The fame of the eloquent friar from Siena spread through the length and breadth of Italy. Through his eloquence and the sanctity of his life Bernardine proved himself a genuine "reformer," curing Italy of its moral corruption in the right way a century before the would-be "reformers" of northern Europe sought to destroy the Church in their misguided efforts at a false "Reformation." Bernardine preached a return to God through a return to the Church and its holy sacraments. According to the quaint expression of a contemporary writer, penitents flocked "like ants" to the confessional after his sermons. Huge bonfires were made in which the people burned their "vanities," their amulets and other objects of superstition. Social reforms were also introduced as the result of his preaching, such as the abolition of usury and the establishment of means by which the impoverished people could obtain necessary loans at a nominal rate of interest, later to be developed into the benevolent loan associations that still flourish in Italy under the name of "Monti di Pieta." In several cities Bernardine's sound counsels for social reform were incorporated into written laws, known as the "Reformazioni di Frate Bernardino." When he met with opposition from the high and mighty, he had no fear of rebuking them, even though they were as powerful as Visconti, Duke of Milan.

In every city and town where Bernardine preached, his basic message was that of his holy Founder, the Little Poor Man of Assisi — the message of "Peace," peace between man and God, and peace between man and his fellow man. His efforts at establishing peace between the Guelphs and the Ghibellines and the other warring factions of the turbulent Italian cities met with much success. He urged the nobles to discard their various escutcheons and to substitute for them the genuinely Christian coat of arms, the monogram of the Holy Name, IHS.

Though Bernardine also preached devotion to the Blessed Virgin Mary and to St. Joseph, his special devotion, which he spread in every place where he gave a sermon, was to the Holy Name of Jesus. On his pulpit he would set up a large placard on which the monogram, IHS, surrounded with rays, was painted. At the end of his sermon he presented this to the people for their veneration, having them come up individually to kiss it, while they begged Jesus for pardon of their sins and promised Him amendment of life. He also exhorted the people to make use of this symbol in their homes.

At Bologna a certain man came to Bernardine and complained that his business of making playing cards was being ruined because the Friar was so vehement in his condemnation of gambling. Bernardine urged him to employ his talents at making cards that showed the IHS monogram and selling these to the people. The card-maker followed his advice and soon was doing a better business in this than he had done in his earlier business of making playing cards.

However, this new devotion to the Holy Name eventually brought upon Bernardine no little trouble and persecution. Other less gifted preachers, envious of the extraordinary success of the eloquent Franciscan, began to accuse of him of misleading the people into idolatry by having them pay worship to this new-fangled material emblem. These accusations were finally brought to Rome, and Bernardine was summoned to appear before the Pope and answer the charges of heresy that were leveled against him. When he presented himself to Pope Martin V, he was told that, till he was cleared of the charges, he was to remain in Rome and not engage in any preaching or other missionary activities. Always unswervingly loyal to the Holy See, Bernardine humbly obeyed. All his sermons and other writings were then examined by a committee of three Cardinals, who however found nothing wrong with them.

But the question of his method in propagating devotion to the Holy Name of Jesus still had to be settled. His enemies employed scores of canon lawyers to show that this method was deserving of condemnation, while he himself, no specialist in the niceties of law, stood alone against them. However, as soon as his good friend and fellow preacher, the Franciscan Friar John of Capestrano, who was himself to be later canonized, heard of Bernardine's plight, he hastened to Rome to defend him. At the trial, held in Rome on June 8, 1427, John publicly displayed a large placard of the IHS emblem and gave such a brilliant defense of the use of this sacred symbol that Bernardine was completely vindicated.

The next day Pope Martin V received the two Friars with every mark of kindness and respect, gave them his blessing with his permission to use this emblem and to preach devotion to the Holy Name wherever they went. To show his full approval, the Pope ordered a solemn procession to be held in the Eternal City, with John of Capestrano carrying the sacred emblem through the streets amid hymns of praise to the Holy Name. Yet Bernardine's enemies refused to admit of defeat. In 1432 under Pope Eugene IV they again brought charges of heresy against the eloquent Franciscan, and again Bernardine was vindicated. On this occasion Pope Eugene IV publicly praised him as "a man of upright conduct, solid integrity, and a blameless, pious life, and not only a most faithful Catholic, but himself a most vigorous and severe destroyer of heresy." To commemorate these events, the Franciscans were granted in 1530 the right to celebrate toward the beginning of every January the Feast of the Triumph of the Holy Name of Jesus. In 1727 this feast was extended to the universal Church. At present it is celebrated by all Catholics, under the simple title of the Feast of the Holy Name, on the Sunday that falls between the Feast of the Circumcision and that of Epiphany or, in those years when there is no such Sunday, on the 2nd of January.

In 1433, after accompanying the emperor, Sigismond, to Rome for the latter's coronation, Bernardine retired to Capriola, where he spent the next three years in the seclusion which he felt was necessary for his soul and body. During this time he wrote many sermons, particularly his two series of Lenten sermons on "The Eternal Gospel" and "Holy Religion." These long sermons, written in Latin, show that their author was no mean theologian. But they were intended primarily as storehouses of material for sermons, to be used by himself and other preachers, and were not meant to be delivered as living sermons in their present form. Therefore they give but a very inadequate idea of the real ser-

mons of St. Bernardine as he actually preached to the people. He
himself did not consider as worthy to be preserved the popular
sermons which he gave in Italian. But fortunately a whole series
of his Italian sermons as preached in Siena during the Lent of
1427 was taken down by a layman who knew shorthand, and a
few manuscripts containing copies of these sermons in longhand
have come down to us. Now published under the title of *Prediche
in Lingua Volgare,* "Sermons in the Language of the People,"
they show why Bernardine enjoyed such immense popularity as
a preacher. They are couched in the simple, common dialect of
Siena (Bernardine had a command of numerous Italian dialects),
and are interspersed with stories, illustrations, mimicry and jokes.
Though they thus sparkle with typical Sienese gaiety and Franciscan playfulness, they know when to be serious, and often they
are awe-inspiring in their denunciation of vice and their threats
of divine punishment. St. Bernardine was indeed a "spellbinder"
who could hold his audience entranced throughout sermons that
lasted as long as three or four hours. Incidentally for us mod-
erns these Italian sermons offer a rich source of information on
the customs and manners of the time.

From 1436 to 1438 Bernardine was again active as a missionary. But in 1438 his fellow Franciscans elected him Vicar General of the "Observants" or strict branch of the Friars Minor in
Italy, and the duties of this office now consumed most of the
saint's energies. The regular Friars Minor of today, as distinct
from the Conventual Franciscans, are the lineal descendants of
these "Observants" of the 15th century and, in a certain sense,
they owe more to St. Bernardine of Siena than to anyone else,
except of course their holy Founder, St. Francis of Assisi. Though
he did not originate the "Observant" movement among the followers of St. Francis, he was its main support and propagator.
During the four years of his Generalship he founded or reformed
more than three hundred monasteries of the Observant Friars.

Like Francis himself, Bernardine was deeply interested in the
Christianity of the Near East, the home land of our divine Savior

and the cradle of our faith. To this part of the world he sent many of his Friars as missionaries, and it was mainly through his efforts that a large number of the prelates of the Eastern Churches attended the Council of Florence (1439), where, at least temporarily, they abjured their schism and returned to the unity of the Church. Bernardine himself addressed the assembled prelates of this Council—in Greek!

In 1442, however, Bernardine resigned his office of Vicar General of the Observant Franciscans in order to devote himself once more to his favorite work of preaching. Though he had now evangelized almost all of central and northern Italy, the Kingdom of Naples in the south had not yet had the privilege of hearing his eloquence. In 1444 he answered the appeals of those southern Italians, and set out toward their region. But worn out by his unceasing labors, he was mortally stricken with fever at Aquila, in the mountains of the Abruzzi, northeast of Rome. Here in the monastery of the Conventual Franciscans, lying, as he requested, on the bare ground, he died on the Vigil of the Feast of the Ascension, May 20, 1444, just as the Friars were singing the Divine Office: "Father, I have manifested Thy name to men . . . And now I come to Thee."

Throughout his life St. Bernardine had refused every ecclesiastical honor and dignity—the bishopric of Siena in 1427, that of Ferrara in 1431, and that of Urbino in 1435—saying that all Italy was his diocese. But now that his humble soul had gone to heaven, he could no longer decline the honors which the Church bestowed on him, when in 1450 he was canonized by Pope Nicholas V. The Sienese longed to have his mortal remains brought to their city, but the people of Aquila would not part with them. At first Bernardine had been buried in the church of the Conventual Friars of this city, but through the efforts of his faithful friend, Saint John of Capestrano, a great basilica was erected in his honor at Aquila.

Saint Bonaventure

Bishop and Doctor

1 2 7 4

(July 14)

ALTHOUGH MUCH INFORMATION about the life of Saint Bonaventure can be gathered from the history of his age as well as from his own writings, it is unfortunate that no contemporaneous Life of this great Franciscan saint has come down to us. Of his early life we merely know that he was born in 1221 at Bagnorea, a little town near Viterbo in Tuscany, central Italy. Originally he was named John, after his father, John di Fidanza. When and why his name was changed to Bonaventure is uncertain, but an interesting legend is told in this regard.

It is said that when he was four years old he fell seriously ill and, as Saint Francis of Assisi was passing through that part of the country, the mother of the sick boy took him to the renowned Poor Man of Assisi and begged him to cure her child. Francis not only granted her request and miraculously saved the boy's life, but he also, according to the legend, said on this occasion, *O buona ventura* — Oh, happy meeting!" The mother thereupon vowed that if it was God's will, her son, who was henceforth called *"Bonaventura* — Bonaventure," would become a Franciscan. Be this as it may, Bonaventure himself merely mentions in one place that as a child he was rescued from mortal illness through the intercession of Saint Francis of Assisi. It is indeed quite doubtful whether the two saints ever met, since

Francis died in 1226 when Bonaventure was only five years old. It was probably in 1238, when Bonaventure was seventeen years old, that he became a Franciscan, though some authorities set this date as late as 1243. He must have already received a good basic education in early life for soon after his profession as a Franciscan he was sent by his superiors from his Roman Province to the University of Paris for higher studies in philosophy and theology. Here his first master was the learned Franciscan, Alexander of Hales, the *Doctor Irrefragibilis* or "Irrefutable Teacher," as he was called, whose faithful disciple Bonaventure always remained. Bonaventure remained a student at Paris until 1248 when he received the degree of the Licentiate, or license to teach, and from then to 1255 he taught philosophy and theology at this university.

During this period Bonaventure produced several of his most famous theological works. In fact, it was in 1248, at the age of only twenty-seven, that he wrote (at the command of his superiors) his "Commentary on the Sentences of Peter Lombard," a masterpiece that does not suffer in comparison with the contemporary *Summa Theologica* of the great Dominican theologian, Saint Thomas Aquinas.

It was during these years at Paris that Bonaventure and Thomas Aquinas met each other and became lifelong friends. Both saints were endowed by God with brilliant minds, and both reached sublime heights in philosophy and theology as well as in sanctity. Yet in several respects one differed from the other. While Thomas may have had a keener mind for philosophical thought and speculation, Bonaventure had a more poetic soul and a livelier imagination. To the Dominican saint philosophy and theology were exact sciences to be developed with cool intellectual detachment and presented in clear-cut, though rather dry terminology, almost like a textbook on higher mathematics. The Franciscan saint, on the other hand, made every philosophical and theological treatise that he wrote a piece of genuine literature that not only enlightens the mind but inflames the heart.

It has well been said that in Thomas we behold sublime love of theology, but in Bonaventure a sublime theology of love.

On another point also these two greatest geniuses among the medieval schoolmen differed. Thomas Aquinas chose Aristotle as his chief guide in philosophy. Bonaventure, because of his intense devotion to the traditional thought of the early Fathers of the Church (particularly St. Augustine of Hippo), was influenced more by the philosophy of Plato than by that of Plato's disciple, Aristotle.

In Bonaventure we find the best example of that typically medieval combination of profound learning with tender piety. It is said that Thomas Aquinas once asked Bonaventure where he obtained his deep understanding of the mysteries of the Christian faith. The latter humbly pointed to the books of others which he had studied. "I, too, have the same books," said Thomas, "but what else do you have?" Then Bonaventure showed him the crucifix on the wall of his cell and said, "Here is really the only source of my knowledge. It is from the sacred wounds of Christ that I draw whatever good is in my writings."

In 1255 the lay professors at the University of Paris, who no doubt were jealous of the popularity which the Dominican and Franciscan Friars were enjoying, succeeded for a time in having them expelled from the faculty. In defence of the Mendicant Orders, as the Dominicans and Franciscans were called, Bonaventure wrote at this time his work, *De Paupertate Christi*, "On the Poverty of Christ." The case was ultimately tried before the Pope, who decided in favor of the Mendicant Orders, and the Dominican and Franciscan Friars were again reinstated in their teaching positions at the University of Paris. In recognition of their just merits, the two greatest teachers among the Friars, Thomas Aquinas and Bonaventure, were given the degree of Doctor of Theology on October 23, 1257, a title that was then but rarely bestowed. For this occasion Thomas returned to Paris from Cologne where he had now been teaching, and Bonaventure came back from Italy where he had recently been appointed to the highest office in the Franciscan Order, that of Minister General.

In the General Chapter or meeting of the Franciscans at their monastery of Ara Coeli in Rome, in 1257, John of Parma who had been unjustly suspected of heresy resigned from the office of Minister General, and he himself made the suggestion that Bonaventure (who was then only thirty-five years old) should be made his successor. The members of the Chapter unanimously approved this choice, and Pope Alexander IV confirmed Bonaventure's election.

The office which the saint now assumed was a very difficult one since there were serious dissentions among the Franciscans regarding various points of their Rule. One group of Friars who were rather unjustly called the *relaxti* or "the lax ones," favored certain mitigations in regard to corporate poverty so that they might lead a more orderly "conventual" life. The other group who called themselves the *zelanti* and the *spirituales,* that is, "the zealous ones" and "the spiritual ones," held to a more austere interpretation of the Rule. However, many of the latter had been misled into embracing the heretical doctrine of Abbot Joachim of Floris according to which a new dispensation of the Holy Spirit was soon to replace the Gospel of Christ.

Throughout his term of office as Minister General of the Franciscans which lasted almost to the end of his life, Bonaventure succeeded in keeping peace between these two groups by holding a middle course. While he condemned the heretical tendencies of the *spirituales* and checked their exaggerated zeal for extreme poverty, he also led the *relaxti* to a more perfect observance of the Rule.

In keeping with the Rule he held a General Chapter every three years, and in the Chapter of 1260 (held at Narbonne in southern France) his revised Constitutions or interpretations of the Rule were adopted by all the Franciscans. While they were somewhat modified in later periods, their influence is still felt among Franciscans of the present day. Likewise at this Chapter,

Bonaventure·was commissioned to prepare a new Life of Saint Francis of Assisi which would give an authentic interpretation of the Founder's spirit for the sake of bringing greater harmony and uniformity among his followers. During the next couple of years Bonaventure visited most of the Franciscan monasteries, gathering from the older Friars the traditions current among them regarding the life of their holy Founder. To digest this information and draw up in writing his Life of the Poverello, Bonaventure retired to Mount La Verna, the secluded retreat so beloved by Francis himself. It is said that at this time Thomas Aquinas went to visit his friend Bonaventure and on coming to his cell, he found him rapt in ecstasy. Quietly withdrawing, Thomas said to his companion, "Let us not disturb him. It is fitting that a saint should write the Life of a saint."

The first part of this Life of Saint Francis contains the various traditions which Bonaventure had gathered on his travels; the second half is an abridged version of the earlier "Lives," particularly Celano's Life of Saint Francis. At the General Chapter of 1263 which was held at Pisa, Bonaventure's work was approved as the official version of the holy Founder's Life, and other Lives were to be destroyed. This prohibition of the earlier Lives should not be looked upon as an effort to falsify the true facts of history. It was rather a practical and necessary means to secure harmony among the Friars, and it was, moreover, only concerned with the public reading in the refectory.

Bonaventure's labors for the followers of Saint Francis of Assisi were not limited to the Friars who formed the "First Order"; his zeal also extended to the cloistered nuns of the "Second Order," the Poor Clares, among whom he likewise strove to establish greater uniformity and whose spiritual welfare he entrusted to the Friars. The lay members of the Franciscan "Third Order" were also the recipients of his pastoral zeal. Thus in 1264 he established for them at Rome a Confraternity of the Blessed Virgin Mary, one of the earliest of such lay organizations in the Church which are known as sodalities. In the General Chapter of

1272, again held at Pisa, he instituted a solemn anniversary in honor of that illustrious member of the Third Order, Louis IX of France (1226-1270), and thus began the process which led to the canonization of this saintly king whose personal friendship he had known in Paris.

For the spiritual good of his fellow Franciscans, as well as for all other Christians, Bonaventure found time in the midst of all his other occupations to write several ascetical and mystical works. In his book on mystical theology, the *Itinerarium Mentis ad Deum*, "Journey of the Mind toward God," written on Mount La Verna in 1257, he not only wrote as a master in this field, but showed that he himself had reached the most sublime heights of mystical contemplation. Likewise the commentaries which he wrote on several of the Books of the Bible are filled with pious thoughts that raise the heart and mind of the reader to God. Bonaventure could hardly speak or write without revealing the ardent love for God with which his heart was inflamed. It is for this reason that he was given the title of the "Seraphic Doctor," for like the Seraphim in the vision of the prophet Isaias he seemed to be on fire with raptuous love of the All-Holy One.

Bonaventure had a most exalted concept of the dignity and obligations of the priesthood. Throughout his priestly life he was ever ready to fulfill the duty of preaching the word of God, and almost five hundred of his sermons have come down to us. So also was he ardently devoted to the Blessed Eucharist and the Sacrifice of the Mass. In his theological works he treats of these sacred Mysteries not only with profound learning and understanding, but with tender love. To this day one of the prayers given in the missal and the breviary as recommended for thanksgiving after Mass and Holy Communion is his prayer, beginning, *Transfige, dulcissime Domine Jesu, . . .* "O dearest Lord Jesus, pierce the depths of my heart with the tender, life-giving wound of Thy love, . . ."

Another characteristic of this saint was his great devotion to the Mother of God. In her honor he composed a "Little Office."

At the General Chapter of 1260 he instituted the custom of having a bell rung in the houses of his Order in honor of the Blessed Virgin's Annunciation. Later on, this Annunciation bell was also rung at sunrise and midday, a custom which is now universal in the Church. From the first words of the prayer which is said at its ringing, *Angelus Domini annunciavit Mariae,* "The angel of the Lord declared unto Mary," this is now known as the Angelus bell. Though Bonaventure, like Thomas Aquinas, had not yet discovered the way to a satisfactory explanation of how Mary could have been conceived without the stain of original sin at the very first instant of her existence, yet the Seraphic Doctor outlined the principles that were fully developed by his successor, the Franciscan genius, Dun Scotus, in giving a clear defense of this doctrine of Mary's Immaculate Conception which is now a dogma of the Catholic faith.

Despite his humility which would have led him to remain hidden and unknown, Bonaventure was soon recognized as one of the most influential men in the Church. In 1265, when the archepiscopal see of York in England became vacant, Pope Clement IV offered him this bishopric, but Bonaventure begged so earnestly to be excused from accepting this dignity that the Holy Father finally consented to his plea. In 1271, when the Apostolic See of Rome had been vacant for over a year because the Cardinals could not agree on the election of a new Pope, it was primarily through the efforts of Bonaventure that they finally agreed to elect Theobald Visconti of Piacenza as Pope Gregory X. Yet Bonaventure could not continue forever in evading ecclesiastical honors. Gregory X overrode his protestations, and on June 23, 1273 consecrated him Cardinal Bishop of Albano. On July 14, 1274, when only fifty-three years old, Bonaventure was called away to behold face to face the God Whom he had loved so deeply and served so faithfully all his life. He was canonized by Pope Sixtus IV on April 14, 1482, and subsequently given the title of a Doctor of the Church by Pope Sixtus V on March 14, 1587.

Saint Bridget of Sweden
Widow

1 3 7 3

(October 8)

THERE ARE TWO saints commonly known in English as "Bridget," but in neither case is the spelling exactly correct. The
great Irish abbess of this name should rather be called Saint
Brigid (451-525), whereas the famous Swedish saint is really
Saint Birgitta. The latter is unquestionably the most illustrious
saint of the Scandinavian countries.

Sweden had only been converted to Christianity for about two
centuries when Saint Bridget was born there, at Finstad near
Uppsala, about the year 1303. Her father, Birger Persson, was
governor of the important province of Uppland and one of the
wealthiest landowners in the country. Her mother, Ingeborg
Bengtsdotter, was also of noble descent. A near relative of the
family was Saint Ingrid who died about twenty years before
Bridget was born. Both of Bridget's parents were devout, God-
fearing people, and they gave their children a good Christian
education. When twelve years old, Bridget's mother died. She
was then reared by her aunt to whom she also owed that strength
of will which she was to show in later life. Although Bridget
seems to have had a normal childhood, as early as the age of seven
she began to have the visions which continued throughout her
life and for which she is best known. A sermon on the Passion of
Christ which she heard when she was twelve years old left a

lasting impression on her. On the night following this sermon, Christ hanging on the cross appeared to her and said, "Look at me, my daughter." When she asked Him who had thus treated Him, He answered, "Those who despise me and are insensible to my love for them." From then on the thought of Christ's sufferings became the center of her spiritual life.

In 1316, when Bridget was probably only thirteen years old, she was given in marriage to the eighteen-year-old Ulf Gudmarsson, Prince of Nierck. Their happy marriage was blessed with eight children, four boys and four girls, one of whom was later to be canonized as Saint Catherine of Sweden. For several years Bridget and Ulf lived on their feudal estate at Ulfsa, but her reputation for charity and piety was known throughout the land. She founded a hospital where she nursed the sick with her own hands. Among her personal friends were several learned and pious theologians, especially Blessed Nicholas Hermansson, Bishop of Linkoping, who was her children's tutor.

About the year 1335 Bridget and Ulf were summoned to the royal court at Stockholm where she became the principal lady-in-waiting to Blanche of Namur, the bride of Sweden's young king, Magnus Eriksson. Here she tried to make her influence for good felt on the frivolous king and his well-intentioned but weak, luxury-loving queen. While respecting her sanctity, they did not take her efforts seriously. On the death of her youngest son, Gudmar, in 1340, Bridget went on a pilgrimage to the shrine of St. Olaf of Norway at Tronheim. Finding on her return to Stockholm that she could not curb the excesses of King Magnus and Queen Blanche, she asked and received their permission to go with her husband on a pilgrimage to the shrine of St. James at Compostela, in Spain, which was then the most frequented place of pilgrimage in all Europe. Their journey lasted from 1341 to 1343. On their return north, Ulf fell dangerously ill at Arras in northern France. While he vowed that if he recovered he would enter a monastery on his return home, Bridget received a revelation from Saint Denis assuring her that her husband would arrive

SAINT BASIL THE GREAT

Saint Basil left the peace of a monastery to defend the orthodox faith of
Christianity against the heresy of Arianism which professed that Jesus
was not the Son of God in the strict sense. To combat this heresy, the
Saint consented to be ordained in 363, and during the following years acted
as a bulwark of orthodoxy by his preaching and writing in Caesarea, Asia
Minor. The above was reproduced from a 19th century Russian triptych.

SAINT BERNARDINE OF SIENA

As most informed Catholics know, the symbol "IHS" is our Lord's mono-gram, and consists of the first three letters of the Holy Name of Jesus as written in Greek: IHSOUS. However, there are probably few who know that the widespread custom of using this symbol as a public profession of our Christian faith in Jesus is due above all to Saint Bernardine of Siena, one of the brightest lights of the Franciscan Order.

safely back in Sweden. In answer to her prayers he did recover, and he kept his vow by entering the Cistercian monastery at Alvastra in the region of southern Sweden known as East Gotland. Here, in 1344, Ulf died, when he had just finishèd his novitiate and taken his religious vows. Meanwhile Bridget was living a holy and mortified life nearby. On the death of her husband she gave herself completely to prayer and penance, and practiced such extreme austerities that her confessor had to warn her to be more moderate in this.

Her visions and revelations now became even more frequent, and many of them were words of warning from God directed not only at the king and queen of Sweden, but also at other rulers in Europe. Like a prophetess of old, Bridget fearlessly delivered these messages in God's own name, even though they seldom produced lasting results in these worldly sovereigns.

In her visions Bridget was urged by Christ to found a peculiar type of monastery. Though destined primarily for nuns, it was to have an adjacent wing for monks; the latter were to have the spiritual care of the nuns, but the temporal affairs of the whole institution was to be in the hands of a Mother Abbess who would be superior in temporal affairs over the monks as well as over the nuns. The priests were to number thirteen, in honor of the twelve apostles plus St. Paul; the deacons were to be four, in honor of the Doctors of the Church, who at that time were of that number. There were also to be eight lay brothers, so that in all there were twenty-five monks. The ideal number of nuns would be sixty, thus bringing the total number of men and women religious in the monastery to eighty-five, the number of the seventy-two disciples of Christ plus the twelve apostles and St. Paul. The monks, of course, would be strictly separated from the nuns.

Two years after the death of her husband, Bridget opened the first monastery of this type at Vadstena on the eastern shore of Lake Vattern in southern Sweden. This order, known as the Brigittines, spread throughout most of the countries of Europe. But in the reformation and in the ensuing religious troubles most of the Brigittine monasteries were destroyed, so that now there are but relatively few of them left. One of the remarkable points in the Brigittine rule was that, while religious poverty was to be strictly observed in everything else, the nuns and monks were to be supplied with as many good books as possible. As a result, the mother house of the Brigittines at Vadstena became the literary center of Sweden in the fifteenth century.

At this time the popes had abandoned Rome and were living at Avignon in southeastern France. In several of her revelations St. Bridget was ordered by Christ to appeal to these popes and beg them to return to Rome. When her strongly worded letter to Pope Clement VI did not induce him to leave Avignon, she decided to go personally to Avignon and Rome. In 1349, though the Black Death was then ravaging Europe, Bridget set out with a small group, including her confessor, Peter Olavsson of Skening, to gain the indulgence of the 1350 Jubilee Year in the Eternal City. In order the better to accomplish her mission, which was the moral uplifting of the people, Bridget remained in Rome till her death, except for several pilgrimages which she undertook, particularly one to the Holy Land in 1373. In keeping with her earlier practice in Sweden, at Rome also she accomplished a great deal of good by her devout and charitable life. Her success in bringing back Pope Urban V to Rome was only short-lived, but in 1370 she did succeed in getting him to give papal approbation to the religious order which she had founded.

A few years after Bridget came to Italy her youngest daughter Catherine went to visit her, and Bridget induced her to stay with her. St. Catherine of Sweden proved herself a worthy daughter of her holy mother, to whom she was utterly devoted. At Rome and on their many journeys the daughter shared in all the hardships and sufferings of her mother. The missionary zeal of the saintly seeress was not always well received, and at times Bridget and Catherine were reduced to such straits of poverty that they had to beg their bread at the door of the Poor Clare convent of St. Lawrence in Panisperna at Rome. As Franciscan tertiaries, these noblewomen rejoiced in the poverty of their spiritual father, the Poverello of Assisi.

Worn out by her many labors and austerities, St. Bridget died at Rome on July 23, 1373. Her body was first buried here in the Poor Clare Church of St. Lawrence in Panisperna, but four months later, in the care of St. Catherine and the Cistercian prior of Alvastra, it was carried in triumphal procession across central Europe to Sweden, where it was given its final resting place in the first monastery of Brigittine Order at Varstena. On October 7, 1391, but little more than eighteen years after her death, Bridget of Sweden was solemnly canonized by Pope Boniface IX. Her feast was originally observed on the Seventh of October, the anniversary of her canonization. But when this day was made the Feast of the Most Holy Rosary in honor of Mary's assistance to the Christian forces at their great victory over the Turks in the naval battle of Lepanto on October 7, 1571, St. Bridget's feast was transferred to the following day, the Eighth of October, on which it is now celebrated by the Universal Church.

Bridget of Sweden is a great saint primarily because of the sanctity of life and not because of the extraordinary graces that God bestowed upon her in her visions and revelations. Undoubtedly Bridget was a genuine mystic, and it would be against all the evidence to attribute her visions to mere hallucinations. The Church has examined all her writings most carefully and has approved of them as containing nothing contrary to faith and morals. Though St. Bridget's revelations no doubt had their origin in divine grace, this does not mean that they are "divine revelations" in the strict sense of the term, but rather that the *spirit* behind them is good. In any case, they are and will always remain merely "private revelations," something quite different from the "public" revelation given by Christ and the apostles to the Church which must be believed on divine faith. The famous theologian and canonist, Pope Benedict XIV (1740-1758), was referring specifically to the revelations of St. Bridget, among others, when he wrote: "Even though many of these revelations have been approved, we cannot and we ought not to give them the assent of divine faith, but only that of human faith, according to the dictates of prudence whenever these dictates enable us to decide that they are probable and worthy of pious credence."

What made the revelations of St. Bridget so popular in the late Middle Ages was the fact that they seemingly supplied a great deal of detailed information about the life of Christ and of His Blessed Mother which is lacking in the New Testament. In most cases, however, it can be said that these new details are nothing more than the fruit of a pious imagination engaged in devout meditation on the events recorded in the Gospels.

At the so-called Protestant Reformation of the sixteenth century the Christian people of Sweden, as also of the other Scandinavian countries, were robbed by force of the Catholic faith of their fathers at the hands of their ruler. It is interesting to note that some of the best scholarly research on the life of St. Bridget of Sweden has been made in modern times by non-Catholics of her native country. May St. Bridget, Sweden's national patron, bring back the good people of her land to the unity of the Catholic faith which she so dearly loved!

REVELATIONS OF ST. BRIDGET

Our Lady's Compassion

At the death of my Son, I was like a woman having her heart pierced with five lances. For the first lance was the shameful and opprobrious nudity; because I saw my most beloved and powerful Son standing naked at the pillar, and having no clothing. The second was his accusation; for they accused him, calling him a traitor and a liar, and even an assassin, whom I knew to be just and truthful, offending and wishing to offend no one. The third lance to me was the crown of thorns, which so cruelly pierced his sacred head, that the blood flowed into his mouth, down his beard, and into his ears. The fourth was his piteous voice on the cross, when he cried to his Father, saying: "O Father, why hast thou forsaken me?" as though he would say: "Father, there is none to pity me but thou." The fifth lance that pierced my heart was his most cruel death. My heart was pierced with as many lances as there were veins from which his precious blood gushed; for the veins of his hands and feet were pierced, and the pain of his lacerated nerves came inconsolably to his heart, and from his heart to the nerves again, and as his heart was most excellent and strong, as being formed of the best substance, therefore life and death contended, and thus life was bitterly prolonged in pain. But as death approached, when his heart was breaking with intolerable pain, then his limbs quivered, and his head, which had sunk on his shoulders, was slightly raised. His half-closed eyes were opened midway. His mouth, too, opened, and his tongue was seen drenched in blood. His fingers and arms, which were somewhat contracted, expanded. Having given up the ghost, his head sunk on his breast, his hands sunk a little from the place of the wounds; his feet sustained the greater weight. Then my hands dried up, my eyes were darkened, and my face became corpselike. My ears heard naught, naught could my mouth utter; my feet, too, shook, and my body fell to the earth. But rising from the ground, when I beheld my Son more fearful than a leper, I gave my will entirely to him, knowing that all had been done according to his will, and that it could not have been done but by his permission, and I thanked him for all. A certain joy was blended with my sorrow, for I beheld him who never sinned, willingly, from his great charity, enduring such things for sinners. Let every one, then, in the world, consider what I was at the death of my Son, and keep it ever before his eyes.

Consider the Passion of my Son, whose members were as my members, and as my heart. For he was within me as other children in their mother's womb; but he was conceived from the fervent charity of divine Love, others from the concupiscence of the flesh. Hence, John, his cousin, says well: The Word was made flesh, for by charity he came and abode in me; but the Word

and charity formed him in me. Hence, he was to me as my heart.
Hence, when he was born, I felt as though half my heart was
born and went out of me. And when he suffered, I felt as though
half my heart suffered, as when a body is half within and half
without, when aught wounds what is without, that within feels it
equally. So my heart was scourged and pierced when my Son
was. I was nigher to him in his Passion, and did not leave him.
I stood nearer to his cross, and as what is nearer the heart,
wounds more keenly, so the pain of it was keener to me than to
others. And when he looked upon me from the cross, and I on
him, then tears streamed from my eyes as from veins. And when
he beheld me spent with grief, he was so afflicted by my pain,
that all the pain of his own wounds, was, as it were, dulled at
the sight of the grief in which he beheld me. Hence, I say boldly, that his pains were mine, because his heart was mine. For as
Adam and Eve sold the world for an apple, so my Son and I re-
deemed the world, as it were, with one heart. Think, then, how I
was at the death of my Son, and you will not find it hard to
leave the world. (*Book I, chap. 27*)

THE CONSIDERATION OF THE PASSION

The consideration of the Passion of my Son ought to be frequently in man's thoughts; for let him consider how the Son of
God, and the Son of the Virgin, who is one God with the Father
and Holy Ghost, suffered; how he was led captive, and buffeted
and spit upon; how he was scourged to the very inmost, so that
the flesh was torn away by the lash; how with all his nerves
distended and pierced, he stood dolorous on the cross; how crying out on the cross, he gave up the ghost. If he frequently fans
the spark, then will he grow warm. (*Book V, chap. 20*)

FRUITS OF THE PASSION

Christ speaks

I voluntarily gave myself up to my enemies, and my friends remained, and my mother in most bitter grief and pain. And though I saw the lance, nails, scourges, and other instruments of torture ready, I nevertheless went joyfully to my Passion. And, although my head was bedewed with blood on all sides, and even if my enemies touched my very heart, I would rather have it divided, then be deprived of thee. Thou art too ungrateful, then, if thou lovest me not for so great charity. For if my head is pierced and bowed down on the cross for thee, thy head should be inclined to humility. And because my eyes were bloody and full of tears, so thy eyes should abstain from every delightful sight. And because my ears were full of blood, and heard words of detraction against me, therefore, let thy ears be turned away from scurrilous and foolish discourse. And as my mouth was filled with a most bitter draught, and cut off from good, so let thy mouth be closed to evil and open to good. And as my hands were extended with nails, by reason of thy works, which are signified by the hands, let them be extended to the poor, and to my commandments. Let thy feet, that is, thy affections, by which thou shouldst go to me, be crucified to pleasure; that as I suffered in all my members, so let all them be ready for my services. (*Book I, Chap. 11*)

Saint Camillus de Lellis

Confessor

1 6 1 4

(July 18)

THERE ARE PROBABLY very few people in America who know that the "red cross" as a symbol for the care of the sick and afflicted originated with a Catholic saint, and a very remarkable saint at that, Saint Camillus De Lellis. This man, Camillus, was born on May 25, 1550, in Bucchianico, a little mountain town, situated about 15 miles from the Adriatic Sea in the high rugged region of the Apennine Mountains known as the Abruzzi, directly east of Rome. In the lower land nearer the Adriatic lies the much larger city of Chieti. In this city Camillus' father, Giovanni De Lellis, was born at the beginning of the 16th century.

The De Lellis family had once ranked among the lesser nobility of medieval Italy. Giovanni tried to keep up its traditions as a professional soldier and served at various times in different armies such as those of Naples and of France. Although he wooed and married Camilla de Compellis of the town of Bucchianico and begot two sons by her, he can hardly be said to have settled there since he was off to the wars most of the time. Camilla's older son, Giuseppe, died in childhood. Much later in life—according to one story—when she was sixty years old—which is hardly credible, she gave birth to a very large baby who grew into a giant of a man, six and a half feet tall! She named him Camillus after herself.

With his father usually away from him, Camillus developed into a gay, carefree and completely unmanagable boy. The death of his mother, when he was only thirteen years old, left him still more neglected. Avoiding school as much as he could, he did not learn much more as a youth than to read and write Italian. At an early age he developed a passion for gambling, a vice which he inherited from his father that was to plague him until his "conversion."

In 1569 most of the Catholic states of Europe were united under the leadership of Venice in a war to stop the advance of the Turks into Christendom, a war in which the Turks suffered a disastrous naval defeat in the famous Battle of Lepanto (October 7, 1571). Both Giovanni De Lellis and his nineteen-year-old son Camillus enlisted for the war, but neither took part at Lepanto. They had only gone about halfway to Venice when, at Ancona on the Adriatic coast, a serious disease overtook both of them. The elder De Lellis died a few days later at nearby Loreto. His son recovered from the disease, but at the same time developed running sores on his legs from which he was to suffer the rest of his life. Giovanni De Lellis had squandered all his wealth in gambling and extravagant living; the only things he could leave to Camillus were his sword, his dagger, and "the glory of the family name."

Instead of continuing toward Venice and the war, Camillus decided that he would first go to Rome to receive treatment for the ulcers on his legs. On his way back he had gone about thirty miles when, at Fermo, he saw two friars traveling along, poor but happy in their Franciscan joy. Suddenly he began to feel how empty and senseless was his own disorderly life. Then and there he took a vow that he would be a Franciscan. Forthwith he went to the city of Aquila in the Abruzzi where his mother's brother was superior of a Franciscan monastery, and told this uncle about his vow. Believing that it was only the impetuous gesture of a despondent man, this good Franciscan spoke kindly to the poor youth, and then sent him on his way with a blessing.

On March 7, 1571, Camillus was admitted as a patient in the Roman hospital of *San Giacomo degli Incurabili,* "St. James of the Incurables," a place that was to loom large in the coming years of this man. This hospital (which occupied a whole block near the Piazza del Popolo in the north of Rome) had been founded in the 14th century by Cardinal Giacomo Colonna, and greatly enlarged at the beginning of the 16th century to take care of the immense number of people who were stricken with venereal disease—an affliction that overwhelmed Europe shortly after the discovery of America. During his three-weeks stay there as a patient, Camillus had an opportunity to see how appalling were the surroundings and treatment of the patients. Although richly endowed, this hospital suffered badly from the fact that its present administrators pocketed most of the income and left the actual running of the institution to poorly paid attendants or male nurses who were too ignorant and indifferent to care much what happened to the patients. The records show that Camillus was employed here as an attendant from March 30 to December 31, 1571, when he was dismissed because of his constant gambling and quarreling. At this time, therefore, he seems to have stayed on at the hospital, not primarily from any motive of charity, but principally to use his small salary on his favorite pastime. According to Father Cicatelli, the companion of his later life and his first biographer, Camillus at this time "was a terrible hothead, forever quarreling with the other servants and so obsessed with card playing that he would often desert the services of the sick to go down to the nearby Tiber and play cards with the Tiber boatmen."

In January 1572, Camillus re-enlisted in the army of the Venetians, but after a few months of military service (during which he was stricken with dysentery at Corfu, and was in action at the attack on the Turkish fortress of Barbagno) he was discharged when Venice signed a cowardly peace treaty with the Turks. His next attempt at soldiering, this time in the pay of Philip II of Spain in a war against Tunis, did not last long either, since the

Turkish victory soon put an end to this campaign. During a fierce storm at sea while on his way back from Palermo in Sicily to Naples, Camillus was so terrified that he renewed his vow to become a Franciscan.

At Naples in November 1572, he lost all the money he had made in soldiering. He even gambled away his coat and dagger and sword. With a fellow soldier, Tiberio, he then tramped across Italy to Manfredonia on the Adriatic Sea, supporting himself on whatever alms he could beg. Here, at the end of November, he was offered the opportunity to work as a laborer on the construction of a Capuchin monastery. Tiberio found the labor too degrading and left, but Camillus, thinking he was thus fulfilling his vow to be a Franciscan, resolved to persevere in his menial labor until the building was finished. After two weeks of this he asked for a day off and was refused. Flying into a rage he threatened to quit, but the Capuchin superior, knowing the basic goodness of this hard worker, coaxed him to stay and even offered him higher wages. With plans to earn enough money to go back to his gambling career, Camillus finally agreed to stay.

God, however, had other plans for him. One day Camillus was sent on an errand to another monastery about a dozen miles away. The superior here spoke to him of the need of serving God, avoiding sin, and saving his soul. "Whenever you are tempted to sin," this good friar told him, "spit in the devil's face." These words made a deep impression on Camillus. He kept thinking of them as he jogged back to Manfredonia on his donkey: "How much I ought to do for God and the salvation of my soul!" Suddenly he got off his beast and flung himself on the ground in bitter tears of repentance. The day was the feast of Our Lady's Purification, February 2, 1575, a date which Camillus regarded ever afterwards as the day of his "conversion."

Back at Manfredonia, he begged the superior to let him join the Capuchins. The astonished superior was filled with joy and wonder, and promised Camillus to do what he could for him. Camillus was so happy that he worked as he never did before.

He determined never to commit even a venial sin, and he began a life of rigorous penance. Finally he was sent to Trivento, almost a hundred miles northwest of Manfredonia, where he was to make his novitiate. One evening on this journey which he made barefoot and alone, he came to a river and started to ford it. In the darkness he heard a voice call out to him: "Don't do it! Don't cross it;" He could not tell where the voice came from; it sounded as if it were above him. Thinking it best to heed the warning, he spent the night on the bank of the stream. The next morning he saw that if he had tried to ford the river at this point he would surely have been carried away and drowned in the torrent. He always believed that it was his guardian angel who had saved him.

In the novitiate at Trivento, Camillus was a model of humility, obedience, mortification and even—what is more remarkable in his case—of meekness. Unfortunately, however, the old ulcer in his leg grew worse, so that the novice master was regretfully forced to tell him to leave and have the wound treated.

Since this was the Jubilee Year of 1575, Camillus decided to return to Rome where he could gain both the Jubilee indulgence and treatment in the hospital for his leg, hoping to be able soon to resume the Capuchin novitiate. As on the previous occasion, but now in quite a different frame of mind, Camillus stayed on in the Hospital of San Giacomo after his ulcerated leg was fairly well healed. According to the records of the hospital he was here from October 23 to June 20, 1579, first as a patient, then in various positions as a hired servant. Finally he held the responsible post of *Guardaroba* or manager of all the material effects of the institution. It was during these years that he sustained a severe rupture from which he suffered much for the rest of his life.

All this time he was continually striving to lead a holy, virtuous life. For this he needed expert guidance which he was fortunately able to get from St. Philip Neri, the founder of the Oratorian Fathers, who was then living in Rome. Philip, though bluff, homely and amusing, possessed great charm and warmth and was famous throughout the city as a wise confessor and spiritual director. Camillus introduced himself to Philip by saying, "I who have been so great a sinner have need of a great saint to help me." Philip, who was then sixty years old but always a boy at heart, understood and loved this big-boned strong-willed young penitent. Despite certain differences of opinion between them in later life, these two always remained devoted to each other.

In the summer of 1579, Camillus felt that his leg was sufficiently healed for him to be readmitted in the Capuchin novitiate. He reminded the Capuchin superior of his promise to take him back, and so was once more accepted as a novice. Philip, however, had warned Camillus that the ulcer would get worse again, and that he would be back in Rome because God had work for him to do there. This time Camillus was admitted into the Capuchin novitiate at Tagliacozzo (a village fifteen miles east of the city of Avezzano and about fifty miles east of Rome), but the prediction of St. Philip Neri came true. Camillus' ulcerated leg worsened and he was finally forced to abandon all idea of becoming a Capuchin. By the middle of October 1579, he was once more back in Rome. The authorities at St. Giacomo Hospital welcomed him back and made him *Maestro di Casa*, "General Superintendent," an office which he held until 1584.

In those days hospitals had no trained nursing staff. The men who were hired to care for the sick seldom had any real concern, to say nothing of love, for the patients. The spiritual conditions were almost as bad as the material ones. Many of the patients died without even receiving the last sacraments.

Camillus gave every spare moment to taking care of the sick. He got Philip Neri to let him have a priest to hear their confessions. Philip had also gathered together a small group of men, some young and some older, who used to visit the hospitals of Rome, prepare food, serve it to the patients, and in various ways help these poor sufferers physically and spiritually. The religious orders, especially the Jesuits, sent novices to the hospitals for this purpose, and they now often chose San Giacomo because of Camillus' presence there.

After two and a half years Camillus came to the conclusion that all such efforts were only half measures. What was needed, he decided, was a group of devoted men who would make a profession—a religious profession—of caring for the sick. It was on the feast of Our Lady's Assumption, the 15th of August 1582, that he became convinced that God had called him back to such a task. He spoke of this idea to the men who worked with him at San Giacomo, and a few of them told him that they were willing to go along with him. A little room in the hospital served them as an oratory where they met for prayer and penance.

Camillus was not merely inspired by human pity, or even by a desire to do this work as a means for saving his own soul. He was inspired above all by a close, personal love for his crucified Savior. When he left the Capuchin novitiate for the second time he had resolved "to follow his beloved Crucified at all times and in all places and in all adversities." On returning to the hospital he had determined "to give himself in all and through all to the services of Jesus Christ crucified in His most living image, the sick." His friends had a crucifix made for him. It was about six feet high with a figure of Christ on it almost three feet high. The cross became worm-eaten in time and had to be replaced, but the original figure of Christ is still preserved in Rome. This large crucifix became the center of Camillus' little community, and before it his five volunteers from the nursing staff promised to follow him in prosperity and toil, in life and in death. The future held much toil and little prosperity for them.

Trouble, in fact, started almost at once. The fact that these laymen had banded together in a pious association could not be kept hidden. The other attendants, and even the authorities at the hospital, resented this as a sort of "separatist" movement. They ordered Camillus and his companions to give up their private oratory and to remove the big crucifix from the room. Full of indignation, Camillus tendered his resignation at San Giacomo Hospital and offered his services to the Hospital Brothers of St. John of God who had recently been given charge of the hospital on the Island of the Tiber. However, these good Brothers, knowing that Camillus' vocation lay elsewhere, advised him to return to San Giacomo.

Convinced that he must do God's will, not his own, Camillus returned to his room at San Giacomo and spent the first part of the night in prayer before the big crucifix which he had placed there for safekeeping. Later that night he had a dream in which he heard a voice saying to him, "Don't be afraid! I will be with you and help you." After that he agreed for the time being to resume his office of superintendent at San Giacomo, and he and his friends met for common prayer in the hospital chapel when no one else was there.

Yet Camillus realized that he could not begin his real work as long as he stayed at San Giacomo and remained dependent on its authorities. He must have a house, no matter how small, for himself and his companions. There was a further difficulty. As mere laymen in a city run by the clergy, he and his friends would also work under a heavy handicap. Besides, the other priests of the city, good as they were, could not, with their other duties, take the proper spiritual care of the abandoned poor in the various hospitals of the city. With the firm conviction that God was calling him to the priesthood so that he could carry out his special vocation, Camillus decided at the age of thirty-two to study for the priesthood. The Jesuit Fathers who knew his true worth gladly accepted him as a student in their Roman College and gave him an accelerated course in Latin and the ecclesiastical sciences. In his deep humility Camillus did not mind the fact that young teenagers were his classmates in Latin. After his first year of study in 1583, he received the Minor Orders from Bishop Goldwell of St. Asaph, the last of the surviving Catholic Bishops of England who was then living in exile at Rome. In the spring of the next year, 1584, he received the Major Orders.

After his ordination to the priesthood Camillus returned to his old home town in the Abruzzi where his fellow townsmen (who remembered his wild youth) were astonished at seeing him now a priest. Learning to his surprise that he had inherited a small piece of property here, he sold it and gave the money to the poor. Two weeks later he returned to Rome.

The time had now come for him to begin his cherished plan of establishing a society of priests devoted exclusively to the care of the sick. Almost insurmountable obstacles stood in his way. In order to retain his valuable services at San Giacomo, the authorities of this hospital had arranged that Father Camillus was made chaplain of the small chapel called the *Madonnina*, "the little Madonna," that is, the little church of the Madonna which was situated on the bank of the Tiber a short distance from their hospital. Although he continued for a month or two to work at San Giacomo, he made it clear that he wished to be free to work for the sick poor wherever they might be, and that he believed that too close a bond with this one hospital would prevent him from attaining such an ideal. To make his intentions clear, he solemnly carried his beloved crucifix one day through the street from his room in the hospital to the little room at the *Madonnina* which he now made his residence.

He induced two of his most devoted fellow workers at San Giacomo to join him here, and on September 15, 1584 (when he gave them "clerical dress") they vowed with him to devote themselves to the service of the sick solely for love of God. Thus his new religious institute which was to grow into a mighty Order first saw the light of day. Camillus thereupon began to work in another hospital, the great *Ospitale del Santo Spiritu*, "the Hospital of the Holy Spirit," near the Vatican.

The original manuscript of the first "rules" that Camillus drew up at this time for his institute is still preserved. It is called "The Rules of the Company of the Servants of the Sick." While these rules allowed considerable liberty to the members in regard to their "religious exercise," so as wisely to adjust their time to the

SAINT BRIDGET OF SWEDEN

This most illustrious Saint of the Scandinavian countries is a great Saint primarily because of the sanctity of her life, and not because of the extraordinary graces God bestowed upon her in her visions and revelations. She had the first of these when she was twelve. Jesus, hanging on the Cross, appeared to her, and from that moment on the contemplation of the Savior's suffering became the center of her spiritual life.

SAINT BONAVENTURE   Francisco de Zuberan

Despite his humility which normally would have led to obscurity, Saint
Bonaventure was recognized as one of the most influential men in the
Church during the thirteenth century. Shown here kneeling before the
Papal Crown, it was primarily through his efforts that the College of
Cardinals finally agreed on Pope Gregory X, in 1271, after the Apostolic
See had been vacant for more than a year.

needs of the sick, great stress was placed on poverty. Not only
the personal poverty of the individual members, but the corporate
poverty of the whole community. Camillus rightly feared that
once his Order became wealthy it would lose its love of working
for the poor as has happened only too often before and after his
time to other religious Orders in the Church.

A sad blow, however, soon fell upon the young institute. Camillus and his first companions used to go to confession to St.
Philip Neri whom they all looked upon as their spiritual father,
and whose wise counsel they sought and gladly followed. Now
Philip, for whatever good reasons he may have had, told Camillus flatly that he condemned this new scheme of his outright.
Either Camillus would have to disband his group and return to
San Giacomo, or Philip would no longer hear his confession. Camillus and his companions were heartbroken; this holy man upon
whom they relied in every respect had turned them away!

It was at this time that Camillus had his second mysterious
experience with his beloved crucifix, only this time he was wide
awake. He beheld the image of his crucified Lord raise His arms
from the cross and hold them out tenderly to him while a Voice
spoke in almost the same words as in the earlier vision: "Why
disturb yourself, timid man? I Myself will help you, since this
work is Mine, not yours." Convinced that they were doing God's
will, the little band held on together heroically despite their loss
of the support and sage counsel of St. Philip. The fact that even
saints can have misunderstandings among themselves should not
scandalize anyone; after all, they are still human and liable to
make human errors in judgment. Moreover, God allows such
things to happen for the sake of trying His elect.

The little house attached to the church of the Madonna soon
proved too small. Camillus therefore arranged to take over the
half-abandoned church of St. Mary Magdalene with the fairly
large house attached to it. This was in the heart of sixteenth
century Rome. It has remained the headquarters of St. Camillus'
Order ever since.

For thirty long years, from the day in 1584 when he and his first two followers formed the "Company of the Servants of the Sick," to his death in 1614, Camillus devoted all of his tremendous energies to the "total service" of the sick. Although his work was primarily for the sick in the hospitals, whether in hospitals under the management of others or, as in later years, in those directly managed by his own Order, he did not limit his zeal to such institutions. He nursed the sick and attended the dying wherever they were to be found. No home was too poor for him to visit. He went into hovels in the slums, and he crawled on hands and knees—this giant of a man—into the nooks and crannies of the ruins of ancient Rome where the plague-stricken poor had taken refuge.

In his care for the sick he insisted over and over again on the need of tender love for them. He often told his followers that they must nurse the sick with a "motherly love," with the same gentleness that a mother shows her little infant—a remarkable characteristic in this rugged he-man. In a time when nothing was known of germs and antiseptics, Camillus insisted on absolute cleanliness in everything that concerned the ill. He washed their bodies, changed their bedclothes and cleaned their rooms. Wherever a major disaster struck, Camillus and his men rushed to the aid of the stricken people. As plague after plague, and pestilence after pestilence devastated the cities of Italy, his Servants of the Sick worked night and day to snatch as many people as they could from death, and to bury the many corpses that had fallen. When the Christian armies marched to the defense of Europe against the invading Turks he sent his followers to set up field hospitals for the sick and wounded soldiers—one of the first organized efforts toward mobile medical units.

Camillus' primary motive was not, of course, a merely natural sense of compassion for the suffering poor. He could never have sustained his superhuman efforts were he not inspired with supernatural motives and upheld by divine grace. With St. Paul he could truly say, "The love of Christ impels us" (2 Cor. 5, 14).

In every sufferer he saw an afflicted member of Christ's Body; yes, he beheld the crucified Christ Himself. His care was by no means limited to the physical needs of the sick. He was much more concerned with their spiritual health. It was not in vain that he himself had become a priest and wished most of his followers to be priests. While caring for the bodies of the sick they were, above all, anxious to see to it that the dying were rightly prepared by exhortations, prayers and the sacraments for their journey into eternity. This zeal of Camillus' Servants of the Sick was so well known that they were popularly known in Italy as "the Fathers of the Good Death."

Camillus must have had an iron constitution. While many of his followers fell victims to the plague to which they had to expose themselves in their work, he himself seemed to have thrived in the most pestilential surroundings. Pain and suffering in his own body was his constant companion. The running sores in his legs never healed and, in fact, grew worse as the years went by. Infections on the soles of his feet must have made every step a torture. The heavy iron belt he had to wear all the time because of a bad rupture was an additional torment. Yet in all this he felt he was not doing enough penance to atone for the sins of his youth that had made his beloved Jesus suffer so much on the cross for his sake.

The heroic example of Camillus soon inspired other courageous men to join him in his work. Whenever one of these fell a victim to the plague, two more were ready to leap into the breach. In 1588, three years after he had opened the first house of his Order at St. Mary Magdalene's in Rome, he had enough new members in his Order to make a new foundation in Naples where fourteen years earlier he had gambled away his shirt! Soon other new houses of his Servants of the Sick were springing up in various cities of Italy. When he resigned his office as General of his institute in 1607 (sixteen years after Pope Gregory XIV had given it formal canonical status as religious Order), it had 242 professed Religious, 80 novices, 15 houses and 8 hospitals. In addi-

tion, at least 170 of its members had sacrificed their lives in carrying out their noble vocation.

In 1585, when Pope Sixtus V gave permission for the first
organization of the Servants of the Sick, Camillus also obtained
from the Pope the right for himself and his followers to wear as
their distinctive insignia a large red cross on the front of their
black cassock. Camillus explained that the cross was to remind
its wearers that only by bearing Christ's cross in labor, suffering,
and self-denial for the sick could its members be true followers
of Christ. Its red color, moreover, was to call to their mind that
it was by the precious Blood which Jesus shed on His cross that
we are saved. The symbol of a red cross on a white background
has been adopted by the international Red Cross for different
reasons and with explicit statements that it has no religious significance, yet the fact remains that any truly unselfish nursing of
the sick and care of the unfortunate must in some way be inspired by religious motives. It can hardly be denied that the
familiar sight of the "Camillans," or members of St. Camillus'
religious Order, with the bright red cross on their habits taking
care of the wounded on the battlefields of Europe exercised an
influence on the choice of the "red cross" symbol for the non-
religious organization of that name—even though those who made
the choice may not have been conscious of it.

One reason why Camillus surrendered (seven years before his
death) the supreme command of the Order which he had founded
was the difference of opinion between him and his most devoted
followers over his idea of "total service" for the sick. He wanted
his followers to do everything, even the most menial chores in
the hospital such as sweeping, washing, and cooking, whereas his
followers thought that these jobs were only indirectly connected
with the sick and could be done by hired help. It was not that
these holy men lacked the humility to undertake such lowly
tasks; they felt that their time could be better employed in the
more direct bodily and spiritual care of the sick. Not all men
can reach Camillus' great height of sanctity. If his Order was to

survive and grow, as indeed it has done, it would have to be better accommodated to the somewhat lesser statures of ordinary men.

An additional reason, however, why Camillus resigned from his generalship was that he wished to be free from routine administration to devote the last years of his life with greater liberty to the personal care of his beloved sick. Although during these last seven years his physical sufferings and ailments grew ever worse, this period was probably the happiest of his life. Even toward the end when his body was so bent that he could no longer walk, he used to creep from bed to bed to help his dear invalids and patients.

On July 14, 1614, at the hour he had foretold and when all his many friends had taken their heart-rending farewell, this valiant soldier of Christ was summoned to receive his heavenly crown of victory. Camillus, the inveterate gambler, had wagered all on Christ—and won! The stake had been staggeringly high, but Camillus knew that there was no real risk involved. With God's grace inspiring and carrying through the supernatural charity of the saint, the outcome was certain.

Even during his life Camillus had worked many miracles to help the poor and the sick. With his death these miracles became still more numerous. He was the idol of Rome and all Italy. Everyone venerated him at once as a saint, but the Church had recently made the official process of beatification and canonization a very exacting affair. Thus it was not until 1742 that he was beatified. Four years later, in 1746, he was canonized by Pope Benedict XIV, with his feast to be celebrated each year on the 18th of July. In 1886, Pope Leo XIII declared St. Camillus the heavenly patron of hospitals, nurses, and patients, and he likewise decreed that this saint's name should be added to those of the other saints who are invoked in the Litany of the Dying.

Saint Clement of Rome

Pope

c. 9 9

(November 23)

T HE EARLIEST POPE after Saint Peter of whom anything more than his name and the length of his pontificate are known is Saint Clement of Rome. He was the third successor of Saint Peter, the first two being Linus and Cletus, each of whom reigned for twelve years. Since Saint Peter was martyred in the 12th year of Nero, that is, in 66 A.D., Clement became pope twenty-four years later, or in 90 A.D. The earliest list of the popes, drawn up about the year 160, assigns a reign of nine years to Saint Clement. Therefore, it is quite probable that he died in the year 99, although according to some scholars his pontificate is dated as 88-97.

The term "of Rome" is added to the name of this pope to distinguish him from Saint Clement of Alexandria, one of the great Fathers of the Church who lived during 150-220. Clement of Rome is the first of a special, small group among the Fathers of the Church (including Saints Ignatius of Antioch and Polycarp of Smyrna) who are known as the "Apostolic Fathers" because they belong to the first generation after the Apostles.

Clement's special claim to fame lies in the fact that his rather long letter to the Corinthians is the earliest Christian writing after the New Testament that has come down to us. At least it is the earliest one of known authorship and definite date. It was

634

written toward the end of his pontificate for the purpose of bring-ing peace and harmony into the Christian community at Corinth which was sharply divided by rival factions. This letter of Clem-ent's is of supreme importance to Church historians for various reasons. Suffice it to say that it proves that even at so early a date as the end of the first century, the Church at Rome (as the see of St. Peter) was speaking with authority to the other Chris-tian churches.

Nothing of certainty is known about Saint Clement's death. Although he has always been called a martyr, this in itself does not necessarily signify that he was put to death for the faith since the Greek word *martyr* was still used in his time in its original meaning of "witness," and meant no more than that the bearer of this title was a famous witness to Christ—not neces-sarily a "blood witness" as the term later came to mean. What complicates matters is the fact that this pope was sometimes con-fused with an illustrious martyr of the same name, the Roman consul Titus Flavius Clemens who was put to death for being a Christian at the end of his consulate in 95 A.D. by his cousin, the emperor Domitian. Origen identified Pope Clement I with the Clement mentioned by Saint Paul in Phil. 4,3: "Help them (the ladies, Evodia and Syntyche), for they have toiled with me in the gospel, as have Clement and the rest of my fellow workers whose names are in the book of life." This Clement, however, was most likely a Philippian, and therefore almost certainly not the same as the Roman Clement who would have been quite young at the time Saint Paul wrote his letter to the Philippians. Moreover, "Clement" was a common name at that time.

Such a famous saint, however, as Clement of Rome could not have remained long without having a legendary account of his martyrdom written up for him. According to this legend, the emperor Trajan banished Clement and many other Chris-tians of Rome to the Crimea (on the northern shore of the Black Sea.) Here, to quench the thirst of these Christians at their slave labor, Clement produced a miraculous spring of water.

He was eventually thrown into the sea with an anchor tied to his neck. Angels built a marble tomb for him where his body lay beneath the sea, and once each year the sea receded far enough away from the shore to reveal this tomb.

Toward the end of the ninth century St. Cyril, the Apostle of the Slavs, thought that he had found the relics of St. Clement in the Crimea and brought them to Rome. Here they were placed in the famous ancient Church of St. Clement which was already in existence at the time of Constantine the Great, in the first half of the fourth century. Under the present church of St. Clement in Rome, which is now in charge of the Irish Dominican Fathers, there were found the remnants of a first-century Roman house which may possibly have been the home of St. Clement.

SELECTIONS FROM ST. CLEMENT'S LETTER
TO THE CORINTHIANS

Fidelity to God

These things, dearly beloved, we are writing, not only to warn you, but also to remind ourselves; for we are in the same arena, and the same contest lies before us. For this reason let us abandon empty and silly concerns, and come to the glorious and holy rule of our tradition. Let us see what is good and pleasing and acceptable in the sight of our Maker. Let us fix our gaze on the blood of Christ and realize how precious it is to His Father, seeing that it was poured out for our salvation and brought the grace of conversion to the whole world. Let us look back over all the generations, and learn that from generation to generation the Lord has given an opportunity of repentance to all who would return to Him. Noe preached penance, and those who heeded were saved. Then Jonas announced destruction to the Ninivites and they repented of their sins, besought God in prayer and estranged though they were from God, obtained salvation.

Exhortation to Repentance

The ministers of God's grace preached on repentance with the help of the Holy Spirit. And the Lord of all things Himself spoke of repentance, with an oath: 'For as I live, saith the Lord, I desire not the death of a sinner but his repentance.' He added this kindly assurance: 'Repent, O house of Israel, of your wickedness. Say to the sons of my people: "If your sins reach from the earth to Heaven, and if they be redder than scarlet, and blacker than sackcloth, and you return to Me with all your heart and say, 'Father, I will listen to you as a holy people.'"' And in another place He speaks thus: 'Wash and cleanse yourselves, put away wickedness out of your souls from before my eyes, cease from wickedness, learn to do good, seek judgment, rescue the oppressed, give judgment to the fatherless and justice to the widow, and come and let us consider together, saith the Lord; and if your sins be as scarlet I will make them white as snow, and if they be as crimson, I will whiten them as wool; and if you be willing and listen to me, you shall eat the good things of the earth, but if you be unwilling and listen not to me, a sword shall devour you, for the mouth of the Lord has spoken these things.' Desiring therefore that all His beloved should share in repentance, He established it by His Almighty Will.

The God-governed Order in the Universe

The heavens move at His direction and are subject to Him in tranquility. Day and night complete the course assigned by Him without hindering each other. Sun and moon and the choir of stars revolve in harmony according to His command in the orbits assigned to them, without swerving the slightest. The earth, flowering at His bidding in due seasons, brings forth abundant food for men and beasts and all the living beings on its surface, without reluctance and without altering any of His ar-

rangements. The unsearchable places of the bottomless pit and
the indescribable regions of the lower world are subject to the
same decrees. The mass of the boundless sea, gathered together
in one place according to His plan, does not overrun the barriers
appointed to it, but acts as He commanded it. For He said:
'Thus far shalt thou come, and thy wave shall be broken within
thee.' The ocean, impassable by men, and the world beyond it
are regulated by the same decrees of the Lord. The seasons of
spring, summer, fall and winter give way in turn, one to the
other, in peace. The winds from the different quarters, each in
its proper season, perform their service without hindrance. The
ever-flowing springs, made for enjoyment and for health, unfailingly offer their breasts to sustain the life of man. The very
smallest of the animals come together in harmony and in peace.
The great Creator and Lord of the universe commanded all these
things to be at peace and in harmony; He does good to all, and
more than superabundantly to us who have found refuge in His
mercies through our Lord Jesus Christ. To whom be glory and
majesty for ever and ever.   Amen.

The Resurrection of the Body

Let us consider, beloved, how the Lord is continually revealing
to us the resurrection that is to be. Of this He has constituted
the Lord Jesus Christ the first-fruits, by raising Him from the
dead. Let us look, beloved, at the resurrection in regard to the
seasons. Day and night demonstrate a resurrection: the night
sleeps and the day arises; the day departs and night returns. Let
us take the crops, to see how and in what manner the planting
takes place. 'The sower went forth' and cast each of the seeds
into the ground, and they, falling on the ground dry and bare,
decay. Then from their decay the greatness of the Lord's providence raises them up, and from one seed many grow up and
bring forth fruit.

Let us look at the strange phenomenon which takes place in
the East, that is, in the regions near Arabia.   There is a bird
which is called the phoenix. This bird, the only one of its species,
lives five hundred years. As the time of its dissolution in death

approaches, it makes a nest of incense and myrhh and other spices, into which it enters when its time is completed, and dies. Now, as its flesh decays a worm is born, which is nourished by the moisture of the dead bird and grows wings. Then, growing strong, it picks up that nest, in which are the bones of its predecessor, and carries them from the country of Arabia as far as Egypt, to the city called Heliopolis. And in the daylight, in the sight of all, flying to the altar of the Sun, it places them there and so sets out on its return. Then the priests look up the records of the years, and they find that it has come at the end of the five-hundredth year.

Do we think it something great and marvelous, then, if the Creator of the universe shall bring about a resurrection of those who served Him in holiness, in the confidence of a good faith, considering that He demonstrates the greatness of His promise by means even of a bird? For He says somewhere: 'And Thou shalt raise me up, and I will praise Thee,' and 'I lay down and slept; I rose up for Thou are with me.' And again, Job says: 'And Thou shalt raise up this flesh of mine which has endured all these things.'

With this hope, then, let our souls be bound to Him who is faithful in His promises and just in His judgments. He who commanded us not to lie will be far from lying Himself. For nothing is impossible to God, except to lie. Let faith in Him, then, be enkindled in us, and let us reflect that all things are near to Him. By the word of His majesty He has set up all things, and by a word He can overturn them. 'Who shall say to Him, "What hast Thou done?" or who shall stand against the force of His power?' When He wishes, and as He wishes, He will do all things, and none of the things decreed by Him shall fail. All things are before Him, and nothing is hid from His planning.

The Heavenly Reward of Virtue

The good laborer receives the bread of his labor with confidence; the lazy and careless one does not look his employer in the face. We must, therefore, be zealous in doing good; for all things are from Him. He warns us: 'Behold, the Lord comes, and his reward is before his face, to pay each man according to his work.' He therefore urges us who believe in Him with all our heart not to be lazy or careless in any good work. Let our glorying and our confidence be in Him; let us be subject to His will. Let us consider the whole multitude of angels, how they stand and minister to His will. For the Scripture says: 'Ten thousand stood by him, and thousands of thousands ministered to Him, and they cried, "Holy, Holy, Holy, Lord of hosts, the whole creation is full of His glory.'" We, therefore, gathering together in concord in our conscience, also should cry out earnestly as with one voice to Him, that we may become participants in His great and glorious promises. For He says: 'Eye has not seen, nor ear heard, nor has it entered into the heart of man, what great things the Lord has prepared for those who wait for him.'

How blessed and wonderful are the gifts of God, beloved. Life in immortality, joyousness in justice, truth in confidence, faith in trustfulness, continence in holiness. And all these things fall within our understanding. And what shall we say of the things that are being prepared for those who persevere. Only the Creator and Father of the ages, the all-holy One, knows their greatness and beauty. Let us strive, therefore, to be found in the number of those who wait for Him, that we may share in the promised gifts. But how shall this be, beloved? If our mind be fixed by means of faith on God; if we seek what is pleasing and acceptable to Him; if we perform what is proper to His faultless will and follow the path of truth, casting from us all injustice and wickedness, covetousness, strife, malice and deceit, gossiping and evil speaking, hatred of God, arrogance and boasting, vainglory and inhospitality.

Harmony in the Mystical Body of Christ

Brothers, let us be His soldiers, therefore, in all earnestness, under His faultless commands. Let us consider those who are enrolled under our rulers, how well ordered, and how readily, how obediently they carry out commands. Not all are prefects, or tribunes, or centurions, or in charge of bands of fifty, and so forth; but each one in his own rank carries out the commands issued by the emperor and the officers. The great cannot exist without the small, nor the small without the great; there is a certain organization, and it is of benefit to all. Let us take our body. The head without the feet is nothing, and so also the feet without the head are nothing. The smallest members of our body are necessary and useful to the whole body. But all conspire together and unite in a single obedience, so that the whole body may be saved.

Therefore, let our whole body be saved in Christ Jesus, and let each be subject to his neighbor, according to the position which grace bestowed on each. Let not the strong neglect the weak, and let the weak respect the strong. Let the rich man supply the wants of the poor, and let the poor man give thanks to God, because He has given him someone to supply his needs. Let the wise show his wisdom not in good works. Let the humble-minded not testify to his own humility, but allow others to bear him witness. Let us consider, brothers, of what matter we are made; who and what we are and who have come into the world; from what a tomb and what darkness our Maker and Creator brought us into the world and prepared His benefits for us before we were born. We who have obtained all these things from Him ought to thank Him for all, to whom be glory forever and ever. Amen.

Saints Cosmas and Damian

Martyrs

c. 3 0 3

(September 27)

THE EASTERN CHURCH venerates a special small group of saints who are called in Greek *hoi anargyroi,* "the no-money ones." These were holy physicians who, out of love for Christ, practiced their profession without accepting any recompense from their patients. The best known and most popular of these generous doctors are Saints Cosmas and Damian. Their fame soon spread to the West, and ever since the fourth century they have also been highly venerated in the Roman Church. Their names are included in the Canon of the Roman Mass and in the Litany of the Saints. During the pontificate of Pope St. Felix IV (526-530), a church was built in their honor at Rome, and the mosaics in this church which date from that time are among the most valuable pieces of ancient Christian art. Cosmas and Damian have always been regarded as the special patrons of physicians and surgeons and are often invoked, especially in Italy, for the blessing of good health.

Yet practically nothing is known with certainty about their lives. Various so-called "Acts" of their martyrdom have come down to us, but it is almost impossible to separate what might be the historical kernel from the many purely legendary elements with which these stories are adorned.

According to the most common legend, Cosmas and Damian were twin brothers who were born in Arabia and studied medicine in Syria. It was principally in the seaport town of Aegeas (modern Ayas) situated on the Gulf of Alexandretta (Iskenderun) in the southeast corner of Asia Minor that they are said to have practiced their healing arts. Being devout Christians they wished to imitate Christ (the divine Physician of souls) who went about the towns and villages of Galilee curing the ill and infirm and, therefore, they, too, refused to accept any fees for their services as doctors. In 303, during the persecution of the Christian Church by the Roman emperor Diocletian (though according to some accounts it was as early as 287), they were arrested and suffered for their holy faith. They remained true to Christ under torture and were finally beheaded. Legendary stories were added about the many miraculous ways in which they were rescued from death before the sword put an end to their lives. These include: when they were thrown into the water, they were saved from drowning; when fire was enkindled around them, it could not burn them; when hung on crosses, the stones that were thrown at them and the arrows that were shot at them bounded back at the persecutors without reaching the holy martyrs. In the fifteenth century, Fra Angelico illustrated the story of their lives and martyrdom in a series of beautiful paintings which are still preserved in Florence, Italy.

Saint Eugene I
Pope

6 5 7

(June 2)

FOLLOWING THE FIRST three centuries of its existence during which it had to endure the Roman persecutions from without, the Church was afflicted in the next few centuries by heresies from within. First, in the fourth century, there was the heresy of Arianism which asserted that Jesus Christ was not truly the Son of God in the strict sense of the Second Person of the Blessed Trinity. Then, in the fifth century, there were two additional heresies which departed from the orthodox Catholic doctrine concerning Christ in two opposite extremes. These included the heresy of Nestorianism which, somewhat like Arianism, over-emphasized His humanity, and taught that in Christ there were two distinct persons, one human and one divine. The heresy of Monophysitism in reaction to Nestorianism denied the true human nature of Christ and taught that He had but one nature, His divine nature, in which His human nature was absorbed. These last two heresies left the Church in the East sharply divided.

Large parts of Syria remained Nestorian and thus separated from the unity of the Church, while the vast majority of the Christians in Egypt were permanently lost to the Church by remaining Monophysite. All through the sixth century, therefore, the Church in the East was split between the Nestorians of Syria, the Monophysites of Egypt, and the Orthodox, principally of Asia Minor and Greece. Thus divided, the Christian countries of the East fell easy victims to the Moslems who swarmed out of Arabia in the second quarter of the seventh century.

In order to bring back the Monophysites of Egypt to the unity of the faith, and thereby give Christendom a more united front against the invading Moslems, certain men in the second quarter of the seventh century proposed a compromise between Monophysitism and Orthodoxy by teaching that while Christ had two distinct natures, one human and one divine, He had only one will—a divine will. The result was the creation of a new heresy called Monothelitism meaning the doctrine of a "single will."

One of the Popes who was active in the defense of the orthodox faith against the heresy of Monothelitism was Saint Eugene I. The son of Rufinianus of Rome, Eugene, or Eugenius ("well born") according to the Latin form of his name, was born and raised in Rome. From his earliest years he was in the service of the Roman church and was known for his gentleness, generosity and holiness.

During the pontificate of Pope Martin I (649-655), the conflict between the Monothélite heresy and Orthodoxy came to a climax. The emperor of Constantinople, Constans II (641-668), had embraced the Monothelite heresy, and when Pope Martin condemned the heresy and ordered the heretical archbishop of Constantinople deposed, the emperor had the pope arrested (June 18, 653) and taken from Rome to Constantinople. Saint Martin I was cruelly tortured and then sent as an exile into the Tauric Chersonese (modern Crimea, on the northern shore of the Black Sea) where, as the result of his ill-treatment, he died a martyr on September 16, 655.

After Saint Martin's banishment from Rome the Church was left for more than a year with no active head. Thus it had to be governed by the leading churchmen of Rome in the same manner as during the vacancy of the Holy See following the death of a pope. However, on August 10, 654, Eugene had been elected pope while Martin was still living. It is not known how this election was brought about; whether with the previous approval of Martin or not. In any case, when the latter heard that a successor had been appointed for him, he endorsed the new pope. If the emperor thought that he was getting a weak man whom he could use as his tool in Eugene, he was soon to find that the opposite was true.

Pope Eugene, to be sure, first tried to be on friendly terms with the emperor. One of his first acts was to send delegates to the imperial court at Constantinople. The delegates returned with a letter from the emperor which pretended to be friendly, but which failed to show that he had any intention of giving up his Monothelite heresy. When this letter was publicly read before the pope and people in the church of St. Mary Major at Rome, the clergy and the people raised such a protest that the pope could not continue the Mass he was then celebrating until he promised that he would refuse to accept this compromising letter.

The imperial envoys were so furious at this contemptuous rejection of their master's letter that they threatened to roast Eugene and his Roman followers as they had roasted Martin I. This dire threat may well have been carried out against the holy pontiff had not the Moslems, who had taken the Island of Rhodes in 654 and defeated the emperor's forces in the naval battle of Phoenix in 655, kept Constans II too busy for the next few years with military and political matters to meddle in the affairs of the Church. Eugene was, therefore, enabled to carry on his pontificate in peace until his death on June 2, 657.

Saint Fidelis of Sigmaringen
Martyr
1 6 2 2
(April 24)

A CERTAIN AMOUNT OF fame is always attached to being "the first" in doing something. To Saint Fidelis of Sigmaringen belongs the honor of being the first martyr to die for Christ under that branch of the government of the Church known as the Sacred Congregation for the Propagation of the Faith. In the last half of the sixteenth century there had gradually evolved in Rome a governing board of cardinals for the spread of the Catholic faith among the pagans in the newly discovered parts of the world, as well as for the return to the true faith of the heretics of those countries of northern Europe which had left the Church in the so-called Protestant Reformation. On January 6, 1622, Pope Gregory XV firmly established this committee of the cardinals into a permanent organization (which still flourishes) under the title of the *Sacra Congregatio de Propaganda Fide*. Less than four months later, in a region of Switzerland subject to this Pontifical Congregation, Fidelis of Sigmaringen sacrificed his life in his effort to "propagate" or spread the faith—the first of the many martyrs who would shed their lifeblood in this noble cause.

This saint received the name "Fidelis" when he became a Religious. His baptismal name was Mark. He was born in 1577 in the little town of Sigmaringen on the upper Danube River in what was then the principality of Hohenzollern, but is now in the

district of Baden-Wuettemberg (southwestern Germany). In the
Protestant revolt a half century before, this part of Germany
(known in general as Swabia) remained faithful to the Catholic
Church. Sigmaringen was, therefore, a thoroughly Catholic town.

The father of the saint, John Rey, was of Flemish descent and
the mayor of Sigmaringen. The saint's mother, Genevieve Rosen-
berger, came originally from Tuebingen situated about 30 miles
north of Sigmaringen. Mrs. Rey lost her husband in death a few
years after the birth of their son Mark. Her second husband
proved a truly devoted stepfather to young Mark and saw to it
that he was well educated. After elementary schooling in his
home town, Mark Rey attended the University of Freiburg in
Breisgau in the southwest corner of Germany. Here his diligent
spirit of study did not prevent him from growing in piety and
virtue. In 1604, before he had finished his course of studies for
a legal degree, he accepted the position of tutor and guide to
three young noblemen on a long tour through various parts of
Italy, southern Germany, and France. One of the members of
this tour, Wilhelm von Stotzinger, later testified at the saint's
cause of beatification that Mark Rey gave them a shining example of charity, mortification and piety on these travels and frequently spoke to them of the things of God.

In 1611 Mark was back at university in Freiburg where he received the degree of Doctor in Canon and Civil Law. For a year
he practiced law at Colmar and Enisheim in Upper Alsace. His
sole aim in the cases which he handled was the establishment of
justice. If his client's case was just, he undertook to defend it
whether he made any personal profit from it or not. Thus he became known as "the poor man's lawyer." On the other hand, he
refused to be the advocate in an unjust case no matter what fees
were offered him. His fellow lawyers disliked him for his refusal
to drag out a case unnecessarily for the sake of increasing the
fees. Such corruption in the practice of law soon filled him with
so much disgust that he resolved to give up the world and enter
a religious order.

Just a century earlier a group of Franciscan friars in Italy had started a "reform" movement in their order. Seeking a return to the primitive spirit of the utter poverty and simplicity of St. Francis of Assisi, they restored the short pointed hood, or *cappuccio*, of the early Franciscans, and so were called *Cappuccini*, or Capuchins, by the people. At the beginning of the seventeenth century they had established several houses in southern Germany where, together with the Jesuits, they rendered yeoman service in the defense of the Catholic faith against the onslaughts of the Protestants.

Mark had an older brother who had already become a Capuchin at Freiburg, and the holy lives led in poverty and austerity by these friars appealed to him also. When he decided to give up the practice of earthly law for the sake of the Kingdom of God and His justice, he naturally applied for admission among the Capuchins at Freiburg. Their superior, however, advised him to be ordained a priest before entering the Capuchin novitiate. Since Mark had already completed the course of ecclesiastical studies, he soon was ready for his sacerdotal ordination.

On the 4th of October, the Feast of St. Francis, in the year 1612, he celebrated both his First Mass and received the Capuchin habit. The name "Fidelis" was given him, and the preacher on the occasion took as his text the words from the Apocalypse (2,10): "Be thou faithful (*fidelis*) unto death, and I will give thee the crown of life." The new novice proved that this name was well chosen. Right up to his martyr death he was always completely faithful, not only to all the laws of God, but to all the evangelical counsels and to the smallest point of the rules of his religious order.

In his novitiate he doubled his zeal for prayer and penance, and these devout practices he continued for the rest of his life. Not satisfied with the strict fasts imposed by the Franciscan Rule, he limited his nourishment during Lent, Advent and on the vigils of the greater feasts to bread and water and a little dried fruit. He always prayed that he might be preserved from lukewarmness and sloth. "Woe betide me," he was heard to exclaim, "if I should be found to be a half-hearted soldier in the service of my thorn-crowned Captain." His spirit of humility was so deep that he seemed to take delight in being humiliated. The last and lowliest tasks of the house were his choice, even later in life when he was superior of his community.

After his novitiate at Freiburg, Fidelis was sent to the Capuchin friary at Constance situated on the border of Germany and Switzerland where he deepened his knowledge of theology under the guidance of Father John Baptist, a Polish nobleman who had become a Capuchin at Milan. The training he received from this holy scholar was to serve him well in his later disputes with the Calvinist and Zwinglian Protestants in Switzerland.

Although he would have preferred to remain a simple subject throughout his life, as soon as he had finished this theological training his outstanding qualities of mind and soul led his fellow religious to elect him "guardian" or superior of their friaries, first at Rheinfelden (at the southern end of the Black Forest), then at Freiburg, and finally at Feldkirch near the Swiss border in Vorarlberg (the westernmost province of Austria). His duties, however, as superior of his community did not keep Fidelis from exercising a very active ministry. Whenever he could, he preached the word of God to the spiritually starved people. His style of preaching was entirely in keeping with true Franciscan simplicity, with no effort at rhetoric or high-sounding phrases but in the ordinary language of the people. His topics were dictated by the needs of the time: loyalty to the Catholic faith and to the Pope; devout reception of the sacraments, especially confession and Holy Communion; devotion to the Blessed Virgin Mary, and the need of praying for the poor souls in purgatory. His preaching produced extraordinary conversions, not so much from his natural eloquence as from the holiness of his life which spoke more loudly than words.

The charity of Fidelis toward the poor was one of his outstanding characteristics. While he demanded that his fellow Capuchins should live as poorly and simply as he did, he could not see a family in want, a needy widow or an indigent orphan, without doing all he could to help them. When an outbreak of the plague played havoc with the Austrian troops that were quartered near his friary in Feldkirch, he gave himself wholeheartedly to nursing the sick soldiers with no thought of the danger he incurred of catching the dread disease himself.

Fidelis had once confided to a friend that he often prayed for two things: to be preserved from ever committing a mortal sin, and to be granted the grace of dying a martyr's death. Both prayers were answered—the grace of martyrdom sooner perhaps than he expected.

While he was superior at Feldkirch, the Holy See entrusted to his Capuchin province the task of trying to bring back to the true Church the people of the easternmost Swiss canton that is called Graubuenden in German and the Grisons in French. Many of the mountain villages here had become Protestant. To complicate matters, this canton (part of the ancient Roman province of Rhaetia) bordered on Austria, and its inhabitants looked upon Protestantism as a defense of their hard-won liberty against Catholic Austria. As superior of the Capuchin friary at Feldkirch, Fidelis was also made superior of the Capuchin friars engaged in this difficult mission.

Nothing daunted, this heroic soldier of Christ set out on his mission of preaching to the heretics of Graubuenden with no other supplies than a Bible, a breviary, a crucifix, and a copy of the Rule book of his order. He left it to God to take care of his other needs.

In Advent of 1621, Fidelis began this first attempt since the outbreak of the Reformation a century before to reclaim for the true Church the Protestants of Graubuenden. Throughout the winter he preached several times each day in the cities, towns and villages of this canton, not only in the Catholic churches, but also in the streets and market places and even in the meeting houses of the heretics. The bishop of Chur, in whose diocese this region lay, sent a glowing report to Rome of the brilliant success of this zealous missionary, and the newly established Congregation for the Propagation of the Faith confirmed the appointment of Fidelis of Sigmaringen as superior of this mission. It was not merely the simple mountain folk who were led by his fervent preaching and holiness of life to come back to the Church of their forefathers; several of the leading citizens, such as Conrad von Plata and especially Rudolph von Salis, one of the most influential men of the canton, renounced their errors and were received by Fidelis into union with the one true Church.

This, however, was too much for the die-hards among the heretics. If they could not stop by arguments this widespread conversion of Graubuenden to Catholicism they would put an end to it by violence. Fidelis had more than a premonition of what was in store for him. On April 24, 1622, knowing that he was about to enter into one of the most violent centers of Protestantism, he left for the mountain villags of Seewis after he had gone to confession, said Mass and preached at Grusch. Pretending to be willing to renounce their errors, the heretics at Seewis had sent word to him on the previous day inviting him to come to preach to them. In the midst of his sermon there on the text, "One Lord, one faith, one baptism," a wild tumult suddenly broke out. A few friends of Fidelis who were standing guard for just such an emergency were overpowered, and he himself barely escaped a bullet that was fired at him. To save their own skins, the people fled from the church. Alone before the altar, Fidelis commended his soul to God, and then went out bravely to meet his enemies. When these men had let him start out a short distance towards Grusch, they suddenly waylaid him and offered him the alternative of accepting the teaching of Calvin or being put to death. Calmly, Fidelis replied: "I did not come here to embrace heresy, but to oppose it." Knocked to the ground by a blow, he rose to his knees, spread forth his arms in the form of a cross, and prayed, "Lord, forgive my enemies. They are blinded by passion and do not know what they are doing." In a moment his head was cracked with another blow and his body riddled with sword thrusts. He was forty-five years old, and had been a Capuchin for only ten years, but he was true to his name: *fidelis usque ad mortem*, "faithful unto death."

The Catholics in the neighborhood were allowed to gather up his remains. His body was carried to Feldkirch and buried in the Capuchin church there; his head and left arm were brought as relics to the cathedral at Chur.

As Fidelis had predicted, the armed revolt of the Protestant peasants in this part of the country was soon crushed by the military forces of the emperor. One of the Protestant ministers, who had witnessed the holy death of the martyr, was so impressed by the fulfillment of this prophecy, that he publicly renounced his errors and returned to the true Church.

St. Fidelis was beatified in 1729, and canonized in 1745. He is usually shown in art as holding a crucifix and bleeding from a wound in his head, or with a bludgeon as his emblem.

Saint Frances of Rome
Widow

1 4 4 0

(March 9)

ITALIANS ADD THE epithet "Romana" to the name of the holy
widow "Francesca," not only because she was born and
spent her life at Rome—as a matter of fact, in the heart of old,
Medieval Rome, but also because *Santa Francesca Romana*, Saint
Frances of Rome, has ever been the pride and joy of the Roman
people. Though she was an astonishing mystic, for whom marvelous visions and amazing miracles were every-day occurrences,
Frances had such a charm and loveliness about her in her tender
love for God and neighbor, that she has captured forever the
hearts of her fellow citizens of the Eternal City.

Both Frances' father, Paul Bussi, and her mother, Giacobella
Rofredeschi, belonged to families of the old Roman nobility,
closely related to the Orsini and the Savelli. As soon as their
daughter was born in 1384 these devout parents had her baptized
in the Church of St. Agnes on the Piazza Navona, where she received as her name the feminine form of the name of the Poverello of Assisi, and it was in the same church in the ancient Campo
Marzo of Rome that she was confirmed six years later.

From her very infancy this child of grace seemed different from
other children. Endowed with a sweet and gentle disposition, she
had a certain angelic air about her. She learned to pray as soon
as she learned to speak. Taking no interest in childish games,

654

just as later she was to find no pleasure in worldly amusements, she began even as a little girl to love solitude and seek her happiness in communing with God and in doing good to others. For even the little faults which every child commits she used to punish herself with hard penances. At the age of six she stopped eating meat, and soon she began to fast as rigorously as her age would permit. Daily she went with her mother to pray in one or the other of the churches in her neighborhood, and before long her mother's confessor and spiritual director, Padre Antonello, also became her own.

This priest was one of the Olivetan Benedictines attached to the Church of Santa Maria Nuova at the end of the ancient Roman Forum. Within the Forum itself was the much older church, then as now in ruins, of Santa Maria Antica, with its quaint mural paintings going back to the early Middle Ages. When this "ancient" Church of St. Mary was abandoned, the "new" Church of St. Mary was built not far away. This church always remained Frances' favorite among the numerous churches of Rome. Today it is also known as the Church of "Santa Francesca Romana" because here the saint's mortal remains are buried.

When Frances was eleven years old, her confessor allowed her to make a vow of virginity, as she confided to him her longing to devote her life to God as a nun. Yet shortly after this her father told her that he had promised her in marriage to Lorenzo de Ponziani, a rich young nobleman of Rome, and that their wedding should soon be celebrated. Frances was utterly heartbroken. On her knees she begged her father not to make her marry, but to let her enter a convent. Signor Bussi, however, was adamant; he had already given his word, and he would not go back on it.

With her eyes full of tears Frances took her heartache to her Father confessor. This good man told her that this might well be God's will and, if so, she should accept it and offer Him the sacrifice of her own will. In this case she could easily be dispensed from her vow. Then as she prayed for light and strength to know and do God's will, she saw clearly that to obey her parents in this was what God was asking of her. Actually, though she did not realize it at the time, God was calling her to a special mission in life, which she could not fulfill if she entered a convent while still a teen-age girl. Later, when her father again brought up the matter, Frances gave her consent to the marriage and asked his forgiveness for her earlier misbehavior.

Though it may seem to us a shockingly early age, it was quite in keeping with the customs of the time that Frances Bussi was married to Lorenzo de Ponziani in 1395 when she was not yet twelve years old. Their marriage proved to be a happy one in every respect. Lorenzo was as virtuous and talented as he was rich, and he could not have found a more devoted wife than Frances. Moreover, it was through this marriage that Frances also found a most dear friend in her sister-in-law Vannozza, the wife of Lorenzo's older brother. Few sisters were ever knit together as closely in heart and mind as these two were. Vannozza confided to Frances that she too had wished to become a nun, but she now found her happiness in doing God's will in the married state. For some thirty years these two saintly women consoled and helped each other, praying together, doing penance together, and going about together doing good.

Frances was quite willing to fulfill all the social duties that were expected of her as the wife of a Roman nobleman. At her husband's request she wore fine clothes and splendid jewelry; but under them, with her confessor's permission, she wore a hair-shirt. Since Lorenzo did not insist on her dancing, going to shows or playing cards, as most of the frivolous ladies of Roman society were accustomed to do, Frances abstained from such amusements. It is really astonishing to see how this twelve-year-old bride was able to keep her quiet dignity and deep piety and to persevere in her religious and charitable activities without giving offense to anyone. Naturally there were a few who resented her devout mode of life and suggested to Lorenzo that he should put an end to his wife's "eccentricities"; but he was a sensible man who tenderly loved his young wife, and so the busybodies got nowhere with him.

After Frances had been married about a year she fell seriously ill, and for several months it was uncertain whether she would survive this affliction. The family was plunged in grief, her father in particular being disconsolate because he blamed himself for having refused her request to become a nun. But Frances herself was calm; the only thing she desired was to do God's will, whether in life or in death. Only once did she become indignant: when some friends suggested that a spell had been cast on her and that magical means should be used to remove it, she replied that she would much rather die than permit such an abomination. For a time she seemed to rally; but thereafter she grew much worse, so that it appeared almost certain that she would soon die.

Then there happened to her one of those marvels which were to become more and more frequent in her later life. As she lay in bed, racked with pain and with her eyes fixed on the crucifix, she suddenly saw the room fill with brilliant light and she beheld a young man in pilgrim garb that shone like gold. He approached her bed and said, "I am Saint Alexis. God has sent me to you, faithful servant of Christ, that I might cure you of your illness." He then spread his mantle over her, and vanished. At once Frances felt completely cured. Arousing her dear Vannozza from sleep, she told her what had happened. At daybreak the two of them slipped out of the house and, after hearing Mass at the Church of Santa Maria Nuova, they went to the Church of St. Alexis, where they venerated his relics and thanked him for what he had done.

Thereafter Frances and Vannozza led even more austere and charitable lives. Since Lorenzo was delighted with his wife's recovery, he allowed her to erect a small hut in the rear of their garden, and here, as in a little oratory, she and Vannozza used to pray and do penance together without being seen by the rest of the household. A good part of each day the two women spent in visiting and assisting the poor and in nursing the sick in the hospitals, especially in the Hospital of the Holy Spirit situated near the Vatican.

In 1401, when Frances was married seven years, her mother-in-law, Cecilia, died. Till then this woman had acted as the mistress of the household. From now on this duty devolved on Lorenzo's young wife. Though only eighteen years old, Frances began to take full charge of the De Ponziani palace. More with gentle tact than with severity she knew how to put an end to the bad language and disedifying conduct of some of the servants. Since her husband allowed her a free hand in dispensing food, clothing and money to the poor, she gave orders to the servants that no poor people were ever to be sent away from the door without giving them something in charity.

During one of these years Rome was stricken with a severe famine. Frances was giving away so much grain and wine to the endless flow of beggars that came to her door, that her father-in-law Andrew decided to sell most of their remaining supplies and to lock the door of the cellar with his own special key where a small amount of the supplies was left for the family's needs. Nothing daunted, Frances, accompanied by Vannozza, went about in the city begging food for the poor. God came to her aid, and the little that the good women were able to beg was miraculously multiplied over and over again. Andrew, seeing that his daughters-in-law were still distributing food and wine, became angry and rebuked his sons for having such disobedient wives. But Frances told him to open the cellar and see that she had not taken any of his supplies. On looking into the cellar, he found to his amazement that it was full of grain and wine, much more, in fact, than he had left there. Apologizing to his saintly daughters-in-law, he told his neighbors what had happened, and soon the miracle was known all over Rome.

Six children, it seems, were born to Lorenzo and Frances. But we have knowledge of only three of them; the other three had apparently died in infancy. In 1400, when Frances was sixteen years old, she gave birth to a son who was christened Giovanni

Battista (John the Baptist). Another son, born in 1403, was baptized Giovanni Evangelista (John the Evangelist). These two boys were ordinarily called merely Battista and Evangelista. In 1408 a daughter, Agnes, was born.

Woeful misfortunes, however, began to come upon the De Ponziani family in 1408, when Frances was twenty-six years old. Lorenzo, an officer in the Papal army, took an active part in the defense of Rome against King Lancelot of Naples. In the battle of 1408 he was severely wounded and carried home, more dead than alive. Everything was in wild confusion, but Frances remained calm. She nursed him night and day till he was out of danger, finding that her hospital experience now stood her in good stead. Contrary to expectations he recovered. But the city fell to the King of Naples, and Lorenzo had to go into hiding. The Neapolitan soldiers pillaged Frances' home, maltreated her servants, and demanded her son Battista as a hostage. Bringing the boy first to the Church of Ara Coeli on the Capitoline Hill, she knelt before the image of the Mother of God and with tears in her eyes she offered up her sacrifice. As she gazed on Mary's image, she saw the Virgin's eyes grow soft and tender and she heard a voice say, "Do not be afraid. I am always here to befriend you."

How long the little Battista remained a hostage is not known, but eventually he was brought back home. In 1413, however, the Neapolitan army was again in Rome, and this time Lorenzo was captured and taken away as a prisoner. Once more Frances saw her house plundered. Yet she could look on it all with resignation and repeat the words of Job: "The Lord has given; the Lord has taken. Blessed be the name of the Lord!"

These were terrible years for Rome. Besides the devastation caused by the wars, famine and pestilence stalked the streets. Frances and Vannozza, forgetting their own troubles, spent almost all their time assisting the poor and the sick. God gave Francesca the gift of healing, and many people whom the doctors despaired of curing were restored to health through her prayers.

What made her so endearing to the poor was the fact that she literally made herself one of them. On one occasion she attended a solemn feast at the Basilica of St. Paul, which attracted all the important people in Rome. Seeing some paupers begging at the door of the basilica, she not only gave them the little she had with her; she took her stand with them and begged for them, let the nobles of Rome think what they would of her conduct!

One sorrow after another now befell Frances. In 1411 God took from her in death her eight-year old son Evangelista. He had been a precocious child and had shown signs of wonderful spiritual gifts ever since his infancy. Then in 1413 her little five-year-old daughter Agnes died. We have Frances' own account of this, taken down as told to her spiritual director. One night, as the little girl was sleeping soundly, her mother saw a dove come with a lighted candle in its beak and touch with it each sense organ of the child just like a priest administering Extreme Unction to a dying person. On the following night Frances had another vision. Her son Evangelista, who had died two years before, appeared in a bright light, and by his side was a young man in brilliant garments. The mother longed to embrace her boy, but she could feel nothing when she touched him. She could only hear him say, "Do not mourn for us who are in heaven. We have no pain or sorrow, but enjoy unspeakable bliss, as we gaze on the infinite goodness of God and praise His adorable majesty. My sister Agnes will soon join me in glory. But God has sent you this archangel to comfort you." The words which Frances heard in the vision were soon fulfilled. Little Agnes died in a short time and joined her brother Evangelista in heaven.

The life of St. Frances of Rome abounds in stories of such visions. They differ from the visions of other mystics by the fact that they are almost always presented in the form of dramatic actions carried out by heavenly personages. Another characteristic of this saint is her familiarity with the angels. Throughout her life she was always conscious of her guardian angel at her side. She always *saw* her guardian angel. At times she even felt him.

SAINT CAMILLUS DE LELLIS

For thirty years following his founding of the *Company of the Servants of the Sick,* Camillus devoted all of his tremendous energy to the "total service" of the sick. Although his work was primarily for those in hospitals, he nursed the ill and attended the dying wherever they were to be found. It was with this remarkable Saint that the "red cross" as a symbol for the sick and the destitute originated.

SAINT BRUNO   Ledoux

Born in Cologne, Germany, of noble parentage, Saint Bruno became a leading theologian of the 11th century. In 1804, he founded the Carthusian
Order, the most austere monastic organization of the Church. Pope Urban
II offered Bruno the archbishopric of Reggio, Italy, to no avail, and
finally permitted him to retreat into Calabria.

When she failed to follow his instructions, she received a resounding slap on the face from him. Others have testified that they heard these slaps, though they could see no one but Frances. After the vision which she had announcing the death of her daughter Agnes, the place of her ordinary guardian angel was taken by the special archangel whom God then sent to her. Toward the end of her life the place of this archangel was taken by one of those high angelic spirits called "Powers." From this great spirit she received sublime visions of hell, purgatory and heaven.

About the year 1417 Frances herself became seriously ill. Grief, labors and austerities had undermined her health. Except for her faithful Vannozza, few people ever came near her, and some of these only came to reproach her for her "absurd infatuation." Yet she was always sweet and gentle with them and never defended herself against their accusations. Her soul was at peace and she was ready to die. But God still had work for her to do, and her time had not yet come.

Eventually Lorenzo came home from his military imprisonment, bringing back with him their only remaining child, Battista. Frances continued her life of prayer, penance, and charity, with the full approval of her husband, who rightly thought her a saint. While relatives and friends were displeased with Frances' life of poverty, which, from a merely human viewpoint, was no longer necessary, the people of Rome generally recognized and respected her holy apostolate. Through her words and good example she was able to wean away from their frivolous amusements and sinful pleasures many of the ladies of Rome. Miraculous favors granted through her prayers grew more and more frequent. On receiving Holy Communion she often fell into an ecstasy that lasted for quite a while. In time a wound opened in her side, as though God had set His seal on her heart. Although this caused her great pain, only Vannozza, who dressed it, and Padre Antonello, her confessor, to whom she revealed everything about herself, knew of it. But when in a vision she was transported to the cave of Bethlehem and beheld the Infant Jesus With His Mother,

Mary bathed the wound with water from the rock of the cave and at once it was healed.

When Frances' son Battista was eighteen years old, he married a girl named Mobilia. Frances received her with love into the family, but she neither returned this love nor seemed even aware of it. Her head was turned by her new stately life and she gave herself up to gay amusements and fine clothes. Basically she was not a bad girl, but she had been utterly spoiled, and the saintly life of her mother-in-law was a continual reproach to her own worldly life. "How can anyone," she used to say, "feel respect for a woman who thinks of nothing but the poor, and dresses like one of them, and goes about the streets carrying wood and old clothes to them?" One of her favorite jests was to mimic and ridicule Frances. Ever patient and kind to the girl, Frances prayed earnestly for her. One day when Mobilia was carrying on outrageously in running down her mother-in-law, she suddenly began to tremble and then fell down in a faint. When she came to herself and saw Frances lovingly taking care of her, all her bad behavior stared her in the face. Overcome with shame and remorse, she begged Frances' forgiveness, which was of course instantly granted. From that day on she was a changed young woman, and her love and veneration for Frances grew more and more. She even kept a sort of notebook on the saint, and from it was later taken evidence that was used in the canonization of St. Frances. Eventually the younger woman took over the management of the De Ponziani palace and thus left Frances free to carry on her service of the sick and the poor.

Lorenzo's veneration of his saintly wife now became so intense that he finally told her he did not think it right for them to live together as husband and wife; he would gladly regard and treat her as if she were his sister. Frances was deeply touched and joyfully accepted this arrangement. But as his health was now failing, she continued to nurse and care for him.

Meanwhile Frances' final destiny in life was taking shape. Several pious women of Rome had taken her as their model and were imitating her devout and charitable life as far as they were able. They would often accompany her on her journeys to the sick and the poor and would join her in prayer at her favorite Church of Santa Maria Nuova. At first this was a rather informal sodality, but under the guidance of her confessor, Padre Antonello, Frances drew up certain simple rules for them, which made them a more closely knit organization. This confraternity was eventually approved by Padre Antonello's highest superior, the Father General of the Olivetan Benedictines and it was affiliated to his Order. Since these women took no formal vows but merely made an oblation of themselves to God, they were called "the Oblates of Mount Olivet." It was on the Feast of Mary's Assumption into heaven, August 15, 1425, that Frances, Vannozza, and eight other Roman ladies made the first oblation of themselves to Christ in common at the Church of Santa Maria Nuova. Frances did not wish to be their head, but they forced her to act as such.

On Christmas in the year 1433 Frances had a marvelous vision that affected the future of her little group. First she beheld the Infant Jesus come to her and nestle in her arms. Then St. Peter, assisted by St. Paul, came and gave her Holy Communion, in the presence of St. Benedict and St. Mary Magdalen. After Frances had renewed before the Prince of the Apostles the consecration of herself to God, he gave her certain instructions regarding her confraternity of pious women, telling her in particular that it was God's will that they should, as far as possible, no longer live in their own homes but rather in common as in a sort of convent.

Frances found a suitable place in a small house at the Tor dei Specchi ("Tower of Mirrors"), an old medieval construction in her neighborhood. Here, on the Feast of Mary's Annunciation, March 25th, in the year 1434, the first ten Oblates of Mount Olivet took up their residence, some of them unmarried young women and some of them widows. Frances herself had to remain at home to care for her invalid husband; her beloved Vannozza had already gone to her eternal reward; so one of their earliest

companions, Agnes de Selli, was elected as their first superior.
Nowadays we are so used to the innumerable religious congregations of Sisters in the Church, that we might not realize what a
daring innovation it was that St. Frances of Rome was making.
Till then a woman either became a strictly cloistered nun, or she
remained "in the world," even though she might dedicate herself
to God by a private vow. There were then no "Sisters" in the
sense of women living under vows in a community who, free from
the obligation of strict enclosure, could devote themselves charitable works, such as nursing and teaching. Frances, though not
the first to conceive this idea of a non-cloistered sisterhood, was
certainly one of the first to establish such a religious congregation
on a successful basis. To this day her original foundation at Tor
de Specchi, naturally much enlarged by this time, is still the fervent center of her Oblates of Mount Olivet. Her plan, of course,
met at first with much opposition. But aided by her powerful
prayers, her convent received the approval of the Pope the year
after it was founded.

In 1436, a little more than forty years after Lorenzo Ponziani
had married Frances Bussi, their marriage ended in his holy
death. All this time his wife had devotedly and tenderly cared for
him. But now at long last, the fifty-two-year-old Frances, who
had longed to enter the convent as a twelve-year-old girl and who
had always been a nun at heart, was free to enjoy her soul's desire. Despite the pleadings and grief of her family, Frances left
her home on March 21, 1436, and presented herself at the convent of Tor de Specchi, not as its foundress, but as a humble suppliant begging admission. The Sisters of course received her with
joy and all of them asked her to become their superior, Agnes
Selli herself being most insistent in this. But Frances refused. It
was only some months later that obedience to her confessor forced
her to accept the superiorship of the community. Yet even after
this she continued to live as if she were the last and least in the
house, using her privilege as superior to appoint herself to the
most menial tasks.

Though Frances had but four years to live at Tor de Specchi, they were no doubt the holiest and happiest of her life. She could now give free rein to her desire for penance, even if it's hard to understand how she could increase her austerities. All her life she took but one meal a day, consisting of some bread and vegetables in the evening. Under her hairshirt she constantly wore a chain with sharp points around her waist. Every night her short sleep was preceded by a self-inflicted scourging. Yet her spirit was always so cheerful and gay that one would have thought she was living in luxurious comfort.

During these last years of her life she was also favored by endless visions and miracles. Padre Mattiotti, her confessor after the death of Padre Antonello, later drew up such a long account of these in the cause of her beatification, that it would be impossible even to summarize them here. Only a sample of one or the other of her astonishing miracles must suffice. One day it was found that the bread in the house was hardly enough for three people. But Frances blessed it and began to distribute it to the fifteen Sisters, till they all had as much as they could eat, with plenty left over for the next day. On another day Frances was out in the fields beyond the city with her Sisters gathering wood for the poor, as was their custom, when one of the Sisters complained of hunger and thirst. Instead of chiding her lack of mortification, charitable Frances told the Sisters to go to a nearby vineyard and gather grapes for themselves. The Sisters would have thought she was raving, had they not known she was a saint. It was the middle of January, and there would be nothing but sticks on the vines! But when they looked, the vines were full of grapes and, thanking the Lord for His goodness, the Sisters enjoyed the delicious fruit.

One day in March of 1440 Frances was called to her old home to attend her son, who was very ill. She had been there but a short time when he became so much better that he got up from bed, miraculously cured. But she had given her life for his. As she got ready to leave, she was suddenly stricken herself, apparently with a heart attack or a stroke. Against the protests of her family she tried to walk back to her convent. But she did not go far before she became so weak that she had to be carried. She was not brought to her convent, but to her old home in the palace of the De Ponziani, where she had for so many years served her divine Lord so faithfully. In a short time her last vision on earth was changed to the face-to-face vision in heaven. Her last words, spoken in obedience to her confessor, were: "The heavens are open and the angels descend. My archangel has finished his task. He stands before me and beckons me to follow him." It was on March 9, 1440 when she thus closed her eyes in death. Her face, which had been prematurely aged with labor and suffering, now took on the radiance of youth and beauty. Her body found its last resting place in Santa Maria Nuova, the church she loved so dearly. All Rome cried out: "Frances is in heaven! Frances is a saint!"

Her canonization was taken for granted. But with the tumultuous times the process of her cause was unduly delayed. Finally on May 29, 1608, amid glorious solemnities at St. Peter's, Pope Paul V pronounced her canonization.

St. Frances of Rome is known and venerated all over the world. Thus, in 1917 there was founded in France a "League of Prayer and Good Works" for widows under her patronage, which has been blessed and approved by Benedict XV and Pius XI. But it is especially in Rome, her Rome, where Santa Francesca Romana is loved. Her feastday on March the 9th is observed with great devotion both at her Church of Santa Maria Nuova and at her convent of Tor de Specchi. An odd custom grew up at her church on this day. Motorists began to bring their cars to receive the blessing of St. Frances of Rome at her church, and the custom has continued. In 1925 Pope Pius XI made her, together with St. Christopher and St. Elias, patroness of motorists: St. Christopher, because this giant once carried the Christ Child across a stream; the prophet Elias, because he went to heaven in a fiery "car."

Saint Francis Borgia

Confessor

1 5 7 2

(October 10)

W HAT IS SAID of many other saints, that they were born of poor but pious stock, cannot be said of Saint Francis Borgia. Not only were all his ancestors of the richest and highest nobility; many of them led lives that were far from exemplary. On his mother's side Francis was the great-grandson of King Ferdinand of Aragon, who, together with his wife, Queen Isabel of Castile, sponsored the famous 1492 voyage of Christopher Columbus which led to the discovery of America. King Ferdinand's illegitimate son Alfonso, who was made archbishop of Zaragoza, though not at all worthy of this office, begot several children by Ana de Gurrea, and one of these, his daughter Juana, he gave in marriage to Juan Borgia, third Duke of Gandia. The first child of this marriage was Saint Francis Borgia.

On his father's side Francis had ancestors who were even more amazing as forebears of a saint. His paternal grandfather, Juan, second Duke of Gandia, was the illegitimate son of Cardinal Rodrigo Borgia, a native of Valencia in Spain, and the latter's mistress, the Roman lady Vanozza Catanei. This is the Cardinal Borgia who has become infamous in history as Pope Alexander VI (1492-1503). Actually, as ruler of the Church, Alexander VI was a very capable administrator and, in his official capacity as pope, he deserves much more credit than is usually given him. The trouble was with his private life as a cardinal. Nature had fashioned him to be a father, and indeed he showed himself a devoted, if over-indulgent father of his illegitimate and equally infamous children, Juan, Caesar, and Lucretia Borgia. The primary fault lay with his uncle, Cardinal Alfonso Borgia, who, as Pope Callistus III (1455-1458), had made his unworthy twenty-year-old nephew Rodrigo Cardinal-Bishop of Porto. It was left to Francis, the great-grandson of this pope and the fourth Duke of Gandia, to remove, with God's grace, the infamy attached to the name of Borgia. Rightly is he often called "the greatest of the Borgias."

Gandia is a small seaport city in the southeast corner of the Spanish province of Valencia, about seventy miles south of the capital city of the same name, Valencia, about halfway down the Mediterranean coast of Spain. Here, on October 28, 1510, in his family's castle, our saint was born. He was named after St. Francis of Assisi because it was especially through the intercession of this saint that his mother Juana was able to bring him safely into the world. Suffering greatly in labor pains, with her life despaired of, she asked to have "St. Francis' cord" brought from the Poor Clare convent of Gandia, and only after she had bound this around her body did she succeed in giving birth to this, her first-born son.

Not all the ancestors of Francis Borgia were sinners. His mother Juana, though born out of wedlock, was a truly virtuous woman. His paternal grandmother, Dona Maria Enriquez de Luna, likewise led a life of piety and virtue, and she it was who was primarily responsible for Francis' early growth in holiness. Her daughter, Isabel Borgia, refused the offer of marriage to the Duke of Segovia, and one day, as she followed a priest who was bringing the Viaticum into the convent of the Poor Clares in Gandia, she went into this convent and refused to leave. Here she became Sister Francis of Jesus and was soon called a saint by all who knew her.

Francis proved to be an intelligent and precocious child, ever eager to learn. He knew his prayers when he was three, and by four he knew the whole little catechism and could follow the Mass when it was said in the chapel of the castle. His first school was at the convent of the Gandia Poor Clares, where not only his aunt Isabel, but also his grandmother Maria was now a nun. Dona Maria had followed the example of her daughter and entered this convent in March of 1512, after Juana's second child, Alfonso, was born, and she was now Sister Gabriela. Later that year a little daughter, Luisa, was born to Juana, and she was very dear to her older brother Francis.

Because of his contact with this convent and its atmosphere of spirituality, Francis soon showed signs of exaggerated piety, which his mother promptly checked. "I asked God for a son," she said, "who would be a duke, not a friar." His father also, who was now a religious man and good to his people, spoke bruskly: "Clear away those altars, my boy. Your great-grandfather, King Ferdinand, was busy with valor in the field, not with altars." As was often the case with youngsters in those days, Francis, helped by Luisa, used to erect little altars and play at being a priest. Consequently he was taught riding and fencing, and in these arts too he was an apt pupil. One of his favorite pastimes was to go hunting with his father.

The Duke, however, had a pious custom which he also taught his oldest son. No matter where he was or what he was doing, at the tinkling of the bell which meant that the Viaticum was being brought to some dying person, he would hurry to follow, bareheaded, the priest carrying the Blessed Sacrament. When Francis was a man, he in turn trained his own sons to do the same thing.

After Francis lost his mother in death, he and his sister Luisa were sent to his maternal grandmother, Dona Ana de Gurrea, at Zaragoza, and it was many years before the boy again saw his father.

Life at the worldly court of Zaragoza was a very different thing from what Francis had known in Gandia. Yet, though he was only ten years old, his faith was strongly rooted in him and, regardless of the way things were here, he went to Mass every morning and made his confession and received Holy Communion as often as he could.

While Dona Ana watched over her little granddaughter Luisa, Francis' uncle Juan, the archbishop of Zaragoza, set up a princely household for him. The boy was kept busy, not only with his regular studies, but also with lessons in riding and fencing and music. He had a special gift for music, and in later life he composed many works that were sung in the cathedrals. He was still writing Church music when his fingers were so gnarled from rheumatism that he could no longer play the organ.

When Francis was twelve years old, he was appointed page boy to his distant cousin, the young Infanta (or, Crown Princess) Catalina. He had just recovered from a serious illness of six months, and it was a strange thing to send him into an atmosphere such as this. For Catalina's mother, Queen Juana, the daughter of Ferdinand and Isabel, had gone completely crazy, and she made the life of her little daughter an utter misery, keeping her locked up all alone in a small room. It was in answer to a letter that Catalina wrote to her brother Charles that Francis was sent to give her some companionship. Soon the two teen-age children became greatly devoted to each other.

When Catalina was eighteen years old a marriage was arranged for her with John III of Portugal. She wished to have Francis go with her to Lisbon, but his father, the Duke of Gandia, refused to grant his permission for this move. Back at Zaragoza with his uncle, the archbishop, Francis resumed the arduous training which this ambitious prelate set for him. The archbishop of Zaragoza thought there was too much reserve under the charming gaiety of the young man. He did not want him to become a virtuous "prig," for chastity was not highly prized at his court. He hinted to Francis that the quickest way to gain experience in the ways of the world was through a woman. The handsome seventeen-year-old youth presented a fascinating challenge to the young ladies of the court. Everyone and everything joined forces to tempt the young man, who, after all, was no plaster saint. It was truly a hard struggle for him. St. Francis' biographers pass swiftly over this time, ignoring his passionate blood, his vicious surroundings and the subtle or flagrant temptations with which he was besieged on all sides. He prayed and visited the Blessed Sacrament and practiced stern discipline. It was one of the most arduous battles of his life, and he bore its scars for the rest of his days. But through it he also developed an iron will, perfect self-control, and a still deeper reserve.

Before starting his nephew out on the world, the archbishop decided to send him home to visit his father in Gandia. The Duke of Gandia had meanwhile remarried and already had three children by his second wife. Francis was saddened at the sight of a stepmother in his own beloved mother's place. He had been invited to the imperial court at Alcala de Henares and he was not certain that his father would give him permission to go there, but the permission was after all granted.

On his arrival in Alcala de Henares, Francis had his first sight of Ignatius Loyola, though of course he had no idea who he was. He then beheld Ignatius merely being led through the street as a prisoner of the Spanish Inquisition.

Francis was received with warm friendliness by the Emperor Charles V and the Empress Isabel, and at once there sprang up a deep and sincere friendship between Francis and Isabel that lasted till her death. The young nobleman was soon recognized as the handsomest of all the courtiers, and he was outstanding in every activity. But his first allegiance was always to his divine Master, the King of kings.

After a year at court Francis had fallen in love with a young Portuguese lady-in-waiting at the court, Eleanor de Castro, and he realized that the wisest course for him to take in the morally dangerous surroundings was to ask her hand in marriage. The sympathetic empress furthered the match by requesting Charles' permission for them to marry, and she prevailed upon him to write a letter to the Duke of Gandia about it. As was expected, Duke Juan refused to let his son marry a "foreigner." But Francis was well enough acquainted with his father's ways to know that he would never leave his home to come to the imperial court, so he cleverly suggested that the Duke be ordered to come to court and there discuss the matter. The ruse worked, and the Duke wrote back that they could do whatever they wanted. The marriage contract was signed on July 26, 1529, at Barcelona. Francis was given half the barony of Lombay, which the emperor raised to the dignity of a marquisate, and he was also appointed to the office of Huntsman-in-chief, while Eleanor was made Mistress of the Royal Household.

Regardless of the power he wielded and the honor of the close friendship which he and Eleanor shared with the emperor and the empress, the young man still held fast to his practices of piety. Two very serious illinesses befell him, but they brought him ever closer to God than he had been before, and he resolved never to miss confession and Communion every month and to do all things solely for the glory of God.

Francis and Eleanor were a truly devoted couple and lived in perfect harmony. During the ten years of their married life at the court they had eight children, whom they brought up carefully and piously. Theirs was indeed a very happy family.

In 1539, however, the empress was again stricken with a fever such as she had had six years before. But now she was pregnant. On May 1 of that year her baby was born dead, and she herself died in childbirth. The emperor was heartbroken, for he dearly loved his good wife. The Marquis Francis was in charge of her funeral cortege. He was not only wretchedly unhappy at the loss of his gracious, lovely friend; he was also deeply worried about the future for himself and his family. He felt sure that the emperor would leave Spain now that his beloved empress was dead, and this would mean the loss of his own position at the court. He was not a soldier; that fact he had learned in the war which he had fought in Charles' army in Provence.

When the funeral cortege reached Granada, which was in deep mourning, the Requiem Mass was sung for the deceased empress by the Cardinal of Burgos. That evening the coffin would be buried in the crypt of the cathedral, where it was dark, dank and gloomy. As part of the ceremony the Marquis of Lombay had a special duty to perform: he would have to uncover the face of the corpse and swear to its identity. When he stepped forward for this purpose, the pall was removed and the outer leaden coffin opened. Then Francis lifted the cloth from the face of the dead empress. The sight of the corpse sent those present reeling back; only seething corruption, stench and sheer horror met their eyes. Francis felt sick to death, but he controlled himself and pronounced the words of the oath, for although every vestige of her previous beauty, grace and loveliness was gone, he knew this was the empress and no other.

Without even stopping to see his wife Eleanor, Francis hastened to his room in the palace where they were quartered. He had reached the breaking point, and he had to be alone with God. John of Avila, the great preacher of Andalusia, had preached the funeral sermon. Francis now sent for him and revealed to him the state of his soul. John gave him sound spiritual advice and warned him of the dangers of his life at the court. Francis always regarded this as his "conversion," even though his previous life had ever been most devout and exemplary. Yet in a certain sense he was now a changed man. On his return to Toledo, he had a meeting with the Admiral of Castile, Don Fernando Enriquez, with whom he had once had a violent quarrel. The Admiral, who expected a duel, was dumbfounded when he saw Francis kneel at his feet and humbly beg his pardon. From that time on they were firm friends.

The emperor, who would have liked to take Francis with him, for to him he could empty the sorrows of his heart, realized with the empress now dead there was no longer any place for Eleanor and her husband at the court; but he appointed him his Viceroy of Catalonia, one of the highest dignities he could confer in Spain. During the years that followed, as Francis carried out this office with his customary vigor—years filled with honors, hard work, and great difficulties—Francis grew ever nearer the destiny that awaited him. He had saved his chastity when he fell in love with Eleanor and married her, but the hot blood of the Borgias still ran in his veins and temptations still surrounded him. He used his scourge on himself till the blood flowed and, when compelled to attend magnificent functions, he wore a hairshirt under his splendid clothes. Every day he spent a long time in prayer, and he asked his guardian angel to watch over his soul and body. Besides his great devotion to Our Lady, he had a special devotion to his guardian angel.

On January 7, 1543, Francis' father, the third Duke of Gandia, died; but it was not till April of that year that Francis went home with his family to Gandia. He had written to the emperor for a short leave of absence, saying that he had stayed on at his post in Catalonia until he felt that he could be spared for a few months. But as things turned out, he stayed with his family for a long time in Gandia, where he was now the fourth Duke. His good wife Eleanor was ill for a long time. When her death seemed imminent, Francis stormed heaven with pleas for her life. One day he heard Christ tell him that he could keep her if he wished, but that this would not be the best thing for him. Thereupon he made the supreme sacrifice and offered up everything to God. His sacrifice was accepted, and on March 27, 1546, Eleanor died in the same room where he himself had been born.

Francis sent for Peter Faber, one of St. Ignatius' first companions in the Society of Jesus, to come and comfort him. There was a deep friendship between Duke Francis of Gandia and Father Faber, and the holiness, understanding sympathy and good advice of the simple Jesuit from Savoy did as much as could humanly be done to heal the nobleman's grief and put him on the right path spiritually. After his wife's death Francis decided to devote himself entirely to God's service in a religious order. He considered the possibilities of several orders, particularly those of the Franciscans and the Dominicans, but he finally chose that of the newly founded Jesuits, among whom he felt he could most surely avoid receiving ecclesiastical honors. He had already been in contact with Ignatius Loyola and other early Jesuits through correspondence and had arranged for the establishment of a Jesuit college at Gandia. Father Faber did not have the time to give the Spiritual Exercises, or Jesuit form of retreat, to Francis, but he delegated this task to his companion, Father Oviedo.

This was the last time that Father Faber and Francis Borgia saw each other. Faber died at Rome on August 2, worn out from ceaseless work and travel, shortly after he had delivered to Ignatius the letter which Francis wrote telling of his desire to enter the Society of Jesus. Fearing that Faber might have died on the way and not brought his letter to Rome, Francis again wrote to Ignatius and told him of the vow which he had made before Father Oviedo on June 3, 1546, to enter the Jesuits, if his request was granted. Ignatius' reply was wise, courteous and holy. He counseled Francis to take time to arrange everything for his family and also, while attending to these matters, to begin his theological studies and to take his doctor's degree in the Jesuit college of Gandia. Ignatius warned him, moreover, to observe strict secrecy about the whole matter because of the violent reaction which he feared would come when the world learned of the Duke of Gandia's decision to become a Jesuit. It was four years before Francis got all his affairs in order and before he finished his studies, and a trying period indeed was this for a nature as impatient as his. On August 20, 1550, he received his doctor's degree at the Gandia college which he himself had founded.

During these years, despite his studies and other occupations, Francis devoted much time to prayer and practiced severe penance. Ignatius gave him sound advice on these matters in his letter to Francis of September 20, 1548: "When temptations weaken and die and are replaced by good and holy desires, we no longer need the same arms to conquer our enemies. Your Grace would be wise to give to study, to the management of your estates and to spiritual talk the hours you now devote to prayer. Wait till your soul

is calm and at peace and ready to do all that our Lord asks of
you. It is a higher virtue to be able to enjoy God in different occupations and in all places than only at prayer in your oratory.
As for fasting and abstinence, I wish your strength to be increased, not lessened ... Body and soul alike belong to their Lord
and Creator, who will demand an account of them. Health must
not be injured, for if the body is weakened the soul cannot act ...
The end of all this fasting will be that your stomach will cease to
work and no longer digest the food necessary for health . . . As
for scourgings, I advise you to stop those which draw even a drop
of blood." On the floor of Francis' small oratory at Gandia can
still be seen the dull marks of his blood where he scourged himself, not only for his own sins, but also for the terrible crimes of
his kinsmen, the Borgias.

Francis' frugal diet did accomplish one good thing for him. He
had previously gained so much weight that, when he came back
to Gandia in 1543, he was dubbed "the fattest man in Valencia."
Now he lost a good deal of this excess weight and in later years
he became extremely emaciated. Pictures and statues of him
which are based on his appearance in the last years of his life
give the impression that he was not only a very austere aescetic,
but also an inhumanly rigid fanatic. The latter idea is far from
the truth. Just as in earlier life Francis had been gay and witty,
a true friend, a loving husband and a devoted father, so now in
his later life he still remained a charming, generous, kindly
gentleman.

Even after Francis had gotten his children's lives and estates
in order, the way was not yet clear for him to devote himself
wholly to God. A command came to him from Charles V for
him to come to the aid of the imperial cause in its trouble with
Protestant princes of Germany. The emperor needed money for
his war, and who could get it better for him than the Duke of
Gandia? When Francis had accomplished this task, which he
found extremely repugnant, the emperor wished him to remain at
court. But the Duke had planned otherwise. Before leaving

SAINT CLEMENT OF ROME

Clement's claim to fame lies in his letter to the Corinthians, the earliest
Christian writing after the New Testament to come down to us. It was
written for the purpose of bringing harmony into the Christian community at Corinth, and proved that even at so early a date as the end
of the first century, the Church at Rome was speaking with authority. The
artist has depicted the pontiff with his stigmata.

SAINTS COSMAS AND DAMIAN

Saints Cosmas and Damian were twin brothers, born in Arabia, who came
to Rome and suffered martyrdom under Diocletian in the third century. As
holy physicians they practiced medicine without compensation. Their fame
spread, and since the fourth century they have been highly venerated in
the Roman Church. Their names are included in the Canon of the Mass.

Gandia on the emperor's command, he had, with the authorization of Ignatius and the permission of the pope (who did not yet know to whom he gave it), made his profession as a Jesuit to Father Oviedo in secret on February 1, 1548. Eighteen months later he was free of all his responsibilities, with all his affairs in order.

In 1550 Francis went to Rome, to see Ignatius and to gain the indulgence of the Jubilee Year. He had hoped to travel as simply as possible, but instead he was obliged to go in pomp as usual. He said his goodbyes and departed, followed by a long cavalcade, including his favorite son Juan and nine Jesuits. There is a spot a little north of Gandia, on the road to Valencia, that is marked by a stone to show where Francis turned to take a last look at his city. The words which he quoted here from the Psalms are symbolic: "The snare is broken and we are freed."

On reaching Rome, Francis at long last met Ignatius. Later he said of him, "Till now I have looked upon Faber as a giant and myself as a child, but compared to Ignatius, Faber himself is but a child." While in Rome, where he was received with every mark of distinction, Francis furnished the main funds for the building of the famous Jesuit institute of learning in this city, the "Collegium Romanum."

After saying farewell to Ignatius and leaving Rome, Francis traveled to Onate in northeastern Spain. Here he spent many happy days in holy retreat and heavenly contemplation, and here, after formally resigning his dukedom in favor of his oldest son, Juan, he was ordained a priest on May 23, 1551. His enthusiasm led him to holy excess, not only in matters of penance, but also in regard to humility. Ignatius, for instance, had to make him stop signing his letters with the words: "Francis the sinner."

The newly ordained priest now found his first and most enjoyable occupation in traveling around the Basque country of northeastern Spain, preaching and instructing the poor, abandoned people and administering to them the sacraments. He would have continued indefinitely in this zealous work, had not

Ignatius given him a special commission to carry out in Lisbon.
Francis had no natural desire to go there, but he obeyed at once.
Everywhere he went he was mobbed by the enthusiastic people,
and once he said with some indignation, "One would think I were
some kind of wild beast the way they come to stare at me"; but
quickly calming himself, he added: "After all, what am I but
a half-tamed beast?" Owing to certain circumstances he was
spared the Lisbon visit at this time, and he gratefully returned
to Onate. Though he longed for solitude and contemplation, most
of his life was to be spent in almost continual travel and heavy
responsibilities.

Francis also had his share of heartaches with his children.
His son Juan suddenly kicked over the traces, plunging into
amusements and then getting married without even asking his
father's consent. Ignatius was greatly displeased at this marriage,
for the bride was his own niece, Dona Lorenza de Loyola, and he
feared that people would say he had used his influence with Francis to negotiate this match. Francis, however, forgave his son and
gave his blessing to the young couple. Then another son of his,
Carlos, caused real trouble by killing a man. Evidently the
Borgia blood was still running its wild course. There is a touching
story of Juan coming unexpectedly into his father's room and
finding him on his knees shaking with sobs. When the young
man spoke to his father, the latter looked at him with a face that
was radiant despite its streaming tears. "Juan," he said, "your
mother has just visited me, and before she returned to heaven she
asked me to give you her blessing."

Francis' great figure was now skeletonlike, which made his tall-
ness even more noticeable. His hair and beard had become gray,
and his fine hands were now rough and scarred from his labor of
laying bricks, gardening, scrubbing and working in the kitchen.
One day the regent, the Infanta Juana, whose spiritual director
he now was, called on him while he was helping in the kitchen.
When told that he had a visitor, he asked the cook's permission
to go to the parlor. "Well, don't be long," answered Brother

Cook, who was harassed with many unexpected dinner guests. So Francis made his interview with the Royal Infanta very brief. Even after he was raised to high office in the Society of Jesus Francis' love of humility led him to perform the most lowly tasks in the community. Thus, when he was the Superior General of the Jesuits, he once visited one of the Jesuit houses where the Brother who was cook had never seen him before. Having a little time to spare, Francis went to the kitchen and volunteered his services. "Can you cook?" asked the Brother who did not know him. "No," answered Francis, "I am not much good at anything except cleaning up." "Well, then," said the Brother, "hurry up and clean all those dirty pots and pans in the scullery." And Francis did as he was ordered. Imagine the unhappiness of the brother when he learned whom he had been ordering about! But Francis was not at all unhappy at the job he received.

Francis had not given up his high position in the world in order to receive offices of honor either in the Church or in the Society of Jesus. When shortly after his ordination he was offered the cardinalate by Pope Julius III, it was only through his earnest pleadings, seconded by Ignatius, that he succeeded in avoiding this dignity, which he would have found a calamity. Yet when Ignatius in 1554 appointed him his Commissary General over all the Jesuits in Spain, Portugal and the Indies, Francis had no choice but to obey. In this office he showed extraordinary ability and succeeded in establishing many new and thriving Jesuit colleges. Even after St. Ignatius died in Rome on July 31, 1556, and was succeeded by Father Lainez as second General of the Jesuits, Francis was asked to retain his office as head of the Jesuits in the Iberian Peninsula and the Spanish and Portuguese colonies.

Francis sorely missed Ignatius. He himself was far from well— overworked, suffering from attacks of fever and gout and chronic indigestion from too much fasting, with his body worn out by labor and cruel penances. In 1557 he had a severe hemorrhage, and as a result his nerves were highly overstrung. There is a well-known story of his journey to Simancas, where he loved to stay. He made the journey alone from Valladolid, traveling on foot through wind and snow, but he arrived so late that no one was up to hear his knocks on the door. Eventually a novice did hear him and, on opening the door, was overcome to find Francis, snow-covered and almost frozen, yet smiling and cheerful. "Do not worry, good Brother," said the saint, "for the Lord has cheered me up while I was waiting. I remembered that it was He who sent the snow and icy winds on me, and I know that all His works are full of infinite joy and beauty. So I rejoice that He should thus chasten me."

In 1557, when Francis happened to pass through the city of Avila, he visited its great mystic, St. Teresa. She used the opportunity to ask him about the "prayer of quiet," which she was experiencing without comprehending its nature. She was happy when she heard his lucid explanation, and in her written works she spoke of him as being a saint.

After Father James Lainez, the second General of the Jesuits, died on January 19, 1565, Francis Borgia was elected to succeed him. Concerning his election to this highest office in the Society of Jesus, he wrote to his friend, Antonio de Cordova: "I know you will be sorry for me because of your great love for me and because you know how much against the grain this is with me." But God had called him to this office on account of his great zeal and administrative ability. During the seven years in which he was the General of the Jesuits he labored so effectively for the spread of the Society of Jesus that he has sometimes been called its "second founder."

The short life of St. Francis Borgia that is given for his feast-day in the Roman Breviary sums up his activity as General of the Jesuits in these words: "In this office he was dearly loved both by secular princes and by the supreme pontiffs because of his prudence and the holiness of his life. Besides the many houses which he founded or enlarged in the existing provinces of the Society, he sent his confreres into the kingdom of Poland

and the islands of the distant seas, as well as into Mexico and Peru, and the apostolic men whom he sent into these and other regions spread the Roman Catholic faith by their preaching, their sweat, and their blood."

Long before his death legends grew up about this man. He was already considered a saint, and miracles were multiplied wherever he went. He prophecied, and his prophecies came true. He healed the sick and cast out devils. To avoid too much publicity, he used to laugh and make a joke of his miraculous powers. Francis clearly had a strong sense of humor, though his biographers seldom refer to it. He made good use of it to soften disappointing denials and to straighten out matters that seemed set on going awry.

In 1571, when Francis was sixty-one years old and worn out by labor and illness, Pope Pius V turned to him for aid. The year before, the Turks had conquered the island of Cyprus and now threatened the whole Christian Mediterranean Sea. Therefore, to enlist the aid of Philip II of Spain in a crusade against them, the pope asked Francis Borgia to accompany his Cardinal Legate to that country. Francis of course obeyed. When the papal delegation reached Barcelona on August 28, 1571, it was received in triumphal procession. Carlos Borgia sent from Gandia a large sum of money, together with riding boots and a new cloak for his saintly father. Francis refused to accept them, saying they were too smart and fashionable for him, but Brother Mark took them over for him. The General of the Jesuits was pathetically shabby. Even his rosary was homemade, of seeds strung on an old violin string!

Francis refused to visit Gandia, so all of Gandia streamed to Valencia over rough roads to visit him. The Cardinal Legate traveled in great magnificence, while the saint journeyed along in humble poverty. At one ceremony no train-bearer had been supplied for the Cardinal, so Francis slipped from his place and acted as his train-bearer. One day a message came for the saint from the Viceroy of Sardinia addressed to "The Most Illustrious

Lord, Don Francisco de Borja, Duke of Gandia." Francis did not open it, but gave it back to the messenger, saying, "I do not know where in the world you will find this most illustrious duke."

Francis was in chapel during the First Vespers of the Feast of All Saints when it was whispered in his ear that on October 7, 1571, Don Juan of Austria, the half-brother of Philip II, had won a tremendous naval victory over the fleet of the Turks at the Battle of Lepanto. He kept at his prayers undisturbed.

The long journey back to Rome had been made under excruciating conditions for the saint. Again and again it was thought he was dead, but he lived to return to his small room in the Eternal City. Then, a little after midnight on Tuesday, October 1, 1572, his faint breathing stopped and Francis Borgia's long and arduous life in this world had come to an end.

In 1617 the saint's body was taken from Rome to Madrid, where it perished in the destruction of the Jesuit house and church during the Spanish Revolution of 1931. He was beatified by Pope Urban VIII in 1624 and canonized by Pope Clement X in 1671. In 1683 Pope Innocent XI set his feastday for the universal Church on October 10.

Saint George

Martyr

c. 3 0 3

(April 23)

I N THE YEAR 495 Pope Saint Gelasius I issued a decree called *De Libris Recipiendis*, "On the Books that are to be received," in which he condemned certain apocryphal Acts of Saint George as being a spurious life of one of those saints "whose names are justly revered among men but whose deeds are known only to God." It is certain that there was a holy martyr called George. It is probable that he suffered martyrdom in Palestine at the city of Lydda (which the Greeks also called Diospolis), some time before Constantine, perhaps in the persecution of Diocletian (303-305). The tradition that he was a soldier is so early and constant that this can also be taken as probably true. Beyond that, all the stories told of St. George must be put down as fictitious legends.

Few saints have been as popular as Saint George. Fabulous stories of his wondrous doings circulated in various forms in all the languages of Christendom. Some of the earlier forms of his "Legend" contain the most fantastic elements, for example, that on three occasions George was put to death in the most thoroughgoing fashion—once he was chopped up into small pieces, once he was buried deep in the ground, and once he was consumed in fire—only to be miraculously restored to life each time by God.

One of the milder forms of his legend is that found in the *Legenda Aurea* or "Golden Legend," a collection of the lives of the saints that Blessed Jacovo de Voragine wrote in the second half of the 13th century. This is one of the earliest accounts of Saint George's encounter with the dragon, a story which cannot be traced back beyond the 12th century. The Golden Legend was so popular in the late Middle Ages that it was one of the first books printed in England by the first English printer, William Caxton. Caxton's English version of it was printed in London in 1483.

According to the Golden Legend Saint George was born in Cappadocia, Asia Minor. One day, as he rode about the world as a Christian knight on his steed, he came to a city called Sylene in the province of Lybia. In a marshy swamp near this place there lived a great dragon, "which envenomed all the country." The people tried to kill it, but were forced to flee from its fiery breath. To keep it contented in its swamp they had to give it two sheep to eat every day.

When their supply of sheep was exhausted, a human victim, determined by lot, was fed to it each day. Now the lot chanced to fall on the maiden daughter of the king. He offered all his wealth to any one who would take her place but, since they had pledged themselves against allowing a substitute, the poor maiden had no choice but to sacrifice herself for the people. She was walking to the dragon's marsh, dressed like a bride, just as Saint George happened to come to the place. Good knight that he was, he at once rushed to the rescue of the damsel in distress. Charging on his gallant steed, he first pierced the dragon with his spear, but this did not kill it. Then, borrowing the maiden's sash, he tied it around the neck of the monster which then became so gentle that the maiden could lead it by the other end of the sash into the city. "It followed her as if it had been a meek beast and debonnaire." When the people were about to flee in mortal terror, Saint George told them to have no fear; all they need do was to believe in Jesus Christ and be baptized, and he would slay the dragon for them. The king and the people were only too happy to agree.

When Saint George cut off the beast's head, four ox carts were required to haul its carcass away. "Then were there well XV thousand men baptized without women and children." In gratitude the king would gladly have given George great treasures, but the saint told him to give his wealth to the poor. Before riding on to other adventures, St. George bade the king be mindful of four things: to maintain God's churches, to honor the clergy, to attend religious service diligently, and to be charitable to the poor.

Now, at this time, the Roman emperors Diocletian and Maximian unloosed a violent persecution against the Christians. When St. George noticed that some of the Christians were so afraid of torture and death that they were in danger of denying the faith, he decided to give them a good example. Going into the public square, he cried out: "All the gods of the paynims (pagans) and gentiles are devils. My God made the heavens and is very God." Thereupon Datianus, "the Provost," had him arrested. When St. George was not moved by flattery, he was strung up and beaten with clubs and then burned with red-hot irons. That night, however, our Lord came to console him and restore his health. After that a magician tried to kill George with a poisoned drink, but when the poison had no ill effect on him, the magician became a Christian and died a martyr's death.

An attempt was then made to crush George between two spiked wheels, but he suffered no injury. An effort to boil him in a cauldron of molten lead was likewise useless. Datianus then went back to his original method of trying to coax George to be reasonable. Only for the purpose of letting God give a still greater display of His power, the saint pretended to be weakening in his faith and so invited all the pagans to witness his sacrifice to their gods. When they had all assembled, he prayed to his God, and the heavens sent down fire that destroyed the pagan priests, idols and temple, and the earth opened and swallowed them all up. The sight of these marvels made a Christian of Datianus' wife, but left him unmoved. He then ordered the beheading of

Saint George, the only means that always proved effective in the legendary martyrdom of the saints. After Saint George was beheaded, a final outburst of fire from heaven burned up Datianus.

Though Saint George was very popular in all the countries of medieval Europe, it was especially in England that he found his most zealous devotees. Even in pre-Norman England he was known and venerated, but it was particularly the Anglo-Norman knights who took him for their special patron, no doubt because of his fame as a valiant knight himself. The brave crusaders from England stormed the bastion of the infidel with the war cry: "For Saint George and merry England!"

In the 14th century a large red cross, called "the arms of Saint George," became the distinguishing mark of English soldiery. Even in the days of Queen Elizabeth, Spencer says of his hero in the *Faerie Queene,* who thought continually of wreaking vengeance "Upon his foe, a dragon horrible and stern."

"But on his breast a bloody Cross he bore,
The dear remembrance of his dying Lord,
For whose sweet sake that glorious badge he bore,
And dead, as living, ever him adored."

The English navy still flies a jack consisting of the red cross of St. George on a white background, and the same cross forms part of the union jack. About the year 1347, King Edward III made Saint George the patron of the Order of the Garter, an order of knights which he then founded. Known for centuries as the principal patron of England, Saint George was officially pronounced by Pope Benedict XIV (1740-1758) England's Heavenly Protector.

Saint Gregory VII

Pope

1 0 2 0

(May 25)

I N EVERY GREAT crisis of the Church its divine Founder (Who
established it on the rock of Peter) raises up a man as His
chosen instrument to ensure the fulfillment of His prophecy that
the gates of hell shall never prevail against it. In the eleventh
century when the Church was in grave danger from internal corruption and external oppression, God's chosen instrument to purify it of its evils from within, and to defend its liberty against the
trespasses by the power of the state from without, was Hildebrand, the monk, who became Pope under the name of Gregory
VII. The principal internal evil in the Church at that time was
the crime of simony (the sin of buying and selling ecclesiastical
offices) which resulted in the presence of utterly unworthy men
among the clergy, and the consequent collapse of morals among
the laity. The external evil was the so-called "right of lay investiture," that is, the claim of the civil government to appoint the
bishops, abbots, and other members of the governing body of the
Church by "investing" them with, or bestowing on them, the
symbols of their office. Essentially this was the age-old question
whether the state is supreme over the Church, or the Church over
the state.

To understand the nature of this problem in that particular
age it is necessary to know something of the origin and constitu-

tion of what is known as the feudalism of the Middle Ages. This
may briefly be described as follows. After the collapse of the
ancient Roman Empire in the fifth century, Europe was overrun
by barbarian hordes from the north. There was general confusion
and lawlessness all over. The prime thought in everyone's mind
was the need of protection. The wealthy landowner turned his
house into a small fortress. When the barbarian chieftains settled
down, they also lived in fortresses. The hills of Europe were
crowned with these semi-independent fortified castles. The lords
of these castles, the "nobility" of Europe, were not fully independent since they needed protection against one another. Some
of them would league together as vassals of a more powerful lord.
The latter, in turn, would owe loyalty to a still more powerful
suzerain, or overlord. Thus all society was graded from the emperor or king through the various ranks of the nobility down to
the peasants who were serfs or semi-slaves of the lord of their
local castle. All land was said to be held "in fief," that is, held
under certain conditions imposed by one's higher lord who "invested" his vassal with the title to his land.

Now, the Church also owned large tracts of land which had
been bequeathed to the Holy See of Rome (the Papal States of
central Italy), or to the various other dioceses by devout persons
of the nobility. The prelates of the Church, therefore, were not
merely spiritual heads of their territory; they were also temporal
lords of their domain, and in the merely political sphere they
would naturally be vassals of the overlord who controlled the
larger region in which their territory was situated. Obviously the
overlord's claim to the right of "investing" the princes of the
Church who were his vassals was bound to lead to various abuses.

Hildebrand, who as Pope Gregory VII did more than anyone
else to break this strangle hold by the political princes on the
Church, was born about the year 1020 of peasant stock in the
Tuscan city of Sovana in central Italy. His Germanic name of
"Hildebrand" (which means something like "battle flame"), was
symbolic of his character and future mission. When seven or

eight years old, he was sent to Rome to be educated at the school attached to the Benedictine monastery of St. Mary (on the Aventine Hill) where his uncle was abbot. Displaying a keen mind for studies, Hildebrand later attended the "Pontifical School" at Rome. This institution, which served as the training center for the sons of the nobility who were destined for high office in the Church, was then under the directorship of a man called John Gratian (not to be confused with John Gratian, the famous canon lawyer of the next century).

Even in his youth Hildebrand had plenty of opportunity to observe the depths into which the Papacy had fallen during the ninth and tenth centuries which are not too unjustly called "the Dark Ages." In 1032, a twenty-year-old son of the powerful Count of Tusculum was forced by his father on the Roman clergy as their Pope under the name of Benedict IX. He proved to be utterly unfit for the office. Thus in 1044, one of the factions of the Roman nobility drove him from Rome and elected their own Pope who took the name of Sylvester III. A year later the house of Tusculum expelled Sylvester and restored Benedict. The latter, however, after only a few weeks of his second term on the Papal throne, offered to sell his office to John Gratian for a large sum of money. Gratian, honestly thinking that the good he could do the Church would counterbalance his act of simony, accepted the offer and became Pope Gregory VI in 1045. To aid him in reforming the corrupt morals of the Romans, Gratian made his apt pupil Hildebrand his "chaplain" or special assistant. Hildebrand, who was later made a Cardinal-Deacon of Rome, began his work of reform with vigor, but his efforts were brought to nought after a year and a half. Benedict decided that he wanted ed the papacy back again, while Sylvester claimed that he was the lawful Pope. For the sake of peace a group of the Roman clergy appealed to the emperor, Henry III (1039-1056), to settle the dispute.

Happy at the privilege (to which he knew he had no right) of appointing a Pope, Henry deposed all three claimants and nominated Suidger, Bishop of Bamberg, who was then consecrated Pope under the name of Clement II. When the latter died less than a year later, Benedict came back for the third time to Rome where he ran riot for eight months until the emperor intervened once more. The new imperial nominee, another German, Damasus II, lasted only three weeks. The reader who feels confused should remember that this was an age of confusion.

Meanwhile, when John Gratian (ex-Pope Gregory VI) went as a voluntary exile into the emperor's domain, north of the Alps, he was accompanied by his faithful friend Hildebrand. The latter used this ocasion to stay for about a year at the monastery of Cluny in northern France. This great abbey, whose monks followed a revised form of the Benedictine rule, was one of the strongest forces working for religious and moral reform throughout Europe in the 10th and 11th centuries. It also had great influence on Hildebrand who was to become the first of several Popes connected with what is known as the "Cluniac reform," that is, the abolition of abuses in the Church according to the spirit of the Abbey of Cluny.

After the papal throne became empty at the death of Damasus II in 1048, the next nominee of the emperor was Bruno, bishop of Toul in Lorraine (then part of Henry's domain) who refused to accept the office unless he was freely elected by the clergy and people of Rome. Since he was a virtuous and capable man, the Romans enthusiastically welcomed Bruno, and he became Pope under the name of Leo IX. The new Pope had asked Hildebrand to accompany him to Rome, and now the two of them began to carry out the long-desired reform in the Church, condemning simony and clerical incontinence. Their campaign against worldly ways, slackness and sin extended from Italy into France and Germany. By his insistence that Rome had the right to accept or reject his nomination by the emperor, Leo had thrown down the gauntlet between the Papacy and the Empire. Through Hildebrand the strict spirit of Cluny penetrated Leo's administration. Both, however, agreed that the Pope had the right to use his sword as a soldier, as well as his papal staff, to defend the rights of the Holy See. It was primarily as a soldier that Leo came in conflict with the Normans of southern Italy who were destined to play an important role in the history of the papacy during the next few decades.

Originally Scandinavians (whence their name of Normans or "Northmen"), these adventurous men had first settled on the coast of northern France, named Normandy after them. At the beginning of the 11th century, a group of them sailed in force into the Mediterranean avowedly to wage war on the Moslems, though their conquest ended up with their seizure of southern Italy. Here they made their headquarters at Salerno, a city on the Italian coast south of Naples which became famous in World War II as the first beachhead of the American army on the mainland of Italy. When Pope Leo IX heard of the sufferings which these Normans inflicted on the inhabitants of southern Italy, he mustered his soldiers and marched against them. Though defeated on the field of battle, Leo was graciously received by the Norman leader, Robert Guiscard, who offered the Pope the services of his own army in the defense of the Holy See and thus became a vassal of the Pope, though a rather unruly one.

Eight months after his battle with the Normans, Leo IX died on April 19, 1054. A saintly as well as a capable Pope, he was later canonized by the Church. When Leo died, Hildebrand was in France combatting heresy, simony and moral laxity among the clergy. The candidate whom he recommended to the emperor as Leo's successor was Gebhard, bishop of Eichstatt in Bavaria. Gebhard was canonically elected Pope in 1055 by the Roman clergy and took the name of Victor II. Hildebrand had made a good choice. Victor continued the policy of his predecessor and, because of his cordial relations with the emperor, he was even more successful in suppressing simony and vice. Unfortunately he died after a reign of only a little more than two years.

Meanwhile Henry III died in 1056, and his seven-year-old son, Henry IV, was crowned emperor. This was the prince who, after he began to reign independently of regents in 1070, was to be Hildebrand's chief opponent in the bitter struggle for supremacy between State and Church.

After the death of Pope Victor II in 1057, Cardinal Frederick, the son of the Duke of Lower Lorraine, was elected Pope under the name of Stephen X without even consulting the imperial regent, the empress-mother Agnes. Hildebrand, however, who was still the strong man behind the papal throne, was willing to go through the formality of obtaining Agnes' approval of Stephen's election. On his way north to see the empress-mother, he stayed for some time in Milan to correct certain ecclesiastical abuses in this city of northern Italy. While there, news reached him of the death of Stephen who had been Pope for less than eight months. Before dying, Stephen had left orders for the Cardinals to await Hildebrand's return to Rome before proceeding with the election of a new Pope.

No sooner was Stephen dead, however, than the faction of the Count of Tusculum promptly elected Cardinal John Mincius, a Tuscan, as Benedict X. At the insistence of Hildebrand this election was declared invalid, and Benedict was deposed. In January of 1059 another of Hildebrand's candidates, Gerhard of Burgundy (now bishop of Florence) became Pope under the name of Nicholas II. A few months later a council was held in Rome which, among other regulations, drew up new rules for the election of a Pope. Essentially such an election was to be the work of the bishops, known as the Cardinal-Bishops (who presided over the suburban dioceses around Rome) and of the pastors (known as Cardinal-Priests) of the principal parishes of Rome, while the Roman laity and the emperor were to have merely the empty formality of approving the election after it was an accomplished fact. This document, which aimed at destroying the influence of both the Roman nobility and the emperor on a papal election, was primarily the work of the Cardinal-Deacon Hildebrand, although he signed it simply as "Hildebrand, monk and subdeacon of the Roman Church." Actually

SAINT GEORGE   Jacopo Tintoretto

Although Saint George was popular in all the countries of medieval Europe, he found his most zealous devotees in England. The brave English crusaders stormed the bastion of the infidel with the cry: "For Saint George and merry England!" This reproduction portrays George (in armor) with Saints Louis and Margaret. The latter is riding the devil who attacked her in the form of a dragon.

SAINT FRANCIS BORGIA

The significance of the skull reverts to the incident in the Saint's life when he was in charge of the funeral cortege of the Empress of Spain. Reaching Granada where the coffin was to be interred in the dank, gloomy crypt of the Cathedral, Francis' special duty was to uncover the face of the Empress and swear to her identity. When the coffin was opened the corroding corpse sent all present reeling back in horror save Francis who stood firm.

Pope Nicholas II gave Hildebrand the title of Archdeacon of Rome.

Two years later Nicholas II died. Now came the test. The party of the reform, under the leadership of Hildebrand, and in keeping with the new regulations for the election of a Pope, chose and consecrated Anselm, Bishop of Lucca, as the new Pope. Anselm, who was another product of the school of Cluny, took the name of Alexander II and proceeded at once (with the help of Hildebrand) to a vigorous enforcement of the Church's laws against simony and clerical incontinence. Yet neither the imperial party nor the Roman nobles would accept the new law on papal elections. At the assembly which the empress-mother convoked at Basel in southern Germany they elected Cadalus, the bishop of Parma, as a rival Pope under the name of Honorius II. For eleven years, till his death in 1072, this antipope carried on his schism (division from the Church) with ever dwindling success. Alexander II, on the contrary, had a notably successful reign of twelve years (1061-1073), though his frequent deposition of simoniacal bishops and abbots gradually built up a strong hostility against him throughout the empire.

At the funeral of Alexander II in Rome the people raised the cry: "Let Hildebrand be Pope! Let Hildebrand be Pope!" Most reluctantly this Archdeacon of Rome, who had long been known as the "Pope maker," acceded to their wishes. Unanimously elected, he was first ordained a priest, but he delayed his consecration as Bishop of Rome till he allowed the emperor, Henry IV (who was now ruling in his own name), time to approve of his election. Against the wishes of most of the German bishops, Henry surprisingly enough gave his approval. Hildebrand, who was then consecrated as Pope Gregory VII on June 29, 1073, saw to it that this was virtually the last time in history that an emperor had the privilege of approving a papal election.

The task that faced Gregory of restoring law and order into the Church was enormous. Even he, stouthearted though he was, quailed at first before it and earnestly begged the prayers of his friends. The eastern half of Christendom was in the process of being lost to the Church. In 1054 Michael Cerularius, the Archbishop of Constantinople, with the flimsiest of pretexts and solely out of ambition, broke with the Pope and made himself head of the Eastern (Orthodox) Church in a schism which has lasted (apart from a few short periods of union) to the present day. At the same time, the Moslem Turks were advancing across Asia Minor and gradually subjugating amost all the lands where the eastern Christians lived. To stop the advance of these infidel hordes, Pope Gregory VII urged the princes of Europe to organize a Crusade, but his plea fell on deaf ears.

In Europe itself the situation of the Church looked desperate. Many of the most important dioceses in Germany, France and northern Italy were ruled by bishops who, as appointees of the emperor, were primarily concerned with worldly matters and consequently sold the church offices in their jurisdiction (such as the charge of parishes) to the highest bidder.

At the beginning of his papal rule, Gregory tried by peaceful means to get the emperor to aid him in correcting these abuses, and the emperor at first gave empty promises of cooperation. Henry IV, whose private life was no worse than that of the average prince of his day, was not basically a wicked man. Despite his impetuous nature, he would have made a good ruler in other circumstances. The fact is that many of the German bishops ruled as temporal lords over large and rich regions of the empire. By having his own men in charge of these dioceses the emperor could not only ensure a goodly source of income for the imperial treasure; with their help he could also hold in check his unruly lay nobility. This had the strange result that, when he broke with the Pope, Henry found his best supporters among the German bishops, while many of the lay nobility favored Gregory.

Although Gregory knew that the ultimate source of the evil lay elsewhere, the Pope fired the opening shot in the battle by roundly condemning the incontinent clergy since this was a matter that directly concerned the spiritual welfare of the Church.

In March of 1074, less than a year after his consecration as Pope, Gregory issued a decree that any of the clergy who had obtained a church office by purchase, or who were living incontinently, should resign from their office, and that the laity should refuse the ministry of any of the clergy who disobeyed these injunctions. Most of the emperor's bishops, together with their priests, ignored this edict.

Gregory, therefore, struck at the root of the evil. In 1075 he issued a decree that, "if any emperor, duke, marquis, count, or any other secular power or person should presume to give the investiture of a bishopric or of any ecclesiastical dignity, let him know that we deprive him of the grace of Blessed Peter and debar him from entrance into a church." To put teeth into this decree, the Pope stated that vassals of any ruler thus excommunicated were freed from their oath of loyalty to such a liege lord of theirs.

Hatred for the Pope among his enemies now became intense. This can be seen in a certain dramatic incident that happened in Rome which, while it had no influence on the ultimate outcome of the struggle, gives a good example both of Gregory's courage and of the extremes to which his foes would go.

On Christmas Eve of 1075 a wild storm raged over Rome. The Pope, as usual, celebrated Midnight Mass at the Altar of the Manger in the Church of St. Mary Major, though few people were in attendance because of the storm. At the Communion of the Mass a gang of ruffians invaded the Church. They had been sent by Count Cenci, one of the Roman nobility who hated the reform measures of the Pope. These men with drawn swords seized Gregory, who suffered a head wound in the struggle, and carried him as a prisoner to Cenci's castle tower in the city. The wicked count demanded of the Pope, under pain of torture and death, the surrender of the papal Castle of Sant' Angelo. Gregory, of course, refused to be intimidated. In the morning, the populace of Rome who by now had heard of the Pope's arrest, stormed Cenci's fortress and freed the Pope. Bloodstained and weary, Gregory then celebrated his other two Christmas Masses for the people.

More serious events were happening in Germany. In retaliation for the threat of excommunication that the Pope had hurled at him, Emperor Henry called for an assembly of the bishops and lay nobility who favored his cause. They met at Worms, in the upper Rhine valley, on January 23, 1076, and had the audacity to declare solemnly that Gregory was deposed from the papacy. A few weeks later two meetings of the Lombard bishops in northern Italy reaffirmed the decision of the Worms assembly. A messenger brought the decree of deposition and Henry's insulting letter: "Henry, king, not by usurpation but by the will of God, to Hildebrand, false monk and no longer Pope. Having been condemned by the sentence of our bishops and by Our sentence, come down from the throne you have usurped!"

The nature of Gregory's reply caused no surprise. He formally excommunicated the emperor and all who had approved of his sacrilegious act. Moreover he released all of Henry's vassals from their oath of allegiance to him. Many of Henry's followers now deserted him. In a meeting held at Tribur (near Mainz on the Rhine) in October of 1076, they invited Gregory to come to a council to be held at Augsburg (in Bavaria) on Candlemas Day, February 2, 1077, and ordered Henry to appear at this council.

The emperor knew that his position had become perilous. The Augsburg council would quite likely depose him. Deciding that it would be safer for him to ask the Pope for forgiveness, even with feigned repentance, he took his wife and child and one servant and crossed the Alps through raging winter storms. Gregory, who had meanwhile started north on his way to Augsburg, was staying for a while with his faithful ally, Matilda, Countess of Tuscany, in her castle at Canossa in Emilia (on the northeastern flank of the Apennines). Henry went to Canossa and, as a penitent, begged the Pope for release from his sentence of excommunication. [In the nineteenth century Chancellor Bismarck of Germany made the phrase famous when, during the *Kultur-*

kamp (or fight) between the Catholic Church and the Kaiser's government, he said that *he* "would never go to Canossa."]

Gregory let the royal penitent wait, or in the modern expression, "cool off his heels," for three days. Yet the picture of the emperor standing alone out in the snow of Canossa's courtyard for three days comes solely from the imagination of a later writer who wished to heighten the dramatic scene. Gregory had plenty of reason to doubt the sincerity of Henry's repentance, but he was in a difficult position. If he refused pardon, he could be accused of not acting as a good priest and failing to settle the quarrel through peaceful negotiations. If he granted pardon too easily, he would endanger his whole reform movement. He spent the three days in prayer, begging God for knowledge and guidance. Finally, on January 28, 1077, Gregory agreed to accept the seemingly penitent Henry back into the communion of the Church, but only after the emperor had sworn that he would appear before a council and abide by its decision.

When Henry failed to meet the demands of the council, the party of reform in Germany deposed him and elected a new emperor in the person of Rudolph of Swabia. A full-fledged war now broke out between Henry (who had the support of most of the south German states) and Rudolph, who depended principally on the Saxon princes of north Germany, Henry's long-time enemies. Gregory tried to remain neutral and even to arrange for a compromise between the two claimants for the throne. However, when Henry again appointed new bishops, the Pope was again forced to excommunicate him. In an assembly held at Brixen (or Bressanone) just south of the Brenner Pass in the Alps, in June of 1080, Henry's feudatory bishops, supported by the Lombard nobles, declared Gregory deposed and elected an antipope, Guibert (Archbishop of Ravenna) who took the name of Clement III. There were now two Popes as well as two emperors.

The fortunes of war first smiled on Rudolph, and his fierce Saxon warriors put Henry's forces to rout in several encounters.

Rudolph, however, fell in the battle of Merseburg (Saxony) in October of 1080 and, lacking a leader, the party of reform in Germany was temporarily scattered.

Henry used the opportunity to invade Italy in 1081. Though supported by the Lombard princes, he met so much opposition that it was not until 1084, after a three-month's seige, that he gained possession of Rome and had himself crowned emperor in St. Peter's Basilica by his antipope, Clement III.

Meanwhile, Pope Gregory, who took refuge in his impregnable castle of Sant' Angelo, called on his southern ally, the Norman Robert Guiscard, for aid. When Guiscard finally arrived with a large army, Henry abandoned Rome and fled north, back to Germany. The Norman soldiers, however, pillaged and ravaged Rome to such an extent that the Romans were enraged at Gregory for having called in these wild allies. When the Normans, therefore, withdrew to their southern domain, the Romans forced the Pope to go with them. Full of sorrow and disappointment, he left his beloved city for the last time. After staying for a short time at the Abbey of Monte Cassino, he proceeded to the castle of Salerno by the sea. Here, abandoned by almost all his friends, broken in body but not in spirit, he gave back his valiant soul to God on May 25, 1085. Three days before his death he had absolved from excommunication all of his enemies except the emperor Henry IV and the antipope Clement III. On his death-bed, alluding to the words of Psalm 44,8, he said, "This is my only consolation: I have loved justice and hated iniquity; therefore I die in exile."

Though it had suffered a temporary setback in the death of its champion, the cause of the Church, for which this brave monk and Pope had ever fought, was soon to triumph. Henry IV was now so involved in family troubles and rebellions at home that he could not afford to antagonize the Church. The successors of Gregory VII continued his policy of reform with such vigor that by the end of the 11th century the evils of simony and lay investiture were almost completely wiped out. The night of the

"Dark Ages" was past; the dawn of the glorious 12th and 13th centuries was at hand. Now "Gothic" Europe reached the apex of medieval learning, art and architecture, all Christendom was harmoniously united in one Faith, with the Pope of Rome as the acknowledged overlord of every emperor, king and prince. The heroic struggles of "Hildebrand the monk" had not been in vain.

The body of St. Gregory VII still lies in the Cathedral of Salerno, the city where he died in exile. His namesake, Gregory XIII, beatified him in 1584, and Benedict XIII canonized him in 1728. The Roman Breviary says of him: "Mighty in word and work, Gregory labored with such zeal in reforming ecclesiastical discipline, in propagating the faith, in restoring the liberty of the Church, and in rooting out error and corruption, that it can be said that no Pontiff since the time of the Apostles bore greater labors and sufferings for the Church of God or fought more strenuously for its freedom."

Saint Hilary of Poitiers

Bishop and Doctor

c. 3 6 8

(January 14)

IN THAT REGION of western France formerly known as Aquitaine lies the ancient city of Poitiers, situated about fifty miles southwest of Tours and 125 miles northeast of Bordeaux. Originally the central fortress of the Gallic tribe called the Pictavi, this settlement of the Romans in Gaul was named "Pictavium," whence its modern French form. Although famous for several reasons, Poitiers is probably best known on account of its connection with Saint Hilary, "the Hammerer of the Arians" and "the Athanasius of the West," who was a native and a bishop of this city.

Hilary was born here in the early years of the fourth century. His parents were well-to-do pagans who provided their son with an excellent education in the Latin classics and — what was becoming a rarity in his day, especially in Gaul — even some training in Greek. The prime purpose of such an education was to teach a man to write and speak eloquently in public life. Hilary was later to put this training to good use in his defense of the orthodox teaching of the Church. Yet at the same time the excessive imitation of classical models, as was customary in the schools of that period, gives to his Latin at times an artificial, stilted tone and makes his long, involved paragraphs difficult to follow intelligently.

He was already married and had a daughter when he embraced the Christian faith and was baptized. His philosophical studies led him to see the foolishness of ancient paganism, while his reading of the Bible brought him to a knowledge and love of Christianity. About the year 350 or 353, probably not long after his baptism, he was chosen by his fellow Catholics at Poitiers to be bishop of this city. Throughout almost all of the y e a r s of his episcopacy Hilary was engaged in combatting Arianism, the great heresy of the age. To understand his work, therefore, it is necessary to know something of the nature and history of this heresy, the earliest serious threat to the unity of the Christian faith.

Named after Arius, a priest of Alexandria in Egypt, who was its first effective proponent rather than its originator, the heresy of Arianism was an attempt to rationalize the doctrine of the divinity of Jesus Christ by saying that as the Son of God He was not of the same divine nature as God the Father, and therefore not the *eternal* Son of God. In its extreme form this heresy was condemned by the Ecumenical Council of Nicaea in the year 325. However, since the emperor Constantine the Great was a personal friend of Eusebius, bishop of Nicomedia, who held a milder form of this heresy known as Semi-Arianism, Constantine himself often favored the Semi-Arians. Moreover, Constantius, one of Constantine's three sons (who was emperor of the East from 337 to 350, and of both the East and West from 350 to 361), was a Semi-Arian, or even an outright Arian.

On his accession to power in the West in 350, Emperor Constantius endeavored to impose his variety of Arianism even on the bishops of the Latin Church. At the councils of Arles (in southern France), Milan, and Rimini (in northern Italy), Constantius, through a combination of intrigue, deceit and threats, succeeded in getting the majority of western bishops present to condemn St. Athanasius, the great defender of orthodoxy, and to subscribe to a form of Semi-Arianism. The leading Arian in Gaul was Saturninus, bishop of Arles. At the council of Beziers, held in 356, where Saturninus tried to defend his position, there were but few bishops present who had the courage to speak up against him. But here he met a valiant defender of orthodoxy in Hilary of Poitiers, who condemned Arianism in all its shapes and forms in no uncertain terms.

When Saturninus reported this to the emperor, Constantius sent orders for Hilary's banishment. They were carried out by Julian, who was then imperial commander in Gaul but who later, as emperor, would be known to all Christians as "the Apostate." Hilary was then conducted to Phrygia, in Asia Minor, and here he remained in exile for three years. His time here, however, was well spent; for it was mostly during these years that he composed his masterpiece, the twelve "books" (really long chapters) of the work called "De Trinitate — On the Trinity." This consists of a complete exposure of all the varieties of heresies that had arisen against the true divinity of Christ, as well as a positive exposition of the orthodox teaching on the Blessed Trinity, the Catholic doctrine that, while there is only one God and therefore only one divine nature, this one God is three divine Persons, the Father and the Son and the Holy Spirit, each of whom is "consubstantial" with the others, that is, has the *same* divine nature as the others have. Although later theologians would refine the terms used to express this doctrine, to Hilary belongs the credit of being the first Latin writer to treat this matter in a professional way, and of being the first to acquaint the West with the theological speculations of the East, the orthodox as well as the heretical ones.

Nor was Hilary content with merely writing in defense of the Catholic faith during his years of exile. Though he was reproached with over-indulgence by some Catholic bishops, such as Lucifer of Cagliari, Hilary endeavored to win back to orthodoxy the more pious among the Semi-Arian bishops of the East. In this he was so successful at the council of Seleucia in southern Asia Minor, and again at a meeting held at Constantinople in the same year, 356, that the extreme Arians induced the emperor to send him back home to Gaul, "because he was a trouble-maker here."

Hilary's journey through Illyricum (modern Yugoslavia) and northern Italy on his way back home was a veritable triumphal procession. But it was especially the churches of Gaul that welcomed him back enthusiastically. Particularly overjoyed to have him back was his disciple, Martin, who was later to become bishop of Tours and a famous saint himself.

His monumental work on the Trinity was not the only literary product of his years in exile; Hilary also wrote other books at this time against the Arians. Now back again in his own diocese, he resumed his more peaceful writings on the Scriptures. Before he became involved in his controversies with the heretics, Hilary had written a commentary of the Gospel of St. Matthew. After his exile he published a commentary on the Psalms, in which he borrowed largely from Origen. He also composed a Latin translation of Origen's commentary on the Book of Job, which is no longer extant. Though the Biblical commentaries of Hilary may not have much exegetical value, since they abound in allegorical accomodations, they are replete with pious considerations and, as St. Jerome said of them, they are free from any trace of false doctrine.

In his last years of peace, following his return from exile, Hilary proved himself a capable administrator of his diocese, removing scandals and restoring piety together with purity of faith. The council of the bishops of Gaul, which he convoked at Paris in 361, condemned Saturninus, the Arian bishop of Arles, and removed him from his see, thereby stamping out the last traces of Arianism in Gaul. The death of Emperor Constantius in the same year and the accession of Julian the Apostate, who was more interested in trying to resurrect ancient paganism than in defending any heretic sect, gave the deathblow to Arianism, which found its chief support thereafter only in the barbarian Goths, who had invaded the empire.

Hilary of Poitiers was well named, for the Latin word *hilarius*, like the Greek word *hilaris* from which it is derived, m e a n s "cheerful, gay," without connoting the idea of boisterous merriment now signified by its English derivative, "hilarious." According to all the reports of his contemporaries, he was of kind, gentle and lovable disposition. It was merely the force of circumstances that drove into endless controversies this otherwise essentially peace-loving man.

Though St. Augustine of Hippo had already called Hilary of Poitiers "the illustrious doctor (that is, teacher) of the churches," it was not till 1852 that Pope Pius IX formally declared him a Doctor of the Church.

SELECTIONS FROM SAINT HILARY'S WORK

On the Trinity

Many people find the Lord's words obscure when He says: 'I in the Father and the Father in Me,' and there is nothing blameworthy in this, for man's natural power of reasoning does not grasp the meaning of this statement. It does not seem possible that the very thing which is in another is at the same time outside of it, and, since those things which we are discussing cannot exist apart from themselves, and, if they are to preserve the number and position in which they are, it seems that they cannot mutually contain each other, so that he who contains something else within himself and remains in this position and always remains outside of it can likewise be always present within him whom he contains within himself.

Human knowledge will certainly never grasp these truths and a comparison drawn from human things does not afford any similarity to divine things, but what man cannot conceive is possible to God. In thus expressing myself on this subject I have not meant that, because God has spoken these words, His authority alone suffices to apprehend them. We should examine and seek to realize the significance of this declaration: 'I in the Father and the Father *in* Me,' provided we shall grasp it such as it really is, in order that what is regarded as incompatible with the nature of things will be obtained by the wisdom of the divine truth.

And that we may penetrate more easily into the knowledge of this most difficult question we must first understand the Father and the Son according to the teaching of the divine Scriptures, in order that, when we have learned to know them and have become familiar with them, our words may become clearer. As we explained in the preceding Book, the eternity of God transcends places, times, appearances, and whatever can be conceived by the human mind, He is outside of all things and within all things; He comprises all things and is comprised by none; He does not change either by increase or decrease, but is invisible, incomprehensible, complete, perfect, and eternal; He does not know anything from elsewhere, but He Himself is sufficient unto Himself to remain what He is.

This unbegotten One, therefore, brought forth the Son from Himself before all time, not from any pre-existing matter, because all things are through the Son; nor from nothing, because the Son is from Him; nor as an ordinary birth, because there is nothing changeable or empty in God; nor as a part that is divided, cut off, or extended, because God is incapable of suffering and incorporeal and these things are characteristic of suffering and the flesh, and according to the Apostle: 'In Christ dwells all the fullness of the Godhead bodily.'

But in an inconceivable and ineffable manner, before all time and ages, He gave birth to the only-begotten God from that which in Him was unbegotten, and through His charity and power He bestowed upon His birth everything that God is, and thus from the unbegotten, perfect, and eternal Father there is the only-begotten, perfect, and eternal Son. But that which belongs to Him because of the body that He assumed results from the eagerness of His good will for our salvation. For, since He as one born from God is invisible, incorporeal, and inconceivable, He has taken upon Himself as much matter and abasement as we possessed the power to understand, perceive, and comprehend, adapting Himself to our weakness rather than abandoning those things which belonged to His own nature.

He is, therefore, the perfect Son of the perfect Father, the only-begotten offspring of the unbegotten God, who has received everything from Him who possesses everything. He is God from God, Spirit from Spirit, Light from Light, and He proclaims with assurance: 'I in the Father and the Father in Me.' As the Father is Spirit, so the Son also is Spirit; as the Father is God, so the Son also is God; as the Father is Light so the Son also is Light. From those things, therefore, which are in the Father are also those things which are in the Son, that is, from the whole Father the whole Son is born; He is not from anywhere else, because nothing was before the Son; He is not from nothingness, because the Son is from God; He is not a God in part only, because the fullness of the Godhead is in the Son, not in some things because He is in all things, but as He willed who could, as He knows who begot Him.

Whatever is in the Father is also in the Son; whatever is in the unbegotten is also in the only-begotten, one from the other and both are one substance, not one person, but one is in the other because there is nothing different in either of them. The Father is in the Son because the Son is from Him; the Son in the Father because He is not a Son from anywhere else; the only-begotten is in the unbegotten because the only-begotten is from the unbegotten. Thus, they are mutually in each other, because as all things are perfect in the Father, so all things are perfect in the Son. This is the unity in the Father and the Son, this is the power, this the charity, this the hope, this the faith, this the truth, the way, and the life, not to spread false reports about God concerning His attributes, nor to disparage the Son because of the mystery and power of His birth, not to place anything on an equality with the unbegotten Father, nor to separate the only-begotten from Him in time or power, but to acknowledge Him as the Son of God because He is from God. . . .

I realize that I have undertaken to write these treatises, at a most trying and unfavorable moment, against the idiotic heresy of the blasphemers who affirm that the Son of God is a creature. Throughout almost the entire Roman Empire, many churches have already become infected with the disease of this fatal teaching, and by long familiarity with its doctrine and its deceptive name of the true worship of God have become attached to this maliciously and unlawfully appropriated belief, as if it belonged to this pious faith. I know that it is difficult to bring about an improvement in the will when it has become rooted in the error, because many have approved of it and the weight of public opinion is in its favor. An error among a large number of people is serious and dangerous, and many of them fall away. Even if they become aware of their predicament, they presume upon their prestige to prevent them from undergoing the shame of rising from their error, and because of their numbers they are impudent enough to wish that their false doctrine be regarded as wisdom, and to assert that an error, which they share in common with others, is the knowledge of the truth, since they assume that a false doctrine is less likely to be found among so many.

In addition to the obligation of my vocation and office, whereby as a bishop of the Church I must indeed devote myself to the ministry of preaching the Gospel, I was the more inclined to assume the burden of writing, the more threatening was the danger to so many who were being held by this false belief. I anticipated a greater measure of happiness from the salvation of many, if, after they had acquired the knowledge of the perfect faith in God, they would renounce the blasphemous teachings of human folly, would repudiate the heretics and return to God, would soar aloft in freedom and security from the deadly food by which birds are often enticed into a trap, would follow Christ as their leader, the Prophets as messengers, the Apostles as guides, and the complete and perfect salvation in the profession of the Father and the Son, and, when they recalled the words of the Lord: 'He who does not honor the Son, does not honor the Father who sent him,' would seek to give glory to the Father by glorifying the Son. . . .

O holy Father, omnipotent God, I shall indeed acknowledge You as the eternal God and also as the eternal Father so long as I shall enjoy the life that You have granted to me. Nor shall I ever express such folly and impiety, so that I, as the judge of Your omnipotence and mysteries, shall exalt this feeble understanding of my weakness above the reverential belief in Your

infinity and the faith in eternity that You have made known to
me, so that I should teach that You were at any time without
Your Wisdom, Power, and Word, the only-begotten God, my
Lord Jesus Christ. The weak and imperfect words of our nature
do not hinder my understanding of You so that my poverty of
speech chokes the faith into silence. Although the word, the wisdom, and the power within us proceed from our own inner activity and are our work, with You, on the contrary, there is the
complete generation of the perfect God, who is Your Word, Wisdom, and Power, so that He is always inseparable from You
whose birth from You is revealed through these names of Your
eternal attributes. He has been born in such a manner that He
points out no one else but You as His author; at the same time
He does not cast aside the faith in infinity, because we are informed that He was born before the eternal ages.

You have bestowed many things of this kind in human affairs,
and although I do not know the cause, the effect is apparent. A
devout faith is found where there is also a natural ignorance.
When, through my own power of vision, I raised these weak eyes
to Your heavens I believed in nothing else but Your heavens.
While I saw there these starry circles, the yearly revolutions, the
seven stars, and the morning star, to which You have assigned
the various functions of their office, I recognized You as God in
these things even though I do not comprehend them. But when
I beheld the marvelous swellings of Your sea, although I am not
aware of the source of the waters or even of the movement of
this orderly ebb and flow. I hold fast to the faith in some reasonable explanation even if I do not perceive it, and I also recognize
You in these things of which I am ignorant. However, when I
now directed my thoughts to the earth, which, through the
power of its secret energies, causes the decay of all the seeds that
it has received, and that which has decayed is restored to life,
that which has been restored to life multiples, and that which
has multiplied grows strong, I found nothing in these things
which I can grasp with my own powers of reason, but my ignorance helps me to understand You, and, while I know nothing of
the nature that is at my service, I recognize You only through
the use of that which is to my own advantage. Since I do not

SAINT FIDELIS

To Saint Fidelis of Sigmaringen belongs the honor of being the first
martyr to die for Christ under that branch of the government of the
Church known as the *Sacred Congregation for the Propagation of the
Faith*. His martyrdom took place in 1622 following his great success in re-
claiming to the true Church the Protestants of Swiss Graubuenden.

SAINT EUGENE I

This seventh-century Pope was one of the most active in the defense of the orthodox faith against the heresy of Monothelitism (the doctrine that declared that while Jesus had two distinct natures, one human and one divine; He had but one will, a divine will). Saint Eugene was born and raised in Rome, and from his earliest years was in the service of the Roman Church. He is portrayed in a mosaic, the 7th century artform.

even know myself, I am so impressed that I admire You all the more because I am ignorant of myself. Without comprehending it, I perceive either the movement, or the reason, or the life of my mind that passes judgment, and, which I perceive, I am indebted to You for what I perceive, since You grant me something beyond the beginning of the nature, namely, the understanding of the nature that fills me with delight. And since I know You, although ignorant of what pertains to myself, knowing You, I worship You. And I shall not lessen my belief in Your omnipotence because I do not apprehend things pertaining to Yourself, as if my own power of reasoning could grasp the origin of Your Only-begotten, make myself the master of this subject, and there would then be something in me which would enable me to proceed further than my Creator and my God.

His birth is before the eternal ages. If there is anything which precedes eternity, it will certainly be something that transcends the idea of eternity. It is Your thing, it is Your Only-begotten, not a portion, not an extension, not some empty name to fit the theory that You have made it, but it is Your Son, the Son who is the true God from You, God the Father, and born from You in the unity of nature. We are to confess Him as being after You as well as with You, because You are the eternal Author of the eternal origin. While He is from You He is second to You, but while He is Yours He is not to be separated from You, because we must not assert that You have ever been without Your Son, in order that no one may accuse You of being imperfect without the generation, or of being useless after the generation. Thus, the birth merely serves the purpose of making You known to us as the eternal Father of the only-begotten Son who was born from You before the eternal ages.

As for me, it is certainly not enough to deny by means of my faith and voice that my Lord and God, your only-begotten Jesus Christ, is a creature. I will not even permit this name to be associated with your Holy Spirit, who has proceeded from You and has been sent through Him, since I know that You alone are unborn and the Only-begotten was born from you, nor will I ever say that He was created. I fear that the stigma attached to this name, which I share with the others whom You have en-

dowed with life, may also be insiduously imputed to You Yourself. According to the Apostle, Your Holy Spirit searches and
knows Your profound things, and my intercessor with You talked to You of subjects that I cannot describe. How can I express
without at the same time defaming the power of His nature,
which is from you through your Only-begotten, by the name
'creation'? Nothing except what is Your own penetrates You, nor
can the intervention of a power, extraneous and alien to Your
own, measure the depths of Your infinite majesty. Whatever enters into You is Yours, and nothing is foreign to You that is
present within You as a power that searches.

I cannot describe Him whose words to me are beyond my
power of description. Just as from the fact that Your Only-begotten was born from You all ambiguity in language and difficulty in understanding are at an end and only one thing remains,
that He was born, so, too, in my consciousness I hold fast to the
fact that your Holy Spirit is from You, although I do not grasp
it with my understanding. I am dull in Your spiritual things, as
your Only-begotten declares: 'Do not wonder that I said to thee,
"The wind blows where it will, and thou hearest its sound but
dost not know where it comes from or where it goes. So is everyone who is born of the Spirit." ' I possess the faith of my
regeneration without any understanding on my part. There are no
boundaries for the Spirit who speaks when He wills, and where
He wills. Shall I place His nature among those of creatures, and
shall I, who do not know the reason for His coming and going,
although aware of His presence, set limits for the beginning of
His origin?

Your St. John says that all things were indeed made through
the Son, who was God the Word in beginning with You, O God.
St. Paul enumerates all the things that were created in Him in
heaven and on earth, both the visible and the invisible. After
mentioning that all things had been created in Christ and through
Christ, he believed that he had designated the Holy Spirit in a
satisfactory manner when he referred to Him as Your Spirit. Such
will be my thoughts about these questions, in harmony with
these men whom You have especially chosen, so that just as I,
following in their footsteps, shall say nothing else about Your

Only-begotten that is above comprehension of my understanding save only that He was born, so, too, I shall assert nothing else about the Holy Spirit that is above the judgment of the human mind except that He is Your Spirit. And I pledge myself not to a futile contest of words, but to the persevering profession of an unquestioning faith.

Keep this piety of my faith undefiled, I beseech You, and let this be the utterance of my convictions even to the last breath of my spirit: that I may always hold fast to that which I professed in the creed of my regeneration when I was baptized in the Father, Son, and the Holy Spirit, together with You, and I may gain the favor of Your Son together with You, and that I may gain the favor of Your Holy Spirit who is from You through the Only-begotten. He is a suitable witness for my faith who says: 'Father, all things that are mine are thine, and thine are mine,' my Lord Jesus Christ, who always abides as God in You, from You, and with You, who is blessed forever and ever. Amen.

Saint Homobonus

Confessor

1 1 9 7

(November 13)

HE NAME "HOMOBONUS" would seem at first sight to be an epithet given later in life to St. Homobonus, for with its meaning of "good (Latin *bonus*) man (Latin *homo*)," it fits his character extremely well. Actually, however, this name, which was occasionally used before his time, was given to Homobonus when he was baptized. During the Middle Ages he was quite a popular saint throughout Europe. However, outside of Italy, instead of calling him by his Latin name, people knew him by a form of this same word as translated into their own local languages. Thus in England his name was given in baptism in the form of "Goodman," and in Germany in the form of "Guthman" —words which still occur as family names.

As is the case with many other saints who lived a long time ago, relatively few details are known about Homobonus. The early accounts of his life, the first of which was written by his own bishop (Sicardus), consist mostly of such generalities about his exemplary virtues as would fit almost any "good man." Still, there can be no doubt about the genuine reputation for true holiness which he enjoyed in his native city of Cremona. The fame of his virtues and miracles was so great that Bishop Sicardus was able to have him canonized by Pope Innocent III two years after his death.

In the 12th century the city of Cremona in Lombardy (northern Italy) was a thriving center of trade. It was in this city that Homobonus was born, lived and died, and to this day Cremona honors him as its prinicpal patron saint.

Homobonus' father was a merchant, and he trained his son to carry on his business. However, he first taught him the much more important matter of being a good Christian. Young Homobonus learned well these basic lessons which his father gave him: to love and serve God with his whole heart, to be devoted to prayer, holy Mass and the sacraments, to be unflinchingly honest in every circumstance of life and, above all, to be as generous as possible in charity to the poor. Only after learning these lessons did he acquire the knowledge necessary to continue his father's trade. Yet this, too, he mastered so well that he could have been one of the richest men in Cremona if he wished to accumulate wealth. He considered his work as God's will in this regard, something that he should do for love of God. He was very careful in every business detail, seeing to it that neither slipshod methods nor a shadow of dishonesty ever entered into his dealings with others. Homobonus would have sacrificed everything rather than stoop to a lie or any form of deceit. Far from hurting his business, this sterling honesty served to increase his trade all the more. No doubt God's special blessing played an important part in this. While the old saying, "Honesty is the best policy," may not always work out well from a worldly viewpoint, it is always true from a spiritual point of view.

Diligent as he was in temporal affairs, Homobonus never allowed them to interfere with his spiritual life. Not only did he go to holy Mass every morning; he made it a practice to attend the singing of the Divine Office every evening.

Even more than honesty and piety, the outstanding characteristic of Homobonus was his unbounded charity to the poor. He considered it merely his duty to give a tenth of his income to the needy. Moreover, he went far beyond that in his generosity in almsgiving, and attended personally to the wants of his less fortunate fellow men. He did not stop, however, with helping them in their temporal needs; he talked with t h e m, consoled them, urged them to repentance, and exhorted them to begin new lives in the service of God. In the prayer to St. Homobonus, to which the Church has attached an Indulgence, he is given the title of the "Father of the Poor."

The good woman who was Homobonus' wife did not always see eye to eye with her husband in this matter of his seemingly excessive almsgiving. She argued that he should provide for her future in case he were suddenly taken from her in death. Gently he answered her: "Do you think, dear wife, that our temporal affairs will suffer harm if we are generous and compassionate toward the poor? The word of God assures us that this will not happen, for Christ says 'Give, and it will be given to you.' "

Eventually Homobonus' wife received proof from God of the truth of her husband's words. Once, when a famine had struck Cremona and its countryside, crowds of poor people came to the house of Homobonus and begged for food. He could not bear to send them away empty, and so he gave them all the bread that was in the house. His wife, who happened to be out of the house at the time, began on her return home to set the table for dinner. She went to the cupboard and found it as full of bread as usual. Noticing that this was of better quality and more delicious than their regular bread, she called the maid. The latter was amazed and told her mistress that her master had just given away all the bread that was in the house and that no one had brought in any new bread. Then the good woman knew that what her husband had said was true: God is never outdone in generosity.

This holy merchant of Cremona knew that true sanctity consists in union with God and that this union is sustained and increased by devout prayer. Therefore, since his many occupations kept him busy during the day, he gave a good part of his time at night to prayer. He had the custom of rising shortly before midnight and assisting at the matins and lauds that were sung in the Church of St. Giles during the first nocturnal hours of the day. Sometimes he would remain at prayer in church till the high Mass at dawn. In any event, even when he went back home for a few hours of sleep after the midnight office, he was always in church for the morning Mass.

On November 13, 1197, Homobonus went to church as usual. At the *Gloria* of the Mass he stretched out his arms and bent his head to the ground. When the Gospel was sung, the people noticed that he did not stand up. On going to him to see why he remained in this strange position, they found him dead.

Tailors and cloth-workers have always regarded Homobonus as one of their special patrons, but he can well serve as a model for all kinds of tradesmen. The example of his life is of real value, especially in our modern world where big business is king and where ethics and morals, not to speak of Christianity, are too often sacrificed in the mad endeavor to become rich as quickly as possible.

Homobonus teaches us where the true riches lie: in piety, justice, and charity. These are the best investments whereby we lay up for ourselves treasures in heaven.

Saint Hugh of Cluny

Abbot

1 1 0 9

(April 29)

ABOUT FIFTEEN MILES northwest of the city of Macon in the department of Saone-et-Loire of east central France lies the little town of Cluny. Although there are enough remains of Romanesque and Gothic buildings in this town to remind the visitor of its glorious past, there is but little left of the great abbey and its church which once made this one of the most famous places in Christendom. In 910, when the Benedictine abbey of Cluny was founded by William the Pious of Aquitaine, with Saint Berno as its first abbot, every Benedictine abbey was autonomous, that is, it elected its own abbot, who was subject to no other abbot. But even in the lifetime of Saint Berno the four or five abbeys which were founded as offshoots of Cluny were not set up as independent abbeys, but as daughter monasteries dependent on Cluny, with their abbots appointed by the Cluny abbot. There thus arose what was known as the Benedictine Congregation of Cluny. Under the following abbots of Cluny not only were many more monasteries of this nature established, but many older abbeys, which had formerly been independent, sought and were granted affiliation and incorporation into this Congregation of Cluniac abbeys. They thereby received two principal benefits: first, improved monastic life, for from Cluny came a revised form of Benedictine life called the "Cluniac Reform", and second, the privilege, guaranteed by the Holy See, that these abbeys would not be subject to secular feudal lords and therefore would be free from the evil practice of having their abbots "invested" in office by secular princes.

During the first two and a half centuries of its existence (910-1157) the abbey of Cluny was fortunate in having a succession of seven extremely capable abbots: Odo, Aymard, Majolus, Odilo, Hugh, and Peter the Venerable. Four of these are venerated by the Church as canonized saints: Odo, Majolus, Odilo, and Hugh. The greatest of all the abbots of Cluny was St. Hugh, who truly merited the title of "St. Hugh the Great."

Some forty miles southwest of Cluny lay the feudal castle of Semur, in the diocese of Autun. Here Saint Hugh was born in the year 1024. His father, Count Dalmatius of Semur and Aremberge was descended from one of the noblest families in Burgundy (eastern France), and he expected his oldest son Hugh to marry and carry on the illustrious family name. But Dalmatius' wife, in keeping with the advice of her spiritual director, who had received a vision in this matter, wished her oldest son to dedicate his life to God's service. From his earliest years Hugh showed such piety and love of things religious that his father soon realized that there was no use in trying to force him to follow the knightly calling. Hugh was therefore placed in the care of his granduncle, after whom he was named, Hugh, Bishop of Auxerre, who had him educated in the monastery school of the Priory of Saint Marcellus.

In 1033, when Hugh was only fourteen years old, he entered the novitiate of the abbey of Cluny, and because of his extraordinary religious fervor he was permitted to make his vows one year later, though a longer period of trial was customary at that time in this monastery. By a special privilege which the Cluny abbey then enjoyed, he was ordained a deacon at the age of eighteen, and a priest at the age of twenty—a remarkably early age for these Holy Orders. Even as a young monk, Hugh showed such ability in administration as well as zeal in religious observance that he was soon appointed to the office of Grand Prior. In this position he was in charge of the domestic affairs in both temporal and spiritual matters and took the abbot's place when the latter was absent from the monastery. When St. Odilo died on January 1, 1049, Hugh, though only twenty-five years old, was unanimously elected to succeed him as abbot of Cluny and was solemnly installed by Archbishop Hugh of Besancon on February 22, 1049.

During his long rule of sixty years as abbot of Cluny, Hugh greatly increased the power and influence of his abbey, so that under his second successor, Peter the Venerable (abbot from 1122 to 1156), it reached the zenith of its power, with 314 monasteries in all parts of Europe subject to Cluny. In 1089 Saint Hugh began the construction of the great abbey church, which was not completed until 1131, twenty-two years after his death. This magnificent basilica, the finest example of Romanesque architecture in France, was 555 feet long, the largest ecclesiastical structure in the world till the erection of the new basilica of St. Peter's at Rome in the sixteenth century. This immense church, which together with the surrounding monastic buildings covered twenty-five acres, was almost completely destroyed in the French Revolution at the end of the eighteenth century.

Saint Hugh won great renown for his unswerving loyalty to the Holy See, his wise discretion in dealing with secular princes as well as in the government of his numerous monasteries, his deep spirit of prayer, his love of the holy liturgy, his faithful observance of monastic discipline, his austerity with himself, and his kindness towards others. Like the other great abbots of Cluny he steadfastly refused to accept the many offers of the bishopric and the cardinal's hat which the various popes made to him. With a keen interest in science, he taught in the monastic school even after he became abbot and he wrote several books, most of which are unfortunately no longer preserved. Widely known for his charity, he built a hospital for lepers, where he loved to labor himself at the most menial tasks. He granted personal and civic freedom to the bondsmen and serfs who were subject to his abbey, and his fostering of guilds for artisans and tradesmen laid the basis for the new towns of Europe which grew into the great cities of today, so that his influence on the social and economic life of the modern world was quite considerable.

For the liturgical services at Cluny Hugh worked to achieve the greatest possible splendor and solemnity which he rightly considered proper to these sacred functions. Some of his ritual ordinances, such as the singing of the hymn, *Veni Creator Spiritus*, at Tierce on Pentecost, were later extended to the whole Latin Church. In Spain he induced King Alphonsus VI of Castile to replace the Mozarabic (Gothic) Rite by the Roman Rite throughout his realm. His zeal likewise extended to the cloistered nuns, especially those in the convent at Marcigny, where his sister was abbess and where his mother later took the veil.

But the most important work of Saint Hugh was undoubtedly his cooperation with his good friend, the great Hildebrand, later Pope Saint Gregory VII, in the latter's struggle against "lay investiture" and the evils which followed from this practice by which secular princes appointed even to the highest offices of the church unworthy men, who often obtained their appointment by "simoniacal" means, that is, by bribery. Hildebrand, though not a monk of Cluny, belonged in early life to a Benedictine abbey in Rome which had accepted the Cluniac Reform. Hence, in Hugh of Cluny he found a staunch ally in carrying out the urgently needed reform measures against lay investiture. Cluny and its widespread network of affiliated monasteries served as a powerful weapon in the hands of the popes, since William the Pious of Aquitaine, when he founded the abbey of Cluny in 910, had made it directly subject to the Holy See and free from the feudal jurisdiction of all secular princes.

In the sixty years of his rule at Cluny Saint Hugh was closely connected with the work of no less than nine popes. In 1049, his first year as abbot, Hugh, as requested by the newly elected pope, Leo IX (1049-1054), appeared at the Council of Reims and spoke so strongly against the evils in the Church that even the boldest of the simoniacal bishops were afraid to stand up against him. Pope Victor II (1054-1057), who succeeded Leo IX, had a like high regard for the young abbot of Cluny, and in the year 1055 he confirmed all the privileges of this monastery. When Hildebrand came to France as Victor's legate in 1054, he first went to Cluny, to consult with Hugh and solicit his aid for the Council of Tours. Victor's successor, Stephen X (or IX, as sometimes reckoned) (1057-1058), insisted that Hugh should accompany him on his journeys, and when he died at Florence on March 29, 1058, it was in the arms of the saintly abbot of Cluny that he breathed his last. After the brief interregnum of the antipope, Benedict X (1058-1059), Pope Nicholas II (1059-1061) also made Hugh his companion and had him play an active part in the important Council of Rome at Eastertime of 1059, which introduced the present regulation whereby popes are no longer chosen at the dictation of secular princes or by the acclamation of the Roman people, but solely by the votes of the college of cardinals. After this council Pope Nicholas II sent Hugh to France with Cardinal Stephan, a former monk of the monastery of Monte Casino, where they enforced the decrees of Rome against the simoniacal bishops. In this matter Hugh addressed the synods held in 1060 at Avignon and Vienne, and in the same year he presided over the Synod of Toulouse. Back again in Rome for the Roman Council of 1063, Hugh vigorously defended the privileges of Cluny, which were under severe attack in France. As a result of this, Pope Alexander II (1061-1073) sent Saint Peter Damian, the Cardinal-Bishop of Ostia, as his special legate to France, where, at the Council of Chalon, Damian gave his decision in favor of Cluny. When Hildebrand, who had really been the power behind the throne during all these preceding pontificates, succeeded Alexander II as pope under the name of Gregory VII (1075-1085), he enjoyed the fullest cooperation of Saint Hugh in carrying out his reform measures in France. Hugh, however, despite Gregory's urgent entreaties, found it impossible to go to Italy till the lamentable conflict between Gregory and the emperor, Henry IV, had come to a climax in the winter of 1067-1077. He now hastened to Canossa, where he was able to bring about a reconciliation, short-lived though it unfortunately was, between the emperor and the pope. It was also at Gregory's request that Hugh went to Spain and there introduced certain necessary reforms in several monasteries. Needless to say, the intimate cooperation between the abbot of Cluny and the Holy See continued undiminished during the pontificates of Gregory's successors, Victor III (1087), who had been abbot of the affiliated monastery of Monte Cassino, as well as Urban II (1088-1099) and Paschal II (1099-1118), both of whom had been former monks of the Cluny abbey. Pope Urban II expressed his heartfelt thanks to Hugh for composing and promulgating the decrees of the Council of Clemont in 1095, which inaugurated the First Crusade. Surrounded by cardinals and bishops, this same pope consecrated the high altar of the new abbey church at Cluny on October 25, 1095. Pope Paschal II also visited Cluny in 1107 and bestowed on its abbey several new privileges.

Not only popes and bishops, but emperors and kings as well loved Hugh as a friend, respected him for his wisdom, and revered him for his holiness. This was partly due to the fact that Hugh concerned himself primarily with spiritual matters and kept aloof from merely secular politics. Thus, he did not take sides either with the Guelphs, the anti-imperialist party in Italy, or with the Ghibellines, the pro-imperialists in that country. Consequently he was on good terms with the German emperors. Emperor Henry III (1017-1056) used to call him his "father" and he invited him to be the godfather of his son, Henry IV (1050-1106). Hugh made good use of this spiritual relationship of his with Henry IV when he induced him to be reconciled with Pope Gregory VII. So also the other rulers of Europe had great respect for the holy abbot of Cluny. Thus, in 1066, shortly before the Battle of Hastings, William of Normandy, "the Conqueror" of England, sent rich gifts to Cluny and asked to be received as a lay oblate.

After serving Christ and His Church so valiantly for eighty-five years, sixty of them as abbot of Cluny, Saint Hugh felt that death was near. Having received the Last Sacraments, he called for his spiritual sons and gave to each of them a farewell kiss of peace. Then he asked to be taken to the Chapel of Our Lady, where, lying in sackcloth and ashes before her altar, he died on the evening of Easter Monday, April 28, 1109.

Ten years after the death of Saint Hugh, Pope Gelasius II (1118-1119) made a pilgrimage to his tomb at Cluny, and there he himself died on January 29, 1119. The conclave to elect a new pope was consequently held at Cluny. Callistus II (1119-1124), who was elected at this conclave on February 2, 1119, began at once the process of Hugh's canonization, and on January 6, 1120 he solemnly declared him a saint of the Church, with the 29th of April set as his feastday.

Saint James the Greater
Apostle

4 4

(July 25)

AT THE TIME of Christ many Jews were named "Jacob" after the forefather of the Israelites, Jacob, the father of the twelve sons who became ancestors of the twelve tribes of Israel. The Greek form of this name which was borne by two of the twelve apostles is *Iakobos*. In the Middle Ages, when the shrine of St. James the Greater at Campostela (in northwestern Spain) was one of the greatest places of pilgrimage in all Christendom, Christian families were very fond of giving this name to their sons. Consequently, this Apostle's name occurred in various forms according to the different languages of Europe. Directly descended from the full form of "Jacobo" are the forms "Jacopo" and "Jacomo" of older Italian, and "Giacomo" of modern Italian. From this form in which the labial "b" shifted to the labial "m," we have the Spanish "Jaime" (pronounced "Haime"), the Portuguese "Jayme" (pronounced "Zhaime"), and, through the Norman-French, the English "James," with a further variant in the Irish "Shamus" or "Shemus." From the contracted form of "Jaco" are derived the older Spanish "Iago," which, when prefixed with "santo," the word for "saint," became "Santiago," and this, in turn, being wrongly analyzed as "San Tiago," produced the variants "Diago" and Diego." Finally, from the French contracted form of "Jacques," we get our English word "Jack," which surprisingly is now used as a nickname, not for "James," but for "John."

723

In Mark 15, 40, one of the two apostles who are called James is given (in Greek) the distinguishing epithet, *ho mikros,* which means "the small one" and most likely refers to his size, although it is poorly translated as "the Less" or "the Lesser," in English Bibles. As a consequence, the other apostle James, with whom we are here concerned, is commonly called, by way of contrast, "James the Greater," a term never found in the New Testament. In any case, this distinction should not be understood as if it referred to the relative importance of this apostle. Both of these apostles play important roles in the New Testament, and it would be unfair to make a distinction between them in this regard.

St. James the Greater was the brother of the apostle St. John. Several times in the Gospels these two are called "the sons of Zebedee"; as, for instance, in the list of the twelve apostles where their names occur immediately after the first two, Peter and Andrew (Matt. 10,3.) Like their father Zebedee, James and John made their living as fishermen in the Sea of Galilee, but when Jesus called them to be His intimate companions, "they left their nets and their father, and followed Him" (Matt. 4,22; see also Mark 1,20). Their partners in the fishing business were another pair of brothers, Simon Peter and Andrew, who also became apostles (Luke 5, 10). There is good reason to think that Zebedee's wife, the mother of James and John, was called Salome. If we compare the lists of women who witnessed our Lord's death on Calvary as given in the different Gospels, "the mother of the sons of Zebedee" (Matt. 27,56) seems to be the same woman as "Salome" in Mark 15, 40.

Christ gave Zebedee's sons, James and John, the nickname of "Boanerges," which is interpreted in Mark 3,17 to mean "sons of thunder." No doubt this epithet was given them because of their tempestuous nature. Their zeal for Christ had at first a little too much of the zealot's fire in it. They were thunderheads, ready to hurl bolts of lightning to their Master's enemies. Thus when the inhabitants of a certain Samaritan town would not let Jesus enter it because "His face was set for Jerusalem," James

SAINT JAMES THE GREATER   El Greco

During our Lord's public ministry, Saint James the Greater was one of
the three apostles who formed a special group within the twelve; the other
two were Saints Peter and John. These three were the only ones permitted
to be with Jesus when he raised Jairus' daughter. They, alone, were present
at the Transfiguration, and close to Jesus in the Agony in Gethsemeni.

SAINT JAMES THE LESS   Peter Rubens

The Gospels seldom speak of Saint James the Less. It is only from Saint Paul that we learn of a special apparition of the risen Savior to Saint James. We do not know on what occasion this took place, but this signalling out of James by Jesus shows what an important role the Saint was to play in the early Church—that of bishop of the Jerusalem Church.

and John on seeing this said, "Lord, wilt Thou that we bid fire come down from heaven and consume them?" Jesus had to "rebuke" them for this: "You know not of what manner of spirit you are; for the Son of Man did not come to destroy men's lives, but to save them." (See Luke 9,51-56).

During our Lord's public ministry, James the Greater was one of the three apostles who formed a special inner group in the twelve; the other two were Peter and John. These three apostles were the only ones permitted to be with Christ when He raised the little daughter of Jarius from the dead (Mark 5,37; Luke 8,51) They alone were present on the high mountain at the Transfiguration of Jesus (Matt. 17,1; Mark 9,1; Luke 9,28), and Christ chose no one but these three to be near Him when He prayed in agony at Gethsemane (Matt. 26,37; Mark 14,33).

Zebedee's wife could not help noticing that Jesus was treating her two sons as His special favorites. She therefore thought that the Master should publicly appoint these two as His first and second assistants, "to sit at His right hand and at His left hand when He would reign as King." He realized, however, that this good woman had no true conception of the nature of His Kingdom which was to be a spiritual kingdom, entered into by suffering. Therefore He asked James and John: "Do you know what you are asking for? Can you drink the cup of which I am about to drink?" Probably with no idea that by "His cup" He meant the lot of suffering and ignominious death which His heavenly Father had destined for Him, James and John answered quite confidently: "We can." Jesus then said to them, "Of My cup you shall indeed drink. But as for sitting at My right hand and at My left, that is not mine to give you; it belongs to those for whom it has been prepared by My Father." (See Matt. 20, 20-23; Mark 10,35-40).

As our Lord had foretold, James the Greater did in truth "drink of the cup" of suffering and death for the sake of his divine Master. He was the first of the twelve apostles to shed his blood as a martyr of Christ. Within a few years after the death of Christ, violent opposition arose in Jerusalem against the followers of Jesus. The Jews, who believed in Jesus of Nazareth as the true Messiah and Son of God, were looked upon by the rest of the Jews as renegades to the faith of their forefathers. The holy deacon, St. Stephen, was the first to fall a victim to the rage of the unconverted Jews. (See Acts 6,8-8,3.) After Saul of Tarsus was converted and changed from a persecutor into the zealous apostle, St. Paul, the Church in Palestine had peace for a few years (Acts 9,31). Then when Herod Agrippa I, (the grandson of Herod the Great) ruled as king of Judea under Roman overlordship in 41-44 A.D., to ingratiate himself with the Jews he renewed the persecution of the Church. This is the Herod of which Acts 12,1f speaks: "Now at this time Herod the king set hands on certain members of the Church to persecute them. He killed James the brother of John, with the sword." It must have been a trumped-up political charge that was brought against St. James the Greater, for beheading, or rather, the cutting of the jugular vein with a sword, was the ordinary Roman method of execution; the common Jewish means of capital punishment was stoning to death. It seems that it was not long after the death of St. James the Greater, and the miraculous deliverance of St. Peter from prison, that Herod himself died, "eaten by worms" (Acts 12,23). Therefore St. James must have been martyred in Herod's last year, that is, in 44 A.D.

The question of the relationship of St. James the Greater with Spain is a ticklish matter, since the Spaniards are very proud of their tradition that he was the first to establish the faith of Christ in their country. However, this tradition was unknown in Spain before the early Middle Ages. The first clear reference to it is in the 9th century by Notker, a monk of the monastery of St. Gall in Switzerland. On the other hand, the intrinsic evidence of the Acts of the Apostles makes it most unlikely. After all, it was not much more than a dozen years after our Lord's death when St. James the Greater died. There is no reason to believe that this apostle had ever left Palestine. As a matter of fact, it seems quite likely that during these first dozen years of the Church none of the apostles had preached the Christian faith beyond the Holy Land. Moreover, when St. Paul wrote to the Romans about the year 58, he who made it a principle "not to preach the gospel where Christ had already been named lest he might build on another man's foundation" (Rom. 15,20), said that he hoped to visit the Romans in passing while on his way to preach the gospel in Spain (Rom. 15,23.28). It would appear, therefore, that in the year 58, fourteen years after the death of St. James the Greater, Christianity had not yet reached Spain.

It is, however, a different matter regarding the relics of this St. James. There can be no denying the possibility of the transference of his relics at some unknown date from the place in Palestine (where they had first been buried) to the site in northwestern Spain where in the Middle Ages the great Church of Santiago de Campostela was erected in honor of this apostle. In fact, the authenticity of these sacred relics is vouched for by Pope Leo XIII in his Bull, *Omnipotens Deus*, of November 1, 1884. All honor then to the Spaniards who have spread the glory of their great Santiago or San Diego throughout the world!

Saint James the Less
Apostle

6 2

(May 11)

I T IS RATHER surprising that half of the twelve Apostles were paired off as brothers. There were three pairs of brothers: Peter and Andrew, James and John, James and Jude. Two of them, with the same name of "James," complicated matters. What was more natural than that one of these two Jameses should be given a distinguishing nickname? He was called *ho mikros* (Mark 15,40). The dictionary tells us that this term means "the small one," although we would probably not be far from wrong if we imagined that the other Apostles used it affectionately, somewhat as if they called this James "the runt" or "peewee." In any case, it does not signify that he was of "less" importance than the other James, even though the English Bibles render it as "the Less" or "the Lesser," and even though the other Apostle James is therefore, without any warrant from the Bible, called "the Greater."

If we had only the Gospels to go by, we might indeed think that St. James the Less was one of the more insignificant among the Apostles. Apart from the mention of his name in the list of the chosen Twelve, the Gospels seldom speak of him. In each of the four official lists of the Apostles (Matt. 10,2ff; Mark 3,16-19; Luke 6,14ff; Acts 1,13) he is called "James, the son of Alpheus." St. Paul says in his Epistle to the Galatians (1,18f) that, when he went to Jerusalem three years after his conversion in order to pay his respects to Saint Peter, he "saw none of the other Apostles except James, the brother of the Lord." At that time, it is true, both of the Apostles who had the name of "James" were still living, but it is certain that Saint Paul referred to St. James the Less because in other passages of his Epistle to the Galatians (2,9.12) he mentions this same James as still living at a time when Saint James the Greater had already been dead for some years (cf. Acts 12,2). Therefore, James the Less must also be the James whom the people of Nazareth knew as one of the "brothers" of Jesus. When they refused to accept as the Messiah their fellow townsmen whom they called "the carpenter's son" and Himself "a carpenter," they exclaimed: "Is not this the carpenter, the son of Mary, the brother of James, Joseph, Jude and Simon?" (Mark 6,3; cr. Matt. 13,55).

Much nonsense has been written about "the brothers of Jesus," as if they were other sons of Mary and Joseph. Anyone who knows anything about the Semitic languages knows that the word "brother" can be used in Hebrew and in Aramaic merely in the sense of a "relative." That James the Less was not a "brother" of our Lord in the strict sense of having the same father and mother is certain from the fact that we know who the father and mother of James were, and they were not the same as the parents of Jesus. First of all, as mentioned above, the father of James was called Alpheus, not Joseph. Then, even though the name of James' mother was Mary, it is clear that this Mary was not Mary, the mother of Jesus. When Matthew (27,56) says that, among the pious women who witnessed the death and burial of Christ, there "were Mary Magdalene, and Mary the mother of James and Joseph, and the mother of the sons of Zebedee," and when Mark (15,47) similarly lists these women as "Mary Magdalene and Mary the mother of Joseph," these Evangelists are surely not referring to the mother of the Savior. If they had wished to speak of Mary the mother of Christ, they would have said so expressly, just as John (19,25) did: "There were standing by the cross of Jesus His mother, and His mother's sister, Mary of Cleophas, and Mary Magdalene."

Who is this "Mary of Cleophas" whom John mentions? Almost certainly the term means "Mary the wife of Cleophas." Now, if this "Mary of Cleophas" is the same as "Mary the mother of James and Joseph" of whom Matthew and Mark speak—and this seems quite probable, then Cleophas must be the same as Alpheus, the father of James. Either the man had two names, as many men had at that time, or these two names are merely dialectic variants of one and the same name. In speaking of Mary of Cleophas as the "sister" of Christ's mother, John must be using the word "sister" in a broad sense; two daughters in the same family would hardly have the same name of "Mary." Mary of Cleophas was rather a "relative" (in some unknown way) of Mary the mother of Jesus; perhaps her sister-in-law, or possibly her niece, aunt, or cousin. That is why James and Jude and the rest of their family could be spoken of as the "brothers," that is, the "relatives" of Jesus. Finally, in connection with this family history the fact should be pointed out that the little Epistle of St. Jude begins with the words: "Jude, the servant of Jesus Christ and the brother of James, to the called, who have been loved in God the Father. . ." Evidently this humble Apostle Jude, who preferred to call himself the "servant" rather than the "relative" of Jesus Christ, wished in his lowliness to identify himself by his more famous brother, James. Yet James also shows his humility by beginning his own, much longer Epistle with the words: "James, the servant of God and of our Lord Jesus Christ to the twelve tribes that are in the Dispersion. . ." Both of these humble men who could have boasted of their blood relationship with Christ glory rather in being His "servants."

It is only from St. Paul that we know of a special apparition of the risen Savior to Saint James the Less. After mentioning the first appearances of Christ after His resurrection, Paul says, "After that He was seen by James, then by all the apostles" (I Cor. 15,7). We do not know on what occasion or in what circumstances this took place, but this singling out of James the Less by Christ shows what an important role he was to play in the early Church.

As head of the whole Church, Saint Peter did not act as "bishop" of any particular Church, at least not in the first couple of decades after Christ's ascension into heaven. Contrary to what one might think, Peter was not the bishop or head of the Jerusalem Church; it was James the Less who held this important office. After Peter was miraculously freed from prison and thus escaped the sword of Herod of Agrippa which had already shed the blood of James the Greater, he made a hasty visit to the Christians and told them how the angel of God had come to his rescue, and he added: "Tell this to James and to the brethren." Peter would not have been quite so anxious to have James the Less know of this unless the latter were the head of the faithful at Jerusalem. Then again, from the way that Saint Paul speaks in his Epistle to the Galatians of James the Less, it is clear that he regarded him as a very important personage in Jerusalem. Thus when the Apostle of the Gentiles made his second official visit to the Holy City after his conversion, he conferred with the leading apostles there on the gospel which he preached among the Gentiles. "When they recognized the grace that was given me," says Paul, "James and Cephas and John, who were considered the pillars, gave to me and to Barnabas the right hand of fellowship, that we should go to the Gentiles, and they to the circumcised" (Gal. 2,9). The apostle whom Paul calls "Cephas" (from the Aramaic word meaning "the rock") is certainly the same as Peter (from the Greek word with the same meaning). The order, however, of the three names should be noticed. James is mentioned first, even before Cephas-Peter! He was thus obviously one of the three "pillars" of the Church in Jerusalem which is what would be expected if he was bishop of this city.

It should not scandalize anyone to hear that for a while there was some disagreement among St. Paul and these three "pillars" of the Church in Jerusalem on a certain matter of practical policy, not on any matter of doctrine. All of the apostles, of course, held with firm faith that they and all Christians were saved solely through faith in Jesus Christ, and that the observance of the precepts of the Mosaic Law had nothing to do with man's salvation. Paul, moreover, agreed with the original apostles that it was perfectly permissible for the Christian converts from Judaism to continue their national custom of eating nothing but kosher food, and the original apostles likewise agreed in theory that the Christian converts from paganism were not obliged to observe the Jewish kosher laws. Yet they held at first that in practice it would be better for them to keep these laws for the sake of not offending the Jews and the Judeo-Christians. Peter, who was of a generous and accommodating nature, hesitated for a while on the question. The crisis came in Antioch of Syria where there was a minority of converts from Judaism, but where the majority of Christians were converts from paganism. "When Cephas came to Antioch," Paul wrote to the Galatians, "I withstood him to his face, because he was deserving of blame. For before certain persons came from James, he used to eat with the Gentiles; but when they came, he began to withdraw and to separate himself, fearing the circumcised" (Gal. 2,11f). It is hard to avoid the conclusion that "the persons who came from James" and were causing a split in the Christian community at Antioch had, or at least claimed to have, the authority of James the Less, the bishop of Jerusalem, behind them. Evidently James thought that there was hope of converting the majority of Jews as long as Christianity held to the externals of Jewish religious practice and worship. Paul, on the other hand, saw clearly that the future of the Church lay with the Gentiles, and that these would never be converted in any great number if they were obliged to observe Jewish customs which they found repugnant.

Since both men were saints and therefore not stubbornly glued to their own opinion, Paul and James worked out a satisfactory compromise at the Council of Jerusalem which was held about the year 50 to settle this question. At this distinguished gathering of "the apostles and presbyters" of the Church of Jerusalem, Peter (as head of the whole Church) gave the first speech in which he insisted on the freedom of the Gentiles from the Mosaic Law. Then "Barnabas and Paul told of the great signs and wonders that God had done among the Gentiles through them." Finally, James proposed that the Gentile Christians should be asked to observe only a few points of the Jewish religious law which he judged as "indispensable": that they abstain from meat which had been sacrificed to idols or which had not been properly drained of its blood, and that they keep the Jewish laws regarding marriage. The whole assembly, including Paul and Barnabas, agreed to this, and it was then put in the form of a remarkably worded decree: "The Holy Spirit and we have decided to lay no further burden upon you but this indispensable one. . ." This decree, moreover, concerned only "the brethren of Gentile origin in Antioch and Syria and Cilicia." It was not enforced in the other churches founded by the Apostle of the Gentiles. Thus St. James the Less, for all his love of the ancient religious practices of his people, had nevertheless shown himself first and foremost a Christian, primarily interested in the good of the whole Church of Christ. (See Acts 15,6-29.)

At the end of Paul's third missionary journey about the year 58, Luke tells us: "On our arrival at Jerusalem the brethren gave us a hearty welcome. On the next day Paul went with us to James, and all the presbyters came in. After greeting them, he related in detail what God had done among the Gentiles through his ministry. They praised God when they heard it" (Acts 21, 17ff). However, the advice which they then gave Paul, that he should placate the Jews by fulfilling a Nazarite vow in the temple and thereby show that he still respected the Mosaic Law, unwittingly caused his arrest and imprisonment.

That is the last thing we heard of Saint James the Less in the New Testament. At some unknown date, however, he wrote a very interesting Epistle "to the twelve tribes who are in the Dispersion," that is, to the Christians, especially the Judeo-Christians who lived outside of Palestine. The moral teachings in this letter have a close resemblance to the teachings of our Lord as contained in the Gospel according to St. Matthew, the most "Jewish" of the four Gospels. Since the ideals which Saint James here sets before his readers were undoubtedly those by which his own life was regulated, we are justified in concluding from this letter of his that he was of a kind and calm, albeit serious disposition, a defender of the rights of the poor, devoted to prayer and the reading of the Sacred Scriptures, and resigned to God in all afflictions and persecutions—in all things worthy of the title given him in the early Church, "James the Just."

The Jewish historian, Flavius Josephus, who wrote toward the end of the first Christian century, records that when Festus, the Roman governor of Palestine, had died and Albinus, the newly appointed governor, had not yet arrived in the country, the Jewish high priest Ananos II "assembled the sanhedrin of judges and brought before them James, the brother of Jesus who was called Christ, and some of his companions; and when he had laid accusation against them as breakers of the law, he delivered them to be stoned" (Antiquities of the Jews, Book 20, Chapter 9,1). The death of Saint James the Less can, therefore, be definitely dated as having occurred in the year 62.

The Christian historian, Hegesippus, who wrote in the second half of the second century, has a more detailed account of the martyrdom of Saint James the Less which has been preserved in the "Church History" of Eusebius (4th century). According to Hegesippus, when James the Just gave testimony to Jesus as the Christ, the Jews pushed him from the high platform of the temple down into the deep valley of the Cedron. As the fall did not kill him, they cast stones on him; "and one of them, a fuller, took the club which he used for beating clothes white and smashed James' head with it" (Eusebius, *Hist. Eccl.* II, 23). Like the dying words of his "brother" Jesus, the last words of James the Less were, according to Hegesippus: "I beg Thee, O Lord God, Father, forgive them, for they know not what they do!"

The feast of Saint James the Less is celebrated on the same day as that of the Apostle Saint Philip. Up until 1956 this combined feast of Saints Philip and James fell on the first of May, but in that year Pope Pius XII transferred its future annual celebration to the eleventh of May in order to observe the newly instituted feast of "Saint Joseph the Worker" on the first of May which is "Labor Day" in Europe. It is no longer known why these two apostles have a feast in common on the same day. As early as the year 563, Pope John III dedicated a church in Rome to the Holy Apostles Philip and James. There is some evidence, however, that the earlier church on this site was sacred to Saint Philip alone. How Saint James the Less came eventually to be associated with him there is still a mystery.

Saint John Berchmans

Confessor

1 6 2 1

(November 26)

THE ONLY THING that all saints have in common is their sublime holiness, that greater abundance of sanctifying grace which makes them the special friends of God. Their sanctity, however, is not all of the same stamp. To some is given what at least their fellow men consider the good fortune of having an early biographer record their life in a most attractive manner. Thus they are known and loved even by people who have no appreciation of genuine supernatural virtue. Other saints, on the contrary, have nothing particularly remarkable recorded that would make them especially appealing to later generations, though the unquestionable miracles that are wrought through their intercession prove that they are genuine saints of God. Again, there are certain saints whose names go down in history for the great things they have done for the Lord as writers, missionaries, founders of religious orders, prelates of the Church, and so forth. Similiarly there are other saints who have never done anything at all that could bring them fame in the world, and yet whose hidden lives may have been more pleasing to God than the renowned careers of some of their fellow saints.

Perhaps God wishes to have a certain number of these "plain" saints canonized in order to teach us that it is not the external circumstances of a man's life, but rather the internal dispositions of his heart, the purity of his love for God and his fellow man, that makes him a saint. It may even be that the good Lord wishes, by occasionally having such a "plain" saint canonized, to encourage ordinary mortals that they too, even if they do not reach the "heroic" degree of sanctity of always doing their little duties in the most perfect manner, may hope to reach true holiness in their own small way. After all, every one in heaven is a "saint," whether canonized or not. One of these simple, hidden saints, whose life seems to have nothing at all of the extraordinary about it, is John Berchmans.

John was born on March 13, 1599, the oldest of five children, of middle-class parents in a little town of Belgium called Diest (between Brussels and Louvain). His father, whose name was also John Berchmans, was a "master leather dresser," or more simply, a shoemaker. His mother, Elizabeth Van den Hove, was a typically pious woman from whom young John learned his first lessons in piety. Both parents were of that stolid Flemish stock which may never do anything flashy, but which has the "stick-to-it-ness" to make a success of any undertaking.

Little John was a good child, causing no trouble to anyone. His nature was sweet and sunny and he was serious in his religious duties. Even when only seven years old, he used to go to school at an earlier hour than necessary to serve two or three Masses before his classes began. For this reason he is now regarded as the special patron of altar boys.

The parish priest of Diest, Father Peter Emmerick of the Order of St. Norbert, had the custom of boarding and training in his house a certain number of boys who wished to be priests. When John Berchmans was ten years old, he also, with his parents' consent, was received into Father Emmerick's home. However, he still continued to attend the school of Valerius Van Stipout, who now began to teach him the rudiments of Latin.

John lived with Father Emmerick for three years, during which time his father paid both for his board at the priest's house and for his education at Van Stipout's school. Unfortunately the

Berchmans gradually became poorer and poorer, until John's parents were forced to tell him that they could no longer keep up these payments. He would have to give up the idea of becoming a priest and begin to contribute by his own work to the support of the family. Young John was heartbroken. He pleaded with his parents not to force him to give up the hope of some day becoming a priest. Since they were devout people themselves, they tried to find a way to help him, and they succeeded.

Another priest in Diest, Father Aymon Timmermans, offered to take John into his house as a servant and to pay for his schooling in recompense for the household service rendered. This arrangement turned out to be a joy both for the priest and for his little servant, although it was soon realized that John would receive a better education in the nearby city of Mechelen (or Malines, as it is called in French). In 1613, therefore, he moved to this city where Monsignor Froymont (choirmaster of the Mechelen Cathedral), who ran a sort of boarding house for schoolboys, agreed to let the Berchmans boy work for him. Here John not only performed various menial chores about the house; he also acted as tutor for some of the smaller boys. All these tasks he carried out with such simple humility and constant cheerfulness that everyone grew to love him.

Meanwhile John attended the classes that were held in the Minor Seminary of Mechelen for aspirants to the secular priesthood. In 1615, when the Jesuits opened a college in this city, he decided to continue his studies in this new institution. Having passed his entrance examination, he was admitted as a student, though he still continued to live with Monsignor Froymont.

Under the guidance of the Jesuit Fathers, Berchmans' spirituality deepened. Always fervently devoted to Our Blessed Lady and her Immaculate Conception, he was one of the first to enroll in the college Sodality of Mary. To prove his love for her he practiced many devotions in her honor and fasted on Saturdays and the vigils of her feasts. Though never a mystic, he always found delight in prayer, in speaking heart to heart with God.

John had always longed to be a priest. Now his desires became more specific: he wished to be a priest in the Society of Jesus. Yet in his humility he sincerely doubted if he was worthy of such a high vocation. With his prayers for God's guidance he combined sacrifice: he divided his entire worldly "wealth" of twenty-five florins into three parts, gave one part to the poor and the other two parts for Masses to be said at Our Lady's altar that through her intercession he might have the grace of recognizing and following his true vocation.

At the advice of his confessor he wrote to his parents, telling them all that was in his heart. They were far from being happy about it. A secular priest, they said, all well and good! Their son could then support them in their old age, but a Jesuit, never! The elder Berchmans then hurried to Mechelen, but his entreaties had no affect on his son who was steadfastly determined to become a Jesuit. After the father returned home, he wrote to his son begging him at least to come back to Diest to say good-bye to his family and friends. In reply the youth wrote a touching letter in which he explained that it was impossible for him to come home. Instead he asked his parents to come to Mechelen to say goodbye to him there. A few days later, on September 24, 1616, when he was seventeen years old, he entered the Jesuit novitiate in Mechelen.

Novices often have a hard time severing the bonds that have previously tied them to their home and the world. John, however, did not have to go through this ordeal. He was long since detached from home ties. In the hard school of poverty and privation he had already learned how to make sacrifices cheerfully. Since his whole life had been directed toward God, now in God's house of the novitiate he felt completely at home. From the first, he displayed perfect ease to the wonderment and respect of his fellow novices. Father Bauters, his novice master, said of him, "He is an angel in a body that is mortal." Coming from this learned Jesuit, who had had much experience with hundreds of novices, this was not merely a pious platitude.

John began every act of the day by raising his heart to God. His devotion to the Blessed Eucharist was at the basis of his spiritual life. Seven times a day he used to go to the chapel to adore the Blessed Sacrament, and he would have stayed there for longer periods if possible. After Our Lord in the Holy Eucharist he loved the Blessed Virgin best, and he would often say that he owed his vocation to her and hoped for his salvation through her intercession. This young man had the rare gift of being able to talk on subjects of piety with no effort, and of pleasing rather than repelling others when he did so.

All who knew him as a novice and a scholastic agreed that his outstanding virtue was his obedience. With unhesitating compliance he carried out every order that he received, not only from his superiors but also from any of his equals when asked to do something. For him the rules of his religious society were in every sense God's commands. He always did his utmost to obey them to the letter. That is why, when later artists wished to portray him with some characteristic symbol, they pictured him as holding the rule book in his hand. Although he would have gladly practiced severe self-denials, he said that his best penance was to carry out every obligation of his rules in the most perfect manner.

The basic reason why the virtue of obedience pleases God so much is because it is the glad acceptance of the divine will. John Berchmans had that unfailingly cheerful disposition which made him loved by all with whom he lived because from love of God he accepted anything that befell him as God's will. There is a simple test that any man can make if he wishes to find out how much he is devoted to God and how much to himself. All he has to do is to see how much he complains when adversity befalls him. Knowing that nothing happens in this world unless it is ordained, or at least permitted, by God, the true saint accepts from God's hands the bitter things in life just as willingly as the sweet. Not that it is always easy to do so. Even Christ was in an "agony," a struggle of soul, to make human

SAINT GREGORY VII

This monk who became Pope under the name of Gregory VII during the
11th century was God's chosen instrument to purify the Church of internal corruption and external oppression. The external evil was the "right of
lay investiture," that is, the claim of the state to the right of appointing
the clergy. The eradication of this is symbolically illustrated here as Pope
Gregory crushes the tyrannical German state and elevates the Papacy.

SAINT JOHN CHRYSOSTOM

John Chrysostom's fame as a saint rests not merely upon his reputation
as one of Christianity's most popular and influential orators. His glory as
one of the most renowned heroes of the Church is solidly established on
his holy and dramatic life of labors and sufferings for the cause of Jesus.
He is depicted here with St. John the Baptist by reproduction from the
panels of a sixteenth-century iconostasis.

nature accept the bitter chalice which His Father gave Him to drink. By such sacrifices true love proves itself.

Berchmans had his trials in life, too. Three months after he entered the novitiate his mother, whom he dearly loved, was taken from him. As a novice he could not, of course, go to her funeral. After he made his first vows on September 25, 1618, at the end of his two-year novitiate, he was first stationed for three weeks in Antwerp and then told he was to go to Rome for his seminary studies. He wrote to his father to meet him when he passed through Mechelen. On his arrival there young Berchmans learned to his sorrow that his father had died eight days before. His brothers and sisters had not even notified him of the death. Looking on this cross, too, as God's will, he said, "Now I have a double reason for saying, 'Our Father, who art in heaven.' "

During the three years that John Berchmans spent in the philosophy course at the "Roman College" of the Jesuits, his simple, unpretended holiness made a deep impression on all with whom he lived. Some of the older Fathers, who had known St. Aloysius Gonzaga, went so far as the say that they liked this Belgian scholastic even better than the saintly Gonzaga because of his great friendliness. While not a brilliant student, John was a model, at least, in the absolute diligence with which he devoted himself to his studies. He regulated every hour, almost every minute of the day, and he followed these regulations exactly: a fixed time for study, for prayer, and for all his other duties. Perseverance in such a rigorous program requires solid virtue indeed.

In March of 1621, John successfully passed the examination on the whole of his course in philosophy, and he then began to prepare for the public defense of certain propositions. During July, while still working hard despite the oppressive heat, his health began to fail and he had a premonition of death. As was customary at the end of each month, on the last day of July he received a patron and a motto from the Bible for the following month. This time his text was from Mark 13,33: "Take heed, watch and pray, for you know not when the time is." He took this as a message from heaven and went with joy to tell his superiors that God would soon call him home.

On August the 5th he was not feeling well, but with characteristic determination he would not quit. On the next day, despite his fever (which he concealed from the others), he gave an excellent account of himself in an hour's talk as the representative of the Roman College in the scholastic affair known as the "public defense." The ordeal left him exhausted. Confined to bed, he never rose again. Day by day he grew weaker, and on August 13, 1671, he fell asleep in the Lord.

The outburst of popular devotion to John Berchmans that followed his death soon grew to almost extravagant proportions. In a certain sense it can be said that the people canonized him at once. Various events delayed the formal process in which the Church investigates the virtues and miracles attributed to any candidate for sainthood. He was finally beautified by Pius IX in 1865, and canonized by Leo XIII in 1888. His feast was not extended to the universal Church, but the Jesuits celebrate it on November 27th.

Saint John Chrysostom

Bishop, Doctor of the Church

4 0 7

(January 27)

E VER SINCE the middle of the 6th century the title of "Chrysostom" (which is Greek for "Golden-mouth"), has been given to Saint John, priest of Antioch and archbishop of Constantinople, on account of his great eloquence. Yet the fame of John Chrysostom as a saint rests not merely on his reputation as one of Christianity's most popular and influential orators. His glory as one of the most renowned heroes of the Church is solidly established on his holy and dramatic life of labors and sufferings for the cause of Christ, whose doctrine he preached with so much fervor in season and out of season.

When John was born at Antioch (on the Orontes River in northwestern Syria) about the year 347, scarcely one generation had passed since Christianity had come forth victorious from the crucible of the Roman persecutions. Although Constantine the Great by his "Edict of Milan" had given official toleration to Christianity throughout the Roman empire in 313, it was not until the time of Theodosius the Great in 394 that Catholic Christianity was made the official religion of the whole empire. During most of the lifetime, therefore, of St. John Chrysostom probably only about half the people of the empire were Catholics, the remainder being pagans, Jews, or Christians of various heretical sects. Even among the Catholics, now that the acceptance of the

Faith no longer involved the danger of persecution, a large number of the new converts were still half-pagan in spirit.

This was especially true both in John's native city of Antioch, and in the upstart metropolis of Constantinople where he was later to preside as archbishop. During the first three centuries of our era, Antioch ranked as the third most important city in the Roman empire. It was surpassed only by the capital itself, Rome, and by Alexandria, the great commercial and intellectual center of Egypt (at the mouth of the western delta of the Nile). Correspondingly, in the first three centuries of the Church the three most important bishoprics of Christendom were those of Rome, Alexandria and Antioch. While the bishop of Rome, as St. Peter's successor, was recognized by all orthodox Christians as head of the entire Church, the individual dioceses had more autonomy than they have at present. The clergy of each diocese ordinarily elected their own bishop. In matters of dispute, appeal was made to the "Patriarch" or leading archbishop of the region, while the Apostolic See of Rome was regarded as the court of highest appeal. Originally there were only three such Patriarchs: the bishop of Rome, who was Patriarch of the West, that is, of the Latin-speaking Church in the western half of the Roman empire, and the bishops of Alexandria and of Antioch who were, respectively, the Patriarchs of the southern and northern parts of the Greek-speaking Church in the eastern half of the empire.

It was only after Constantine in 330 changed the hitherto obscure city of Byzantium on the Bosphorus into the "New Rome," the capital of the empire, that this place which was renamed "Constantinople" or "the City of Constantine" in his honor, rapidly grew in both political and ecclesiastical importance. At the Second Ecumenical Council (in 381) the bishop of Constantinople was recognized as the second-ranking Patriarch in Christendom, inferior only to the bishop of Rome.

Theodosius the Great was the last ruler of a united Roman Empire. When he died in 395, his realm was divided between his sons, neither of whom inherited the ability of their father. Arcadius became emperor of the East, with Constantinople as his capital, and Honorius emperor of the West.

(Some knowledge of this historical background is necessary for a correct understanding of the events in the life of St. John Chrysostom.)

John's father, Secundus, who had been an officer of high rank in the Roman army of the East, died soon after the birth of his son, but he left his twenty-year-old wife Anthusa with ample means to raise their two children, John, and an older daughter. The latter, however, soon followed her father to the grave. Anthusa, who never remarried, was a devout Catholic and exercised a beneficial influence on her son, although according to the custom of the time he was not baptized until he was twenty years old.

John's mother saw to it that her son received the best possible education which at the time consisted mostly in what was called "rhetoric" in the original meaning of the word, that is, the art of expressive speech particularly for the purpose of oratory. The prime aim of such an education was to prepare a man for public life. John's principal teacher was a pagan named Libanius who was regarded as the greatest civic orator of his time. This training was truly providential inasmuch as the young "golden-mouth" orator was later to use it for so much spiritual good. Had not God intervened to achieve His own ends, John might well have become nothing more than one of the famous lawyers and leading figures in the political life of his time—and his name now completely forgotten. During his student days he became acquainted with St. Meletius, the Catholic archbishop of Antioch, and under the benign influence of this holy man he soon gave up his classical and profane studies in favor of a deeper knowledge of the Christian faith which he first studied in preparation for his baptism (about the year 367).

Shortly after being baptized, John was ordained a "lector," that is, a cleric who publicly read the "lessons" or readings from the Sacred Scripture at the liturgical services in church. It was probably around this time that he began his special studies in Sacred Scripture under the Antiochean priest Diodorus of Tarsus, the founder of the famous "Antiochean School" of Biblical interpretation. The latter, in opposition to the allegorical method of the "Alexandrian School," explained the Bible in a rational, scientific manner.

John always remained a diligent student of the Bible, and in later life he constantly urged people to read it. He used to say that the Christian who does not know his Bible is like a workman without tools. Once, when he was preaching on the Scriptures, he had to scold his inattentive audience. "Please listen to me," he said. "You are not paying attention. While I am talking to you about the Holy Scriptures, you are looking at the lamps and the men who are lighting them. It is very frivolous of you to be more interested in what the lamplighters are doing than in what the preacher is saying. After all, I too am lighting a lamp—the lamp of God's word."

After his mother's death, about the year 374, John, who ever since his baptism was filled with a desire to lead a more perfect spiritual life, joined one of the communities of monks in the mountains to the south of Antioch. For four years he followed the austere life of fasting, prayer and study that was led in this monastery. His earliest written works, concerned with the ascetic and monastic life, probably date from this period. Seeking a still more perfect life of detachment from the world, John then spent two years as a hermit, living alone in a cave. In his zeal he overdid things; too much fasting, too many vigils, too much exposure to the inclement weather. When his health broke down, he wisely returned to Antioch and resumed his duties as a "lector" in the ministry of his church.

Here, in 381, St. Meletius ordained John a deacon. This was shortly before Meletius left for Constantinople where he died as the presiding prelate at the Second Ecumenical Council. The new archbishop of Antioch was Flavian. John served as his deacon for five years. Besides functioning in the important part of the liturgy which a deacon has to perform in the Eastern Rite of the Church, John was also connected with the financial administration of the diocese, and in this capacity was responsible for the collection and distribution of alms for the care of the poor and the sick.

During these years he obtained a thorough, firsthand knowledge of the social and economic conditions of the people. He came to know and love the ordinary, hard-working men and women, and they loved him in return. Throughout his life he never ceased to write and preach against social injustice, the misuse of wealth, and the neglect of the poor. In all his later troubles it was primarily the common people who remained most loyal to him. Not that he lacked faults of his own, but he humbly acknowledged them and did his best to overcome them. Irritability and indignation were strong characteristics which he always had to combat in himself.

In 386 Archbishop Flavian ordained John to the priesthood. Toward the end of his five years as a deacon, or during his first years as a priest, John composed one of the greatest of his literary works, *On the Priesthood*, a masterful treatment of the dignity, office and responsibility of priests and bishops that is as pertinent today as when it was written. On his ordination day, when he was about forty years old, he preached his first sermon. From that time on, the aged archbishop delegated almost all the preaching in the cathedral of Antioch to him, and to him also was entrusted most of the religious instruction of the people, especially the large groups of "catechumens" or converts. For the next twelve years preaching remained John's principal occupation. His fame as a preacher spread throughout the whole Roman empire. People from everywhere came to Antioch, and later to Constantinople, just to hear him.

The sermons of Saint John Chrysostom, more than seven hundred, have come down to us. Conditioned by his time and place, they perhaps would not be listened to as avidly now as they were when delivered by this "golden-mouth" orator of the 4th century. His style strikes a modern reader as often too florid, but such was the height of style in those days. This should not be understood in the sense that everything he said was roses and honey. Far from it! John could be brutally frank in his sermons, and he never hesitated to denounce in the most vigorous terms whatever he considered to be an evil or an abuse. A modern audience would also find his sermons far too long. In those days, however, listening to a good sermon was almost as popular a pastime as watching a chariot race. A sermon that did not last an hour was hardly worth going to hear. What especially attracted people to John's sermons was the worthwhile things he had to say, and the forceful words with which he expressed his ideas. His delivery was in no way remarkable, since he seems to have had a rather weak voice. Nor was his appearance particularly attractive, with his large bald head, his wrinkled forehead that overshadowed his bright, deep-set eyes, a pale complexion, straggly gray beard, and a short, thin body. Once he jokingly likened himself to a spider, but he had great dignity and his words were golden, indeed.

His more elaborate sermons were delivered on special occasions, such as the great feasts of the Church, or in connection with certain events in Antioch. An example is his remarkable series of sermons "On the Statues," which won him world-wide fame. Most of his sermons, though, were in the form of "homilies" on the Scriptures. The "homily" of the Fathers is a type of sermon which unfortunately has gone out of fashion. It consists of a running commentary on some book of the Bible, explaining it verse by verse, and drawing doctrinal and moral lessons from the inspired word of God as it proceeds. A series of several scores of sermons may be required to cover a single Biblical book. Saint John Chrysostom delivered such homiletic commentaries on many of the books of the Holy Scriptures. His homilies on the Epistles of Saint Paul rank among the best commentaries ever written on these letters of the Apostle of the Gentiles. Strictly speaking, however, John did not "write" these homilies; usually he deliver-ed them merely from notes, and a stenographer or "tachygrapher," as the "speed-writer" of ancient times was called, wrote down what the preacher said and his copy was then corrected for pub-lication.

Chrysostom had but little inclination for speculative theology. In this field he cannot be compared with St. Augustine of Hippo of the Latin Church, or with Saint Basil or the two Saint Gre-gories of Nanzianzus and Nyssa of the Greek Church who were roughly his contemporaries. Yet he is of prime importance as a witness to the doctrines of the Church since he explains these in a very clear and detailed manner. Thus he is rightly ranked among both the Latins and the Greeks as one of the great "Doc-tors" (or "Teachers") of the Church. His theology is an explana-tion of the revealed truths not so much as aided by the light that philosophy can cast on them, but rather as interpreted by a clear understanding of the passages in the Bible where these truths are revealed—always guided, of course, by sound Catholic tradi-tion. Contrary to the practice of the Biblical exegetes (i.e. those skilled in explanation) of the Alexandrian School, such as the great Origen who often read a "spiritual" meaning into a passage where the words themselves did not really have this sense, Saint John Chrysostom held to a strictly literal interpretation of the words of the Bible. With his keen mind, however, and his vast knowledge of all the Scriptures, he was able to draw from this literal sense valuable doctrinal and moral conclusions.

Although Chrysostom never fell a victim to that besetting sin of popular orators—vainglory over the power of one's words, he did lapse at times into those faults which are almost inherent in enthusiastic eloquence—exaggeration and overvehement expres-sions. In condemning various vices he sometimes painted them in too black a color. Besides, while ever careful to avoid explicitly naming rich and influential persons as guilty of injustice, he would occasionally use such unmistakeable terms that the per-sons concerned would know he was referring to them. Thus in later life he made enemies of certain powerful individuals, who succeeded in wreaking their vengeance on him.

Chrysostom was ordained only about one year when his name as a preacher became known throughout the empire, especially at its capital, Constantinople, as a result of his series of twenty sermons, *On the Statues,* that were delivered at Antioch during Lent of 387. In February of that year, the emperor Theodosius I imposed a special tax levy on the wealthy cities of his domain. At Antioch this caused a riot, in the course of which the mob smashed some statues of the imperial family. The emperor was furious. He would make an example of this rebellious city by giving it up to his soldiers for plunder, and by having hundreds of its citizens massacred. While Flavian, the Archbishop of Antioch, hastened to the capital to beg the emperor for mercy, a group of holy monks induced the imperial commissioners to delay the chastisement for a while. In the meantime, Chrysostom preached his Lenten sermons *On the Statues* in which he exhorted the people to repentance and penance to win God's mercy on their city. These vigorous sermons prevented the people of Antioch from fleeing in panic, and helped them hold out in patience and hope. On Easter Eve, Archbishop Flavian returned with the good news of the emperor's pardon.

In the ordinary course of events John Chrysostom would, no doubt, have succeeded Flavian as archbishop of Antioch. Actually, though, when Flavian died in 404, John had already been archbishop of the more important see of Constantinople for six years. At the death of Nectarius, archbishop of Constaninople, on September 27, 397, several candidates competed for the appointment to this primatial (first) see in the capital of the empire. Theophilus, archbishop of Alexandria, was particularly anxious that his candidate, Isadore, a priest of his own diocese, should be the successor of Nectarius. Theoretically the clergy and laity of any diocese elected their own bishop, but actually the decisive vote at Constantinople lay with the emperor. Arcadius, who succeeded his father Theodosius to the imperial throne in 395, was a weakling; first under the domination of his vicious prime minister, the ex-slave Eutropius, and later under that of his clever, unscrupulous wife, the empress Eudoxia. Surprisingly enough, Eutropius decided that Nectarius' successor should be John, the famous orator-priest of Antioch. John, knowing nothing of this, was invited one day by the imperial commissioner at Antioch to visit one of the shrines of the martyrs outside the city. The chariot, however, passed the shrine and started on its way to Constantinople. John was literally kidnapped. The people of Antioch would never have consented to give up their beloved preacher. Knowing the good that he could accomplish at the imperial capital, John saw in his abduction the will of God, and thus accepted his election to the see of Constantinople. The clergy and laity of this city welcomed him wholeheartedly, but the other competitors were bitterly disappointed. On February 26, 398, John Chrysostom was consecrated archbishop of Constantinople. Theophilus of Alexandria was forced to act as his consecrator, but this rival of John's bided his time and was eventually to have his revenge.

The new archbishop of Constantinople soon saw that his easygoing predecessor had let many abuses creep into the diocese. The need for reform was obvious, and John began it at once. As his first biographer, Palladius, says of him, he started by "sweeping the stairs from the top." His first act was to reform his own household; he would live as simply as he did when he was a monk and an ordinary priest. He sold the rich furnishings of the archbishop's palace and used the proceeds to build a hospital for the poor. He also put an end to unnecessary banquets and preached the need of simpler living among the luxury-loving people of the city. Despite his frequent sermons against the abuse of wealth, he was at first on friendly enough terms with the rich nobility, including the empress Eudoxia.

Unfortunately this feeling of friendship toward the archbishop did not last long. When John preached against the foolish extravagances of the rich, and especially against the ridiculous style of dress and cosmetics affected by the wealthy ladies (whose age should have put them past such vanities) several of them in the imperial court took this as spoken directly against themselves, and did not hide their resentment from the empress. Eudoxia, herself, soon felt herself personally offended by the archbishop when he interceded for a certain widow whose country estate she had taken to herself by rather dishonest means. There is no evidence, however, that he publicly called her a Jezebel, as she claimed. In any case, by 401, only three years after John was consecrated as archbishop of Constantinople, Eudoxia was looking for a way to get rid of this troublesome reformer whom Eutropius had brought from Antioch. Her first opening came when Eutropius, himself, fell into disgrace with the emperor.

Although Eutropius had previously tried to abolish the right of asylum at the altar, he, himself, when misfortune befell him, fled to the cathedral altar for refuge from his many personal enemies. With the fallen prime minister cringing at the altar, the archbishop gave a dramatic sermon on the text, "Vanity of vanities, all is vanity." While urging the poor wretch to repentance, John vigorously defended the right of the victim to asylum and a fair trial. A few days later, however, Eutropius thought he could safely make his escape. He was quickly caught and executed, and the empress Eudoxia became the real power behind the imperial throne. In her schemes for revenge on John she soon found a capable ally in Theophilus of Alexandria.

The story of John's fall and banishment from Constantinople is a long, sad and complicated affair. The occasion for it was the controversy over the orthodoxy of Origen's writings. Origen (c. 185-254), the first great Biblical scholar of the Church, had expressed certain views on Catholic doctrine which could be understood in an heretical sense. Out of personal animosity against some monks in Egypt, particularly their leaders who were known as the "Tall Brothers," Theophilus, archbishop of Alexandria, accused them of holding these heretical teachings of Origen, and drove them out of his jurisdiction.

In 402, these monks fled to Constantinople where John received them with kindness and sympathy and gave them hospitality in one of the buildings belonging to his diocese. He refused, moreover, to give a decision on the doctrinal controversy until he had heard the other side of the case. Thereupon the emperor Arcadius summoned Theophilus to appear before a synod (or ecclesiastical meeting) at Constantinople over which John would preside. Theophilus, however, plotted his course carefully. He really was not concerned about the doctrinal questions involved in the dispute over Origen's teachings (As a matter of fact, later in life he, himself became an ardent Origenist), but he was able to persuade certain highly respected churchmen to condemn John as an heretical Origenist. Saint Jerome thus let himself be drawn into writing a vehement letter in condemnation of the archbishop of Constantinople. Saint Epiphanius also, the learned bishop of Salamis (on the island of Cyprus), was induced by Theophilus to go to Constantinople and throw the weight of his great authority against the Tall Brothers and their fellow monks. Realizing too late that he had merely been used as a dupe, the aged Epiphanius left the capital and died on the voyage back home.

Theophilus likewise endeavored to win the Pope to his side. He sent certain carefully selected statements from the works of Origen to Pope Anastasius I who said that, while he had not studied the works of Origen, these statements, if authentic, certainly looked heretical. Then, aware of the fact that there were several disgruntled bishops in John's jurisdiction, as well as many influential persons at the imperial court who thoroughly detested their zealous archbishop, Theophilus knew exactly how to use these people to his own advantage. Moreover, it so happened that just about this time John delivered one of his forceful sermons against the scandalous dress and conduct of the rich women of the city, and the empress Eudoxia took this as a personal insult to herself.

Only after he had thus set the scene for his triumph at Constantinople did Theophilus sail from Alexandria, and not as a humble suppliant answering a summons, but accompanied by twenty-nine of his suffragan (assistant) bishops and a rich supply of gifts for buying additional friends at the capital. In the palace given him for his use by the empress, he held private conferences with John's enemies, and then retired with his suffragan bishops to a country estate known as "The Oaks," situated near Chalcedon (beyond the Dardanelles opposite Constantinople), where they held a synod of their own. Meanwhile, John went his customary way, attending to his pastoral duties and doing nothing to save himself from the plotting of Theophilus. Forty-two archbishops and bishops had come to Constantinople in answer to the original summons of the emperor for a local council, but now that they had lost the support of the imperial court they could do little to help John, who told them, "I know Satan's ways, and he will not stand my preaching against him any longer."

Theophilus then struck his first blow. He ordered John to appear before the Holy Synod assembled at "The Oaks" and justify himself for having given aid and comfort to the refugee monks from Egypt accused of heresy. John, of course, refused to recognize the legality of the assembly at "The Oaks," and therefore ignored the summons. When he failed to answer the third summons, the Synod declared him disobedient and had the rashness to depose him from his see. The emperor was asked to have him banished from Constantinople, and even to try him on the capital charge of treason, apparently for the alleged reason that he had called the empress a Jezebel.

With the popular support that he enjoyed among the common people, John could have defied the emperor's order of banishment. Preferring to suffer injustice rather than cause bloodshed in his defense, he voluntarily surrendered to the soldiers and was secretly ferried across the Dardanelles. The next day, when the people found out what had happened, the riot that John had feared really broke out. The infuriated populace stormed the royal palace. The troops were called out and many were killed.

Then a certain mysterious event thoroughly frightened Eudoxia. Disclaiming any share in John's banishment, she hurriedly
sent a messenger asking him to return to the capital. He came
at once to one of its suburbs, but he wished to wait until he was
officially cleared of the charge against him before entering the
city itself. The people, however, who were ready to give him an
enthusiastic welcome would not listen to delay. Against his better
judgment, John finally consented and was given a triumphant
ovation as he returned to his cathedral.

The peace did not last long. Two months after John's return
Eudoxia again became furious with him. She had a silver statue
of herself erected in the public square on which the cathedral
faced. At its unveiling the pagan revelry in the square, which
lasted for many days, was so noisy that the archbishop could
scarcely conduct the services in his cathedral. He complained to
the chief of police about it, and the latter, no friend of John, reported his complaint to the empress. She again took it as a personal affront, and once more sought the aid of Theophilus. This
crafty man, who had fled back to Alexandria on John's triumphant return to Constantinople, wisely excused himself from com·
ing again to the capital. He advised her, however, that she could
have the emperor banish John from his see on the grounds that
he had violated the canon of an earlier synod held at Antioch
which had decreed that a bishop who had been deposed by a
synod could not be reinstated in his see except with the approval
of a still more important synod.

John refused to be intimidated. He would not abandon his
flock. Several months passed before the emperor felt himself
strong enough to strike. On Easter Eve of 404, the imperial soldiers, many of whom were pagans, broke into the cathedral and
attacked the numerous men and women being baptized, and even
desecrated the sacred Eucharist. The archbishop was rescued by
his faithful people and was safely guarded by them in his palace
where he remained until Pentecost. Then for the sake of peace he
secretly surrendered himself to the emperor's soldiers who were un-

der orders to exile him to Cucusus in the Taurus Mountains (southeastern Asia Minor).

As soon as the people heard the news a fierce riot broke out in the city. In the midst of this bloody battle the cathedral caught fire and burned to the ground. (On its site the emperor Justinian I was later to erect the still more magnificent cathedral of Sancta Sophia, "Holy Wisdom," which is now a Turkish museum.) The fire, which spread to the senate house and other public buildings, was blamed on John's followers. A violent persecution broke out against them, and many of them were cruelly tortured to make them confess the alleged crime.

During the next three years John remained at Cucusus where he suffered much from the inclement climate and the dangers of attack by the wild mountaineers called the Isaurians. Nevertheless, he carried on a large correspondence, conforting and guiding his persecuted flock even from this great distance. Some two hundred and thirty-eight letters of his, written at this time, have come down to us. They not only make interesting and even exciting reading; they reveal the heroic character of this great man at his best—a genuine saint of God, full of wisdom, holiness and love of Christ. As a result of the long letter which John sent to the Pope telling him the full story of his persecution, the latter, Saint Innocent I, excommunicated all three Patriarchs of the East; the emperor's puppet who succeeded John as archbishop of Constantinople, the archbishop of Antioch who, after succeeding Flavian, had become an enemy of John, and Theophilus, archbishop of Alexandria, who was the ringleader in the outrage.

The emperor retaliated by banishing John to a still more isolated spot. Two rough soldiers were sent in June, 407, to take him to Pityus in the Caucasus Mountains (in the extreme northeast corner of the empire). John was now sixty years old. He had never been robust, and the forced marches which the soldiers ordered him to make proved too much for his health. Exposed to the scorching heat of the sun by day and to the cold rain of the mountains by night, he fell deathly ill near Comana in Pontus (northern Asia Minor) on September 13, 407. The soldiers let him spend the night in the chapel of St. Basiliscus (the bishop of Comana who had suffered martyrdom here in 307 during the persecution under Maximinus). That night Basiliscus appeared to John in a dream and said, "Be of good cheer, brother; tomorrow we shall be together." On the morrow, September 14, 407, the golden voice of John Chrysostom was finally stilled in death.

After several years, John's enemies were reconciled with the Pope, and his cause was at last vindicated. In 438 his holy remains were brought back to Constantinople, and on January 27, the day on which his feast is now celebrated, they were solemnly enshrined in the church of the Holy Apostles in that city. In 1909, Pope St. Pius X declared St. John Chrysostom the model of sacred eloquence and the heavenly patron of all preachers of the word of God. In addition to this patronage, the saint is invoked against epilepsy.

John was a brave man as well as a "golden voiced" orator, and his stirring cry still rings down through the centuries: "You are but a poor soldier of Christ, O Christian, if you think that you can overcome without fighting, or suppose that you have the crown without the contest."

SAINT JOHN CHRYSOSTOM ON THE
HOLY EUCHARIST

From his 46th Homily on the Gospel according to St. John

"How can this man give us his flesh to eat?" (John 6, 52)

If thou seekest to know the "how," why askest not thou this in the matter of the loaves, how He extended five to so great a number? Because they then only thought of being satisfied, not of seeking the miracle. "But," saith someone, "their experience then taught them." Then by reason of that experience these words ought to have been readily received. For to this end He wrought beforehand that strange miracle, that taught by it they might no longer disbelieve what should be said by Him afterwards.

These men then at that time reaped no fruit from what was said, but we have enjoyed the benefit in the very realities. Wherefore it is necessary to understand the marvel of the Mysteries, what it is, why it is given, and what is the profit of the action. We become one Body, and "members of His flesh and of His bones." (Eph. 5, 30). Let the initiated follow what I say. In order then that we may become this not by love only, but in very deed, let us be blended into that flesh. This is effected by the food which He hath freely given us, desiring to show the love which He hath for us. On this account He hath mixed up Himself with us; He that kneaded up His body with ours, that we might be a certain One Thing, like a body joined to a head. For this belongs to them who love strongly; this, for instance Job implied, speaking of his servants, by whom he was beloved so exceedingly, that they desired to cleave unto his flesh. For they said, to show the strong love which they felt, "Who would give us to be satisfied with his flesh?" (Job 31, 31). Wherefore this also Christ hath done, to lead us to a closer friendship, and to show His love for us; He hath given to those who desire Him not only to see Him, but even to touch, and eat Him, and fix their teeth in His flesh, and to embrace Him, and satisfy all their love. Let us then return from that table like lions breathing fire, having become terrible to the devil; thinking on our Head, and on the love which He hath shown for us. Parents often entrust their offspring to others to feed; "but I," saith He, "do not so, I feed you with Mine own flesh, desiring that you all be nobly born, and holding forth to you good hopes for the future. For He who giveth out Himself to you here, much more will do so hereafter. I have willed to become your Brother, for your sake I shared in flesh and blood, and in turn I give out to you the flesh and the blood by which I became your kinsman."

This blood causeth the image of our King to be fresh with us, produceth beauty unspeakable, permitteth not the nobleness of our souls to waste away, watering it continually, and nourishing it. The blood derived from our food becomes not at once blood, but something else; while this doth not so, but straightway watereth our souls, and working in them some mighty power. This blood, if rightly taken, driveth away devils, and keepeth them afar from us, while it calleth to us Angels and the Lord of Angels. For wherever they see the Lord's blood, devils, flee, and Angels run together. This blood poured forth washed clean all the world; many wise sayings did the blessed Paul utter concerning it in the Epistle to the Hebrews. This blood cleansed the secret place, and the Holy of Holies. And if the type of it had such great power in the temple of the Hebrews, and in the midst of Egypt, when smeared on the doorposts, much more the reality. This blood sanctified the golden altar; without it the high priest dared not enter into the secret place. This blood consecrated priests, this in types cleansed sins. But if it had such power in the types, if death so shuddered at the shadow, tell me how would it not have dreaded the very reality? This blood is the salvation of our souls, by this the soul is washed, by this is beautiful, by this is inflamed, this causeth our understanding to be more bright than fire, and our soul more beaming than gold; this blood was poured forth and made heaven accessible.

Awful in truth are the Mysteries of the Church, awful in truth is the Altar. A fountain went forth out of Paradise sending forth material rivers; from this table springeth up a fountain which sends forth rivers spiritual. By the side of this fountain are planted not fruitless willows, but trees reaching even to heaven, bearing fruit ever timely and undecaying. If any be scorched with heat, let him come to the side of this fountain and cool his burning. For it quencheth drought, and comforteth all things that are burnt up, not by the sun, but by the fiery darts. For it hath its beginning from above, and its source is there, whence also its water floweth. Many are the streams of that fountain which the Comforter sendeth forth, and the Son is the Mediator, not holding mattock to clear the way, but opening our minds. This fountain is a fountain of light, spouting forth rays of truth. By it stand the Powers on high looking upon the beauty of its streams, because they more clearly perceive the power of the things set forth, and the flashings unapproachable. For as when gold is being molten, if one should (were it possible) dip in it his hand or his tongue, he would immediately render them golden; thus, but in much greater degree, doth what here is set forth work upon the soul. Fiercer than fire the river boileth up, yet burneth not, but only baptizeth that on which it layeth hold. This blood was ever typified of old in the altars and sacrifices of righteous men. This is the price of the world, by This Christ purchased to Himself the Church, by This He has adorned Her all. For as a man buying servants giveth gold for them, and again, when he desireth to deck them out, doth this also with gold; so Christ hath purchased us with His blood, and adorned us with His blood. They who share this blood stand with the Angels and Archangels and the Powers that are above, clothed in Christ's own kingly robe, and having the armor of the Spirit. Nay, I have not as yet said any great thing: they are clothed with the King Himself.

Now as this is a great and wonderful thing, so if thou approach it with pureness, thou approachest for salvation; but if with an evil conscience, for punishment and vengeance. "For," It saith, "he that eateth and drinketh unworthily" of the Lord, "eateth and drinketh judgment to himself" (1 Cor. 11,29); since if they who defile the kingly purple are punished equally with those who rend it, it is not unreasonable that they who receive the Body with unclean thoughts should suffer the same punishment as those who rent it with the nails. Observe at least how fearful a punishment Paul declareth, when he saith, "He that despised Moses' law dieth without mercy under two or three witnesses; of how much sorer punishment, suppose ye, shall he be thought worthy, who hath trodden under foot of the Son of God, and hath counted the blood of the covenant, wherewith he was sanctified, an unholy thing?" (Heb. 1, 28). Take we then heed to ourselves, beloved, we who enjoy such blessings; and if we desire to utter any shameful word, or perceive ourselves hurried away by wrath or any like passion, let us consider of what things we have been deemed worthy, of how great a Spirit we have partaken, and this consideration shall be a sobering of our unreasonable passions. For how long shall we be nailed to present things? How long shall it be before we rouse ourselves? How long shall we neglect our own salvation? Let us bear in mind of what things Christ has deemed us worthy, let us give thanks, let us glorify Him, not by our faith alone, but also by our very works, that we may obtain the good things that are to come, through the grace and loving kindness of our Lord Jesus Christ, by whom and with whom, to the Father and the Holy Ghost be glory, now and ever and world without end. Amen.

SAINT JOHN CHRYSOSTOM ON THE VANITY OF EARTHLY WEALTH

From his first Sermon on Eutropius

"Vanities of vanities, all is vanity"—it is always seasonable to utter this, but more especially at the present time. Where are now the brilliant surroundings of thy consulship? Where are the gleaming torches? Where is the dancing, and the noise of dancers' feet, and the banquets and the festivals? Where are the garlands and the curtains of the theatre? Where is the applause which greeted thee in the city, where the acclamation in the hippodrome and the flatteries of spectators? They are gone—all gone: a wind has blown upon the tree shattering down all its leaves, and showing it to us quite bare, and shaken from its very roots; For so great has been the violence of the blast, that it has given a shock to all those fibres of the tree and threatens to tear it up from the roots. Where now are your feigned friends? Where are your drinking parties, and your suppers? Where is the swarm of parasites, and the wine which used to be poured forth all day long, and the manifold dainties invented by your cooks? Where are they who courted your power and did and said everything to win your favor? They were all mere visions of the night, and dreams which have vanished with the dawn of day: they were spring flowers, and when the spring was over they all withered: they were a shadow which has passed away—they were a smoke which has dispersed, bubbles which have burst, cobwebs which have been rent in pieces. Therefore we chant continually this spiritual song—"Vanity of vanities, all is vanity." For this saying ought to be continually written on our walls, and garments, in the market place, and in the house, on the streets, and on the doors and entrances, and above all on the conscience of each one, and to be a perpetual theme for meditation. And inasmuch as deceitful things, and maskings and pretence seem to many to be realities it behooves each one every day both at supper and at breakfast, and in social assemblies to say to his neighbor and to hear his neighbor say in return "vanity of vanities, all is vanity."

Was not I continually telling thee that wealth was a runaway? But you would not heed me. Did I not tell thee that it was an unthankful servant? But you would not be persuaded. Behold actual experience has now proved that it is not only a runaway, an ungrateful servant, but also a murderous one, for it is this which has caused thee now to fear and tremble. Did I not say to thee when you continually rebuked me for speaking the truth," "I love thee better than they who do flatter thee?" "I who reprove thee care more for thee than they who pay thee court?" Did I not add to these words by saying that the wounds of friends were more to be relied upon than the voluntary kisses of enemies? If you had submitted to my wounds, their kisses would not have wrought thee this destruction: for my wounds work health, but their kisses have produced an incurable disease. Where are now thy cup-bearers, where are they who cleared the way for thee in the market place, and sounded thy praises endlessly in the ears of all?   They have fled, they have disowned thy friendship, they are providing for their own safety by means of thy distress. But I do not act thus, nay in thy misfortune I do not abondon thee, and now when you are fallen I protect and tend thee. And the Church which you treated as an enemy has opened her bosom and received thee into it; whereas the theatres which you courted, and about which you were oftentimes indignant with me have betrayed and ruined thee. And yet I never ceased saying to thee, "Why doest thou these things?" "Thou art exasperating the Church, and casting thyself down headlong," yet thou didst hurry away from all my warnings. And now the hippodromes, having exhausted thy wealth, have whetted the sword against thee, but the Church which experienced thy untimely wrath is hurrying in every direction, in her desire to pluck thee out of the net.

And I say these things now not as trampling upon one who is prostrate, but from a desire to make those who are still standing more secure; not by way of irritating the sores of one who has been wounded, but rather to preserve those who have not yet been wounded in sound health; not by way of sinking one who is tossed by the waves, but as instructing those who are sailing with a favorable breeze, so that they may not become overwhelmed. And how may this be effected? By observing the vicissitudes of human affairs. For even this man, had he stood in fear of vicissitude, would not have experienced it; but whereas neither his own conscience, nor the counsels of others wrought any improvement in him, do ye at least who plume yourselves on your riches profit by his calamity: for nothing is weaker than human affairs. Whatever term therefore one may employ to express their insignificance it will fall short of the reality; whether he calls them smoke, or grass, or a dream, or spring flowers, or by any other name; so perishable are they and more naught than nonentities but that together with their nothingness they have also a very perilous element we have a proof before us.

For who was more exalted than this man? Did he not surpass the whole world in wealth? Had he not climbed to the very pinnacle of distinction? Did not all tremble and fear before him? Yet lo! he has become more wretched than the prisoner, more pitiable than the menial slave, more indigent than the beggar wasting away with hunger, having every day a vision of sharpened swords and of the criminal's grave, and the public executioner leading him out to his death; and he does not even know if he once enjoyed past pleasure, nor is he sensible even of the sun's ray, but at midday his sight is dimmed as if he were encompassed by the densest gloom. But even let me try my best, I shall not be able to present to you in language the suffering which he must naturally undergo, in the hourly expectation of death. But indeed what need is there of any words from me, when he himself has clearly depicted this for us as in a visible image? For yesterday when they came to him from the royal court intending to drag him away by force, and he ran for refuge to the holy furniture, his face was then, as it is now, no better than the countenance of one dead: and the chattering of his teeth, and the quaking and quivering of his whole body, and his faltering voice, and stammering tongue, and in fact his whole appearance were suggestive of one whose soul was petrified.

Saint John of the Cross
Confessor, Doctor of the Church

1 5 9 1

(November 24)

THE LIFE OF St. John of the Cross is so closely connected with the history of the Carmelite Order that it is difficult to understand the former without some knowledge of the latter. For many centuries devout hermits had lived their solitary lives of contemplation on Mount Carmel in Palestine. In the second half of the 12th century they became organized into a community, and in 1210 they accepted a rule of life that was prepared for them by St. Albert, the Latin Patriarch of Jerusalem, who was then living at Tyre, a town on the Palestinian coast just a little north of Mount Carmel. This original rule of the Carmelites, which is ordinarily called the "Primitive Rule," was very austere and penitential as befitted a group of men who wished to give up the world completely and devote themselves solely to a life of prayer and penance. Within a few decades several separate communities of these monks were established in various parts of Palestine. On account of the church dedicated to the Blessed Virgin Mary at their original foundation they became known as "The Friars (that is, the Brothers) of the Order of Our Lady of Mount Carmel."

When in the course of the 13th century the Saracens conquered most of Palestine from the Crusaders, many of these Carmelite monks, who had not been killed there by the infidels, fled to Sicily and Italy where they established new monasteries. Other Carmelite monasteries were soon founded in all parts of Europe, including England. At the first general meeting or "chapter" of their order in 1247, an Englishman, St. Simon Stock, was elected General of all the Carmelite Friars. This is the saint to whom Mary gave the "Scapular of Our Lady of Mount Carmel" or the "brown scapular," as it is commonly called.

In order to facilitate the work of his friars in the ministry and in teaching, St. Simon Stock obtained from the Pope a "mitigation" or lessening of some of the austerities of the original rule. This new rule which is known as the "Mitigated Rule" in distinction to the "Primitive Rule," would still be considered quite strict from a modern viewpoint. However, it did change the Carmelites from an essentially contemplative order to an essentially "active" one, that is, one engaged in the active ministry.

In the course of the next three centuries further "mitigations" were introduced, and in many monasteries the friars, though still good and devout men, lived a life which their spiritual ancestors of Mount Carmel would have considered quite lax. Several attempts to "reform" or correct these abuses were made, but without much success. That is where St. Teresa of Avila and St. John of the Cross appeared on the scene. Neither of these two saints ever left their native country of Spain, but through their efforts many monasteries and convents where the Primitive Rule was observed by the Carmelite friars and nuns were founded, not only in Spain but in several other countries of Europe. Their restoration of the Primitive Rule is known as the Carmelite "reform." One of the characteristics of the "reformed" or more austere friars and nuns is the use of sandals on their bare feet instead of shoes and stockings. Hence their branch of the Order is called the "Discalced" or "barefooted" Carmelites, as distinguished from the branch still observing the Mitigated Rule, and which is called the "Calced" or "shoe-wearing" Carmelites. To this day both branches are flourishing throughout the world, especially in America.

The Carmelite nuns had been founded in the 15th century, and naturally at that time they observed the Mitigated Rule. When St. Teresa became a Carmelite nun in the Convent of the Incarnation at Avila (in Old Castile) she, too, lived according to this rule. However, finding that it allowed far too much contact with the world to permit her to devote herself to prayer and contemplation, she was inspired and, finally, after much difficulty, was able to establish a number of convents of nuns where the Primitive Rule of the Carmelites was observed in all its rigor.

While Teresa was founding a convent of her New Rule at Medina del Campo, about a hundred miles north of Avila, a young Carmelite friar came to speak with her about his longing to lead a more secluded and austere life than was possible among his fellow friars who observed the Mitigated Rule. He had heard of her success in establishing convents of Carmelite nuns where the Primitive Rule of their order was zealously observed. Doubting if it were feasible to found similar monasteries among the Carmelite friars, he was thinking of leaving them and joining the Carthusian monks. Teresa had talked with him for only a few minutes when she joyously realized that she had found a treasure. She had already met another friar, Antonio del Campo, a prior of one of the Carmelite monasteries in Spain who was also desirous of following the Primitive Rule. So she begged her new acquaintance to wait until a place could be found where these two friars could begin a new monastery that would return to the observance of the Primitive Rule. He would please God more by remaining a Carmelite, she told him, than by taking off the habit of Our Lady of Mount Carmel, the Mother of God, to whom he always had a great devotion. He promised to wait, but only on condition, he added, that there would not be too long a delay.

That evening at recreation Teresa happily said to her nuns: "Daughters, we have won a friar and a half!"

The "half!" was Juan de San Matias (John of St. Matthias), who was less than five feet tall. Despite his diminutive size, he was to become a spiritual giant. Under his later name of Juan de

Cruz, or John of the Cross, he is now a Saint and a Doctor (or teacher) of the Church whose writings on mystical theology have won for him world-wide fame.

John was born on June 24, 1542, at Fontiveros, a little town about thirty miles north of Avila (in Old Castile), the youngest of three children. His father, Gonzalo de Yepes, was of an *hidalgo* family (that is, of the lesser nobility), by whom he was disowned for marrying a poor girl of the peasant class, Catalina Alvarez. John's parents made a living as silk weavers. Gonzalo died while John was still a little boy, and Catalina struggled in extreme poverty to raise her three children. At Medina del Campo, where she settled after the death of her husband, John was apprenticed to an artisan and had but little time to go to the town school for poor boys. What free time he had he spent in prayer and in visiting the sick in the hospital. The man in charge of this hospital was fond of him and arranged for him to attend the Jesuit school in Medina while working part-time at the hospital.

After seven years spent in the care of the sick and in studying with the Jesuits, John asked to be received and was admitted into the Carmelite monastery at Medina. He always led an extremely mortified and prayerful life and longed to give himself entirely to God. His deep devotion to the Mother of God led him to choose the Order of Our Lady of Mount Carmel rather than another order for his religious life. He entered the Carmelite novitiate in 1563 and took his vows the next year. His request to remain as a lay brother was denied him. After studying theology for three years at the great university of Salamanca, some sixty miles northwest of Avila, he was ordained a priest in 1567. While he had obtained permission to follow the austere Primitive Rule of the Carmelites and had known the rapture of mystical contemplation amid the supreme denial of self, he felt dissatisfied with the lax surroundings in which he lived among his fellow Carmelites of the Mitigated Observance. Therefore, as said above, he would have left them to join the Carthusians if Teresa of Avila had not dissuaded him from taking this step.

Finally on the first Sunday of Advent in 1568, with the permission of their higher superiors, John of the Cross, Antonio del Campo, and a lay brother, opened the first monastery of the Discalced Carmelites. It was nothing but a poor hut hardly fit for habitation, but the joy of its inmates knew no bounds. Teresa had to restrain their zeal for self-denial which even to her seemed excessive. They could not, however, keep their heavenly joy to themselves; they went about the countryside preaching the love of God to the poor peasant folk.

Spiritual joy is contagious. Soon other poor monasteries of Discalced Carmelite friars sprang up in various towns of Spain under the guidance of John and Teresa, but the little friar who took "the Cross" as his title never really liked being the superior of any of them. He was happiest when he was the last and least of his brothers. For him the only proof of genuine love was sacrifice, and thus his constant prayer was: "Lord, to suffer and be despised for love of Thee!" God, too, heard his prayer and granted his request in a way that only John of the Cross could have accepted with joyful gratitude.

First, there was the outrageous treatment he received from his fellow friars who still lived according to the Mitigated Rule. There is no need of being too hard on them. Their viewpoint and conduct are understandable, though hardly commendable. They had entered the religious life with the intention of living according to the Mitigated Rule and they had no wish to change their manner of life. Yet they feared that, if their barefooted brethren of the Primitive Observance became too numerous, all of them would be forced to keep this strict rule. They therefore succeeded in having their Father Provincial command John of the Cross to go back to his home monastery of Medina del Campo. However, John was ordered by the Apostolic Delegate, who was all in favor of the reform movement among the Carmelites, not to return there. John obeyed the Pope's representative rather than his Provincial Superior. Thereupon, during the night of December 3, 1577, he was taken prisoner by the "unreformed" friars and thrown into a dark cell in the Carmelite monastery at Toledo which is on the banks of the Tagus River about fifty miles south of Madrid. The treatment given to rebellious monks in the Middle Ages was anything but lenient, and in sixteenth-century Spain the tradition was still carried on in all its harshness. John was given scarcely enough food to keep him alive. Once a week he was publicly flogged till his back was covered with blood. Yet in all this his spirit soared to the most sublime heights. Here in his prison cell he wrote some of his greatest poems—short lyrics, perfect in their rhythm, splendid in their finely chiseled language.

After nine months John made his escape under what was, according to some accounts, the direct guidance of Our Lady. Mary herself, it is said, told him to escape and "showed him in spirit" a window high in a gallery above the Tagus River. At any rate, it was a miracle that in his weakened condition he was able at all to get out of his monastery prison. At the appropriate hour he made a rope out of two old blankets and his tunic and obeying an "interior voice," climbed through a small window. Suddenly, as he worked his way down the rope, he realized it was too short! He dangled, a tiny, pitiful figure, above the rock-edged river, and then jumped. He landed unharmed, but to his dismay, in the courtyard of another house with more walls barring his way to freedom. Miracle or not, it must have required superhuman strength for a frail, little man who was almost dead from exhaustion to scale those walls and walk almost a hundred miles to Avila where Teresa's good nuns saw to it that he was hidden till the storm blew over.

Peace was at last restored between the Discalced and the Calced Carmelites by the establishment of a separate province with its own Provincial Superior for the friars of the Primitive Observance. This led eventually to the Carmelites being divided into two distinct Orders, an outcome which neither Teresa nor John had ever intended.

The sufferings of John of the Cross, however, were not over. Since he himself had no desire of ruling, Father Jerome Gratian, who was one of his early companions and a good friend of Teresa, became Provincial of the Discalced Carmelites. Jerome, like John himself, favored the combination of a certain amount of missionary work with the strict monastic life of the friars. Yet another group of the Discalced, under the lead of the rigorist Nicholas Doria, interpreted the Primitive Rule to mean that the friars should be strictly cloistered and not engage in any missionary work at all. After the death of St. Teresa in 1582 the rigorists at first won out. Jerome was deprived of his office, and John was punished for having sided with him. He who had always prayed that he might suffer for love of the Lord now found himself persecuted by the very friars of the Order that he himself had founded. John's last years were spent in intense suffering from various physical ailments in the poor Carmelite monastery at Ubeda of Andalusia, in southern Spain, under a superior who had a strong dislike for him and treated him quite harshly. However, through it all John of the Cross sang with joy in his heart for the love of God who is Love personified, till on the 14th of December in 1591 his pure and innocent soul that had so often been rapt in mystic contemplation was called to the eternal sight of God face to face. No doubt he then experienced the truth of what he had written seven years earlier: "Perfect love of God makes death welcome and most sweet to the soul. He who loves thus dies with ardent longing, his soul in impetuous flight mounting up with vehement desire to its beloved. The rivers of love in the heart now swell almost beyond bounds, about to enter into the ocean of love. The soul seems already to behold that glory, and everything within her seems to turn to love, now that there remains no other separation than a thin web and the prison of the body has almost been broken open."

Like his crucified Savior whose glorious triumph came only after His seeming defeat, so also John of the Cross had but little apparent success until he had drained in death the last dregs of suffering and humiliation. Yet scarcely was he dead when his heroic sanctity was acknowledged by all. With unquestionable

miracles done through his intercession, he was beatified by Clement X in 1675, canonized by Benedict XIII in 1726, and declared a Doctor of the Church by Pius XI in 1926. If these dates
seem rather long after his death, it must be remembered that the
Church wished to be absolutely certain of the orthodoxy of his
writings, and a thorough study and examination of them took
considerable time.

John of the Cross published nothing during his life. In fact, he
never wrote anything at all with the thought that it would eventually be published. The only reason he recorded his thoughts in
prose and poetry was that the Carmelite nuns had begged him to
do this in order that they might be led by him on the higher
paths of mystical prayer. After his death his surviving manuscripts were gathered together and first published in 1619. His
major prose works were given the titles of *The Ascent of Mount
Carmel; The Dark Night of the Soul; The Living Flame of Love,*
and *The Spiritual Canticle.*

John had relatively little formal education, and his writings
show scant knowledge of the Fathers of the Church beyond the
selections from their works which are contained in the Roman
Breviary. Practically the only written source that he used was
the Bible, of which he had a profound knowledge. He apparently
knew nothing of the earlier writers on mystical theology. Although
entirely in line with the tradition of the Church, like St. Teresa,
he based his mystical theology almost wholly on his own experience. For John, the essential condition for mystical union with
God in contemplation lies in being emptied of every last particle
of self-love. His desire for suffering and humiliation, therefore,
had nothing of the morbid about it. They were merely means of
stripping oneself of every inclination for bodily comfort and the
deceitful mental pleasure that comes from pride. Even the natural
happiness that may be felt in prayer must be taken from the
soul before it is pure enough to enjoy the spiritual embraces of
the all-holy God; hence, the need for "the dark night of the soul"
in which the true mystic is deprived of even the spiritual consola-

tions that come from conscious thought and imagination. All these higher stages of the mystical life are granted solely as pure gifts from God. No mortal man can reach them by his own efforts. At best, he can only dispose himself for the reception of these gifts by absolute self-denial. Yet the good Lord is never outdone in generosity; He gives to those who ask and opens to those who knock. St. Teresa's humble little "half friar," not despite, but because of his own share in the sufferings and degradation of Christ's cross, had on earth a keener foretaste of heavenly bliss than is given to few men to experience. To those who have the courage to follow him on the hard path of utter self-denial, his luminous writings shine like a beacon light to guide their steps through *the dark night of the soul* to the mystic dawn where the lover is united to the Beloved.

From

"ASCENT OF MOUNT CARMEL"

St. John of the Cross

We have now to describe the detachment and purity of three faculties of the soul and for this are necessary a far greater knowledge and spirituality than mine, in order to make clear to spiritual persons how straight is this road which, said Our Saviour, leads to life; so that they may be persuaded hereof and not marvel at the emptiness and detachment to which, in this night, we have to abandon the faculties.

To this end must be carefully noted the words which Our Saviour used, in the seventh chapter of S. Matthew, concerning this road, as follows: *Quam augusta porta, et arcta via est, quae ducit ad vitam, et pauci sunt, qui inveniunt eam.* This signifies: How straight is the gate and how narrow the way that leadeth unto life, and few there be who find it! In this passage we must carefully note the emphasis and insistence which are contained in that word. *Quam.* For it is as if He had said: In truth the way is very straight, more so than you think. And likewise it is to be noted that He says first that the gate is straight, to make it clear that, in order for the soul to enter this gate, which is Christ, and which comes at the beginning of the road, the will must first be straight and detached in all things sensual and temporal, and God must be loved above them all; which belongs to the night of sense, as we have said.

He next says the road is narrow—that is to say, the road of perfection—in order to make it clear, to travel upon the road of perfection, the soul has not only to enter by the straight gate, emptying itself of things of sense, but that it has also to constrain itself, freeing and disengaging itself completely in that which pertains to the spirit. And thus we can apply what He says of the straight gate to the sensual part of man; and what He says of the narrow road we can understand of the spirit or rational part; and, when He says 'Few there be who find it,' the reason of this must be noted, which is that there are few who can enter, and desire to enter, into this complete detachment and emptiness of spirit. For this path ascending the high mountain of perfection leads upward, and is narrow, and therefore requires such travellers as have no burden weighing upon them with respect to lower things, neither aught that embarrasses them with respect to higher things; and as this is a matter wherein we must seek after and attain to God alone, God alone must be the object of our search and attainment.

Hence it is clearly seen that the soul must not only be disencumbered from that which belongs to the creatures, but likewise, as it travels, must be annihilated and detached from all that belongs to its spirit. Wherefore Our Lord, instructing us and leading us into this road, gave, in the eighth chapter of S. Mark, that wonderful teaching of which I think it may almost be said that, the more necessary it is for spiritual persons, the less it is practised by them. As this teaching is so important and so much to our purpose, I shall reproduce it here in full, and expound it according to its real and spiritual sense. He says, then, thus: *Si quis vult me sequi, deneget semetipsum: et tollat crucem suam, et sequatur me. Qui enim volurit animam suam salvam facere, perdet eam: qui autem perdiderit animam suam propter me . . . salvam faciet eam.* This signifies: If any man will follow My road, let him deny himself and take up his cross and follow Me. For he that will save his soul shall lose it; but he that loses it for My sake, shall gain it.

Oh, that one might show us how to understand, practise and experience what this counsel is which our Saviour here gives us concerning the denial of ourselves, so that spiritual persons might see in how different a way they should conduct themselves upon this road from that which many of them think proper! For they believe that any kind of retirement and reformation of life suffices; and others are content with practising the virtues and continuing in prayer and pursuing mortification; but they attain not to detachment and poverty or denial or spiritual purity (which are all one), which the Lord here commends to us; for they prefer feeding and clothing their natural selves with spiritual feelings and consolations, to stripping themselves of all things, and denying themselves all things, for God's sake. For they think that it suffices to deny themselves worldly things without annihilating and purifying themselves of spiritual attachments. Wherefore it comes to pass that, when there presents itself to them any of this solid and perfect spirituality, consisting in the annihilation of all sweetness in God, in aridity, distaste and trial, which is the true spiritual cross, and the detachment of the spiritual poverty of Christ, they flee from it as from death, and seek only sweetness and delectable communion with God. This is not self-denial and detachment of spirit, but spiritual gluttony. Herein they become spiritually enemies of the cross of Christ; for true spirituality seeks for God's sake that which is distasteful rather than that which is delectable; and inclines itself rather to suffering than to consolation; and desires to go without all blessings for God's sake rather than to possess them;

and to endure aridities and afflictions rather than to enjoy
sweet communications, knowing that this is to follow Christ
and to deny oneself, and that the other is perchance to seek
oneself in God, which is clean contrary to love. For to seek
oneself in God is to seek the favors and refreshments of God;
but to seek God in oneself is not only to desire to be without
both of these for God's sake, but to incline oneself to choose,
for Christ's sake, all that is most distasteful, whether as to
God or as to the world; and this is love of God.

Oh that someone could tell us how far Our Lord desires
this self-denial to be carried! It must be like to death and
annihilation, temporal, natural and spiritual, in all things that
the will esteems, wherein consists all self-denial. And it is
this that Our Lord meant when He said: He that will save
his life, the same shall lose it. That is to say: He that will
possess anything or seek anything for himself, the same shall
lose it; and he that loses his soul for My sake, the same shall
gain it. That is to say: He that for Christ's sake renounces all
that his will can desire and enjoy, and chooses that which is
most like to the Cross (which the Lord Himself, through St.
John, describes as hating his soul), the same shall gain it. And
this His Majesty taught to those two disciples who went and
begged Him for a place on His right hand and on His left;
when, giving them no reply to their request for such glory,
He offered them the cup which He had to drink, as a thing
more precious and more secure upon this earth than is
fruition.

This cup is the death of the natural self, which is attained
through the soul's detachment and annihiliation, in order that
the soul may travel by this narrow path, with respect to all
that can belong to it according to sense, as we have said; and
according to the spirit, as we shall now say; that is, in its
understanding and in its enjoyment and in its feeling. And,
as a result, not only is the soul detached as to all this, but,
having this spiritual help, it is not hindered upon the narrow
road, since there remains to it naught else than self-denial (as
the Saviour explains), and the Cross, which is the staff whereby one may reach Him, and whereby the road is greatly light-

ened and made easy. Wherefore Our Lord said through S.
Matthew: My yoke is easy and My burden is light; which
burden is the cross. For if a man resolve to submit himself
to carrying this cross—that is to say, if he resolves to desire in
truth to meet trials and to bear them in all things for God's
sake, he will find in them all great relief and sweetness wherewith he may travel upon this road, detached from all things
and desiring nothing. Yet, if he desire to possess anything,—
with any feeling of attachment, he is not detached and has
not denied himself in all things; and thus he will be unable
to walk along this narrow path or to climb upward by it.

I would, then, that I could convince spiritual persons that
this road to God consists not in a multiplicity of meditations
nor in ways or methods of such, nor in consolations, although
these things may in their own way be necessary to beginners;
but that it consists only in the one thing that is needful, which
is the ability to deny oneself truly, according to that which
is without and to that which is within, giving oneself up to
suffering for Christ's sake, and to total annihilation. For the
soul that thus denies itself will achieve this suffering and annihilation, and more also, and will likewise find more than
suffering and annihilation therein. And if a soul be found
wanting in this exercise, which is the sum and root of the
virtues, all its other methods are so much wandering about in
a maze, and profiting not at all, although its meditations and
communications may be as lofty as those of the angels. For
progress comes not save through the imitation of Christ, Who
is the Way, the Truth and the Life, and no man comes to the
Father but by Him, even as He Himself says through S.
John. And elsewhere He says: I am the door; by Me if any
man enter in he shall be saved. Wherefore, as it seems to me,
any spirituality that would fain walk in sweetness and with
ease, and flees from the imitation of Christ, is worthless.

And, as I have said that Christ is the Way, and that this
Way is death to our natural selves, in things both of sense
and of spirit, I will now explain how we are to die, following
the example of Christ, for He is our example and light.
In the first place, it is certain that He died as to sense,

spiritually, in His life; and also, naturally, at His death. For, as He said, He had not in His life where to lay His head, and, in His death, this was even truer.

In the second place, it is certain that, at the moment of His death, He was likewise annihilated in His soul, and was deprived of any relief and consolation, since His Father left Him in the most intense aridity, according to the lower part of His nature. Wherefore He had perforce to cry out, saying: My God! My God! Why hast Thou forsaken Me? This was the greatest desolation, with respect to sense, that He had suffered in His life. And thus He wrought herein the greatest work that He had ever wrought, whether in miracles or in mighty works, during the whole of His life, either upon earth or in Heaven, which was the reconciliation and union of mankind, through grace, with God. And this was, as I say, at the moment and the time when this Lord was most completely annihilated in everything. That is to say, with respect to human reputation; since, when they saw Him die, they mocked Him rather than esteemed Him; and also with respect to nature, since His nature was annihilated when He died; and with respect to the spiritual consolation and protection of the Father, since at that time He forsook Him, that He might pay the whole of man's debt and unite him with God, being thus annihilated and reduced as it were to nothing. Wherefore David says concerning Him: *Ad nihilum redactus sum, et nescivi.* This he said that the truly spiritual man may understand the mystery of the gate and of the way of Christ, in order to be united with God, and may know that, the more completely he is annihilated for God's sake, according to these two parts, the sensual and the spiritual, the more completely is he united to God and the greater is the work which he accomplishes. And when he comes to be reduced to nothing, which will be the greatest extreme of humility, spiritual union will be wrought between the soul and God, which in this life is the greatest and the highest state attainable. This consists not, then, in refreshment and in consolations and spiritual feelings, but in a living death of the Cross, both as to sense and as to spirit—that is, both inwardly and outwardly.

Saint John the Evangelist
Apostle

c. 1 0 0

(December 27)

PROBABLY ONE OF the best known and certainly one of the best loved of the twelve apostles is Saint John, "the disciple whom Jesus loved." We know a good deal about him not only from the first three Gospels and the "Acts of the Apostles" where he is often mentioned by name, but also from his own Gospel even though his name is not mentioned therein. It is certain that the author of the Fourth Gospel refers to himself under the frequent term, "the disciple whom Jesus loved," as the final epilogue of this Gospel explicitly states: "This is the disciple . . . who has written these things" (21,24). Catholic tradition is unanimous in attributing the authorship of the Fourth Gospel to the apostle Saint John despite the objection which some non-Catholic scholars raise against its authenticity. In fact, it is because of his having written this Gospel that he is commonly called "Saint John the Evangelist" to distinguish him from Saint John the Baptist. On account of the sublime theological truths in his Gospel concerning the divinity of Jesus Christ and the eternal Word of God, the Greek Church also calls him "Saint John the Theologian." The corresponding English term, Saint John the Divine, is used more often in England than in America.

John was the brother of James the Greater, and these two are mentioned together several times in the Gospels as "the sons of

Zebedee." Their father Zebedee earned his livelihood catching fish in the Sea of Galilee, and the two sons were also fishermen. When Jesus called them to be His close companions in His ministry, they left their father and mother, their boats and their nets, to follow Him. Their mother, who toward the end of our Lord's public ministry tried to get Jesus to appoint her two sons, James and John, to the most important positions in His Kingdom, probably was called Salome. Since John is almost always mentioned after, not before his brother James, it is quite likely that he was younger than James. In fact, he may have been the youngest of all the apostles. There is no reason for thinking that the apostles were well on in years when Jesus called them to be His followers, despite the fact that artists generally portray them as hoary old men. Quite likely most, if not all, of them were younger than Jesus. St. John, as the youngest among them, would then probably have been only a teen-ager when Christ called him to be a disciple. This would also explain the tradition which says that John never married. When he first became acquainted with Jesus, he had not yet reached the age at which Jewish men were accustomed to take a wife. Saint Peter was certainly married—the Gospel speaks of his mother-in-law (Matt. 8,14)—and so in all probability were the other apostles with the exception of John. Perhaps it was his youth and celibacy that made him, humanly speaking, so attractive to our Lord.

In any case, John was certainly Christ's favorite disciple. He and his brother, James (the Greater), and Peter were the only apostles privileged to be with Jesus when He restored the little daughter of Jairus to life (Mark 5,37; Luke 8,51); when He let some of the splendor of His divinity illumine His human body in a transfiguration of glory (Matt. 17,1; Luke 9,28), and when He fell prostrate on the ground in an agony of grief and fear at Gethsemane (Matt. 26,37; Mark 14,33).

At the Last Supper, John reclined at the table directly next to, or more precisely, in front of Jesus, a position which he himself describes as "reclining in Jesus' bosom" or lap, even though there would, of course, have been some space between them. When John, at Peter's request, wished to ask Jesus secretly who the betrayer was, all he had to do was to bend his head back so that it would be near Jesus' breast (John 13,23f).

Elsewhere John is often mentioned in close connection with Peter, the prince of the apostles. Thus the "two of His disciples" (Mark 14,13) whom Jesus sent alone into Jerusalem to make preparations for the Last Supper were Peter and John (Luke 22, 8). John was probably "the other disciple who was known to the high priest," and who "went out and spoke to the portress and brought Peter in" the high priest's courtyard (John 18,16). So also, on the morning of our Lord's resurrection, when Mary Magdalene "came to Peter and to the other disciple whom Jesus loved" and told them that the Lord's tomb was empty, these two apostles ran to the tomb. As was to be expected of young John, he outran Peter and got there first. Quite prudently he did not touch the shroud of Christ. For him the position of this shroud was such that it convinced him that his Master must have passed through it in some mysterious manner without, in the least, disturbing the way it had been wrapped around His body; "he saw and believed" in the resurrection of Christ (John 20,2-8). A little later, when Jesus appeared to His apostles on the shore of the Sea of Galilee while they were fishing in a boat offshore, it was John who first recognized the risen Savior and said to Peter, "It is the Lord" (John 21,7). On this occasion, after Jesus had foretold to Peter that he would some day die a death similar to His own, Peter asked his Master what John's fate would be and was told that this was none of his business (John 21,18-23). Finally, in the history of the early Church in Jerusalem, John played a prominent part in company with Peter. He is with Peter when the latter cures a blind man at the gate of the temple, and the two of them are arrested by the Jewish rulers for preaching that Jesus of Nazareth is the Messiah (Acts 3-4).

After Philip the deacon had first brought the gospel of Christ to the Samaritans, "when the apostles in Jerusalem heard that

Samaria had received the word of God, they sent to them Peter and John" (Acts 8,14). Several years later, when St. Paul made his second official visit to Jerusalem fourteen years after his conversion, the only apostles whom he met there were James the Less, the bishop of Jerusalem and Peter and John, "who were considered the pillars," and who gave him the right hand of fellowship (Gal. 2,9).

The greatest sign of Christ's love for John no doubt was the bequeathing of His mother to His beloved disciple. As He hung dying on the Calvary's cross, "Jesus saw His mother and the disciple whom He loved standing by, and He said to His mother, 'Woman, behold thy son'; then He said to the disciple, 'Behold thy mother.' And from that hour the disciple took her into his home." (John 19,26f). Christian piety has rightly seen in this act of our Lord not merely His tender concern for the future care on earth of His dear mother, but also the giving of His own mother to all of us in the person of John as our heavenly mother.

Saint John is the author of three Epistles and of the "Book of Revelations" called the "Apocalypse," as well as of the Fourth Gospel. His three Epistles breathe the same spirit of love for God and love for neighbor that is so characteristic of his Gospel. His magnificent "Apocalypse" written to encourage the faithful to bear patiently the persecutions they must suffer for the sake of Christ, and to assure them of the ultimate victory of the Lamb of God over all the powers of hell and Satan, reveals a man who was deeply versed in the prophetic books of the Old Testament and who could speak the same divine fire that burned in the hearts of these seers of old. Though the "Apocalypse" was written while its author, now an old man, was living in exile on the little island of Patmos off the shore of western Asia Minor [where the emperor Domitian (81-96 A.D.) had banished him "because of the word of God and the testimony of Jesus" (Apoc. 1,9)], it still shows him as one of the "Sons of Thunder," one of the *Boanerges*, as Jesus had called him and his brother James for wanting to bring down fire from heaven on their Master's enemies (cf. Mark 3,17; Luke 9,49-56). This gives us quite a different picture of John than that painted by many artists who portray him with a sentimental and somewhat less than manly face.

St. John's symbol in Christian art is most commonly an eagle, symbolizing the soaring flight of the sublime thoughts in his Gospel. He is also sometimes shown as holding a cup from which a small snake emerges. This is based on a story told of him in the apocryphal "Acts of John." According to this legend the high priest of the goddess Diana at Ephesus once tried to kill him by giving him a cup of poisoned wine to drink. John blessed the cup, and the poison had no harmful affect upon him. This legend is probably the origin of the custom of giving a special "blessing of St. John" to wine, and sharing in the community of this blessed "cup of love" on his feast day.

A somewhat more reliable, though by no means certain, tradition is the story of "Saint John at the Latin Gate." This tells how the emperor Domitian had John arrested at Ephesus and brought to Rome for punishment. John was condemned to be boiled in a cauldron of seething oil, but God protected His devoted servant and changed the death-dealing oil into a refreshing bath so that the apostle suffered no harm. The feast on the 6th of May commemorating this event is really the anniversary of the dedication of the Church of St. John at the Latin Gate in Rome— a gate in the wall of Aurelian that was not built until two centuries after the time of St. John.

Both the story of the poisoned cup and that of the miraculous escape from a martyr's death are perhaps due to certain authentic events concerning St. John in the Gospels. There is, first of all, the question of our Lord to him, "Can you drink the cup (of suffering) that I am to drink?" and Christ's assurance that John would indeed drink of this cup (cf. Matt. 20,20-23). Then there are the words of Christ to Peter, who inquired about what death John would suffer: "If I wish him to remain until I come, what is it to thee?" The unknown second-century author of the apocryphal "Acts of John" evidently thought that this apostle must have, in some way connected with a cup or a cauldron, been exposed to martyrdom without dying as a martyr.

Of all the twelve apostles St. John is the only one whom the Church does not consider as having died a martyr's death. On his feast day which at least from the early Middle Ages, is celebrated two days after Christmas, white vestments (not the red ones for a martyr) are used. According to ancient tradition John spent the last decades of his long life at Ephesus in western Asia Minor. Here he returned after his banishment on Patmos, and here about the year 100, when he would have been nearly ninety years old, this disciple whom Jesus loved and whose ardent prayer, "Come, Lord Jesus, come!" closes the New Testament, heard the final "Come, follow Me" from the lips of his beloved Master Who had first called him on the shores of the Sea of Galilee. The once great city of Ephesus is today but a dismal ruin, but the Turkish name for its site, *Aya Soluk*, still recalls in distorted form the Greek name for the famous shrine that once stood here in honor of John *Hagiou Theologou*, "the Holy Theologian."

Saint John of God
Confessor
1 5 5 0
(March 8)

WHEN JOHN CIUDAD (later known as John of God) was born at Montemor-o-Novo in Portugal on March 8, 1495, the Iberian Peninsula of Spain and Portugal was witnessing stirring events. Three years before his birth, in 1492, the Spanish sovereigns, Ferdinand and Isabella, conquered Granada, the last stronghold of the Moors in southern Spain and in the same year (as every schoolboy knows) they sponsored Christopher Columbus' first voyage of discovery to America. Three years after John's birth, in 1498, the great Portuguese navigator, Vasco da Gama, first sailed around Africa and opened the sea road to the enormous wealth of India and Asia.

Although John's parents, Andrew Ciudad and Teresa Duarte, reared their only son in piety and virtue, even as a little boy he caught the spirit of adventure that was in the air and he longed to be off to distant lands for deeds of valor and glory. One day, when he was only eight years old, a journeying priest stayed overnight at the Ciudad's house. Before going to bed, this good man entertained his hosts with tales of the marvelous new world that their compatriots had discovered and of the heroic exploits that these men were performing in those faraway lands.

John listened with bated breath to the story. Acting on sudden impulse, as he was always to do in later life, he then and there decided to leave home at once and see this fabulous world for himself. His home town of Montemor-o-Novo (Mount Major the New) was a sleepy city situated some seventy miles east of Lisbon. Nothing ever happened here. Why wait until one became too old to enjoy adventure in the wide world? So the next morning, shortly after the priest bade farewell to the Ciudads, the eight-year-old boy slipped quietly out of the house and soon caught up with the priest. The latter must have thought that John had the permission of his parents to join him, otherwise he would hardly have taken the run-away boy along with him. In any case, the two went on together, day after day, across Portugal, over the mountains that form its eastern border, and well up the Tagus valley into Old Castile in western Spain. For twenty days all went well. The kindly peasants along their route gave food and lodging to the two travelers. Then at the Spanish village of Oropesa little John fell ill. The priest could not delay. Leaving the boy in the care of Senor Ferrus-y-Navas, the "Majoral" or master-shepherd of the flocks of the local count, he continued his journey alone.

The Majoral took pity on the homeless lad (who was soon cured of his illness) and accepted him as part of the family. Young John had learned his lesson; it would be long before he left his new home. However, he was much too far away from his parents — a good two hundred miles — to go back alone to them. So he lived with the Majoral's family, learning to read and write — the only formal schooling he ever received — and also more of his Christian religion and how to shepherd the flocks by himself in the hot sun and the cold, windy rain.

When John was twenty-six years old and had grown into a fine strong man, the Majoral feared losing the services of so valuable a shepherd. Besides, the Majoral's daughter had fallen in love with John. So this foster father of John, who had no son of his own, offered to adopt him and make him his heir if he would accept his daughter's hand in marriage. Surprisingly enough, John refused this very favorable offer. It can hardly be said that he was a confirmed bachelor, nor is there any reason to think that he was conscious of a supernatural motive for remaining unmarried. No doubt his refusal to marry the Majoral's daughter was ultimately due to the providence of God who wished to keep His servant free for much greater things. At that time though, John's only motive was to stay free for a more adventurous life in the world.

To get out of the embarrassing situation, John enlisted as a soldier in the army of Charles V, the King of Spain, who was then resisting an invasion of the French army which Francis I of France had sent across the border to avenge his allegely injured honor. In itself, this turned out to be only a minor war, not much more than a series of border skirmishes, but it proved to be a turning point in John's life.

Being a soldier was not the glamorous life of adventure that he had expected. There were long, hard marches, small and uncertain rations, and wearisome sentry duty. John found his companions in arms a rough, depraved lot who scoffed at him when he tried to say his prayers, or when he would not join them in their sinful revelry. Gradually he fell in with them, giving up his prayers, using their foul-mouthed language, and engaging in their drinking bouts, gambling, and revelry.

Then one day God's grace literally struck him down. While foraging near the enemy's lines, his horse suddenly bolted and threw him to the ground. When he came to his senses, the throbbing pain in his head and the blood running down his face told him that he had landed headfirst on a rock. His horse had long since run away. There he lay, alone and helpless, too weak to move. Either he would die of exhaustion, he thought, or the French would capture him. In the latter case he would either be put to death at once, or taken away to languish for years in a miserable dungeon. He was still Christian enough to want to die well. Thus he began to pray. The first prayer his good mother had taught him came back to his lips: "Holy Mary, Mother of God, pray for us sinners now and at the hour of our death!"

As he prayed, his whole life passed before his mind. What a sinner he had been! First as a boy he had run away from home, and then as a soldier he had committed so many terrible sins. If only God would rescue him now, he would surely amend his ways. Little by little, he regained his strength, and slowly he found his way back to his own lines. As soon as he could, he went to confession and made his peace with God. All the wicked ways were abandoned; no more gambling or drinking.

When his former companions saw the change in him, they were filled with disgust which quickly changed to hatred. He had even dared to chide them for their wicked ways. This was going too far, and they decided to get even with him. They soon found the opportunity. An officer had collected a large pile of booty which he naturally feared might be plundered in turn from him, so he kept a soldier on guard over it. When John's turn came for this sentry duty his vindictive enemies struck. While one of them lured him away for a few minutes on the pretext that he needed his help, the others removed a part of the goods and then reported to the officer that he had been robbed. The latter flew into a rage and ordered John to be hung at once on the nearest tree. At the last moment, with the noose already around the victim's neck, the chief commanding officer rode up and stopped the execution. However, the negligent sentry was still found guilty and sentenced to be stripped of his uniform and made to run the gauntlet between the soldiers.

The dishonorably discharged soldier, half dead from the beating he had received, trudged his way back to Oropesa. Once he had happily begged his way to this place when people gladly helped him as a little boy traveling with a priest, but now things were different. He did not mind sleeping in the fields. It was the cold refusal he got when he asked for a crust of bread that hurt him. In their eyes — in fact, in his own eyes, he was only a worthless tramp. His lesson in charity he learned the hard way. Who knows if a beggar is "deserving of charity" or not? Henceforth he would never refuse anyone anything.

Back home in Oropesa, John was warmly greeted by the Majoral and his daughter. Again he took up his old life of shepherding. Out on the hills he could give his thoughts to God and to the life of holiness and goodness he now hoped to live. Yet he still felt that he must do more than this to atone for his old sinful ways. So again he became a soldier, but this time in a holy crusade that the Pope had called for. The Moslem Turks were invading the Balkans and threatening Austria and even Italy. John marched with the imperial army into Hungary but the infidels became frightened and retreated. The war was called off.

This time, instead of going to Oropesa, John decided to return to his native town of Montemor-o-Novo in Portugal. Here there was no sign of his father and mother; in fact, no one seemed to remember his family. Finally an old man recognized him as his nephew and told him the sad news that soon after John had run away from home his brokenhearted mother died and his father then became a Franciscan lay brother, only to die a few years later himself. This was a crushing blow to the prodigal who now had to add to his already overheavy burden of sin the sense of guilt for having caused the untimely death of his good parents.

With nothing but sad memories left for him in Portugal, John turned back to Spain and again took work as a shepherd, but this time near Ayamonte, a town in the southwest corner of Spain. Here for two years, alone with the sheep, he thought back on his wasted life. He would have to make some heroic sacrifice to atone for all his years of sin. Suddenly he made up his mind: he would go to Morocco and spend his life in ransoming Christian captives from the Moors. Perhaps he might even take the place of one of these slaves, so he thought, and have the chance of martyrdom. So off he went to Gibraltar to take ship for Ceuta, the fortress city, then held by the Portuguese, on the opposite shore of the Strait. Here he met a noble family in great distress, that of Count Almeyda, who had been deprived of his estates by the king of Portugal and driven into exile with his wife and daughters. John at once offered to serve them without pay. When they were stricken with fever at Geuta, he nursed them back to health. With his own hard work he earned enough for their support.

The only labor he could find at Ceuta was construction work on the fortifications. Most of his fellow laborers were prisoners who were driven to their back-breaking tasks under the lash. Even the neighboring Moors were kinder to their slaves than were these so-called Christian masters to their Christian prisoners. When John's faith was badly shaken by this scandal, a good Franciscan friar whom he consulted advised him to leave Africa and return to Spain. This was fortunately made easier for him when, at the same time, Count Almeyda won a reprieve from his sovereign and no longer needed help.

Back in Gibraltar, which then belonged to Spain, John worked at first as a stevedore. Despite this hard labor in the midst of rough companions, he kept his heart constantly united with God in prayer. His spare time he now largely spent in reading good books. Sensing the need for good reading in that day when romantic novels were the rage among the people, he impulsively decided to sell good books. All that he could save from his wages he invested in the purchase of prayer books, catechisms, lives of the saints, and holy pictures. With a good sense of salesmanship, he also bought a certain number of inoffensive novels with which he could attract the attention of his prospective customers. When he finally had sufficient stock he gave up his job as a stevedore and, with a pack on his back, he became a traveling bookseller. Going from village to village to peddle his wares, he did quite well in his new business. The art of printing was not yet a hundred years old, and people were eager to buy up any kind of book as soon as it was printed. John, however, had no intention of making a rich business of this. For him the whole thing was primarily a missionary undertaking. Whenever a man or woman showed interest in his religious books, but lacked the money to buy them, he promptly gave them away for nothing. Canonized saints in the book business are rare indeed. No wonder then that

Catholic publishers and bookdealers looked upon St. John of God as their heavenly advocate and patron!

One day John had a wonderful and mysterious experience. As he was walking along the road with his pack of books he met a little boy who seemed very weary and footsore. With his usual compassion, this strong, kind man picked up the boy and carried him on his shoulders. Strangely the child seemed to grow heavier and heavier, and John began to feel ashamed of his unaccustomed feeling of weakness. A wayside fountain gave him a chance to rest. Putting the boy on the ground, he went to get him a drink of water, but as he again turned to him, an astonishing sight met his eyes. The boy was surrounded with radiance and in his hand was a pomegranate surmounted by a cross. "John of God," said the boy, offering him the cross, "Granada shall be your cross." With that the boy vanished. The good man thought in all honesty that he must have been dreaming. The Spanish word for "pomegranate" is *granada*. That's it, he thought; it must be merely my imagination. Yet, after all, it might also be God's way of telling me His divine will. So promptly John set out for the city of Granada, about a hundred miles northeast of Gibraltar.

John entered Granada in September of the year 1536. It was a memorable date, for this city was henceforth to be the scene of his great labors for God. Here John opened a small bookshop, but he also used to spend part of his working hours selling his wares in the market place and peddling them through the streets. Thus he soon became a well-known figure in the city. God had told him to go to Granada and he had obeyed. Although he was almost forty-one years old, he still did not know where his real vocation lay.

Then one day an unexpected thing happened to him. The famous preacher and spiritual director, Father John of Avila (a personal friend of Saints Teresa and Francis Borgia, and later to be beatified himself by the Church) came to Granada to give the sermon in the church of St. Sebastian on the feast of this Roman martyr. John, the ex-shepherd and ex-soldier now turned bookseller, went to hear the sermon. He was tremendously moved by the eloquent orator and his words: "We s h a l l never know peace of mind or find true happiness until we cast ourselves into the arms of our Maker." All his past sins overwhelmed him in a flood of contrition. Not only in the church but also on the street all the way back to his bookshop he gave vent to loud cries of grief. The secular books that he had in stock he destroyed; the religious ones he gave away for nothing. Taking Christ's words literally, he sold all that he had and distributed the money among the poor.

Day after day he continued his strange behavior in the streets, weeping and crying with loud moans and beating his breast savagely. He wanted everyone else to know what he really believed himself to be — the worst sinner on the earth. The demonstrative inhabitants of Granada were used to public displays of passionate feeling, but this was going too far. The more staid citizens eventually had the seemingly mad bookseller taken to the ward for the insane in the Royal Hospital of Granada. Far from resisting, John found this quite to his liking. Though he was, in a sense, the sanest man in all Granada, he thought that such a humiliation would be the best thing for his soul. Believing that the penance meted out to one by others is better than the penance that one afflicts on oneself, he gladly submitted to the "medicine" which was then the custom to give to the insane — a sound whipping given them when they did not behave themselves, or administered to them as a matter of routine every day. For forty days John endured this harsh treatment, the same length of time that Christ had fasted in the desert. The only thing that sustained him was his ardent desire to atone for his sins by sufferings and humiliations.

Then Father John of Avila, who was still in Granada, visited the Royal Hospital and to his surprise found his namesake there being treated as a madman. The latter, before being committed to the hospital, had consulted the learned priest on the state of his soul and had revealed to him his whole life and his holy aspirations. When Father John explained to the officials of the hospital that the well-known bookseller of Granada was only pretending to be crazy according to his own ideas of the folly of the Cross, they were willing to declare that their treatments had affected a cure in this patient and released him.

John now followed the advice of his spiritual director and stopped his carrying on like a madman. However, he decided not to leave the hospital. Instead of being a patient, he would work there without pay as a nurse or attendant. As in the other hospitals at that time, the care for the sick here left much to be desired. John was deeply moved to compassion for these poor suffering people. Day by day he went around among them, washing them and cleaning up their surroundings, giving them words of sympathy and consolation, speaking to them of God's love and forgiveness.

After two years spent in this self-sacrificing life of devoted care for the sick, two years of prayer for God's guidance, John finally knew where his true vocation lay. He would be an apostle not only of the sick, but of all the poor and downtrodden in Granada. From his earlier rounds as a bookseller through the streets and alleys of the city, he knew that there were numberless people among the paupers who were in too miserable a condition to be admitted into the Royal Hospital. Never for a moment did he doubt the words of Christ: "What you do for these, the least of my brethren, you do for me."

John now left the Royal Hospital to begin his new life of working for the outcasts of Granada, but first he must dedicate himself entirely to God and His Blessed Mother. He therefore went barefoot on a pilgrimage to the sanctuary of Our Lady of Guadalupe in central Spain, not to be confused with the still more famous shrine of Mary under the same name in Mexico. Arriving here late in the evening, several weeks after his departure from Granada, he found that the curtain had already been drawn in front of the miraculous statue of the Madonna. Nevertheless he humbly knelt and prayed before Mary, whose image he could not see. Suddenly the curtain was withdrawn and the ancient statue exposed to his view. John no doubt thought that some kindly person had done this favor for him, but the sacristan heard the sound of the curtain being pulled back and came to investigate. Seeing no one but John, who looked like a ragged tramp, he naturally thought that this was the villain who had taken this liberty. "Get out of here, you dirty scarecrow!" he yelled at him, while raising his foot to give him a good kick. To his horror, his leg suddenly became so stiff that he could not move it. John, however, went on praying as if no one were there. When the sacristan in his fright began to beg his forgiveness, John said gently, "Let us recite the 'Hail Holy Queen' together." As soon as they had finished this prayer the sacristan felt his leg come back to life and he ran to tell the prior that a saint was in the church. The latter, with his fellow Hieronymite monks, induced John to stay several days in their monastery. There is a tradition that on one of these days, as John was praying before Mary's miraculous statue, it seemed to come to life, and the Blessed Mother offered him the divine Babe whom she held in her arms and told him to wrap Him in swaddling clothes as an indication that she wished him to tend and clothe Christ in the persons of the poor.

Back again in Granada, John had no idea how he could ever get a hospital of his own started, but that he left to God. First he must earn some money himself to help the poor. He did not want to go back in the book business. On his pilgrimage to and from Granada he had supported himself by cutting and selling wood. The outskirts of Granada have plenty of wood. He would gather wood there and sell it in the city. Walking through the streets with a heavy load of wood on his back, he was again laughed at as a madman. For a moment he almost gave in to the temptation to become "respectable." Humiliations in themselves did not disturb him, but now he needed financial aid if he was to get even a little hospital started, and how could he ever get rich people to help him if they thought him crazy? Yet John knew that if God wanted this work done, it would be done in God's way, not by human prudence. So he not only let people laugh at him; he joined them in laughing at himself. Gradually it dawned on them. This fellow is no fool, even though he seems a bit queer. By day he sold his wood; by night he hunted out the poor and sick in whatever holes he could find them. It was little enough in a material way that he could give them, but his mere interest in them and his kindly sympathy filled these unwanted ones with a new thrill of joy and hope.

Then one day John saw an empty house with a sign: "House to let for lodging the poor." Here it was at last! The star of the Magi had finally led him to the house where he would find Jesus in the last and least of His brethren. This was the answer to all his prayers. His real life's work could begin, now that he was forty-five years old. Quickly he made arrangements for renting the house from its owner. The latter asked only a nominal sum; in fact, he was one of those who had seen through John's odd behavior and recognized the gold that lay under that rough exterior. After begging a small sum of money from a good priest, John fitted out the place with second-hand cots, mattresses and blankets to take care of forty-six patients. Now, to get his patients. He knew well enough where to find them, but it was not easy to get them to leave their slums. Gradually he coaxed a few of them to try his new "hospital." When these found that he was lenient and let them come and go as they pleased, they brought others in with them. Those that could not walk John carried on his shoulders, sometimes for miles across the city.

They also had to be fed, and that required money. He could not possibly support them by the little he earned as a woodseller. He would have to go begging for them. For him it was not so much a matter of begging as rather a job of peddling. He went through the city peddling the opportunity to practice charity. Now it was grace, not books, that he was offering to people, but he used the same method. With a sack on his back for holding the food he collected, and rattling the can he held in his hand for collecting coins, he hawked his wares with loud cries of "Do good for yourselves, brothers! Who wants to do good for himself? For the love of God, brothers, do good!" There was a ringing tone of joy in this cry. Why be a cringing beggar when one is offering people the rewards of heaven?

It was mostly in the evenings when the men were home from work that John went about the city on these begging tours. He had a good sense of timing and he knew that most of his help for the poor would have to come from the lowly laboring class, not from the rich. All day he spent with his sick, tending to their needs with the gentleness of a mother. He needed no special time to devote solely to prayer; he was always united in heart and mind with God. Late at night when all the others were asleep, he stayed up to mend their clothes. An hour's sleep on the floor was all the rest he needed. Since he always went barefoot as well as bareheaded, his own clothes consisted only of a worn-out shirt and ragged pants, with perhaps a patched-up coat in winter. Every time some friend gave him better clothes he changed them with the first beggar he met in the street.

Legends naturally grew up around such a man. He himself never spoke of anything marvelous happening to him. He honestly thought that no such wonders could possibly be connected with so great a sinner as he believed himself to be, but the people who lived with him would swear to the truth of these stories. One stormy night as John was returning home from his round of begging, he found a poor cripple huddled against the wall of a church trying to keep out of the cold rain. He knelt at once in the wet street to lift the unfortunate man up and carry him back, but in struggling to get on his feet he slipped and fell with the cripple on top of him. Though he never expected anyone to be near to help him, a noble young man appeared from nowhere and did him this good turn. Thanking him for this kindness, John added apologetically, "Brother, pardon my clumsiness. I have this lazy ass of a body to contend with that is too well

clothed and fed to do much work." The stranger smiled and turned to leave, but John spoke again: "Brother, give me at least
your name that I may remember your kind deed in my prayers."
By now a few people had come up and were standing about.
They heard the stranger say, "John, I am the Archangel Raphael.
God has given me the office of watching over you and over those
who help you in your work of serving the poor." With that he
vanished.

Some time later, when John had come home disconsolate because no one had given him any food and he had nothing for his
patients' supper, the door opened and a young man came in carrying a large basket of fine bread which he put on the table. The
patients stared in astonishment, not only at the noble visitor and
his welcome gift, but also at John who was gazing in silent love
at one he recognized as his archangel friend. The silence was at
last broken by Raphael. "My brother," he said, "take this bread
which heaven sends you. You and I belong to the same Order for
there are some men wearing ragged clothes who are equal to the
angels."

Wonderful as this is, a greater wonder once befell John. One
evening he picked up a sick man from the street and carried him
to the hospital. There, as he always did for any new patient, he
set him on a chair and began gently to wash his feet. Suddenly
in the foot that he held in his hand a gaping wound opened.
John knew, but he dared not raise his head to look up. "John,
My faithful servant," he heard a lovely Voice say, "do not be
afraid. I have come to show you my gratitude for the care you
take of My sick poor." Then John no longer held anything in
his hand. His Patient had vanished, but the room was filled with
such brilliant light that the men came in from the other room
shouting, "Fire! Fire!" John quieted them and told them not to
worry; it was their Lord who had visited them.

Soon the little hospital became much too small for John's
many patients and volunteer helpers, and he was able to get the
use of an old Carmelite monastery that had been abandoned by

its monks. Even the good people of Granada could not help laughing at the sight of the strange procession of John and his helpers and his less crippled patients carrying bedding, furniture and helpless patients on their backs to the new hospital.

The sick poor, however, formed only a part of John's apostolate. There was hardly a needy man, woman or child in the whole city who did not benefit from his loving charity. He also managed to get a separate building where, under the care of devoted ladies, John undertook the reclamation of women and girls who had been leading sinful lives. He aided poor communities of pious women who had banded together to support themselves by spinning and weaving. He provided a shelter for orphans and other homeless children. In all this John was not moved primarily by a merely natural feeling of compassion for the miserable; his basic urge was his deep supernatural faith which made him see Christ Himself in each and every one of his suffering brethren. Therefore, he was not satisfied in relieving their bodily ills and their worldly wants. Much more important in his eyes was the crying need of bringing them closer to God, of instilling in them a love of virtue and holiness.

Naturally, in all this work John had more than his share of troubles. Not all the men and women whom he helped were worthy of his charity, although that did not disturb him for he never inquired into any poor person's background. Quarrels at times broke out among the rough men whom he had taken in from the gutter. Some of the fallen women who relapsed after their first efforts at reform spread scandalous stories about him. Yet he was always willing and ready to defend them all. When told by the authorities that he should be more careful about whom he sheltered in his hospitals and homes, he answered that he himself was the only one who did not deserve to be there—he who deprived the poor of their food by eating some of it himself!

Money problems always beset him. If he could get a loan to obtain more funds to help his poor, he never hesitated to borrow the money without worrying about how he could ever pay it back.

Since he never spent a cent on himself, he did not doubt for a moment that God would provide the means for him to pay his debts. Large gifts came to him in the most amazing ways.

One evening he went to ask alms of the Marquis of Terifa who happened at the time to be playing cards with a group of his friends. Between them these men gave John the sum of twenty-five ducats, quite a handsome sum of money. After he left, they argued whether he was a genuine saint or not. In true gambler fashion they laid bets on the question, but how could they prove the point one way or another? The Marquis had an idea. Disguising himself in old clothes, he caught up with John in the dark street and told him a tale of woe; he was a nobleman who had lost everything and had no food for his wife and children. "Brother, I sympathize with you," said John, who, of course, did not recognize the Marquis, "here is all the money I have." With that he poured the twenty-five ducats of the astonished Marquis back into his hand. The next day the Marquis, no longer in disguise, visited John and told him that he heard that John had been imposed on by an imposter the night before and had been robbed of twenty-five ducats. "No," John calmly answered, "I was not robbed. I gave the money for the love of God. If the man lied about it, that is his concern, not mine." Then the Marquis told him the whole story and gave him not only the twenty-five ducats, but all the money that had been wagered on the question. The Marquis' friends had agreed that John had won the bet hands down.

On a later occasion, when both John's good works and debts had expanded to alarming proportions, the archbishop of Granada called for him and told him to apply personally to the king of Spain for a really worthwhile grant. Nothing daunted, John, now at the age of fifty-two, walked barefooted the two-hundred miles north to Valladolid where the royal family then lived. In the absence of Charles V, his son and regent, Philip II (who ruled half the world and was later to send his ill-starred Armada against England) not only granted the poor man of Granada an audience but gave him large sums of money. Philip, who was always surrounded by fawning courtiers, had never seen a man like this. "Sire," said the outspoken ex-shepherd, "I have the habit of addressing all men as 'Brother,' since we are all brothers in Christ. How do you wish that I should address you?" "John," the king replied, "you can call me anything you like." "Then, brother, I will call you 'Good Prince.'" The only trouble with the immense amount of money that John received at Valladolid was that he would have given it all away in charity in this city had not his companion sent part of it ahead to Granada. The excuse that John gave his companion was quite typical of him: "Brother, what's the difference whether we give it away here or in Granada, as long as we are doing good for the love of God?"

One of the most astounding acts of heroism that John performed was his exploit at the time when the Royal Hospital of Granada caught fire. As soon as he heard of the fire he rushed to this hospital. The lower floors of one of its wings were filled with smoke and flames. The patients on these floors had been evacuated, but those on the top floor were trapped. When John arrived, no one had the courage to go into the building to rescue these poor victims. Without a moment's hesitation he ran in and disappeared into the smoke. A few minutes later the crowd cheered as he reappeared with a cripple in his arms and two other patients clinging to his clothes. Back he went for more. In groups of three or four at a time he succeeded in bringing all of the patients out of the flaming building. Finally he was seen on the roof of the burning wing, vigorously swinging an axe to chop away this doomed section from the rest of the hospital. The crowd gasped in terror when they saw the burning wing fall away from the main section—and John with it, crashing down through the flaming timbers. He would surely perish in the flames. What would Granada ever do without its apostle of charity? Then suddenly John appeared. The crowd went wild with joy. There he was, safe and sound, his eyebrows burnt off, but otherwise unharmed! His amazing survival could hardly have been less than miraculous. Referring to this event, the Church prays on his feastday: "O God, who didst make the blessed John, when burning with Thy love, walk unscathed through the flames and through him didst beget new offspring for Thy Church, grant that by his merits our sins may be purged away in the fire of Thy love and the remedies for everlasting life may be given us, through Christ our Lord. Amen."

The "new offspring" spoken of in this prayer are the members of the religious order which John unknowingly founded, the Hospital Brothers of St. John of God. The sight of his heroic work for the sick poor attracted other men to follow his example and become his helpers. His first two followers, Anthony Martin and Peter Velasco, had once been rough, violent men. Anthony had sworn to avenge the death of his brother whom Peter had killed. When John begged him to forgive his enemy, even as God in his mercy was willing to forgive, Anthony not only pardoned Peter but these two became the best of friends and the most devoted helpers that John had. After the latter's death, they organized his disciples into a religious community with ecclesiastical approbation, though even in John's lifetime he and his helpers really formed a religious congregation in all essentials. His good friend, Bishop Ramirez of Tuy, had given him a cassock as a sort of religious habit and had ordered him not to exchange it for the rags of the first beggar he met. With some slight changes this form of cassock is still the religious habit worn by his religious Brothers. When Bishop Tuy heard from John that a "boy" had once called him "John of God," he gave him this title as his official "religious name," and it was as "John of God" that the saint was universally known during the last ten years of his life. His followers remained the devoted imitators of all his ways, including even his unique method of collecting alms. Like him, they went through the streets crying out, "Do good for yourselves, brothers for love of God!" In Italy this cry struck the people as so odd that they dubbed the Brothers of St. John of God the "Fate Bene-Fratelli," the "Do-Good-Brothers." Everyone who has lived for some time in Rome knows of the famous hospital there on the Island of the Tiber, popularly known as the Hospital of the Fate-Bene-Fratelli. John's brotherhood quickly spread through most of the countries of Europe where it is still flourishing and still faithful to the spirit of its remarkable founder in caring for the sick poor. In the United States it now has foundations in the archdioceses of Los Angeles and Boston.

Though only fifty-five years old, John of God had finished his noble task of utterly unselfish charity. Worn out by unending labors, he was forced to take to bed, but would not stay put. Knowing that his hospital needed firewood to ward off the cold of late winter, he got up from bed and went with a companion to the river outside the city to gather driftwood. The sight there of a drowning youth was too much for him, and he dove into the icy stream. The result was pneumonia. The archbishop of Granada, not knowing of John's illness, sent for him to answer certain charges of wrongdoing at the hospital. John went at once. He listened humbly to the charges and replied to the complete satisfaction of the archbishop. "John," said the latter, "go back to your hospital and run it as you think best. I am satisfied that you have no other purpose than the glory of God and the good of the sick and the poor."

John went back to bed, but he knew that his end was near. He appointed Brother Anthony Martin his successor and arranged for the payment of all his debts. All his followers and patients came to his bed to kiss him farewell, but he was denied the happiness of dying among these poor people whom he loved so dearly. A wealthy lady who meant well had the archbishop order him to be taken to her house for better care. John obeyed; he would drink the cup of sacrifice to its bitterest dregs.

Even before he was called to heaven, God wished to glorify His good and faithful servant. All Granada was grief-stricken at the news of John's fatal illness. Police had to be stationed outside the house where he lay to keep away the crowds that tried to visit him. The archbishop himself came to give him the last sacraments. Then John asked to be left in peace for a few minutes rest. When finally alone, he got up and put on his old religious habit and knelt in prayer before a crucifix. There they found him some time later, still kneeling upright with his head against the cross—cold in death!

During his life John had plenty of critics and enemies who were bitterly opposed to his ways and methods, but now he had none but friends. He became the idol of all Granada, yes, of all Spain. His funeral rivaled that of an emperor. It took three hours for the long funeral cortege to pass through the thick throngs on the way to the church for burial. His lifeless body was carried by four noblemen. His Christ-like soul, though in heaven, was also with his best friends—the thousands of poor along the way, weeping and wailing their hearts out.

It was on March 8, 1550, that St. John of God died; his fifty-fifth birthday on earth was his first birthday in heaven. In 1638 he was beatified by Pope Urban VIII, and in 1690 he was can-onized by Pope Alexander VIII. Pope Leo XIII solemnly declar-ed him the heavenly patron of all hospitals and their patients in 1886.

Saint Joseph Calasanctius
Confessor

1 6 4 8

(August 27)

A SAINT WHO lives to the age of ninety-two and through all the years serves his divine Master with steadfast fidelity, patience and humility; who pours forth his charity on poor children and the afflicted of all sorts; who labors for the conversion of heretics and founds a religious order to carry on his work, is surely worthy at the end of his life to hear Christ's words of praise: "Well done, good and faithful servant! Enter into the joy of the Lord." Such a saint was Joseph Calasanctius.

This saint's last name, "Calasanctius," is a Latinized adjective derived from the Spanish word, "Calasanza," by which a certain castle near the town of Petralta ("High Rock") was called. This town of Petralta de la Sal, to give it its full name, lies in the Pyrenees Mountains of northern Aragon, northeastern Spain. In the middle of the sixteenth century the lord of this castle was Pedro de Calasanza, who lived here with his wife, Maria Gastonia, and their five children. The youngest of these children, born on September 11, 1556, was Joseph, the future saint.

Even as a little boy, Joseph gave signs of his future calling by trying to teach his playmates the prayers and religious instructions he had learned at home. Taking his religion very seriously and his instructions quite literally, when he heard that the Devil was God's enemy, he went out with his toy sword in hand to do

SAINT JOHN THE EVANGELIST   Peter Rubens

Probably one of the best known, Saint John the Evangelist was certainly
one of the best loved of the twelve apostles. It is because of his having
written the Fourth Gospel that he is commonly called "the Evangelist" to
distinguish him from Saint John the Baptist. The greatest sign of Jesus'
love for John was the bequeathing of His mother to His beloved disciple.

SAINT LUKE von Steinle

The fame of Saint Luke rests on his authorship of the Third Gospel and the Acts of the Apostles. Although a wealthy physician, the Saint manifested a special love for the poor, and emphasized Christ's teaching on charity. Another characteristic of his Gospel is the stress placed on prayer, and what would Christmas be without Luke's stirring words!

battle against him. Soon, however, he was to learn that God's battles are fought in quite a different way.

After his elementary schooling at Petralta, Joseph was sent for his classical studies to the city of Estadilla, where he grew in virtue as he progressed in knowledge. Though he showed real talent for composing prose and poetry in Latin as well as in Spanish, he found prayer his favorite occupation, being especially devoted to Christ in the Blessed Sacrament and to Our Lady.

When at the age of fifteen he finished his classical studies, he went to the university of Lerida for the study of philosophy and law, and here he received the degree of doctor in law at the early age of twenty. His father had hoped that he would be a soldier like himself, but the young man, who longed to devote his life, not to the service of arms, but to the service of God, pleaded so effectively that Senor Calasanza finally consented to let him study theology at Valencia. Here, for reasons of courtesy, Joseph was obliged to make occasional visits to the home of some of his relatives. A certain young lady of noble descent, who lived at this house, though only related to him through marriage, fell hopelessly in love with the handsome young Joseph and soon told him of her ardent affections. Since he had already taken a private vow of celibacy, Joseph was filled with consternation at the situation in which he now found himself.

On the advice of his confessor he therefore left Valencia and went to Alcala de Henares (near Madrid) in Castile to finish his theological studies. The calm of his life of prayer and study at this university was troubled by the news, first of the death of his oldest brother, and then of the death of his mother. Don Pedro, his father, urged Joseph to come home, but, fearful of the pressure that would be put on him to marry, he long hesitated to go back home. However, on the completion of his course in theology in 1582, he finally consented to his father's pleadings and went back to Petralta.

The strain under which Joseph was now placed in trying to please his father while struggling at the same time to remain true to his vocation, proved too much for his health, and he fell dangerously ill. At length he told his father that with his permission he would like to take a vow that, if he recovered, he would become a priest. Don Pedro, feeling quite sure that his son had no chance of recovering his health, humored him by letting him make this vow. To everyone's surprise, Joseph soon grew better and in a short time was restored to perfect health. In fulfillment of his vow he was ordained to the priesthood on December 17, 1583, by the bishop of Urgel, the diocese in which his town of Petralta was situated.

Soon after his ordination Father Joseph Calasanctius was invited by his friend, Bishop Figuera, to assist him in his diocese of Jaca, further to the west of northern Spain. With the permission of the bishop of Urgel, Joseph went not only here, but later to other dioceses in northern Spain, where he labored zealously for the salvation of souls. Not only the Pyrenees of Aragon, but also Catalonia along the Mediterranean coast on the east and even Castile in the heart of Spain enjoyed the blessings of his apostolic spirit. Throughout these regions the zealous young priest gave religious instructions to the spiritually forsaken people, made peace between various feuding factions, and restored ecclesiastical discipline in several monasteries which had lost their religious spirit.

In 1588 Joseph returned home to Petralta to assist his father in his last agony, and after the latter's death the bishop of Urgel asked him to remain here in his home diocese. The apostolic priest therefore now labored here among the rough mountaineers with such success that in 1590, when only thirty-five years old, the bishop appointed him vicar general of the whole diocese. He would have, no doubt, been soon made a bishop himself, had not God had other designs for him.

On several occasions while at prayer Joseph heard an inner voice urging him to go to Rome because the Lord had special work for him to do there. Once in a vision he beheld himself at Rome surrounded by a large crowd of children and as he tried, in his vision, to teach them about God, he saw many angels come down from heaven to help him. Not understanding the meaning of this vision, he spoke to his spiritual director and asked him what it meant. The latter advised him to heed the inner voice that was evidently a call from God and therefore go to Rome.

Consequently, he resigned from his office of vicar general and gave up all his other benefices, except one from which he received an annuity of two thousand pounds a year; on the advice of his bishop, who sadly but willingly agreed to his departure, he kept this source of income, since it would be useful to him in the work to which he felt himself called by God. For the same reason he retained a part of the income from his father's estate; the rest of this he divided between his sisters and the poor. Then, in January of 1592 he left Spain forever, as he set sail for Italy. He arrived at Rome some time before Clement VIII, who had been elected pope on January 30, took solemn possession of the Lateran Basilica on April 4; we know that he witnessed this event.

The Eternal City seemed to fill Joseph's soul with a new outburst of spiritual ardor. Afflicting his body with fastings and other austerities, he spent days and nights in heavenly contemplation. One of his pious practices, which he continued for many years, was to walk to all of the seven major basilicas of Rome every night. As most of these ancient churches lie in different directions on the outskirts of the city, his nightly pilgrimages to these shrines must have left him but precious little time for sleep.

Prayer and penance, however, were not to be the only occupation of St. Joseph Calasanctius in Rome. God had brought him here for a special apostolate of charity, and soon the way was opened for him to begin this work. The bishop of Urgel had written beforehand a warm letter of recommendation for Joseph to his friend at Rome, Canon Baltazar Compte. The latter, after searching for a long time and finally locating Joseph in Rome, dressed in lowly pilgrim garb and living in a poor section of the city, introduced him to Cardinal Marc' Antonio Colonna, who was in need of a personal theologian-secretary as well as a tutor for his grand-nephew, Prince Filippo Colonna. Joseph hesitated to take up his abode in such princely surroundings, but when the cardinal assured him that he would be free to continue his usual practices of piety, Joseph consented to live at the Colonna palace.

Through members of the Colonna family, whose spiritual direction he was soon asked to assume, Joseph learned of a confraternity established by Pope Pius IV (1559-1565) under the title of the Holy Apostles, whose members sought out the poor who were too ashamed to ask for assistance, as well as the sick and all others in trouble, whom they helped with alms and counsel and whatever else they needed. He at once asked to be enrolled in this confraternity and thus found his first opportunity to practice Christian charity on a large scale, not only by dispensing the alms of the confraternity, but also by secretly supplementing these from his own personal income. His work with the Colonna family was soon noticed by Cardinal Alexander de Medici, who invited him to join another confraternity, that of Christian Doctrine, of which de Medici was the Cardinal Protector. This confraternity taught children and adults the essentials of Christian doctrine. Joseph's work in this association was so productive of good that in a short time he was elected its president.

In 1595 Rome was ravaged by an outbreak of the plague, and Joseph gladly sacrificed all his time to work for the plague-stricken in their homes as well as in the hospitals. One of the tasks which he did not hesitate to perform was to carry away the bodies of the dead on his own shoulders for burial. St. Camillus de Lellis was carrying on the same heroic work of charity during this plague in Rome, and it is quite probable that he knew of and labored in conjunction with the work of St. Joseph Calasanctius.

In the streets of Rome Joseph saw innumerable children in need of instruction, though there was no school to which they could go. There were indeed some schools for children in Rome, but their teachers were underpaid and they refused to accept children whose parents could not afford to pay at least a small tuition fee. Joseph tried his best to get the orphans and abandoned children off the streets and into these schools, but without success. God allowed him to suffer this disappointment in order to show him that, with divine help, he himself was to take care of these little ones.

One day, as he was walking along the streets of Rome, he passed a group of children whose obscene language he could not help overhearing. Then he heard a voice saying to him, "Look, Joseph, look!" What he saw the children doing was a shock to him, but at the same time it filled his heart with pity for these young souls that were so dear to Christ. Within him he heard the Holy Spirit say, "It is to you that these poor children are confided. Help them!" Suddenly he recalled the vision he had had some years before in Spain. He could doubt it no longer: this was truly the work for which God had brought him to Rome.

In the section of Rome called "Trastevere" ("Across-the-Tiber"), which had the worst slums of the city, there was a parish church dedicated to St. Dorothy. Its pastor, Father Antonio Brendani, offered Joseph the use of two rooms in his house and he volunteered to help with the teaching. Enlisting the aid of two other secular priests, in November 1597 Joseph Calasanctius opened his first school for the children of the Trastevere slums. No child paid even a single *soldo* for its tuition; whatever expenses were incurred, such as the small salary of the hired priest-teachers, Joseph paid for from his own income. The date and place are memorable: this was the first *free* public school in Europe! The only name that its founder gave it was the "Scuola Pia," which means really "the charitable school" rather than "the pious school."

At the end of the first week there were more than one hundred pupils in Joseph's two-room school. His first two fellow teachers soon found the work too arduous and quit. Joseph paid other priests to help him with the teaching, while he always hoped to find some who would work as he did—without pay, for pure charity. The school grew and grew. Twice in 1598, its second year, Joseph had to increase the number of rooms and the number of teachers. Finally he asked Pope Clement VIII if he might move to more spacious quarters, where he and his fellow priest-teachers might live together as well as teach. The pope not only approved of this idea; he also suggested that Joseph should form a sort of religious congregation with himself as head and director. In addition to this Clement VIII promised to give some financial support each year to the project, and he induced others to make similar annual contributions.

In 1600, therefore, Joseph Calasanctius entered on his new life, as he with a small group of priests began to live together in a kind of religious community. He was unanimously elected superior, with the title of "Prefect of the *Scuola Pia.*" His work and expenses were thereby greatly increased. But he still maintained his original principle: no child should be in want of an education for lack of money to pay for it. When his own limited resources were exhausted, charitable donations always came in, quite in proportion to his unfailing trust in divine Providence. One of his customs, worth mentioning, was his practice for him and his fellow teachers to accompany the children home from school at the end of each day, to see that no harm befell them on the way.

The saint's activities were also increased by his enrolling in the Confraternity of the *Santissima Trinita dei Pellegrini* which, founded by Cardinal Camillo Borghese and Cardinal Sfrondati, had for its purpose the serving of poor pilgrims and the instructing of heretics who were attracted to Rome during Jubilee Years and other Holy Years. Joseph Calasanctius had a certain winning way about him that attracted non-Catholics, and he made many converts during his long life. Another act of charity which he engaged in throughout his life was visiting the prisons, where he brought great consolation with his religious instructions and exhortations to the unfortunate inmates.

In 1601 and again in 1602 Joseph's schools had to be enlarged to care for his seven hundred pupils. Monsignor Vestri, Secretary for Papal Briefs, gave him the use of his palace for this purpose. It was about this time that Joseph had a mishap. While pulling the school bell, he fell from from a ladder and broke his hip and his leg. The height of the fall was so great that it was a miracle he was not killed. His fractures were not properly set, and he suffered much from this for the rest of his life.

New troubles, however, awaited Joseph at this time. Some men whom he had trained began to desert him and open independent schools with paid tuition. Not content with this, they tried to stop his free teaching by spreading calumnies against him. They even presented a formal list of charges against him to Cardinal Camillo Borghese, recently appointed Cardinal Vicar of Rome. The latter, however, refused to believe these lies and showed his high regard for Joseph by making him director of the monastery of San Silvestro in Capite. When new accusations were brought against Joseph to the pope himself, the latter, though putting no credence in them, commissioned Cardinals Antoniani and Baronius to make a secret investigation of Joseph's schools and report their findings to him. When they found everything satisfactory, the pope took Joseph's schools under the protection of the Holy See. Yet the jealous teachers in the paying schools continued their petty persecution of the charitable priest.

In 1606 Joseph had nine hundred pupils in his schools, and again he had to look for more rooms and more teachers. He was pressed on every side and worn out by his labors. Since his own funds were gone and his annuities had not yet arrived, he hung an alms box at the door of his school. The same evening he opened it and found in it forty *scudi* in cash and a banker's order for two hundred gold crowns.

Pope Paul V (1605-1621) showed Joseph great esteem, and the people expected that soon Father Calasanctius would be raised to some high dignity in the Church. They did not know that he had recently refused two bishoprics in Spain as well as the archbishopric of Brindisi, to which he had actually been nominated. He wished for no earthly glory. When Cardinal de Torres, the Cardinal Protector of Joseph's schools, died, the pope told Joseph to take his place. This meant that he would have to accept the cardinal's hat. As for Joseph, it amounted to practically a death sentence. He wept and begged and insisted that it would be the end of his schools. The pope saw that he was sincere and dropped the matter for the time being. But on August 17, 1611, at the new nomination of cardinals, Paul V again put Calasanctius name on the list and seemed inflexible, till Cardinal Scipione Borghese begged the pope to let Joseph have his wishes, so that in the end Cardinal Benedetto Justiniani was appointed Cardinal Protector of Joseph's schools, and being a good, generous and friendly man, who highly venerated Calasanctius, he did much good for his schools.

One day the saint had a vision of "Lady Poverty," so beloved by St. Francis Assisi, and he pondered on its possible meaning. Then it occurred to him that there were no Jewish children in his schools, though they too were God's children. He therefore invited the poor children of the Jewish families in Rome to attend his schools, and their parents gratefully accepted the offer.

As Joseph's work grew by leaps and bounds, he thought it well that his rather informal group of priests should be placed on a firmer basis. He therefore applied to the pope for permission to organize his companions into a canonically recognized religious congregation. The pope accordingly, in a Brief dated January 14, 1614, united the Father of the *Scuole Pie* with the small Congregation of the Mother of God, under two conditions: that Joseph Calasanctius alone should be their superior, with all the religious following his rule, and that no children whatever should be admitted to their schools except those who were really poor.

For the first two years things went along fairly smoothly for Joseph. But then trouble started. People began to complain that they were forced to declare publicly that they were insolvent or outright paupers in order to get their children into the schools. Besides, the priests of the Congregation of the Mother of God complained that the school work interfered with the proper duties of their own institute. Joseph went to his Cardinal Protector, and the latter spoke with the pope about it. Consequently, on March 6, 1617, the Holy Father revoked the former Brief of union, and instituted a new Congregation for Joseph's work, called the Pauline Congregation of the Poor of the Mother of God of the Pious Schools. Its members were to take simple, not solemn vows, and in addition to the customary three vows of poverty, chastity and obedience, they were to take an additional vow to teach without taking payment for it. Joseph was to the Prefect General of the Schools, and he with his fellow members were to draw up suitable statutes for the ultimate approval by the Holy See. The restriction regarding only poor children was removed, since it had proved so troublesome. Those priests who did not wish to join this religious congregation were free to leave; the rest would take vows and live in community.

On March 26, 1617, Cardinal Justiniani gave the habit to the founder, Joseph Calasanctius, with faculties for him to give it to his companions. With tears of joy he gave it to fourteen of his companion priests. On this day he dropped his family name of Calasanctius and called himself henceforth "Joseph of the Mother of God."

In 1618 Joseph lost two dear friends, one of them a young man of twenty-four, Antonio Lucchesi. The saint had promised the sick man that he would be with him when he died. But since he was not called in sufficient time, he found to his great grief, when he did arrive, that his friend was already dead. After reproaching the attendants for not having called him on time, he cried aloud: "Antonio! Antonio!" To the utter amazement of the attendants, the dead man opened his eyes and raised his head. Joseph asked him how he had died. Antonio spoke up and said that he had died "with humility" and "with resignation." Then the saint embraced him and blessed him, and Antonio returned to death.

This holy man had the gift of prophecy and of reading thoughts, as substaniated by numberless accounts. He healed the sick, drove out evil spirits, provided food where there was none, and even restored the dead to life. One of his predictions, that Cardinal Ludovisi would be the next pope, was verified when this cardinal became Pope Gregory XV (1621-1623). When the Pauline Congregation began in 1617 it had more than one thousand enrolled pupils in its schools. Since it continued to grow both in the number of its schools and in the number of its teaching priests, Gregory XV, on September 18, 1621, raised it to the rank of a Religious Order with solemn vows, approving its new constitutions on January 31, 1622. On April 29, 1622, its founder, Father Joseph of the Mother of God, had the happiness of pronouncing his solemn vows. The full title of his order is *Ordo Clericorum Regularium Pauperum Matris Dei Scholarum Piarum.* This title proved too much of a mouthful for the ordinary people, when this Order spread throughout Italy and most of Europe. In Spain the last two words alone were used, shortened into the form of "Escolapios." In Italy this became even shorter, and the Fathers were called simply the "Scolopi." But most commonly the last word of the title was alone used, and the Fathers were called the *Piaristae,* or in English, "the Piarists."

The saint's term of office as General expired in 1631, since the constitutions had set it at nine years. He longed for this, so that he might be free to practice his ordinary works of humble charity, such as sweeping the schools. But he was re-elected against his wishes and, bowing his head, he accepted this as God's will.

He had once been warned in a vision by Saint Theresa of Avila that he would still have more afflictions and troubles before he died. This came to pass in 1642, when Joseph was eighty-six years old. One of his own members, a Father Mario Sozzi, filled with ambition to advance his own position, spread vicious calumnies against the aged saint, which eventually were believed by the Holy See. The whole sordid story of Father Mario's machinations is too long and complicated to recount here. Suffice it to say that in 1643 Joseph was removed from his office of General, and his Order was reduced to the status of a simple religious Congregation. The saint bore this last cross with heroic resignation to the will of God and generously forgave all his enemies and calumniators. Although he would have been perfectly willing to die in disgrace, his good name was restored in 1646, when, in his ninetieth year, he was again asked to hold the reins of government as General. He did not live to see the complete vindication of himself and his faithful followers, when in 1669 the Piarists were given the rank of an Order by the Holy See. During the rest of the 17th century and almost all of the 18th the Order of Piarists was one of the great Orders in Europe, famous for its schools, not only for poor children, which it continued to foster, but for its institutions of higher learning. But the French Revolution and the suppression of religious orders at the beginning of the 19th century dealt it a severe blow, from which it is only now recovering.

St. Joseph Calasanctius died a holy, peaceful death on August 25, 1648. His sacred remains are buried in the Church of St. Pantaleon in Rome, at one of his earliest foundations. He was beatified by Pope Benedict XIV on August 7, 1748, and canonized by Pope Clement XIII on July 16, 1767, with his feast set for the 27th of August.

Saint Juliana Falconieri

Virgin

1 3 4 1

(June 19)

I T IS NOT only in regard to genuine saints of the early Church that we are without a detailed account of their lives. Even some of the great saints of the Middle Ages lacked biographers until a century after their deaths, so that authentic knowledge concerning them is quite scanty. One such medieval saint is Juliana Falconieri. Although the many miracles that were wrought through her intercession made her one of the most popular saints in the second half of the 14th century, that is, during the first two generations after her death, it was not until more than a century later (in the second half of the 15th century) that the first short accounts of her life were written. Again, after her canonization in 1737, popular devotion to St. Juliana Falconieri during the following decades of the 18th century was so widespread that it might well be compared to the popular devotion to "the Little Flower of Jesus" during the first half of the 20th century. Yet practically the only thing that people knew about her was that she had led a very holy life, and that many favors were granted by God to those who sought her intercession. In 1954 the Servite Father, Alessio M. Rossi, published a short life of this saint in Italian, based on the relatively few facts that he could discover about her, and well illustrated by an account of the spiritual history of her time.

The year of her birth is given by her later biographers as 1270, though Fr. Rossi could not find a contemporary document to verify this. All that is known of her mother is that her maiden name was Riguardata (the highly "Regarded" one). Considerably more is known about Juliana's father and his family. His full name was Chiarissimo di Falco di Ugo dei Falconieri, which would literally mean, "Most Illustrious, son of Falcon, son of Hugh, of the Falconers." The Falconieri (whose coat of arms showed a pair of falcons) formed one of the most famous familes in medieval Florence which at that time, though troubled with rival factions of the nobility, was the cultural capital of Italy.

Giuliana dei Falconieri (to give our Saint the full form of her Italian name) was not the only child of Chiarissimo and Riguardata dei Falconieri. She had an older sister, Guiduccia, about whom practically nothing is known except that she died a few years before Juliana. It was not the parents of Juliana, but rather her paternal uncle, St. Alexius (Alessio) dei Falconieri, who played the predominant role in her spiritual development.

St. Alexius Falconieri was one of the "Seven Founders" of the Order of the Servants of Mary, or the Servites, as they are now more commonly called. To understand the spirit that inspired Juliana, we should know something of the original spirit of the Servite Fathers, for she was an ardent disciple of her Servite uncle.

As can be seen in the medieval saints, especially St. Bernard of Clairvaux and St. Francis of Assisi, Catholic devotion in the Middle Ages was mostly directed to the sacred Humanity of Christ. These saints, of course, believed with all their heart in the Divinity of Christ, but it was to Jesus as the Son of God made Man, to Him as the Babe of Bethlehem and to Him as the Crucified Savior, that their piety was primarily aimed. Now, one can hardly be ardently devoted to Jesus as Man without being equally devoted to His Mother Mary,, and since Christ was now most commonly thought of as "the Man of Sorrows," His Mother was also especially venerated as the *Addolorata,* the

"Sorrowful" Mother. It is not without reason that the most famous hymn to Mary from the Middle Ages is the "Stabat Mater."

In 1233 seven merchants of Florence (among whom was Alessio dei Falconieri), left their local confraternity to live as hermits, especially devoted to the Mother of Sorrows, outside their native city. In 1240 they organized into a regular religious Order, under the title of "the Servants of Mary." Like the other religious Orders of the 13th century (the Dominicans, Franciscans and Carmelites), the Servites also organized a "Second Order" of cloistered nuns and a "Third Order" of pious lay people who wished to share, to a greater or less degree, in the spiritual life of the First and Second Orders without, however, changing their state, usually of marriage, in the world.

When Juliana was fifteen years old she listened to a sermon on the Last Judgment that made a profound and lasting impression on her. In this, as in so many other traits of her spirituality, Juliana was "a child of her age." In the Middle Ages, despite an overflowing joy in life, there was a strong undercurrent of what the modern world might call pessimism. The vivid spirit of faith which then filled all the people of Europe—even the worst sinners, who would never dream of denying the faith, though they failed miserably to live according to it—led them to view their earthly life in the light of the future world, the only life which really mattered for them. At the same time they were deeply conscious of their unworthiness to attain to eternal bliss, and they stood in dread at the thought of eternal damnation as due to their sins. Hence, the key word of medieval spirituality was "penance," in the sense of austere self-denial that would keep the body in subjection and not allow it to become an occasion of sin. Even acts of Christian charity were viewed primarily as "works of penance." The favorite prayer to Mary in the Middle Ages was the "Salve Regina." In this, the Mother of Mercy is implored to turn her eyes of pity upon the poor banished children of Eve, so that after their exile in this valley of tears she might show unto them the blessed fruit of her womb, Jesus.

On hearing this moving sermon on the Last Judgment, Juliana resolved to devote the rest of her life solely to God. Following the advice of her uncle, St. Alexius, she took a private, perpetual vow of virginity. She would have gladly entered a convent of the Second Order of the Servite Nuns, but she felt that she had an obligation to remain at home with her aged parents. Therefore she had to content herself with receiving the habit as a member of the Third Order of the Servites. In that age a fifteen-year girl was already regarded as a fully grown woman; thus Juliana's parents were considering a suitable marriage for her, one that would link their proud Falconieri family with another of the powerful families of Florence. However, she showed that she had plenty of the fighting blood of the Falconieri in her veins. She gave a strong, decisive "No" to all the plans for her marriage, and her parents finally relented and let her have her way. Throughout her life she proved herself a faithful copy of the *Mulier fortis*, "the Strong Woman," of the Book of Proverbs. Her strong will can be seen in the perseverance with which she adhered to the penitential life she vowed to lead, even though the descriptions of her later biographers regarding her extraordinary fasts and her constant wearing of an iron chain around her waist may be taken as typical exaggerations.

The death of her mother in 1302 and of her father a year or two later left Juliana free to devote her whole life to the service of God as a true "Servant of Mary." All of her biographers stress her acts of charity to the poor and the sick, but unfortunately they record no individual instances which would give us a clearer picture of her work in this matter. There are, however, contemporary records to show that she often acted as a peacemaker between the rival factions in Florence, no small deed of truly Christian charity.

In the Middle Ages, moreover, there were no communities of "active Sisterhoods," such as have grown so numerous in the

Catholic world during the last few centuries. In those days a young woman either entered a cloistered convent as a "nun," or she remained in the world, at best as a member of one of the Third Orders of lay people. The canon law of the Church had not yet taken recognition of what are now known as "Third Orders Religious" of priests, Brothers and Sisters who do not belong to either a First or a Second Order. St. Juliana was definitely centuries ahead of her time when, in 1332, she established a convent where she with other women who, like herself, were members of the Servite Third Order could live in a community under a fixed rule of life (though they continued their active work of charity among their fellow men in the world). Her father had already built the lovely church of the "Annunziata" (Our Lady of the Annunciation) in Florence for the Servite Fathers, and now Juliana used one of the houses belonging to her family in this city as the first convent of the Servite Sisters of the Third Order. Although the many branches of this Order which now exist throughout the world (including England and the United States) have only an indirect connection with the original convent founded by St. Juliana, they rightly regard her as their holy "Foundress."

One of the special devotions of St. Juliana was that which she had to our Lord in the Blessed Eucharist. There was a great surge of Eucharistic devotion in Christendom during the second half of the 13th century and throughout the 14th century, after Pope Urban IV, following the revelations made to Blessed Juliana of Liege (Belgium), instituted the feast of "Corpus Christi" in 1264. Although the daily reception of Holy Communion was not yet sanctioned by the Church, St. Juliana Falconieri received Communion as often as she could, that is, on Sundays, Wednesday and Fridays, and she spent the intervening days either in preparation for, or in thanksgiving, after her Communions.

Because of her extraordinary devotion to the Holy Eucharist, God rewarded His faithful servant Juliana with an astounding miracle at her death in 1341. There was then a custom in the

SAINT JOHN OF GOD

The conversion of John Ciudad, later called John of God, from a life
of sin to that of a saint took place as illustrated above. Henceforth he
dedicated himself to the abandoned and infirm of Granada, Spain. He died
in this dedication in 1550. Beatified in 1638, he was canonized by Pope
Alexander VIII in 1690, and declared a patron of the sick in 1886.

SAINT MARK   Jacopo Tintoretto

This is a reproduction of the painting entitled *The Miracle of Saint Mark*. It was based on the legend that when a certain Venetian Christian who had been captured by the Turks was about to be tortured, he prayed to the patron saint of Venice (St. Mark), and the latter immediately came down from heaven and freed the prisoner.

Church, which is no longer tolerated, of placing the Blessed Sacrament on the breast of a dying person who was unable to receive it as Viaticum. When Juliana was dying she suffered so much from a stomach ailment that there was danger of her vomiting up the Sacred Host if she received it in Communion. She therefore begged and was granted the favor of having the Blessed Sacrament placed on her breast. When the priest was about to remove the Sacred Host from her, it could no longer be found. The radiance of peace on the dying saint's face showed that she had indeed received it as Viaticum in a miraculous manner. After her death, when the Sisters washed her body, they found a cross, such was the one on the Host, indelibly marked on the place on her breast where the Sacred Host had been laid. It was Christ's seal of approval imprinted on the pure heart of Juliana, who, as a faithful servant of His sorrowful Mother, had ever been devoted to Him as the Crucified Savior, and as the sacrificed Lamb of God in the Holy Eucharist.

Saint Lawrence

Martyr

2 5 8

(August 10)

Ever since his death in the year 258, Saint Lawrence, deacon of the Holy Roman Church, has been honored as one of the greatest glories of the Eternal City. Not merely the fact of his martyrdom, but also details, such as the date of his death and place of burial, are known with absolute certainty from contemporary documents. The martyrdom, however, of so great a hero of the Church would naturally be adorned with legendary additions as its story was told and retold by the people. Thus the form in which it appeared in the sermons of the Fathers during the fourth and fifth centuries contained many details of doubtful authenticity.

The manner of his martyrdom (being roasted alive on a gridiron) is taken for granted as true in St. Ambrose's sermon, and in Prudentius' poem on the martyr, both from the second half of the fourth century. Despite the objections of some modern historians, there is no reason to doubt that popular tradition could have preserved this detail correctly. In any case, the gridiron on which he suffered has always been St. Lawrence's best known symbol in Christian art.

The facts which are certain are these. In 257, the Roman emperor Valerian issued a relatively mild edict against the Christians forbidding them to meet for religious services, and threatening to exile their clergy. In August, 258, he put teeth into his decree by ordering at once the arrest and execution of the Christian clergy. From a letter written by St. Cyprian, Bishop of Carthage, who was himself to die a martyr on September 14 of this year, we know that the Bishop of Rome, St. Sixtus II, was apprehended in the catacombs and executed with four of his deacons on August 6. Four days later, on August 10, Lawrence, the last of the pope's seven deacons, was put to death.

There can also be no doubt about the fact that Saint Lawrence was buried in the Catacombs of Cyriaca on the Via Tiburtina (the Tivoli Road) a short distance outside the Tiburtine Gate in the eastern wall of Rome. In the first half of the fourth century the emperor Constantine built a small church in honor of this Roman martyr over his grave in this cemetery. In the course of the following centuries various popes enlarged, beautified and added a much larger basilica to the church. The present complexity of structures on the site goes back to Pope Honorius II (1216-1227). Extensive repairs on this venerable building had to be made at the end of World War II. Adjacent to it are the large railroad yards of Rome, and during the war American pilots, in bombing these yards, accidentally hit the Basilica of Saint Lawrence. The considerable damage which it thereby suffered was later made good by ample American funds.

To understand the fame attached to St. Lawrence's name it is necessary to know that in the early Church the diaconate was an important, permanent office, not merely a sort of stepping stone to the priesthood, as it is now. In imitation of the seven deacons whom the apostles ordained for the church at Jerusalem, each diocese had seven deacons who were primarily entrusted with its temporalities, especially with the distribution of alms to the needy among its faithful. Lawrence was probably the archdeacon or chief of the seven. The poor Christians at Rome remembered him, not only for his great charity toward them, but especially for his heroism in refusing under torture to reveal the place where the funds, small though they no doubt must have been, were kept for help of the needy.

According to the account of his martyrdom as told a century after his death by St. Ambrose, bishop of Milan, and by the poet Prudentius, there was a touching farewell scene between the pope, St. Sixtus II, and his deacon Lawrence on the day when the former was executed. It cannot be called improbable, for the persecutors may well have delayed the martyrdom of Lawrence for a few days in the hopes of finding out from him where the treasures of the church were kept. Lawrence is said to have wept at the sight of his beloved father in Christ being led to death and to have asked him: "Where are you going, father, without your son? Should you, holy priest, offer up the sacrifice without the ministry of your deacon?" To this the pope replied: "I am not leaving you, my son. But a greater combat awaits you, and after three days you will follow me."

When the persecutors asked Lawrence to show them where the treasures of the church were hid, he pointed to the poor Christians who had assembled to witness his martyrdom—the widows and orphans, the sick, the blind and the lame. "These," he said, "are the treasures of the Church." Lawrence was thereupon stripped and bound with chains to an iron grate under which a fire was kindled. But the fire of divine love in his heart, comments St. Ambrose, burned more strongly than did the material flame beneath his iron grate, so that for love of God he disregarded his bodily pain. The grim humor in the remarks Lawrence made to his torturers rings too true to be entirely a fiction of his later biographers. "Turn me over," he told them, after his back was well roasted; "I am done on that side." Toward the end he said to them, "You can eat now; I am broiled enough."

Even apart from the heavenly crown that he won, Lawrence did not die in vain. The later Fathers say that the sight of his heroism won many converts to the faith. Nor has Rome forgotten its great deacon. Wherever the Roman liturgy is celebrated throughout the world, his feast on the tenth of August is of very high rank and is still one of the few feasts that has its special vigil on the preceding day. In the Roman Mass, just as the name of the first Christian martyr, Saint Stephen, the deacon of Jerusalem, is mentioned in the canon after the consecration, so the name of Lawrence, deacon of Rome, is mentioned in the canon before the consecration.

In North America the name of St. Lawrence is attached to one of its great rivers. In 1536, the French explorer, Jacques Cartier, was the first to enter the gulf at the mouth of the mighty river which flows from the Great Lakes. On August 10th of that year he sailed into a bay on the north shore of this gulf, and he named it the "Bay of St. Lawrence" after the saint whose feast was celebrated on that day. Gradually the name of the saint was extended to the great river itself, although Cartier, its discoverer, always spoke of it as the 'River of Canada."

Saint Luke
Evangelist

First Century

(October 18)

THE FAME OF Saint Luke rests almost entirely on his authorship of the third Gospel and the Acts of the Apostles.
Although his name does not occur in either of these two works,
there is no good reason to doubt the very early tradition which
attributes both of them to him. If the early Church had not
known for certain that Luke wrote these books, attempts would
surely have been made to attribute them to more famous persons
of the Apostolic Age.

Luke's name occurs only three times in the New Testament. In
Col 4,14 Saint Paul wrote: "Luke, our most dear physician, and
Demas send you greetings." From this statement we know that
Luke was a medical doctor and that he acted as Saint Paul's
personal physician during certain periods in the life of the Apostle of the Gentiles. In Phlm 24, written at the same time as the
Epistle to the Colossians, Luke is mentioned by St. Paul as one
of five men who send greetings to Philemon. In 2 Tm 4,11,
written near the end of St. Paul's life, that is, about the year 67,
the Apostle says to Timothy, "Luke only is with me." Luke, the
"dear physician," was therefore faithful to his master Paul even
to the end.

From the Acts of the Apostles, however, we can learn a good
deal about the travels and activities of Saint Luke, even though

his name does not occur in this book. Since we know that he is its author, from those parts of it where the narrative is in the the first person plural, known as the "We Sections," information can rightly be drawn regarding the whereabouts of Luke. The first of these "We Sections" is Acts 16,10-17: "As soon as he (Paul) had the vision, straightway *we* made efforts to set out for Macedonia, being sure that God had called *us* to preach the gospel to them. So, sailing from Troas, *we* ran a straight course to Samothrace, and the next day to Neapolis, and thence to Philippi . . . *We* stayed some days in this city; and on the Sabbath *we* went outside the gate to the bank of the river, where there seemed to be a place of prayer. And *we* sat down and spoke to the women who had gathered there . . . And a certain woman named Lydia . . . was listening . . . And when she and her household had been baptized, she appealed to *us* . . . and she insisted upon *our* coming. Now it came to pass as *we* were going to the place of prayer that a girl met *us* . . . She followed Paul and *ourselves* and kept crying out, saying, 'These men are servants of the most high God and they proclaim to you a way of salvation.' "

Since this is the first time that Luke speaks of himself as being with St. Paul, it seems to be a logical conclusion that he first met the Apostle at Troas, near the ancient site of Homer's Troy in western Asia Minor. It is true that there are a few manuscripts which have a short "We Section" as early as Acts 11,27-28: "Now in those days some prophets from Jerusalem came down to Antioch, and there was great rejoicing. But when *we* had assembled, one of them named Agabus spoke and revealed through the Spirit that there would be a great famine all over the world." However, it is certain that the words, "When *we* had assembled," do not form part of the original book of Saint Luke but were added by some editor a generation or two after its composition. Therefore, this passage is of little or no value regarding the early life of St. Luke. Yet it would seem that the tradition which began in the third or fourth century, stating that Luke was a native of

Antioch, is ultimately based on this reading in these secondary manuscripts.

As said above, Luke apparently first met Saint Paul at Troas and accompanied him as far as Philippi in Macedonia, northern Greece. This was during the Apostle's missionary journey (about 49-52 A.D.). The next "We Section" in the Acts (20,5-15) begins, as we would expect, precisely when Saint Paul again came to Philippi, now on his third missionary journey (about 53-57 A.D.). Luke writes: "These (several of Paul's traveling companions), having gone in advance, waited for *us* at Troas; but *we ourselves* sailed from Philippi after the days of the Unleavened Bread, and five days later joined them at Troas, and there *we* stayed seven days" (Acts 20,5-6). It is clear, therefore, that between St. Paul's first visit to Philippi and his second visit there about five years later, Luke remained in this city, probably as head of the Christian community.

From this point on, although the "We Sections" are intermittent in the Acts (21,1-18 and 27,1—28,16), it is clear that Luke now stayed more or less constantly with St. Paul, no doubt because the Apostle's health required the care of a physician and Luke could ably fulfill this need. This period covered the two-year's imprisonment of St. Paul at Caesarea (Acts 21,17—26,32). During this time, Luke, while remaining in touch with the Apostle, had ample time "to follow up all things carefully from the very first" (Luke 1,3) regarding the life and teachings of Christ. Undoubtedly it was during these two years spent in Palestine that he gathered the material for his Gospel by recording the traditions he could learn concerning Jesus, and most likely it was during this time, that is, from 58 to 60 A.D., that he "undertook to draw up a narrative concerning the things that have been fulfilled among us, even as they who from the beginning were eyewitnesses and ministers of the word have handed them down to us" (Luke 1,1-2).

A comparison between Luke's Gospel and the other Gospels enables us to draw certain conclusions regarding the "characteristics" of his Gospel and thus learn something about his own "character." In reading the Gospel according to St. Luke one cannot help feeling that its author was a gentle, peaceful man, with a finely developed aesthetic temperament. Throughout this Gospel special stress is laid on the mercy of God and the compassion of Christ for sinners; for instance, this is the only Gospel that gives us the story of the Penitent Woman of Galilee (7,36-50), and the parable of the Prodigal Son (15,11-32). The author of this Gospel shows a special reverence for womanhood, and many of the famous women of the New Testament are best known from his brief but striking pen sketches of them: the Blessed Virgin Mary, Elizabeth, Anna the Prophetess, the Widow of Naim, the Penitent Woman of Galilee, Mary and Martha of Bethany, Mary Magdalene, and the other "Ministering Women."

Luke, though probably rather wealthy, as physicians usually are, shows a special love for the poor and often emphasizes Christ's teachings on charity and social justice. This can be seen, for instance, in comparing his wording of Christ's Beatitudes and Woes (Luke 6,20-26) with the Beatitudes as given in the Gospel according to St. Matthew (Matt. 5,3-10), or in reading the powerful but unfortunately little known parable of the Rich Fool which is found only in Luke's Gospel (12,13-21).

Another characteristic of Luke's Gospel is the emphasis which is placed here on prayer. St. Luke is often the only Evangelist who mentions certain occasions when Christ prayed, and he gives at greater length than the others our Lord's instructions on prayer.

To his Gospel alone we are indebted for the three beautiful hymns which the Church uses in its daily liturgy: the *Magnificat*, the *Benedictus*, and the *Nunc Dimittis*.

And what would Christmas be without St. Luke? St. Matthew, it is true, is the only Evangelist to tell us the story of the Magi; but it is Luke alone who speaks at length of the birth of the Savior. His stirring words ring the joyful Christmas bells of the angels and the shepherds and the Babe in the manger.

Luke may not have been an artist with a brush, despite the tradition going back to the sixth century which speaks of him as a painter, and despite the innumerable late Byzantine icons which are attributed to him. Yet the fact remains that he was an artist in the use of words. There is deliberate art in the way that he can build up pathos until his punch-lines make the tears flow: "A dead man was being carried out, the *only* son of his mother, and she was a *widow*" (7,12); or again: "She brought forth her first-born son, and wrapped him in swaddling clothes, and laid him in a manger, because there was *no room for them* in the inn" (2,7).

There is some evidence, though it is not entirely certain, that, as a physician, St. Luke occasionally employs somewhat more technical terms than the other evangelists do in speaking of the various physical ailments which Jesus miraculously cured. Be this as it may, there is an interesting sidelight in his Gospel which shows his loyalty to the medical profession. Biblical scholars commonly hold that in writing his Gospel, St. Luke knew and made use of St. Mark's Gospel. Now, St. Mark (5, 25-26) says in regard to the woman whose pathological flow of blood Jesus cured by a miracle: "There was a woman who for twelve years had a hemorrhage, and had suffered much at the hands of many physicians, and had spent all she had, and found no benefit, but rather grew worse." It is interesting to see how St. Luke, while true to the essential facts, tones down this harsh indictment of this woman's physicians; he writes of her merely as a "certain woman who for twelve years had had a hemorrhage, and had spent all her means on physicians, but could not be cured by anyone" (8,43). Luke, the physician, could hardly be expected to say with Mark that "she suffered at the hands of many physicians" and that she "grew worse" under the medical treatment that she received.

Everything points to the fact that before St. Luke became a Christian he had been a pagan and not a Jew, as were all the other writers in the New Testament. As a well educated man, he was able to bring much that was good in pagan culture to the service of Christ. He, more than any other New Testament writer, is a "literary" man. Though he intentionally imitates the "Jewish" Greek of the Bible, especially in his Gospel and in the first half of the Acts, he shows in the second half of the Acts that he can write as pure Greek as the best pagan writers of his time. For all his devotion to the divine message of Christ, Luke shows an interest in secular history, too. As a learned writer, he carefully dates the beginning of the ministry of John the Baptist by giving us the names and countries of all the petty rulers in the Near East at that time (3, 1-2).

Tradition is rather uncertain about the last years of Saint Luke's life. Even if he may not have actually shed his blood in a martyr's death for Christ, the Church is justified in saying in the "oration," or official prayer on his feast day, that "he constantly bore in his body the mortification of the cross for the honor of the Lord's name."

Of the four symbolic creatures in the vision of the prophet Ezechiel—the man, the lion, the ox, and the eagle (Ez. 1,10), which have been traditionally used as symbols of the four Evangelists, Saint Luke is represented by the ox because he begins his Gospel with an account of the priest Zacharias, the father of John the Baptist, and the ox was one of the chief sacrificial animals in the liturgy of the Temple in Jerusalem.

Saint Margaret
Virgin and Martyr

c. 3 0 4

(July 20)

ALTHOUGH THE VIRGIN Martyr Margaret was among the most popular saints of the Middle Ages, the one thing known with certainty about her is that there was once a virgin by this name who gave her life as a martyr for Christ. The Roman Martyrology for July 20th lists as one of the events of this day: "the passion at Antioch of the holy Margaret, virgin and martyr." Even her name is not entirely certain, since the Greek Church venerates her under the name of "Marina." Yet in the Middle Ages there were few more popular "lives of the saints" than the "Legend" of Margaret or Marina. Numerous cities claimed to have her relics. Hers was one of the "voices" heard by St. Joan of Arc. In certain dioceses of England her feast was a holy day of obligation and therefore a "legal holiday" free from work. Her picture was common in medieval art, and many other genuine Saint Margarets received their name in baptism in her honor.

According to her "Legend," Margaret was the daughter of a pagan priest at Antioch in Pisidia of Asia Minor — not the more famous Antioch in Syria. Soon after her birth her mother died, and Margaret was then placed by her father in the care of a Christian woman who lived in the country near Antioch. On growing up, Margaret herself became Christian. When her father heard of this, he disowned her, and she was adopted by her foster mother.

One day while she was attending her foster mother's sheep, a lustful Roman prefect (called Olybrius) caught sight of her beauty and offered to take her as his wife, if she was a free woman, or as his concubine, if she was a slave girl. When neither flattering promises nor dire threats could induce her to accept his offer, he had her arrested as a Christian (since the persecution of Diocletian was then raging, 303-305), and brought to trial at his own tribunal. Having remained steadfast under various tortures, Margaret was sent back to prison, where the devil appeared to her in the form of a dragon that eventually swallowed her alive. While in the dragon's belly, however, she so irritated him by the cross which she held in her hand, that, writhing in cramps, he belched her forth, quite alive and unharmed.

At her next trial before the Roman prefect various attempts were first made to put her to death. When she was tied to a stake, the fire burned her bonds away but left her uninjured. When she was bound hand and foot and thrown into a cauldron of boiling water, the water dissolved her fetters but did her no harm. Thousands of spectators, on witnessing these marvels, proclaimed themselves Christians, and were all promptly put to the sword. Finally Margaret herself was beheaded. Thereupon her executioner also fell dead — not, as one might think, in punishment for his crime, but for the sake of joining her at once in heaven, since God knew that he had carried out his gruesome task unwillingly. Theotimus, who wrote this story and claimed to have seen these events, carried her body away and had it buried by a noble widow in Antioch.

St. Margaret is commonly represented in art as triumphing over a dragon, but also at times as a shepherdess holding a cross, or as standing in a cauldron. As one of "the Fourteen Holy Helpers," she was frequently invoked in the Middle Ages for various needs, especially by women in childbirth.

Saint Margaret of Cortona
Penitent

1 2 9 7

(February 22)

I T WAS NOT Margaret's birthplace that gave her the distinquished epithet "of Cortona." She was born in the little town of Laviano (in the diocese of Chiusi) about twenty-five miles south of Cortona, but it was the latter city that she made famous by spending the second half of her life there. All these places were in the southeast of Tuscany, in the heart of Italy.

Margaret was born in 1247, in the middle of the great 13th century, the age of faith. Saint Clare was still to live five years after Margaret's birth, Saint Francis had gone to Heaven only twenty-one years befor Margaret saw the light of day, and Assisi in Umbria, which these two saints made so illustrious, was only about fifty miles from her birthplace. What Francis was to the First Order of his followers, his friars, and what Clare was to his Second Order, the cloistered Poor Clares, Margaret was to become to his Third Order, his pious penitent men and women of the laity. Yet for the first half of her life Margaret was far from being a saint.

Practically the only source of true information that we have on St. Margaret of Cortona is the *leggenda* or popular life written in Latin shortly after her death by Fra Giunta Bevegnati, her friend and spiritual director at Cortona. Most of this "Life" is taken up with an account of the revelations which she received from God, and which Fra Giunta ordered her under obedience to dictate to him. The critical edition of this *leggenda,* and the scholarly studies of it made in modern times, have shown that the once common picture of Margaret as a woman who was grossly immoral in the early part of her life was due to misunderstanding of the exaggerated description she herself gave of the sinful ways of her youth — a trait common to most saints who felt their utter unworthiness in the presence of God. Margaret, it is true, did go astray and lived in sin for nine years, but there is no reason to think she was ever one to sell her favors lightly.

Since no mention is ever made of any sisters or brothers, it seems Margaret was an only child. Her father, a simple farmer, was too occupied in his daily work to take much interest in his daughter. Her mother may have somewhat spoiled her only child, but otherwise must have planted in her the seed of virtue which was later, despite the weeds which almost choked its growth, to ultimately bear much good fruit. Unfortunately, however, when Margaret was only seven years old she lost her good mother in death, and her father soon took another wife. Probably it was not so much sheer dislike as a lack of understanding which led this woman to treat her stepdaughter rather harshly. Margaret had a nature that craved affection. Not finding it at home, she sought it elsewhere and, with her gay disposition and pretty looks, she did not have far to look. Had she met the right man, no doubt she would have married, settled down as a dutiful peasant wife — and not been heard of in the world.

When she was seventeen, a dashing young nobleman from nearby Montepulciano took a fancy to her, and she fell in love with him. On the promise that he would marry her she eloped with him to his castle near Montepulciano. After a few years a son was born to them. Though he treated her kindly and made her mistress of his house, he constantly postponed the matter of taking her as his lawfully married wife.

From a merely worldly viewpoint these years were not too unhappy for Margaret. Her lover was generous and gave her fine
clothes and jewelry. With her kind and cheerful disposition and
her charity to the poor, this upstart peasant girl gradually won
the friendship of her neighbors. Yet deep in her heart she had
no peace, for she knew she was doing wrong. She could not receive the sacraments, and the thought of her future in eternity
frightened her. Later she was to confess: "In Montepulciano I
lost everything — honor, dignity, peace. I lost everything —
except faith." That is where the Middle Ages differed from the
modern world. At that time men sinned as much as at present,
but they did not try to excuse it by calling wrong right. They
still had a true sense of right and wrong because they still had
a true faith in God. At times Margaret prayed to God to save
her, but she saw no way out of her situation.

Then God came to her rescue in a very dramatic way. One
day, some nine years after Margaret had come to Montepulciano,
her sporting husband left the castle with his hound. A couple of
days later the hound came back alone and tugged at her skirt.
She followed the dog into the woods and there, under a pile of
leaves and branches, lay the body of her lover, murdered by his
enemies! Grief overwhelmed her. It was not merely his loss
to her. He was lost to God forever, dead in mortal sin, and all
because of her!

Her mind was made up. Back at the castle, she returned all
the precious gifts her lover had given her to his relatives. With
her little son walking beside her, she took her sad way back home
to Laviano. She would publicly confess her sins in church, do
penance, and try to begin life anew.

Her father was willing to accept the situation, but her stepmother would have nothing to do with her. Wasn't it bad
enough that this hussy had run away and lived in sin? Must
she now come back and bring disgrace on their honorable family
by making a fool of herself with her public penance in church!
So Margaret and her little boy were driven from her father's

SAINT MARGARET OF CORTONA

What Saint Francis was to the First Order of his followers, and what Saint Clare was to his Second Order (the cloistered Poor Clares), Saint Margaret was to become to his Third Order, his pious and penitent laity. Margaret spent a three-year period of probation before the Franciscan friars gave her the habit of the Tertiaries of Saint Francis. In the United States, members of the order are permitted to wear the habit only at death.

SAINT MARTHA

The life of Martha illustrates that not only those who spend their lives in holy contemplation, but also those who occupy themselves with external affairs can be pleasing to God and become genuine saints. From the Gospels we learn that Martha was the sister of Lazarus whom Jesus resurrected; and of her industrious nature when they say of her that "she served" at the banquet Simon the leper gave Jesus to celebrate the miracle.

house. She went out in the field, weeping her heart out in hopeless misery.

Then Satan came to tempt her. Why not go back to Montepulciano? She had plenty of friends there who would sympathize with her. She was still young — only twenty-seven — and still pretty. Moreover there were other young men left in the world. Margaret knew, however, that if she succumbed to the temptation this time, all would be lost for her. She prayed and prayed. She begged God to be her father, her spouse, her lord and master. Then an inner voice seemed to urge her to go to Cortona. She knew there was a monastery of Franciscan friars there; perhaps they would have pity on her and help her.

Once more she took her small son in hand, and together they trudged the twenty-five miles north to Cortona. Here, at the entrance to the town, as she hesitated, two noble ladies saw her grief-stricken face and took pity on her. They invited her to stay for a while with her son in their house, and they introduced her to the Franciscan friars.

Margaret begged the friars to accept her as a member of their Third Order. Though not doubting the sincerity of her conversion, they put her through a three-year period of probation before giving her the habit of the Tertiaries of St. Francis. During these three years she earned a living for herself and her son by doing jobs as a housemaid and nursing the sick. After she became a Franciscan tertiary she imitated the *Poverello* of Assisi by working for nothing and subsisting only on alms. Even during the first three years at Cortona she had given away most of the money that she had earned, living as poor, and as humbly as possible.

During these three years she still had her son with her. If she had once been spoiled by her mother, she would not spoil her own child. She made him live almost as austerely as she did. When she received the Franciscan habit, the two noble ladies (who always befriended her) arranged to have the boy sent to a good school in Arezzo (the city of the bishop to whose diocese

Cortona then belonged). Both in her own lifetime and ever since there have been people who thought that Margaret's treatment of her son was too strict and lacking in motherly affection. The fact is that she loved her son too tenderly for both his and her own good. She recognized that what is called "mother's love" is often only a hidden form of self-love, that being over-indulgent toward her child makes a mother feel good but is not good for the child. In any case, the repression of too much natural affection for the child of her sin was a sacrifice that God asked of Margaret, and she never hesitated to give Him anything He asked.

When her son grew up, he became a Franciscan Father and lived a holy life himself. A letter that Margaret wrote to him while he was in the Franciscan novitiate has come down to us. Before giving him much sage advice, she began: "My son, may you be blessed by the Lord to whose service you have consecrated yourself. If for love of Him you fight bravely in His army, I will ever remain tenderly attached to you. I will always be your mother, if you faithfully follow my advice." No one can say that a mother who could write like that did not love her son.

Margaret had made a general confession to Father Giunta as soon as she arrived in Cortona. Under his wise direction she then began a life of prayer and penance that was to last for twenty-three years, until the peace of heaven put an end to the ceaseless warfare she waged against her once-sinful body. Now that she was a member of Saint Francis' Order of Penance, she practiced as much mortification as she could beg permission from her director to do. Her food was dry bread, raw vegetables and a few nuts, limited to the smallest amount that was necessary to sustain her life. Her only drink was water. Her days were spent in laboring for the poor and in praying in the church. Her nights, which were passed in a small hut near the Franciscan monastery, were largely spent in prayer and penance. What little sleep she took was on the floor, with a block of wood for a pillow. When her director tried to restrain her zeal for penance, she answered: "Father, there can no longer be peace between my soul and my body. Let me treat my body like a relentless enemy and not pay attention to its protests. It did not complain when it used to live in luxury and comfort. Then it overcame me. Now it is for me to overcome it."

The purpose of so much mortification was not merely to make reparation for past sins; more than that, it was Margaret's way of trying to show God by means of generous sacrifice how much she loved Him. She always felt a strong need of loving and being loved. She had already learned the hard way how unsatisfying and disappointing is earthly love. She now found Love Itself, the God of love, Who alone could satisfy the ardent longings of her soul. Her life was now spent in intimate union with Him, her soul often rapt in ecstacy as she conversed heart to heart with Him.

Much of the account of her life, as recorded by Fra Giunta, is devoted to these conversations between Margaret and her crucified Lord, her "revelations," as they are called. To us who live in a different age and place, some of the expressions that occur in these "colloquies" between Margaret and Christ may seem oversentimental. We may also find it hard to understand why Margaret should make so much of the fact that Christ, after addressing her for quite some time as *poverella*, "My poor little one," finally consented to call her "My daughter." However, we should remember that every age and place has its own language, and this is not merely in the sense that Margaret of Cortona spoke medieval Italian and we speak modern English; she also spoke a different emotional language than we do. The reality, therefore, that stands beneath such seemingly exaggerated expressions of love is not the less genuine and true. Despite the sentimental terms in which it was expressed, Margaret's love for her divine Savior was far from being a merely sentimental thing. It was a living reality that expressed itself clearly in her actual life.

For one thing, Margaret proved the genuineness of her ardent
love for Christ by her sincere and deep love for all her fellowmen
that found expression in her active charity toward them. She
saw Christ in the last and least of His brethren and, as such,
they were objects of her constant, self-sacrificing service. In this
regard she was also eminently practical. Not satisfied with her
own personal care of the sick poor, she prevailed upon the civil
authorities in Cortona to open a hospital for them. Here they
were nursed by her and her followers, the members of the congregation of Tetiary Sisters, known as *le poverelle,* "the Little
Poor Women," which she founded. To supply the necessary
financial and material aid for this work she also established a
pious society among the better-off citizens known as the Confraternity of Our Lady of Mercy who contributed to the support
of her works of charity. On several occasions she intervened
between fueding parties for the sake of public peace. Twice she
carried out the difficult commission given her by God to rebuke
her bishop for living more like a secular prince and soldier than
like a spiritual shepherd of souls.

Margaret's love for Christ was also tested and found true in
the crucible of trials and tribulations. There were long periods
when her soul enjoyed no sensible consolations in prayer and
she felt utterly alone and forsaken by God. The devil then came
to tempt her with the thought that all her efforts were in vain,
that she was lost because of her sins. In fact, that her very penance was displeasing to God since it might be shortening her life
and thus be a form of suicide. Yet through all this she clung to
her beloved Lord with unshaken confidence in His infinite love
and goodness. Finally, toward the end of her life, she had to
stand the painful trial of slander. Malicious rumors were spread,
no doubt from the instigation of the devil, that all was not as it
should be in her relations with the Franciscan friars. To squelch
these rumors, Fra Giunta was transferred to another city, and
for several years Margaret was deprived of his spiritual guidance.
She herself moved her abode away from the friars' monastery to

the ruined church of Saint Basil in another part of Cortona. Here she worked on the repair of this edifice, here she spent the last years of her life, and here she was buried.

Her ardent longing to be inseparably united with God was finally satisfied when on February 22, 1297, fifty years after her birth, her heavenly host came to take her soul into its eternal home. Although she was always venerated in Cortona and the rest of Italy as a *beata,* a "blessed one," it was not until 1728 that she was formally canonized. Her body still rests in a silver shrine over the high altar of the Church of Saint Basil in Cortona.

Saint Margaret of Scotland
Widow

1 0 9 3

(June 10)

STRANGE TO SAY, the most famous queen of Scotland, Saint Margaret, had no Scottish blood in her veins. On her father's side she was English or, correctly, Saxon; on her mother's side she was Bavarian. To complicate matters still more, Queen Margaret of Scotland was born and reared as a girl in Hungary. A brief review of English history is necessary if one would understand how it came about that a Hungarian-born, English-Bavarian princess became queen of Scotland.

In the 9th century England suffered from a series of Viking or Danish invasions which wiped out all but one of its petty kingdoms. The only English kingdom to hold out against the Danes was that of Wessex, of the West Saxons, in the south of England. King Alfred the Great (871-901) of Wessex finally drove the Danes from a good part of the land they had occupied, and his valiant descendants annexed the remaining sections of the "Danelaw" to the realm of the Wessex kings. However, during the weak reign of Alfred's great-great-grandson, AEthelred II (979-1016), known as "the Unready" (though his Saxon epithet of *Redeless* really means "ill-advised"), England was again invaded by the Danes under Sweyn, whose son, Canute the Great, succeeded AEthelred II as king of England (1016-1035). AEthelred's hard-fighting son, Edmund Ironside, had indeed beaten Canute in several battles and regained much of the land that his father had lost to the Danes, but in the first year of his reign (1016) he suddenly died or, as some say, was treacherously murdered.

Now that the Dane Canute had complete control of England, the Saxon heirs to the throne were forced to leave England. Edward, later known as "the Confessor," one of AEthelred's sons by Emma, the sister of Duke Richard of Normandy, had fled to his mother's relatives in Normandy where he lived from 1013 to 1040, so that he was more Norman than English in culture. His nephews, Edmund and Edward, the young sons of Edward Ironside, likewise went to the Continent and eventually found refuge with St. Stephen, the first Catholic king of Hungary. Here Edmund died without issue. His brother Edward "the Exile," however, married Agatha, the niece of Stephen's queen, Ghisela (of the Imperial House of Bavaria) and a kinswoman of the Emperor (973-1024), St. Henry II. Three children were born of the marriage, Margaret, the future queen of Scotland; Christina, who was later to become the saintly abbess of a monastery in Romsey, Hampshire; and Edgar, known as "the AEtheling," Saxon for "the Prince." The family of King Stephen of Hungary saw to it that these royal children were reared in an atmosphere of fervent faith.

Meanwhile in England the throne reverted to the old Saxon line. Canute's two sons died without heirs after reigning but a short while, and St. Edward the Confessor (the son of AEthelred II) had been invited back from Normandy in 1040 and received the English crown in 1042. Since he had no son of his own, St. Edward offered to make his nephew and namesake, Edward the Exile, his successor. Therefore, in 1057, when Margaret was about ten or twelve years old, "the Exile," with his wife Agatha and their three children, left Hungary for England.

Tragedy awaited their arrival on the English shore. The father of these young children suddenly died within a short time after his return to England. There was some suspicion that his was not a natural death, but no foul play was ever proved. This then left Edgar the Aetheling, who was still but a boy, the next in line for the throne of England. Edward the Confessor took the widow Agatha and her three children under his protection at court which was already more Norman-French in culture and politics than it was English. During the nine years, therefore, that Margaret lived at St. Edward's court in London the atmosphere around her was one of art, scholarship, chivalry and fresh religious zeal. The young girl could hardly remain unimpressed by the example which her saintly granduncle Edward gave her in fervent piety and generosity to the Church and the poor.

Then on January 5, 1066, St. Edward the Confessor died and was buried in his favorite Abbey of Westminster. The leaders of the English nobility met and decided that Edgar the AEtheling, the rightful heir to the throne, was too young and inexperienced for it. They offered it to Harold, the son of Godwine, Earl of Wessex. Godwine's daughter Edith had been married to King Edward in 1045, and Harold, who had actually been governing in place of the aged king for several years, felt that as brother-in-law of the deceased king he had a claim to the throne. Scarcely had Harold accepted the crown when a new powerful claimant appeared in the person of Duke William of Normandy who had even less right than Harold to the throne. The fortunes of war, however, smiled on William. On September 28, 1066, he safely landed his large force at Hastings on the English Channel while Harold's fleet was engaged with a Viking invasion in the north. Harold's forces went back south in a weakened condition and suffered a disastrous defeat in which he himself lost his life. This was the famous battle of Hastings on October 14, 1066.

With William the Conqueror, as he was now called, in complete control of England, Agatha ("the Hungarian") with her three children and a small band of faithful followers fled to Northumbria in northern England. The ancient accounts differ regarding their next move. According to one story they put to sea with the intention of returning to Hungary, and were driven by a storm to the shores of Scotland. According to another story, they deliberately sailed to Scotland to seek refuge with King Malcolm III of that country. In fact, some say that Malcolm had already met Margaret in London and that Edward the Confessor had suggested a marriage betweeen them.

In any case, within a few years after the Battle of Hastings Agatha and her family were welcomed by Malcolm at his fortress tower in Dunfermline. According to one tradition, as they sailed into the Firth of Forth they found shelter from a violent storm in a little bay on its north shore that is still called "St. Margaret's Hope." About five miles inland lay Malcolm's Tower of Dunfermline where the refugees were given a warm welcome.

Malcolm III, known in Gaelic as the *Canmore* or "Great Head," was the son of King Duncan I of Scotland who had been murdered by Macbeth of Shakespeare fame. Having found a safe refuge at the court of Edward the Confessor, Malcolm, with the aid of Godwine's son Harold, returned to Scotland where he defeated Macbeth in July 1054, and where he was crowned in April 1057 at Scone (just northeast of Perth) the traditional crowning place of the Scottish kings. The ancient English chroniclers were inclined to call Malcolm savage and ruthless, but St. Ailred of Rievaulx, his contemporary, says of him: "He was a king very humble in heart, bold in spirit, exceedingly strong in bodily strength, daring, though not rash, and endowed with many other good qualities." The fact is that Malcolm irritated the Anglo-Normans by making several raids into Northumbria in an unsuccessful endeavor to restore Edgar the AEtheling to the throne of his fathers, and in doing so naturally wrought much havoc on that English province. However, there are records to prove that he could also be kind and merciful to his enemies. Therefore, though this king was not a ruthless savage, but a brave and intelligent man, still, according to the high standards of culture at the Anglo-Norman court, he must at first have seemed rather crude to Agatha and her children, and his rough Tower at Dunfermline a poor place indeed.

Margaret had grown into a beautiful, charming, intelligent and cultured young woman. It is not to be wondered at, therefore, that Malcolm soon asked her hand in marriage. He had already lost his first wife, Ingibiorg (widow of the Earl Thorfin of Sweden) who had given him a son, Prince Duncan. Though Margaret had desires (like her sister Christina) to enter the convent, she recognized the hand of God in so directing the course of events for her to do much good as queen of Scotland. Thus in 1070, Malcolm and Margaret were married in the little chapel of Dunfermline Tower by Fothad, Bishop of St. Andrews. Margaret was then about twenty-three years old, and Malcolm about forty. Despite the difference in their ages, this union proved to be a remarkably happy one, and particularly fortunate for their subjects and for the future of Scotland. It lasted for twenty-three years, during which Margaret proved a real helpmate and a wise counsellor to her royal husband.

Turgot, a monk of Dunfermline (and later Bishop of St. Andrews), who was the queen's confessor, is our principal source of information on St. Margaret of Scotland. A few years after her death he wrote her biography in Latin at the request of her daughter, Matilda. After outlining the history of Margaret's noble ancestors, as given above, Turgot shows that she proved herself a worthy descendant of such illustrious forebears. Endowed with a character that was both strong and gentle, she knew how to bring her husband to her way of thinking even while she let him believe that they were largely his own ideas which he put into practice. All the great things that she accomplished in life really arose from her ardent love for God and for His Catholic Church. Turgot says: "The prudent queen directed all such things as it was fitting for her to regulate: the laws of the realm were administered by her counsel; by her care the influence of religion was extended, and the people rejoiced in the prosperity of her affairs."

Margaret had a noble Abbey Church erected at Dunfermline in honor of the Most Holy Trinity, and all across Scotland she rebuilt the fallen churches that had been erected at the time of the glorious Celtic Church but devastated in the Viking invasions. Among the more famous of these ancient churches that Margaret restored were the one on the island of Iona (from where St. Columba and his Irish monks had brought the faith to Scotland), and the one at St. Andrews in honor of the Apostle who was Scotland's oldest patron. She furnished them with splendid ornaments, chalices and other sacred vessels of pure gold, as described by Turgot who saw them. This biographer of Margaret speaks of a beautiful crucifix which she presented to St. Andrews, and particularly of another one given to the Abbey Church of Dunfermline for its Rood Altar: "A cross of priceless value, bearing the figure of our Savior, which she had caused to be covered with the purest gold and silver, studded with gems." It was thus that she brought about a renaissance of the arts and crafts for which the old Celtic monasteries had once been so famous. At the court she personally supervised the work of the women engaged on the embroidery of the vestments and the hangings for the solemn liturgy.

Queen Margaret also brought to her court, first at Dunfermline and later at Edinburgh, many learned clerics, and she gathered a considerable library there of precious manuscripts, especially of the Sacred Scriptures. Turgot tells of her keen intellect and her ability to hold her own in the learned arguments that were a common occurrence at the court. "It very often happened," he says, "that these doctors went from her much wiser men than when they came." These discussions were probably held in Latin, but it is interesting to note that it was under Queen Margaret and King Malcolm that English first became the regular language of the Scottish court, instead of Gaelic. The annexation to the Scottish realm by Malcolm's father, Duncan, of the district of Lothian in northern Northumbria (where English had already been the common language for several centuries) no doubt hastened this displacement of Gaelic by English, first in southern Scotland, and then even in most parts of the Highlands.

King Malcolm, who could speak both Gaelic and English, never learned to read. Yet for the sake of his wife whom he adored, he revered the books that she loved. "Hence it was," wrote Turgot, "that, although he could not read, he used to page through and examine the books that she used either for her devotions or her study; and whenever he heard her express a liking for a particular book, he also would look at it with special interest and often take it into his hands and kiss it. Sometimes he sent for a worker in precious metals, whom he commanded to ornament a certain volume with gold and gems and, when the work was finished, the king himself would carry the book to the queen as a loving proof of his devotion."

A curious legend of the miraculous preservation of one of these books, a copy of the four Gospels, was told by the people and recounted by Turgot. While carrying this precious manuscript on a journey, a cleric accidentally dropped it in a stream, and only after some days of diligent search was it found, lying deep in the water with its illuminated pages turning over in the current. Wonderful to relate, on being rescued and dried out, all but two end pages were left unharmed by the water. Be this as it may, the truth is that this very book is now one of the treasures of the Bodleian Library at Oxford, and it is more of a miracle that this ancient Celtic volume escaped the destructive fury of the sixteenth-century Protestants than that it was not harmed by the water.

Margaret also encouraged trade and commerce with foreign countries. Merchants now came to Scotland with valuable and useful goods unknown there before. New cloths of various colors and elegant fashions were introduced. The increase of foreign commerce greatly aided the prosperity of Scotland which until then had been a poor, semi-barbarous hinterland. It was, of course, especially in the castles at Dunfermline and on the Rock at Edinburgh where most of this new magnificence was to be seen. The king was now attended by a splendidly liveried retinue, befitting his royalty. Elegant tapestries adorned the walls,

and gold and silver dishes were on the royal table. All this state-
liness was not part of Margaret's nature, but she knew it was a
requirement of kingly dignity. Within she was a humble woman,
and her gorgeous clothing covered a heart whose real richness
was its love for Christ.

Most of all, Margaret labored for religious restoration. The
ancient Celtic Church had largely fallen into a state of decay,
its monasteries in ruins and its communities cut off from the rest
of Christendom by the Viking invasions. Ancient customs, long
since revised by the universal Church, were still in use, and even
worse, certain surprising and almost barbarous rites had crept in.
Margaret worked to bring about the necessary reforms, and Turgot tells of one council, convened by Malcolm, that lasted for
three days when the "holy queen" prevailed upon the assembled ecclesiastics to discard their local customs and conform to
the practices of the Holy Roman Church. Margaret addressed
these men in English since she could not speak Gaelic very well,
but to make sure they understood her Malcolm then repeated her
words in Gaelic.

At the very time when the great Hildebrand, St. Gregory VII,
was fighting moral decay in the Church on the Continent, Margaret was doing the same thing in Scotland, and her methods
closely followed those of the reforming popes. She sought counsel
from such men as Lanfranc, the Italian scholar who became Archbishop of Canterbury and was one of the foremost restorers of
the Church in France and England. To help her in this good
work, he sent Goldwin and other clerics to Scotland. It is
thought that she even asked the advice of Pope Alexander II
(1061-1073), during whose pontificate she had married Malcolm.
In any case, it seems likely that it was out of veneration for this
pope that she named one of her sons "Alexander," thus introduc-
ing the widespread custom in Scotland of using this for a given
name.

Only in one thing did Margaret meet with partial failure; her
attempt to do away with the holding of ecclesiastical benefices

by laymen. The abuse was too ingrained. Even Lanfranc was forced to tolerate this traditional evil. She did, however, ultimately succeed to a large extent, for gradually during the reigns of her husband and her sons there evolved a Catholic Church in Scotland that was truly spiritual, scholarly, and independent of the laity. By herself she thus achieved greater success than many popes and bishops in other places were able to do.

The basic reason why this otherwise weak woman (who was not a native of the country where she lived) was able to accomplish so much for the glory of God was her genuine personal sanctity. In the Mass for the Feast of St. Margaret of Scotland the Church reads for the Lesson (or Epistle) the passage from the Book of Proverbs (31, 10-31; *Mulierem fortem quis inveniet . . .*), which describes the ideal woman. How perfectly she fulfills this description! It was especially the prayers of this ideal of Catholic womanhood that played a major role in all that she accomplished. Surely it was Malcolm's wife rather than his mother whom Shakespeare describes in his "Macbeth":

> "The queen that bore thee,
> oftener upon her knees than on her feet,
> died every day she lived."

Turgot wrote: "Of all living persons I know or have known, she was the most devoted to prayer and fasting, to works of mercy and almsgiving." At night she often arose for the Divine Office in the abbey church; in the morning she was at Mass, and on great festivals she sometimes assisted at five or six low Masses before she attended the high Mass. In Dunfermline there is a grotto, still called St. Margaret's Cave (and still visited by many pilgrims), where the queen often used to go alone at night to spend hours in contemplation and penitential prayer.

Perhaps the greatest, certainly one of the most surprising accomplishments of this saintly woman lay in the success she had in teaching her warrior husband to seek the spiritual, to keep vigils of prayer before God. Turgot says that he was "astonished to see in the king such a steady earnestness in his devotions" and he "wondered how it was that there could exist in the heart of a man living in the world such an entire sorrow for sin." Even more, Margaret taught the king humility. It must have astounded the court to see Malcolm kneel to wash the feet of the poor whom his wife devotedly attended every day. He also helped her wait on them at table as she fed them.

The queen's charity was amazing. The poor came not only from all over Scotland, but even from foreign ports. It is not possible to list here all her daily acts for her beloved poor, or the variety of those that she ministered to. Often her gifts outran her means, but the courtiers vied with each other to offer her their own belongings to aid her charity. Charity after all is contagious. She was even known to pilfer from the king, who, though he gave generously himself, was much amused at her doing this and, when at times he caught her with his money in her hands, would laugh and tell her he would have her arrested.

She also found a good opportunity to practice charity toward the many serfs who were then in Scotland as a result of Malcolm's raids on the English in Northumbria during the reign of William the Conqueror. Life was cruel for them, and the queen did all she could to lighten their hardships and, when it was possible for her, she ransomed them and returned them to their homes.

Margaret also erected hostels at St. Andrews for the pilgrims who came to venerate the Apostle's relics there. For the pilgrims who came from the south and would otherwise have had to make a long detour inland to get to the north side of the Firth of Forth (where St. Andrews lay), she inaugurated a free ferry service at a relatively narrow part of the Firth west of Edinburgh and south of Dunfermline. This ferry service, though no longer free, was the only crossing of the Firth until the end of the last century when a great cantilever bridge was built at the same site. The towns on each side of the Firth here are still known as North Queensferry and South Queensferry, both named after Queen Margaret.

To be easily accessible to everyone, Margaret used to hold open court in the fields. On the North Queensferry road near Dunfermline there is an old stone, shaped like a seat, which is still called by the people thereabouts "St. Margaret's Stone," because it is believed to have been one of her judgment seats. Though Malcolm was by nature a violent man, Turgot says "there was in him a sort of dread of offending Margaret, whose life was so venerable; for he could not but perceive from her conduct that Christ dwelt within her."

With all her devotions, her care of the poor, and her duties of state, Margaret never neglected her children. She took the word of the Lord literally that "he who spares his rod hates his son" (Prv. 13,24), and the royal children were not spared its use, when necessary. They were thus well-behaved and carefully instructed in their religion, and in all the branches of learning of that time. Hence, "her children rose up and praised her; her husband, too, extolled her (Prv. 31,28).

Malcolm and Margaret were blessed by God with eight children: six boys—Edward, Edmund, Edgar, AEthelred, Alexander, and David, and two girls—Matilda (or, Maud), and Mary. Edward fell with his father in the Battle of Alnwick. Edgar, Alexander, and David were each in turn kings of Scotland. AEthelred became Abbot of Dunkeld. The only black sheep among Margaret's sons was Edmund, who, probably under the influence of the trouble maker, Malcolm's brother, Donald Bane, proved treacherous and disloyal to his father, and was stripped of his royal rank and the right of succession. It is good, however, to hear from the ancient chroniclers that he later repented and died a monk in the monastery of Montecute in Somersetshire. Margaret's daughters were educated in the convent of their aunt, Christina, and later entered into illustrious marriages. Princess Matilda became the wife of King Henry I of England (1100-1135), and was long remembered by the English as "good Queen Maud." Princess Mary married Count Eustace III of Boulogne, and when their daughter and only child became the wife of King Ste-

SAINT LAWRENCE, COSMAS and DAMIAN (*Courtesy of the Metropolitan Museum of Art, Rogers Fund,* 1935)

This Italian altarpiece enthrones Saint Lawrence, deacon of the Holy Roman Church, who has been honored since his death, in 258, as one of her greatest glories. When his persecutors asked him to reveal where the treasures of the Church were hidden, he pointed to the poor Christians who had assembled to witness his martyrdom—the widows, orphans, the sick and the blind. "These," he said, "are the treasures of the Church!"

SAINT MARGARET

Saint Margaret lived in Antioch of Pisidia (Asia Minor), and suffered martyrdom under Diocletian during the third century. She was swallowed by a dragon, but survived. Subsequently she was beheaded for her faith. Her cult was widespread in medieval England, and she was one of the saints who counseled Joan of Arc. As one of the *Fourteen Holy Helpers*, she was frequently invoked in the Middle Ages for various needs.

phen of England, the nephew and successor of Henry I, the English had another Queen Matilda.

For two hundred years Scotland was fortunate in being ruled by descendants of St. Margaret, all of them very good kings: her three sons, Edgar, Alexander, and David; then David's two grandsons, Malcolm IV and William; and finally, William's son and grandson, Alexander II and Alexander III. Throughout their reigns the traditions established by Queen Margaret were carried on. Thus this period is rightly reckoned as Scotland's golden era. David was an especially fine man, and after his death he was venerated locally as a saint. Continuing his mother's work, he rendered great service to the Church, particularly by his construction of many splendid ecclesiastical edifices. Like his mother, he was wholeheartedly devoted to God and God's cause. As an old poem says of him,

> The day he was both king and knight;
> a monk devout he was by night.

It was God's will that St. Margaret's heroic virtues had their final testing in the tragedy that attended her deathbed. For six months she lay in Edinburgh castle broken in health and racked with pain. Then the fire of war again flared up between Scotland and England. The English king, William Rufus (1087-1100), violating the treaty of peace which his father, the Conqueror, had made with Malcolm (and which he himself had confirmed), seized several Scottish castles in Northumberland. When the army of the Scots, led by their king and his two sons, Edward and Edgar, went to recover the castle at Alnwick, Malcolm and Edward were treacherously slain. Even as Margaret was praying for them at the very time of the battle, she had a foreboding of the disaster. Three days later, on November 16, 1093, she seemed to rally from her illness and went to her little oratory, the small chapel that still stands on the walls of Edinburgh Castle. Here she heard Mass and received the Holy Viaticum. Scarcely had she returned to her chamber when her illness became worse than ever. Knowing that her death was imminent, she begged the clergy to recite the prayers for the dying. Then she asked them to bring her the Black Rood.

A word might be said here about this famous relic, a richly ornamented cross of pure gold containing in itself a relic of the True Cross. It is quite possible that she herself had brought it to Scotland. When David I died at Carlisle in 1153, he venerated it on his deathbed. In 1291 it was carried off to England with other treasures by Edward I. In 1328 it was returned to Scotland. David II carried it into battle in 1346, and with his defeat it again fell into the hands of the English who placed it in the Cathedral of Durham. Here it remained until 1540, when it disappeared from history in the despoiling of Durham Cathedral by the hordes of Henry VIII.

When this precious relic was given to St. Margaret, she blessed herself with it, kissed it, and held it tenderly while she said the "Miserere." At that moment Edgar arrived from the scene of battle, and his mother asked him about his father and brother. As he hesitated to speak, she cried out: "I know it, my boy, I know it. By this Holy Cross, by the bond of our blood, I adjure you to tell me the truth!" In tears, he told her what had happened. Margaret, who had never refused God anything, accepted with loving resignation this final sacrifice. Then she said the prayer used before receiving Holy Communion: "Lord Jesus Christ, who according to the will of the Father, through the cooperation of the Holy Ghost, hast by Thy death given life to the world, deliver me . . ."—and died. Her face, so pale and worn with pain, became "suffused with fair and warm hues."

Because Donald Bane had started to besiege Edinburgh Castle to usurp his dead brother's throne, the queen's body had to be carried away secretly "in a myst" to Dunfermline where it was buried in the Abbey Church. From the day of her death the veneration of Margaret as a saint grew constantly. Dunfermline, instead of Iona, became the sacred house of eternal sleep for the Scottish kings. The numerous pilgrimages of the Middle Ages to this national shrine are again resumed in our times.

A century and a half after Margaret's death, King Alexander II and the bishops of Scotland petitioned the Holy See to canonize the holy queen, and on August 5, 1249, Pope Innocent IV solemnly pronounced her a saint. Thereupon a new and more fitting tomb was prepared for the relics of St. Margaret in the once lovely Lady Chapel of the Abbey Church at Dunfermline. Here, on July 19, they were solemnly transferred and placed side by side with the remains of her spouse, King Malcolm.

For three centuries vigil lights burned night and day before this venerated shrine of St. Margaret of Scotland, but in the sixteenth century the monks of Dunfermline, rightly fearing for the safety of the saint's relics, removed them to a more secure place. Thus when John Knox's fanatics stormed the Abbey Church in 1560 with their "pure gospel," they could vent their fury on the building alone, not on Margaret's relics. The Lady Chapel they smashed to the ground and left only the marble base on which the holy queen's shrine tomb stood. For a while St. Margaret's head was kept by Mary, Queen of Scots, at Edinburgh Castle. Later it was taken to the Catholic College of Douay, in the Low Lands, where it was venerated until the French Revolution. Thereafter its whereabouts remained unknown. The rest of her relics were eventually received by Philip II of Spain who placed them in his Escorial Palace in Madrid. From this source Bishop Gillis of the Eastern District of Scotland is said to have secured the relic of St. Margaret which is now the treasure of St. Margaret's Convent in Edinburgh.

St. Margaret of Scotland has ever been greatly venerated at the Scots College in Rome. In 1646, when the church of this college was built, a magnificent altar was dedicated to her along with a beautiful painting by an unknown Polish artist showing her at prayer; above her is a vision of the Holy Trinity, while in the background is a scene from the Battle of Alnwick in which her husband and oldest son were killed.

The reason is no longer clear why the 10th of June was chosen for St. Margaret's feast in the universal Church. In Scotland her feast is again celebrated on the anniversary of her death, November 16th. With St. Andrew the Apostle, she is venerated as the special patron of the land over which she ruled so well as queen. Even among the Protestants of Scotland there has ever been a remarkable love for their great and holy queen. Thus, when Glasgow University opened its college for women, it was named "Queen Margaret's." The Protestant historian Skene wrote: "Perhaps there is no more beautiful character recorded in history than that of Margaret. For purity of motives, for a deep sense of religion and great personal piety, for the unselfish performance of whatever duty lay before her, and for entire self-abnegation she is unsurpassed."

It is the hope and prayer of the ever growing Catholic Church in Scotland that through the intercession of their beloved St. Margaret all the inhabitants of that fair land may once more be loyal children of the one true Church which she loved and served so well.

Saint Mark

Evangelist

First Century

(April 25)

T HE NEW TESTAMENT speaks of a certain man called "John who was surnamed Mark" (Acts 12, 12.24; 15,37). There is no reason to doubt that this is the same man who is called "John" in Acts 13,5.13, and "Mark" in several other passages. It was quite common at that time for Greek-speaking Jews to have two names, one Hebrew and the other Greek or Latin. In this case he who had the Hebrew name of "John" was also known by the Latin name of "Marcus" or "Mark."

From these various references to John Mark we can gather considerable information about him. First of all, it is to be noted that he was the nephew or cousin (the Greek word being ambiguous) of Saint Barnabas, the early friend and companion of Saint Paul (Col. 4,10). Although Barnabas was a native of the island of Cyprus (Acts 4,36), Mark was probably born in Jerusalem for his mother Mary had her home there, at least about the year 44 when Saint Peter was imprisoned by King Herod Agrippa I (Acts 12,12). Mark's mother Mary seems to have been a woman of some means. She had at least one servant girl (the maid Rhoda, or Rose, who kept Saint Peter waiting at the outer gate of the house), and her house served as one of the meeting places or local churches of the early Christian community in Jerusalem. It is possible that it was in the large "upper room" of this house that Jesus celebrated the Last Supper with His apostles, though this supposition cannot, of course, be proved.

John Mark was probably too young at the time of our Lord's public ministry to be considered one of the disciples of Christ, but it is again just possible that Mark is the unnamed "young man" referred to in his Gospel (Mark 14, 51-52) who, "having a linen cloth wrapped about his naked body," followed Jesus out to Gethsemani. "And they seized him. But leaving the linen cloth behind, he fled away from them naked." On the double supposition that the house of Mark's mother was the place of the Last Supper, and that the young man at Gethsemani was Mark himself, one might reconstruct the occurrence on something like these lines. After Christ and His apostles left the Upper Room in Jerusalem and went to the garden at the foot of the Mount of Olives, His enemies first came there to seize Him at the house of Mark's mother, or word reached there that they were out to arrest Him. Young Mark, who had meanwhile gone to bed, roused by the excitement, takes time merely to wrap his sheet around his body, and runs to Gethsemani to warn Jesus. But he arrives too late. Christ's enemies lay hold of him also. The sheet, however, that he had thrown around himself does not offer a firm hold for his captors. Slipping out of it, he leaves it in their hands while he runs away "naked"—which is the Biblical way of saying that he was not fully and decently clothed. All this, however, is in the realm of sheer fantasy; there is no way of proving that the young man of whom Mark alone speaks in his Gospel is Mark himself.

When we come to the other data about St. Mark in the New Testament, we are on much firmer ground. About the year 47, when Paul and Barnabas had brought assistance from the Christian community at Antioch to the Christians at Jerusalem (who were suffering from the great famine that occurred in the reign of the Emperor Claudius [Acts 11,27-30]), these two apostles, on their return to Antioch, "took with them John, who was surnamed Mark" (Acts 12,25). A few months later the community at Antioch, acting under the inspiration of the Holy Spirit, sent Paul and Barnabas on their first missionary journey (48-49 A. D.), and these two men again took John Mark with them as their "assistant" (Acts 13,1-5).

After Mark had accompanied Paul and Barnabas on their journey from the eastern to the western end of Cyprus, and had sailed with them north to the district of Pamphylia in southern Asia Minor, for some unknown reason he "left them and returned to Jerusalem" (Acts 13,13). It could hardly have been a disagreement over methods or principles, such as Saint Paul receiving uncircumcised pagans into the Church; Mark would surely have been in agreement with his relative Barnabas on these matters. More likely, it was homesickness or fear of the hardships that would await him in the wilds of southern Asia Minor.

Saint Paul, however, did not take it lightly that Mark had proved so unsteady on this first missionary journey. About the year 50, when Mark had come to Antioch again with Barnabas after the question of receiving uncircumcised pagans into the Church had been settled at the Council of the Apostles in Jerusalem, his desertion on the first journey was not forgotten by the Apostle of the Gentiles. Back at Antioch, "Paul said to Barnabas, 'Let us return and visit the brethren in all the cities where we have preached the word of the Lord, to see how they are doing.' But Barnabas wanted to take with them John also, who was surnamed Mark. But Paul asked that he, inasmuch as he had deserted them in Pamphylia instead of going on with them to their work, should not again be taken along. And a sharp contention sprang up so that they separated from each other, and Barnabas took Mark and sailed for Cyprus" (Acts 15,36-39). It was indeed unfortunate that this seemingly minor matter should have been the cause of a "sharp contention" between these two old friends, for Barnabas had been the first in Jerusalem to give the right hand of welcome to the newly converted Paul (Acts 9, 26-27). Yet, after all, the saints are human, and the power of divine grace does not instantly wipe out all human frailties. Later in life St. Paul would become mellower and more considerate of others' weaknesses. For the present he evidently felt that the apostolic ministry was no place for a weakling. Saint Barnabas' loyalty to his young relative on this occasion merely proves the old adage that "blood is thicker than water."

It is consoling, however, to know that St. Paul's dispute with Barnabas and Mark did not have lasting effects. A few years later, when Paul wrote to the Corinthians, he praises Barnabas as the only one who, like himself, preaches the gospel without using his right to receive financial aid from the faithful (1 Cor. 9,6). What is more important for our purpose, Mark, himself, is later one of Paul's companions again. When St. Paul was a prisoner at Rome in the years 60 to 62, or perhaps as some hold, a prisoner at Ephesus about the year 58, he mentions Mark as one of his "fellow workers" who send greetings to Philemon (Phlm 24), and he writes at the same time to the Colossians: "Aristarchus, my fellow prisoner, sends you greetings; so does Mark, Barnabas' cousin, concerning whom you have received instructions: if he comes to you, welcome him" (Col. 4,10).

Mark was thus not only one of Paul's fellow missionaries at this time; he was also sent by the Apostle on some special mission to the Colossians in western Asia Minor. Again, St. Paul at the end of his life writes to Timothy: "Take Mark and bring him with thee, for he is useful to me for the ministry" (2 Tim. 4,11).

Mark, however, was not only a fellow worker with St. Paul; he was also a companion of St. Peter in Rome. The Prince of the Apostles, writing from the capital of the Roman empire which he calls "Babylon," sends greetings to the various Christian communities in Asia Minor in these words: "The Church which is at Babylon, chosen together with you, greets you; and so does my son Mark" (1 Pet. 5,13). The word "son," as used here, may be merely a term of affection, or it may signify that Peter had given spiritual birth in Christ to Mark by baptizing him.

In any case, the tradition in the Church which states that St. Mark's Gospel represents the preaching of St. Peter is very early and completely unanimous. This tradition can be traced back to the early Father of the Church, Papias, who, writing about the year 120, quotes "the Elder" (commonly believed to designate St. John the Apostle) to this effect: "This also the Elder used to say, 'Mark, having become the interpreter of Peter, wrote down accurately, although not in an orderly arrangement, the sayings and deeds of the Lord, as far as he recalled them. For he himself neither heard the Lord nor was he His follower, but he was later on, as I have said, a follower of Peter. The latter used to deliver his instructions as circumstances required, but not like one who draws up an orderly arrangement of our Lord's activity. Therefore Mark did nothing wrong in thus writing down certain things as he remembered them. For his sole purpose was to omit nothing of what he had heard and to falsify nothing in recording this.' " As a matter of fact, it can be demonstrated that there is a striking similarity between the preaching of St. Peter as recorded in the Acts of the Apostles and the Gospel according to St. Mark. That is why St. Justin the Martyr in the middle of the second century calls St. Mark's Gospel "the Memoirs of St. Peter."

Although according to Catholic tradition the original Aramaic Gospel of St. Matthew was the first Gospel written, this is no longer preserved, and the Greek translation that we have of it shows signs of having been composed after St. Mark's Gospel was written in Greek. For all practical purposes, therefore, the Gospel according to St. Mark is the oldest of our present four Gospels. It is indeed a "primitive" Gospel. Its author does not try to write "fine literature;" he simply records the early "oral" Gospel as recited by the Christians at Rome, the church of St. Peter. Its Greek is that of the ordinary people of the time as spoken in the forums and highways of the Roman empire, not the literary Greek of the schools. Yet there is a certain charm in the very simplicity of Mark's language. His style is straightforward and vigorous, full of a realism that would be expected in a "primitive" account. The vividness and graphic touches, the frequent use of the historical present, and the uneven structure of the sentences are typical of a story told by an eye-witness, here Saint Peter himself.

Concerning Saint Mark's later years nothing can be said with certainty. The Church venerates him as a martyr, but this is probably to be taken in the original sense of the Greek word *martyr*, meaning simply a famous "witness" to the faith, but not necessarily one who shed his blood for Christ. A tradition began in the fourth century which claims that Saint Mark founded the Christian Church at Alexandria in Egypt, and to this day the Coptic Christians of Egypt look upon him as the first Father, under Christ, of their Church. This tradition, however, was unknown to such great third-century Fathers of Egypt as Saint Clement of Alexandria and Origen. Besides, it runs into serious historical difficulties. On the one hand, we knew pretty well of the doings and whereabouts of Saint Mark the Evangelist up to the martyrdom of St. Peter and St. Paul in Rome about the year 67, so that St. Mark could hardly have gone to Egypt until after this date. On the other hand, during the time of the apostles, Alexandria (which was next door to Palestine) had by far the largest colony of Jews in any city except Jerusalem. Thus it seems certain that the gospel of Christ may have been preached there even before it reached Antioch in Syria. Perhaps the founder of the Church at Alexandria in Egypt happened to be called "Mark" also, and by the fourth century people began to confuse him with his namesake, Saint Mark the Evangelist.

In the Middle Ages the reputed relics of Saint Mark were brought to Venice in Italy, and ever since then he has been the principal patron of this city. The Venetian cathedral of St. Mark is one of the greatest glories of this City of Canals.

When the four beasts of the prophet Ezechiel's vision (Ez 1, 10) were distributed as symbols among the four Evangelists, Saint Mark received the lion as his emblem for the fanciful reason that he begins his Gospel with the preaching of Saint John the Baptist in the desert, and the lion is *the* beast of the desert.

Saint Martha

Virgin

First Century

(July 29)

T HE LIFE OF Saint Martha of Bethany shows that not only those who spend their lives in holy contemplation, but also those who by nature must keep themselves busy with external affairs, can be pleasing to God and even become genuine saints despite their lack of talent at devout meditation.

Although the Gospels tell us relatively little about Martha, they consistently portray her as a sensible, practical person, full of zeal and industry "to get things done." Martha is mentioned only in the Gospels of Saint Luke (10:38-42) and Saint John (11: 1-44 and 12:1-2). From these texts we learn that she was the sister of Lazarus, whom Christ raised from the dead, and of Mary who is often, but wrongly, confused with Mary Magdalen.

This close-knit family of three, none of whom was apparently married, lived at Bethany (a suburb to the east of Jerusalem, to the southeast of the Mount of Olives). That Martha was older than Mary, is clear, not only from the fact that she is always named before her, but also from Saint Luke's statement that she welcomed Jesus into *her* house. To her was entrusted the management of the household. This family was evidently one of considerable means since Mary could afford to pour a vase of precious perfume on Jesus which the worldly-wise Judas Iscariot estimated to be worth "three hundred denarii." (One denarius was the normal day's pay of the average workman). Hard worker though she was, Martha did not permit her spirit of industry to be spoiled by that of avarice, and there is no reason to think that she objected to this generous gift that Mary made from the family's wealth.

Her industrious nature can be observed at the banquet which her neighbor in Bethany, Simon the leper, gave Jesus to celebrate the miracle of Lazarus' resurrection from the tomb. While her sister Mary makes herself everlastingly famous at this banquet by her anticipation of Jesus' burial anointing, of Martha the Gospel says simply that she "served" at the table.

Martha's dominant characteristic of industry is best seen at an event which happened earlier in the life of our Lord. On this occasion, when Jesus was visiting Jerusalem, "Martha welcomed Him to her house." Anxious to have a suitable meal prepared for her honored Guest, she "was worried about much serving." Meanwhile her younger sister Mary merely "seated herself at the feet of our Lord and listened to His word." Finally this proved too much for Martha. Almost chiding Jesus for being responsible for Mary's seeming laziness, "she came up and said, 'Lord, is it no concern of Thine that my sister has left me to serve alone? Tell her therefore to help me.' But the the Lord answered her and said to her, 'Martha, Martha! Thou art anxious and troubled about many things; and yet only one thing is needful.' "

Perhaps this reply of Christ means directly no more than: "You are worried about too many courses for the dinner. One dish will be enough." Generally a deeper meaning is seen in His words. He wished to teach Martha that she was too much concerned with merely material things, even though good in themselves, and that "the one thing needful" is essentially a matter of the spirit: to know, love, and serve God, and thereby find eternal bliss in Him.

Jesus then takes up the defense of the younger sister. "Mary," He said, "has chosen the best part, and it will not be taken from her." No, He will not order her to help her older sister. Mary has picked a better task for herself, merely to sit and listen to Him, and He is just as well pleased with her rapt attention to His words as He is with Martha's bustling activity in His service.

This saying of Jesus is often used as the classical text to prove that among the clergy the "contemplative life" is a higher state than the "active life." Viewed theoretically, this is no doubt true. St Thomas Aquinas, however, teaches that best of all is a combination of both the contemplative and the active life. As a matter of fact, in every good religious there must be a certain amount both of "contemplation" (in the sense of prayer and meditation), and of "activity." It is merely a question of degree. As far as one or the other element predominates in it, a religious life is called either "contemplative" or "active." Even the most strictly cloistered nuns and monks must engage in a certain amount of profitable work at home for the support of the community, as well as in the necessary household chores. Moreover, their prayers and sacrifices for the good of the Church, and of the individual faithful, can rightly be regarded as an active sharing in the ministry for souls. On the other hand, religious of one of the "active" orders must engage in at least a minimum of prayer and meditation, else their work in teaching, preaching, or in works of Christian charity will be empty of spiritual benefit both for themselves and for others.

One should not think that, because of this little rebuke which our Lord had to give Martha, He did not love her. St. John said clearly, "Jesus loved Martha and her sister Mary and Lazarus." The Evangelist made this statement to explain that Christ's delay in answering the sisters' appeal to come and cure their brother (who was mortally ill) was not caused by any lack of love for them. It was rather the will of His heavenly Father that Jesus should let Lazarus die in order to manifest Christ's divine power in the great miracle of raising Lazarus from the dead.

When our Lord finally came to Bethany four days after the death of Lazarus, it was the practical Martha, not her contemplative sister, who went out to meet Him. "Martha therefore said to Jesus, 'Lord, if Thou hadst been here, my brother would not have died. But even now I know that whatever Thou shalt ask of God, God will give it to Thee.' " Her faith in Jesus remained unshaken. He assured her with the words that are now spoken at every Catholic burial service: "I am the resurrection and the life. He who believes in Me, even if he die, shall live; and whoever lives and believes in Me shall never die." Then He asked her: "Dost thou believe this?" And Martha proclaimd her faith: "Yes, Lord, I believe that Thou art the Christ, the Son of God, who hast come into the world." To reward this faith, Christ then restored her brother to her. Although Martha, the ever practical one, warned Him not to have the tomb of her half-decayed brother opened, our Lord gave the order to have the stone removed from its doorway, and then with His almighty command, "Lazarus, come forth!" He brought the dead man back to life.

Neither the New Testament nor early Christian tradition tells us anything more of Martha or her family. However, in either the 10th or 11th century a legend was invented according to which Martha, Mary and Lazarus eventually came to southern France and preached the gospel there. Apparently this story arose from the fact that at the beginning of the 5th century there was a holy bishop called Lazarus at the city of Aix, near Marseilles. Later veneration of this Bishop Lazarus caused confusion between him and Lazarus of Bethany. To keep the Bethany family together, the legend pictured Martha and Mary accompanying their brother Lazarus even to southern France.

Saint Martin de Porres

Confessor

1 6 3 9

(November 3)

LIMA, THE CAPITAL of Peru, has a unique honor. It is the only city in the Americas that can boast of being the place where two canonized saints were born, lived, and died: Rose of Lima, and Martin de Porres. What is more remarkable, the lives of these saints, who seldom went far from their native city, were contemporaneous. Here Martin came into the world seven years before Rose, and here he left it twenty-two years after her. Both were baptized by the same priest at the same baptismal font, both belonged to the Order of Saint Dominic, and both had the same general mission in life—to love God in His poor and to offer Him the sacrifice of their penitential lives in reparation for the sins committed against the down-trodden Indians and Negroes of Peru.

God's ways are not man's ways, and no one would ever have guessed from the circumstances in which Martin was born that he would some day be one of God's great saints. His father, Don Juan de Porres was a native of Burgos in Spain and a knight of the Order of Alcantara, who, like many other Spanish noblemen of his day, went to the New World to seek his fortune with the conquistadores. In the city of Panama he fell in love with a beautiful young woman, named Anna Velasquez, who was a full-blooded Negro. Though born in slavery, she is mentioned in the records as a free woman. Perhaps Don Juan himself freed her from slavery, but if so, he refused to give her a much better gift. Although both were Catholics, this proud Spanish nobleman would not deign to let his conjugal relations with a woman of so low a caste be blessed by the Church.

Less than fifty years after Pizarro's amazing conquest of the Inca Empire of Peru these lovers moved to Lima, and here their first child was born, a son as dark as his mother. The same day the baby boy was baptized in the Church of San Sebastian, where the record is still preserved: "On Wednesday, December 9, 1579, I baptized Martin; mother, Anna Velasquez; father, unknown; sponsors . . .; (signed) Father Antonio Polanco." After the birth of Martin's sister, Juana, their gallant father coolly abandoned his little family in Lima to accept a higher government post in Guayaquil, Ecuador.

Though Juan de Porres occasionally sent some money for the support of his dark-skinned offspring in Lima, Martin and Juana were raised on the bread of poverty. Anna worked hard to earn enough to keep her children alive, but she hardly loved her unwanted son. He had inherited all the African color and features of his mother, and she rightly concluded that this was the reason why the boy's white father had left her. Almost everything contrived to give Martin a sad and tragic boyhood; that is, almost everything but the grace of God. Far from becoming resentful of his lot, the boy prized it highly because it gave him a deeper sympathy and a warmer love for all the other poor and despised of his city. For the rich and mighty, too, he had a loving pity since he saw how miserable their lives were made by sin. In every one of his fellow men he always saw his Savior, Jesus Christ.

We do not know who taught him how to pray so well even as a little boy. We would like to think it was his poor mother. In any case, it was hardly this harassed woman who inspired him with his irrepressible love for the poor. On more than one occasion she let him have a sound whipping for giving away to the poor what little money she earned with her hard work.

SAINT PAUL OF THE CROSS

For Saint Paul of the Cross, the Passion of Jesus Christ was the all-consuming passion of his soul. The story of the external events of the life of this Saint is essentially a record of his activity to win men to God by preaching Christ crucified, and by founding a religious order, commonly known as *The Passionists,* for this same purpose.

SAINT MARY MAGDALENE   Batoni

Mary Magdalene was one of the devoted women who joined Jesus' company during His public ministry in Galilee, and stood by the cross when
all the Apostles, except John, had fled. She not only saw the Savior die;
she also watched Him being buried. Thus she was an important witness to
the fact that He was truly buried, without whom, His empty tomb would
not have been valid testimony to His Resurrection.

When Martin was eight years old, his father came back to Lima and took his two children with him to Guayaquil. Here he placed his son in the care of a tutor who taught him how to read and write Spanish. But after two years Don Juan de Porres was made governor of Panama, and Martin was sent back to his mother in Lima. God's Providence again arranged things for the future of the poor little black boy. When he was twelve years old, his mother apprenticed him to a "barber." In those days, however, a barbershop was much more than a tonsorial parlor; it was a sort of dispensary or clinic. Besides shaving and cutting hair, a barber then set broken bones, pulled troublesome teeth, dressed wounds, performed minor surgery, and administered simple drugs. Martin loved his work; it gave him a greater opportunity for being of service to the poor. Soon he learned his trade so well that countless poor people came flocking to his barbershop-dispensary. Even then he was already working wonderful cures which the primitive remedies at his disposal could hardly account for.

Yet Martin longed to do good to the souls as well as to the bodies of his dear poor. Morever, he felt an urgent need of dedicating himself more closely to God's service. Thus when he was eighteen he asked to be admitted to Lima's Monastery of San Domingo. But here he did not even aspire to be a Dominican lay brother. It may have been the knowledge of his illegitimate birth, but more likely it was the thought of his own personal unworthiness that made him ask that he might merely be accepted as a Dominican tertiary, a layman working as an unpaid servant in the monastery. The prior, who already knew his virtue and value, gladly accepted him in this capacity. For nine years Martin remained in this position, a secular coadjutor of the Third Order living inside the cloister. Then, when he was twenty-four, his religious superiors, who were now completely certain of his heroic virtues, dispensed with the impediment caused by his illegitimate birth and allowed him to make the solemn vows of a Dominican lay brother.

During all his years in the monastery Martin rejoiced in doing the lowliest, menial tasks. Popular pictures of him used to represent him as "the saint with the broom," as he became known soon after his death. But his superiors also gave him ample opportunity to use his medical skill and to exercise his practical charity to the poor. Almost from the beginning they made him infirmarian of this large community of several hundred members, as well as the dispenser of its alms to the poor. Though the monastery itself was very poor, its prior knew that Martin's boundless generosity would somehow not impoverish it still more. For Martin suddenly appeared in the room with fresh sheets and ways the clearest expression of God's will.

So many marvels were told of what he did in life that only the most skeptical would doubt that many of them must have been true miracles. Yet to Martin himself they all seemed quite normal and natural; his childlike faith took for granted God's power and will to do the miraculous. A novice, for instance, was lying awake one night with a high fever; scarcely had he said, "O Brother Martin, if you were only here to help me," when Martin suddenly appeared in the room with fresh sheets and medicine, and soon comforted the astonished youth who was completely cured the next morning. But the strange thing was that Martin's room was in a distant part of the monastery, separated by several locked doors from the locked door of the novice —and Martin had no keys! Similar things happened on several later occasions; all a sick man had to do was to say, "Brother Martin, come and help me," and there was the Negro lay brother, mysteriously present after having passed through numerous locked doors.

The sick of the city and the surrounding countryside, Spaniards and Indians, Negroes and mulattos, came to his dispensary for treatment. Those too ill to go back home he put in his own bed or, with the superior's permission, in other parts of the house. Whenever he had free time he nursed the sick throughout the city. To all of them he also spoke words of spiritual advice or encouragement. And not only the sick, but every one in any kind of human misery moved his heart to compassion.

He was too practical, however, to think that he could take care of all the needy in Lima by himself. Because he combined skillful organization with genuine charity, he has rightly been called the first social worker in the Americas. From the wealthy, who knew his goodness or had even been benefited by his marvelous gift of healing, he begged enough money to build and operate the Orphanage of the Holy Cross which is still in existence. Here he housed and fed and taught the many unwanted children of the city—orphans and neglected foundlings, homeless boys and girls. To care for these little ones he hired the best nurses and teachers available whom, he insisted, must be paid a good salary. No wonder Peru has officially declared him their National Patron of Social Justice!

Even dumb animals found in him a friend and helper. He set and cured the broken wing of a hawk which acted as meekly as a dove in his hands. Stray cats and dogs followed him as if their instinct told them where to go in need. Or was it only their instinct? Charming tales are told about how he could speak to animals and how they understood and obeyed him. Once, when he had a stray cat and dog which became so friendly that they ate from the same dish, he noticed a timid mouse watching them from a corner. "Brother dog and brother cat," he asked, "why don't you let the mouse eat with you?" Then he said, "Brother mouse, come out and eat at the dish, too." And with that all three animals ate in peace together. On another occasion the sacristan of the monastery was angry because the rats gnawed at his candles and tore his altar linens to pieces for nesting material. "Brother Martin," he said, "it's your fault for having so many animals around." "That's right," answered Martin in happy surprise; "it really is my fault. I should have thought of it sooner. I have forgotten all about feeding the rats." So he called a rat and said to it, "Brother rat, tell your sisters and brothers, your nieces and nephews, your aunts and uncles and cousins, that, if they keep out of the sacristy, I promise to feed them every day in the old barn." So into the barn the tribes of rats trooped, and every day, after Martin had said his prayer over the bread that he gave the poor, "Lord, bless this bread and make it enough to feed all Your poor ones," he would hand it out till all the poor were fed, and then, gathering up the fragments lest they be lost, he brought the rest to the rats in the barn, and the rats thereafter never went back to the sacristy.

While Martin was kindness itself to everyone else, on himself he was mercilessly hard. Filled with an insatiable longing to make reparation for all the sins committed against his good Lord, he led such an austerely penitential life that it was literally a miracle that he lived till his sixtieth year. He fasted every day, often for months at a time, on only bread and water. Despite his long days of exhausting labor, he allowed his worn-out body only a few hours sleep, and that mostly on the ground.

Though at other times Martin had been stricken with fever and made light of it, there came a time when a strange malady struck him and he calmly told his brothers in religion, "Four days from now I shall die." All his friends, high and low, from the Archbishop and the Viceroy to the poorest Negroes and Indians, came to the rude boards on which he was dying to receive in tears his last blessing. On the day he had foretold, November 3, 1639, he closed his eyes in everlasting sleep as peacefully as a baby dozing off on its mother's lap.

All Lima turned out for his triumphant funeral. He who had always regarded himself as a good-for-nothing slave was carried to his grave by the Viceroy of Peru, the Archbishop of Mexico, and two other high dignitaries of Church and State. In the years and centuries that followed, this lowly Negro lay brother continued to shower down from heaven miracles on all who called on his aid. Recognizing these miracles as God's testimony to the sanctity of his life, Pope Gregory XVI, on September 8, 1837, solemnly pronounced him "Blessed," and on May 6, 1962, Pope John XXIII added the Church's highest honor, canonization.

Saint Mary of Egypt
Penitent

c. 4 2 1

(April 2)

THE INTERESTING "LIFE" of St. Mary of Egypt is a good example of how early Christian hagiography took a short historical fact and developed it into an elaborate "legend" which made for more exciting reading. The fact, itself, that there was a certain woman who, after a youth spent in sin, lived a solitary life of great holiness and severe penance for many years in the desert during the beginning of the fifth century, is so early and well attested to that its basic historical truth can hardly be doubted. Mary may have been her name, and she may have come originally from Egypt. However, in the fully developed form of her "legend" which enjoyed immense popularity in the Middle Ages, the story of Mary of Egypt can be shown to contain numerous elements borrowed from the lives of the "Fathers of the Deserts." The elaborate form of this legend used to be attributed to Saint Sophronius, Patriarch of Jerusalem, who died in the year 638. There is reason to believe that even this full form was in existence before the sixth century, so that it is probably older than Saint Sophronius. The legend is unfortunately too long to be translated here in full. It may be summarized as follows.

There was a holy priest called Zosimas who lived as a monk in one of the monasteries of Palestine. When he had spent fifty-three years here serving God with great fervor, he began to be tempted to vainglory at the thought that no one could teach him anything new in virtue. The Lord therefore directed him to go to a certain monastery near the Jordan River, and here he would learn that no one is so perfect that he cannot still be taught by others. Obedient to the divine command, Zosimas left the monastery where he had lived since his youth and proceeded to the monastery at the Jordan. He found monks of this monastery living even more virtuous lives than those of his old monastery, fasting always on bread and water and conversing only on heavenly things. They had the custom here that on the First Sunday in Lent, after hearing Mass and receiving Holy Communion, they would leave the monastery and scatter one by one into the Syrian Desert east of Jordan. Here they would live in complete solitude with even more rigorous fasting until Palm Sunday, when they would again return to the monastery for the divine services of Holy Week and the Easter Liturgy. Never would they tell one another of their spiritual experiences in the desert lest they be tempted to vainglory.

When the beginning of Lent came around about the year 420, Zosimas also departed with the other monks for the desert. Each day he walked farther and farther into the desert, hoping to meet some hermit from whom he might learn greater spiritual doctrine, but not a soul did he meet. At noon on the twentieth day, when he had reached the farthest point in the desert to which he could go (if he were to return on time for Palm Sunday), he stopped to say his midday prayers. While he prayed he noticed a human figure walking to the south. Its naked body was darkly sunburnt; its hair hung like white wool down its neck. Thinking it was a hermit, Zosimas arose and hurried after it. The strange being, seeing that it was being followed, began to run. Zosimas cried out: "Servant of God, why do you run away from me? Wait for me and give me your blessing." The two ran on until they came to a dry river bed. Here the fugitive was able to run up the other bank, while Zosimas was forced to rest in the gully, exhausted. From over the bank he then heard a voice say, "Father Zosimas, forgive me in the Lord for not turning and showing you my face. I am a woman and unclothed, but if you have pity on a sinful woman, throw me your cloak that I may cover my nakedness. Then I will come back to receive your blessing."

Astonished at being called by name, but knowing that the woman could not know his name unless it were revealed to her by God, Zosimas complied with her wish and threw her his patched and frayed cloak. Having wrapped this around herself, she came down to the monk and begged his blessing. He, however, insisted on her blessing him, so that both knelt opposite each other and kept saying to each other, "Bless me. Bless me." Finally the woman said, "It is right for you to bless me and pray over me, for you are a priest and have stood for many years at the altar offering up the divine Sacrifice." All the more astounded that she should know of his priesthood, the monk cried out: "O spiritual mother, it is clear from your divine knowledge that you are more than half dead to the world and already near to God. Bless me, then, and pray to the Lord for me, since I need your prayers." Ceding to the old man's insistency, the woman said, "Blessed be God who takes care of the salvation of human souls!" To which the man answered: "Amen."

The woman then asked him: "How do the Christians fare? Who governs the Church? Who rules the empire?" "Thanks to your prayers, O mother," answered the monk, "Christ has granted lasting peace to us all. But do pray now for all the world and for me, a sinner." Turning toward the East, with eyes raised to heaven and arms extended, the woman prayed for a long while. Zosimas could see her lips move, but he could not hear what she said, except for the oft-repeated phrase, "Lord, have mercy! Lord, have mercy!" And as she prayed, he beheld her raised from the ground in ecstacy.

When she had finished praying, the monk begged her to tell him why she had lived so long in the desert, adding that she was so holy she need not conceal for fear of vainglory the great graces that she had received.

"It is not the fear of vainglory," she began, "that would keep me from telling you of my life, but rather the fear of you running away from me in horror at learning of the utterly shameless life that I led.

"I was born in Egypt. When only twelve years old, I ran away from my loving parents and went to Alexandria. How I lost my virginity there and burned with an insatiable lust for sexual pleasure it would be too shameful for me to tell you or even for me to think of. Only this will I say, that I became a prostitute not for profit, but solely for the pleasure it gave me. In fact, I would never accept anything for the favors of my body, but I kept myself alive by begging or working as a weaver.

"One day in summer, as I was living this wicked life, I saw a large crowd of men standing at the seashore. Asking one of them where the men were going, he told me that they were going to sail to Palestine, to be present at the Feast of the Exaltation of the Holy Cross, which would be celebrated within a short time at Jerusalem. I decided that I could not let so many fine young men escape me. Although I had no money to pay the fare nor food for the journey, I managed to induce the men to let me come along on board the ship by promising them I would be of use to them. How I blush to confess that I seduced many even of these men who were going on a holy pilgrimage! Father Zosimas, I am ashamed to say more about these vile things."

But when the monk begged her to tell him the rest of her life's story, the woman continued: "At Jerusalem on the Feast of the Exaltation of the Holy Cross I saw that great crowds of people were hurrying to the basilica even at daybreak. So I joined the crowds and tried to enter the sacred building with them. But though I pushed and was pushed along with the rest, while the others were entering, I could not get past the doorway. Over and over again I tried, but each time I was pushed to the side without being able to go into the building.

"As I was standing there alone at the side of the entrance, I began to realize that it was because of my sinful life that I was being prevented from entering this holy place where the True Cross on which Christ had died was to be venerated. A deep sense of shame and contrition came over me. Noticing that above me on the building there was an image of the Mother of Christ, I cried out to her: 'Virgin Lady, you who have given birth to the Word of God! I know that it is not right that I, who am so vile, should even look at the image of your spotless purity. It would not be surprising if you, who have always remained chaste and immaculate, should loathe and despise me, who am so impure. Yet the God whom you bore became man, as I heard, that He might call sinners to repentance. Help me who am desolate and destitute! Do allow me to enter the church that I may not be deprived of the sight of that Wood on which He Who was born of you shed His blood for my redemption. If you will let me enter, I swear to you and to your divine Son that I will never again give my body to impurity but, as soon as I have adored the Cross of your Son, I will leave the world and all that is in it and I will go where you, the mediatress of my salvation, tell me to go.'

"Having thus prayed and feeling confident that through the mercy of the Mother of God my prayer would be heard, I once more went to the doorway of the basilica, and now I had no trouble at all in going in with the others. Once within, I gazed on the life-giving Cross and beheld the mysteries of God and saw how ready He was to welcome repentant sinners. Having lain prostrate in adoration on the sacred pavement of the church, I hastened back to my mediatress, who had accepted my oath, and, kneeling before her image, I begged her to tell me where I should go. Then I heard a voice say, 'If you go across the Jordan, you will find perfect rest.'

"On leaving the holy image, someone gave me three coins with which I bought three loaves of bread for the journey. The baker and that evening I reached the Church of St. John the Baptist from whom I bought the loaves told me how to go to the Jordan, on the bank of this river. Having first prayed and washed my hands and face in the sacred waters of the stream, I went into the church of the Precursor and received the Holy Eucharist. When I had eaten half of one of my three loaves of bread and had drunk of the water of the Jordan, I spent the night sleeping on the ground. The next morning a man rowed me across the river and, as I walked up the other side, I prayed our Lady to guide me. Thus I came into this desert, and from that day to this I have been here in this distant solitude, waiting for my God, who saves those who turn to Him from storm and weakness of spirit."

On hearing this remarkable story, Zosimas said, "How long has it been my lady, since you have come to this desert?" "As far as I can remember," she answered, "It is now forty-seven years since I left the Holy City." "But what have you eaten in all this time?" asked the monk. "The two and a half loaves of bread," she said, "which I took with me over the Jordan soon became dry as I ate but a small piece of bread each day. After that I subsisted on what little foodstuff I could find on the ground."

When Zosimas begged her to tell him of her experiences during all these years, she replied: "After some years my clothes fell from me in tatters till in the end I was left completely naked, to burn with heat of the sun by day and freeze with cold at night. But my worst physical torture was thirst, as I, who had drunk so much wine in Egypt, now often roamed for days without even a drop of water to drink. Despite all this I suffered for seventeen years even more terrible torments from the vile temptations which afflicted me. The sweet songs of the harlots came back into my ears, and my flesh longed for the sensual delights in which it had once reveled. Beating my breast as hard as I could, I recalled with tears and sighs the oath I had taken before the image of God's Mother. Kneeling again each time in spirit before that image, I besought the spotless Virgin to free me from these temptations and to give me the strength to keep my vows. And each time, after I could beat my breast no more nor wring any more sobs from my heart, a radiant light surrounded me and a deep peace came into my soul. Yet it was only after seventeen years that these agonizing temptations completely left me. From then on my Protectress, who had accepted my repentance, always led me safely on the paths of peace.

"During the forty-seven years that I have been in the desert I have not seen a single person, and not even an animal, till today, when God sent you to me. This is then the favor I would ask of you. Return in peace to your monastery at the Jordan. But tell no one of what you have heard from me until the Lord has taken me from this world. Next year at the beginning of Lent do not leave your monastery with the other monks; if you try to do so, you will be prevented. Then on the evening of the Last Supper bring with you to the bank of the Jordan a vessel containing the sacred Body and Blood of Christ. Stay on the Holy Land side of the Jordan. There I will come to you to receive the life-giving Sacrament. I have not partaken of the Holy Eucharist since I last crossed the Jordan, and I long with inexpressible desire to share again in the Sacred Mystery."

This Zosimas promised to do. After they had again given each other their blessing, the woman departed into the desert, and the monk returned to his monastery, just in time for the Holy Week services.

For the whole year Zosimas kept the secret, but none seemed to him so long. Finally when the next Lent came around, he was laid up with a fever, and he remembered the words of the woman that, even if he tried, he would not be able to go into the desert this year. He was soon cured, but he remained at the monastery for the rest of Lent. On Palm Sunday the other monks returned, and on the evening of Holy Thursday they celebrated the Lord's Supper together. At the end of the liturgy Zosimas took a small cup containing the Body and Blood of Christ and, carrying along a basket of figs and dates and soaked beans, he went to the bank of the Jordan.

For a long time he waited in vain and began to think that because of his sinfulness he was not worthy to set eyes again on the

holy woman. Then it struck him that there was not even a small
skiff at hand, and how could she ever cross over to him?

Suddenly in the light of the full moon he beheld the blessed
sight of the woman coming down to the Jordan from the desert.
When she reached the bank of the river, she made the sign of the
cross over the water and forthwith proceeded to walk out on top
of the water. Overcome with fear at the sight of the miracle,
Zosimas began to fall prostrate on the ground. But the woman
cried out: "What are you doing, Father, you who are a priest
and carry with you the Holy Eucharist!" Then she added: "Give
me your blessing, Father." Overwhelmed with wonder, the monk
could only praise and thank God for having let him witness so
marvelous a sight.

When the woman reached him on his side of the Jordan, she
asked him to say the Creed and the Our Father. This he did
and then, according to the liturgical custom, he gave her the kiss
of peace and administered to her the Body and Blood of the Savior. Having received the Holy Eucharist, she raised her hands to
heaven and prayed: "Now Thou dost dismiss Thy handmaid, O
Lord, according to Thy word, in peace; because my eyes have
seen Thy salvation."

The woman then said to the monk, "Pardon me, Father, if I
ask you one more favor. Return now to your monastery. Then
next Lent go again into the desert as you did a year ago, and for
love of Christ look for me in the same dried-up river bed where
you first met me; there, as the Lord wishes, you will find me."
"Would to God," answered the monk, "that I might follow you
now and enjoy the sight of your blessed countenance forever! I
will do as you say, but first do me this little favor: do take some
of this food that I have brought you." And with that he showed
her the basket of figs and dates and beans. But she merely took
and ate three beans, saying that the grace of the Holy Spirit was
sufficient to keep body and soul together. "Pray to God," she
said, "pray for me and remember my lowliness." Kneeling down
and embracing her feet, he begged her to pray to God for the

Church and for the empire and for himself, a poor sinner. When they had finally bid each other farewell, she turned toward the Jordan, and again made the sign of the cross over it, and once more she walked across on top of the water.

When she had disappeared into the desert, the monk returned to his monastery near the Jordan, and again waited impatiently for the following Lent. But it was only now that he remembered that he had never thought of asking the holy woman her name. Once Lent again came around, he went into the desert as on his first journey there. Carefully following the landmarks, like a hunter on the track of game, he finally reached the gully where he had first met the saintly woman. But look as carefully as he could, he did not succeed in finding any trace of her here. "Show me, O Lord," he prayed, "where Thou hast hidden Thy sacred treasure, Thy angel incarnate, of whom the world is not worthy." Finally he spotted her. There she was, lying there dead! She lay on her side, facing the East, with her hands devoutly folded.

Having washed her feet with his tears—the only part of her body that he dared touch, he recited the customary Psalms and prayers for Christian burial. As he thought to himself whether it was right to bury so holy a body here in the desert, he noticed these words scratched on the ground: "Father Zosimas, bury in this place the body of lowly Mary, returning dust to the dust, and always pray to the Lord for me, who departed this world on the night of Our Lord's Passion after partaking of the divine mystic Banquet." By this the old man understood that within the space of an hour Mary had traversed the distance into the desert which had taken him twenty days to cover, and that she had then forthwith departed for the Lord.

He looked for some means of digging a grave for her mortal remains. But all he could find was a little stick. Struggling and sweating with this, he had only succeeded in digging a small hole, when suddenly he looked up and a terrifying sight met his eyes. There beside the corpse crouched a big lion, which was licking the feet of the holy woman. Trusting in the power of the departed saint to save him from the lion, the monk made the sign of the cross over it. With that the lion walked slowly to the old man, not as if it were about to leap on him, but rather to show that it wanted to help. "O lion," said Zosimas, "since the holy woman wished to be buried, and since I am too old to dig a grave for her, it is up to you to use your paws for this purpose." Scarcely had he said this when the lion began to dig fiercely with its forepaws until a grave large enough to receive the corpse had been dug. Tenderly laying St. Mary, in this grave, with nothing on her body but the old torn cloak he had given her at their first meeting, he covered her with the dug-up earth, and departed. And as he left her sacred grave, the lion, too, departed into the desert as meek as a lamb.

On his return to the monastery, Zosimas now told all these things to his fellow monks. He lived to be almost 100 before he departed for the Lord. These facts have been handed down by word of mouth in this monastery where I, too, am a monk. Now God has commanded me to record them in writing, that all may learn what wonderful things He does for those who take refuge in Him, to whom be honor and glory for ever and ever. Amen.

Saint Mary Magdalene
Penitent

First Century

(July 22)

ALL OF THE four Gospels have something to say about a certain woman they call "Mary Magdalene," which means "Mary of Magdala," a town in the plain of Genesareth on the western shore of the Sea of Galilee. The Gospels of Luke and John also speak of a certain woman whom they call "Mary," who was the sister of Martha and Lazarus, and who lived at Bethany (near Jerusalem), while the Gosples of Matthew and Mark agree with John in giving an account of how this woman anointed Jesus shortly before His death, although they do not mention her name. Finally, in the 7th chapter of Saint Luke's Gospel, a touching story is told of an unnamed penitent woman who anointed the feet of Jesus while He was at table in the house of Simon the Pharisee. Since the time of Saint Gregory the Great (at the end of the 6th century) it has been customary in the Western (Latin) Church to consider Mary of Magdala, Mary of Bethany, and the Penitent Woman of Luke 7 as one and the same person. This idea, which was unknown to the earlier Fathers of the Western Church and has always been unknown in the Eastern (Greek) Church, is regarded by almost all modern Biblical scholars, Catholic as well as non-Catholic, as lacking in any solid foundation in the Bible and therefore mistaken. However, since the Western Church has only one feast, on July 22,

883

during which all these three women are honored under the general name of "Saint Mary Magdalene," it seems fitting to set forth here what the Gospels tell us of each of these women.

Mary Magdalene is first mentioned as one of the wealthy women who joined Jesus' company during His public ministry in Galilee, and "who used to provide" for Him and His apostles "out of their means." The passage in Luke 8:2, which speaks of this, also says that "seven devils had gone out" of Mary Magdalene, and Mark 16:9 also states that Jesus "had cast seven devils" out of her. This does not, of itself, mean that she had once been a great sinner. What we would now regard as any kind of mental affliction was sometimes viewed at the time of Christ (not entirely without good reason) as something caused by the devil. The Biblical number "seven" is merely an expression for "quite a few"; hence, to be plagued by seven devils is to be seriously afflicted. By working a miracle for her, Christ cured Mary Magdalene of her affliction, and out of gratitude for this favor she became one of His most faithful followers.

We next find Mary Magdalene among the devoted women who stood by the cross of Jesus when all the apostles except John had fled (Matt. 27:55-56; Mark 15:40-41; John 19:25). She not only saw how the Savior died; she also watched how He was buried (Matt. 27-61; Mark 15;47), and she was thus an important witness to the fact that He was truly buried. The evidence of His empty tomb would not be valid proof of His resurrection unless there were witnesses to guarantee the truth that His body had really been laid in this tomb.

Finally, Mary Magdalene plays an important part in the events of Easter morning. She is mentioned first among the holy women who went at sunrise on that Sunday morning to the tomb where Jesus had been buried to complete the anointing of His body which they were unable to do on the Sabbath (Matt. 28:1; Mark 16:1; Luke 28:10). The risen Savior "appeared first to Mary Magdalene" (Mark 16:9). The account of this apparition is told at considerable length in John 20:1-18. When she found the

SAINT PETER CANISIUS

Born in the same year (1521) that Martin Luther started his revolt against
papal authority, probably no one did more than this Saint to save southern Germany for the Catholic Church in the tumultuous period of the
sixteenth-century Protestant Reformation. Most important of all was
Canisius' prodigious literary activity which culminated in his being
declared a Doctor of the Church.

SAINT MATTHIAS   Peter Rubens

The account of how Saint Matthias was chosen to fill the ranks of the
twelve Apostles (following the treachery and death of Judas) is told in
the *Acts of the Apostles*. The choice was made during the nine days between the Ascension and the Descent of the Holy Spirit which the Apostles spent mostly in prayer with Mary, the mother of Jesus, in the first
"novena" of the Church. (The cracks which appear in this reproduction
are present in the original Rubens' masterpiece).

tomb empty, Mary Magdalene hastened to the house where the Apostles were staying in Jerusalem and told them, "They have taken the Lord from the tomb, and we do not know where they have laid Him." At once, Peter and John ran to the tomb and verified for themselves the fact that Jesus was no longer there. By the time that Mary got back to the tomb they had already left. She was so distraught in her anguish at the loss of the body of her beloved Master that the two angels who appeared to her failed to console her. Then, through her tears, she saw a man whom she thought was the gardener. "Sir," she cried, "if thou hast removed Him, tell we where thou hast laid Him and I will take Him away." But all she had to hear from this Man, who was really Jesus, was the word "Mary!" and she cried out "Rabboni—My Master!" Falling at His feet in adoration, she hugged Him with such fervor that Jesus had to assure her that He was not leaving at once to ascend to His heavenly Father; rather she should go to His apostles, whom He called His "brethren," and tell them of His resurrection. She was thus the first to announce the glad tidings: "I have seen the Lord!"

That is all that the Gospels tell us of the woman whom they call Mary Magdalene. But it is sufficient, however, to give us a picture of her as an ardent, energetic woman, a natural leader among the good women who followed Jesus, and utterly devoted to Him—characteristics not too dissimilar from St. Peter.

Mary of Bethany, on the other hand, was quite a different type. This Mary, together with her sister Martha and her brother Lazarus, lived in the pleasant little town of Bethany (which lay a couple of miles east of Jerusalem at the southeast foot of the Mount of Olives) through which one passed on the way from Jerusalem to Jericho. On one of our Lord's journeys to Jerusalem He was a guest at the house of these three people, who evidently were already acquainted with Him and believed in Him as the promised Messiah. The account of this visit is given in Luke 10: 38-42. While the older sister, Martha, was working hard preparing the meal that she would serve to her honored Guest, her

younger sister, Mary, sat quietly at the feet of Jesus listening entranced to His words of wisdom. When Martha begged Jesus to
tell her sister to get busy and help her, He defended the young
girl. "Mary has chosen the best part," he said, "and it will not
be taken away from her."

The same characteristics of the practical, energetic Martha and
the calm, mystical-minded Mary appeared in the story of Jesus'
raising of Lazarus from the dead as told in John 11:1-44. When
Lazarus became mortally ill, his sisters sent word to Jesus, im-
plicitly asking Him to come and cure Him, although their message was merely: "Lord, behold, he whom Thou lovest is sick."
Jesus intentionally delayed His coming to Bethany so that, when
He arrived there, Lazarus was already dead. As soon as Martha
heard that Jesus was approaching her town, this courteous lady
of the house went to greet Him, whereas Mary, too absorbed in
her grief, did not hear the report of the Lord's coming. But
scarcely had Martha's message reached her, "The Master is here
and calls thee," than she ran to Him, fell at His feet, and sobbed:
"Master, if Thou hadst been here, my brother would not have
died." In utter simplicity the Gospel then says, "And Jesus
wept." Ignoring Martha's sensible advice not to open the tomb
of a half-decayed corpse, Jesus ordered the stone to be rolled
away from its entrance and with a loud voice He spoke the command which only the divine Author of life can utter with authority: " 'Lazarus, come forth!' And at once he who had been dead
came forth." What greater tribute can be given to any man or
woman than that which the Evangelist gave to these three holy
persons of Bethany: "Jesus *loved* Martha and her sister Mary
and Lazarus"?

The last time that Mary of Bethany appears in the Gospels is
in connection with her anointing of Jesus less than a week before
His death (Matt. 26:9-13; Mark 14:3-9; John 12:1-8). One of
Jesus' friends, Simon the leper (so called probably because he
once had leprosy and had been cured of it by Christ), gave a
banquet at his house in Bethany in honor of the revered Master

from Galilee, and one of the distinguished guests was Lazarus whose resurrection from the dead was now being celebrated. As usual, Lazarus' sister Martha was busy serving at table. However, his other sister, Mary, performed a generous act of devotion for her beloved Master which had a deeper, prophetic meaning than she herself was aware of. While Jesus was reclining at the banquet table, she brought in a large alabaster vase of precious perfume and poured it not only on his head, but also on his feet which she then wiped with her hair. Judas Iscariot, the business man among the apostles and the treasurer of their little company, estimated that this perfume was extremely expensive, and complained bitterly at this waste of good money which could have been used in helping the poor—though John adds that Judas, the old thief, was more concerned about what he could pocket for himself of this money than he was about the poor. Jesus defended Mary's act. "In pouring this ointment on my body," he said, "she has done it for my burial."

As a matter of fact, the burial of Jesus had to be done so hastily in the late afternoon of Good Friday that there was then no time for the usual anointing of a dead body. When the holy women wished to make good this omission on Easter Sunday, they came to the tomb with their ointment too late; Christ had already risen from the dead. Therefore, what Mary of Bethany did at the banquet in the house of Simon the leper was really an anticipation of the burial anointing of Jesus. For this reason He foretold that this good deed which she then did for Him would be proclaimed to her everlasting honor throughout the whole world wherever His gospel would be preached.

The story of the anointing of Jesus by the unnamed Penitent Woman as told in Luke 7:36-50 bears a slight resemblance to the above account of His anointing by Mary of Bethany, but the two are clearly separate and different events. Possibly there had been some mutual influence of one story on the other while they were being handed down by oral tradition among the people before being recorded in writing by the different Evangelists. In both cases the anointing takes place at a banquet, and in both instances the name of the host is Simon. In Luke's Gospel he is called "Simon the Pharisee," whereas in the Gospels of Matthew and Mark he is called "Simon the leper." The latter Simon is evidently a friend of Jesus, but the former Simon hardly acts friendly toward Him. Besides, if one may conclude from the context in which it is placed, the event of Luke 7:36-50 takes place in one of the towns of Galilee and relatively early in our Lord's public ministry. The anointing by Mary of Bethany, on the other hand, was done in Bethany and only a few days before Christ's death.

However, like Mary of Bethany, the Penitent Woman also brought an alabaster vase of perfume and, silently stealing into the banquet hall, she knelt at the feet of Jesus while He was reclining on a couch at the table. Here "she began to bathe His feet with her tears, and she wiped them with the hair of her head, and she kissed His feet and anointed them with ointment." Jesus repays her repentant love by saying to her, "Thy faith has saved thee; go in peace." Except for the purpose of reassuring her, He really had no need to say to her, "Thy sins are forgiven"; her sins had already been forgiven by Him from the first moment that she knelt at His feet. That is the whole point of the little parable that Jesus spoke to Simon the Pharisee.

Simon knew that this woman was a public sinner; everybody in the town knew this fact. It is true, Simon thought, a stranger in town, like this Nazarean preacher, might not be acquainted with this fact. If this Jesus were a genuine prophet sent by God, He would know by a revelation from God that this woman was a sinner, and therefore, as a good Jew, He would not let Himself become defiled by contact with this impure creature. Jesus argued that He was letting the woman touch Him because she was no longer a sinner. The proof she gave of her grateful love showed that her sins had already been forgiven.

Jesus told Simon a little parable or story: a certain creditor had two debtors, of whom one owed him ten times as much as the other, but he remitted the whole debt for each of them. Now, which of the two, Jesus asked, would be expected to give him greater proofs of grateful love? Simon thought the question rather foolish; obviously the man who had the bigger debt remitted would show himself more grateful. Jesus then made the application. Simon had shown Him no special signs of love: he did not give Him the kiss of friendship, he did not have the servants wash His feet, nor did he have perfume poured on His head—acts of courtesy that every good host at that time did for his guests. Obviously, Simon did not feel that he had any sins which Jesus may have forgiven, since he gave such scant signs of grateful love. Yet this poor woman, kneeling in humility at the feet of Jesus, kept kissing them, washing them with her tears, drying them with her hair, and anointing them with her perfume. Therefore, it was clear that her sins, great though they were, must have already been forgiven, or she would not have given such abundant signs of her grateful love. Unfortunately, the whole point of our Lord's argument is lost by the faulty translation which is commonly given of His words: "Wherefore I say to thee, her sins, many as they are, shall be forgiven her, because she has loved much." The sense really should be: "Therefore I tell you that, since she has given so many signs of love, her sins, many though they were, must have been forgiven her." Of course, Christ never intended His words here to mean, as some insanely imagine: "Her sins are forgiven her because the reason why she committed them was that she loved so much her human lover"!

Apart from this passage in Luke's Gospel we know nothing else of this Penitent Woman. We can, of course, rightly suppose that, ever after this impassioned demonstration of her repentance, she lived a holy, innocent life. Since St. Gregory, however, identified her with St. Mary Magdalene, the word "magdalen" has come to mean a "reformed prostitute."

There is another curious thing that happened to the name of Mary Magdalene in English. The common pronunciation of "Magdalene" in England used to be "Maudlin." Now, popular art in the Middle Ages often represented "St. Maudlin" with eyes red and swollen from excessive weeping. Thus the word "maudlin" came to mean "excessively sentimental," as in the expressions, "a maudlin poem," "a maudlin orator."

Although St. Gregory was no doubt mistaken in thinking that Mary of Magdala, Mary of Bethany, and the unnamed Penitent Woman were one and the same person, we can be grateful to him for the fact that the tradition which he started led to a unique feast on which we honor three Saints in one, all of whom Jesus held in affection.

Saint Matthias
Apostle

First Century

(February 24)

I N THE BIBLE a sacred symbolism is attached to the number "twelve." Just as the people of Israel (the Church of God in the Old Testament) consisted of the twelve tribes that were descended from the twelve sons of Jacob, so also in the New Testament Christ wished to found His Church upon Twelve Apostles. These disciples of Jesus (who were most intimately joined to Him in His public ministry) formed such a special group among His followers, and were so conspicuous by their particular number that, besides being known as "the Apostles" (that is, "the ones sent" by Him) they are often spoken of in the Gospels merely as "the Twelve."

When Judas, one of the original Apostles, not only brought about the death of Jesus by his treachery, but also committed suicide in remorse over this sin, Saint Peter reminded the other Apostles that it was necessary for them to choose another man to take the place of Judas so that the number of the Apostles would still be twelve. The choice was made in the days that intervened between our Lord's ascension into heaven and the descent of the Holy Spirit on the Apostles, that is, during these nine days that they spent in prayer together with Mary, the mother of Jesus, in the first "novena" of the Church.

The account of how Saint Matthias was chosen to fill the ranks of the twelve Apostles is told in the first chapter of the Acts of the Apostles. An essential condition that was required in Judas' successor, whoever he might be, was that he should be, as Saint Peter said, "one of these men who have been in our company all the time that the Lord Jesus moved among us, from John's baptism until the day that He was taken up from us, in order to be a witness with us of His resurrection." There is no doubt that among the 120 persons present at this election there were several of the disciples of Jesus who could have fulfilled this condition. Of these possible candidates two men were selected. One of them had no less than three names, "Joseph, called Barsabbas, who was surnamed Justus." The other was simply known as "Matthias," which means "gift of the Lord."

The Apostles, however, did not take it on themselves to make the final choice between these two; they left this up to God. The text says, "They prayed and said, 'Thou, Lord, who knowest the hearts of all, show which of these two Thou has chosen to take the place in this ministry and apostleship from which Judas fell away to go to his own place.' And they drew lots between them, and the lot fell upon Matthias; and he was numbered with the eleven apostles." This drawing of lots probably consisted in picking one of the two names from a box or vessel.

That is all that we know with any certainty about St. Matthias. He is not mentioned anywhere else in the New Testament. Later traditions about him are so vague and contradictory, that they can hardly be taken seriously. A secret Gospel was attributed to him, and it is probably from this document that St. Clement of Alexandria quotes a statement which certain heretics attributed to St. Matthias: "We must combat our flesh, set no value upon it, and allow it nothing that can flatter it, but instead we must increase the growth of our soul by faith and knowledge."

According to one tradition, Saint Matthias, after preaching the Gospel in Judea, went to Ethiopia, where he was crucified. According to another tradition he was stoned and then beheaded by the Jews in Jerusalem. His body is said to have been sent by St. Helen, the mother of the Emperor Constantine, from Jerusalem to Rome, but the ancient Roman city of Trier (now a part of Germany, near Luxembourg) claimed to have at least a part of his relics.

In the ancient Latin calendar the days of the second half of each month, that is, the days following the Ides (15th), or middle of the month, are called the 1st to 16th days before the Calends (or first day) of the following month. The feast of Saint Matthias is celebrated in the Latin Church on "the fifth day before the Calends of March;" in ordinary years this is the 24th day of February, but in leap years it is the 25th of February.

Saint Maurice

Martyr

c. 2 8 7

(September 22)

NEAR THE SOUTHWEST CORNER of Switzerland, not far from
the French border, there nestles in the valley of the
Rhone River (between the Bernese and the Pennine Alps) the
picturesque town of Martigny. This town is on the site of an
ancient settlement of the Gauls that was called Octodurum, the
name by which the place was also known in the early Christian
centuries. In the same valley, about six miles north of Martigny
(and a dozen miles from the entrance of the upper Rhone into
the Lake of Geneva), there is a small village now known as Saint-
Maurice-en-Valais, but which was originally called Agaunum.
This village owes its fame to the Church of St. Maurice that was
first erected here in the fourth century when Saint Theodore, the
bishop of Octodurum (present Martigny), had a vision telling
him that at this place in his diocese the bodies of the Christian
martyrs, Maurice and his companions, were buried. Theodore
found their relics here and built a basilica (or large church) in
their honor. From that time to the present day this Church of
St. Maurice has been a very popular place of pilgrimage. The
venerable monastery that is still attached to this church was
founded at least as early as the beginning of the sixth century.

Around the middle of the fifth century, the bishop of Octodurum was a certain Salvius. Wishing to know more about these

saints who had been martyred in his diocese, he wrote to St. Eucherius, the archbishop of Lyons in the lower Rhone valley of southeastern France. The latter's reply is our principal source of information regarding the martyrdom of St. Maurice and his companions, although we have other means of checking and correcting the story about Maurice which Eucherius said he learned from Theodore and other Christians who had in turn learned it from their ancestors. There is, therefore, no good reason to doubt the substantial truth of Eucherius' account, even though certain details of it may be legendary. The story of St. Maurice, as told by St. Eucherius to Bishop Salvius, can be summarized as follows.

Maurice was in command of a body of Roman soldiers known as the "Theban Legion." This unit of the Roman army was thus called because it was recruited at Thebes in Upper (that is, southern) Egypt, a region which contained a large number of Christians at the end of the third century. In any case, according to the account, the Theban Legion of St. Maurice was made up entirely of Christians. During the early Christian centuries Roman soldiers were mostly employed in guarding the borders of the empire against invasions from the barbarians who lived in the hinterland. One of the danger spots along the far-flung boundaries of the Roman Empire was the northern border which was strongly fortified to ward off the attacks of the Germanic tribes not yet subdued by Rome. Along this border, in the Alps, the Theban Legion was stationed.

The martyrdom of Saint Maurice and his companions took place during the reign of the Emperor Maximian Daza. According to the account given by Saint Eucherius, Maurice and his soldiers refused to obey Maximian when he ordered them to put certain Christians to death because of their faith. According to another account, Maximian was about to start a campaign against the barbarian tribe of the Bagaudae that had revolted against the Romans and, when he ordered his soldiers to offer sacrifice to the gods for the success of his expedition, Maurice and his companions refused to take part in these pagan sacrifices. If this is the correct version of the story, then their martyrdom took place about the year 287; for, as known from other sources, it was at this time that Maximian waged his war against the Bagaudae.

In any case, it is certain that it was solely on account of their Christian religion that Maurice and his companions refused to obey the emperor and, as a result, lost their lives. Maximian, enraged at their disobedience, ordered his pagan soldiers to "decimate" this unit of Christian soldiers, that is, to kill every tenth one among them. When the Christian soldiers who survived this first slaughter still remained firm in their refusal to carry out the sinful command, the emperor ordered a second decimation of the loyal soldiers of Christ. Finally, as Saint Maurice and his two subordinate officers, Saints Exuperius and Candidus, kept urging their men to remain true to the Christian faith, Maximian gave orders for a general massacre of all the rest of these Christian soldiers, including their leaders. Preferring martyrdom to a bloody combat with their pagan comrades in arms, these heroes calmly allowed themselves to be cut down to the last man.

All the accounts call this Christian group of soldiers the "Theban Legion." Now, at this period a "legion," which was the largest unit in the Roman army, consisted of between five and six thousand men. There were probably only two or three Roman legions engaged in the expedition against the Bagaudae. It is, of course, possible, but most unlikely that even such a bitter persecutor of the Christians as Maximian would have destroyed a half or a third of his entire expeditionary force on account of their religion. Moreover, it seems quite improbable that all the soldiers of a whole Roman legion at this period should have been Christian. Therefore, even Catholic historians are inclined to regard the word "legion" in the account as a merely general term for any kind of military unit. Perhaps only a few companies of soldiers, amounting to not more than a couple of hundred men, were martyred on this occasion.

The fact, however, that Maurice and a fairly large number of his soldiers gave their lives for Christ toward the end of the third century cannot be seriously questioned. The tradition of their martyrdom is too early and too constant to be mistaken. Throughout the centuries that followed, pilgrims flocked to the place of their martyrdom and burial in the upper Rhone valley. Saint Maurice was venerated in many places in Europe, and especially in Switzerland. At the other end of this little country, in the eastern Canton of the Grisons, there is another place that bears his name, the well-known winter-resort town of St. Moritz.

For various reasons Saint Maurice became the patron of sword makers, of weavers and dyers, and for obvious reasons, the special patron of soldiers, especially the fighting men of the infantry. Many groups of American GIs in recent years have made him their spiritual protector and model. Soldiers who put God's cause first are far from being cowards. On the contrary, they make the bravest fighters; for, with their conscience right with God, they are not afraid to face death in battle. They are ever loyal to their country and gladly defend it against its enemies. Yet their first duty is to God. As Saint Maurice said to his emperor, they also say to their country: "We are your soldiers, but we are also servants of the true God. We owe you military service and obedience, but we cannot renounce Him Who is our Creator and Master."

Saint Nicholas of Tolentine
Confessor

1 3 0 6

(September 10)

ALONG THE ADRIATIC Sea about halfway down the "boot" of Italy, that is, to the east of Saint Francis' Umbria, lies the region known as the Marches. It is a rugged land where the eastern spurs of the Appenine Mountains reach to the sea and where the hard-working peasants know the simple but deep joy of wringing a livelihood from the stubborn soil of their hills and valleys.

Here in the little village that bears the big name of "Sant' Angelo in Piceno," situated near the larger town of Fermo, there was born about the year 1245 a saint whose holy life of humility, simplicity and austerity exemplified all the best qualities of his sturdy compatriots of the Marches. Because his devout parents had long been childless, they took a vow and made a pilgrimage to Bari (on the Adriatic coast of Italy) to implore the intercession of the great Saint Nicholas of Bari—the same holy bishop who appears at our modern Christmas with his name distorted into Santa Claus—so that through his prayers they might be blessed with a child. Having been reassured in a vision that their petition would be granted they returned home. Within a year they had a baby boy whom they named Nicholas after the saint of Bari who had obtained this favor for them. As this Nicholas spent the last half of his life at the town of Tolentino in the Marches, he is commonly known as "Nicholas of Tolentino," or in anglicized form as "Nicholas of Tolentine." As a matter of fact, except for one year, when as a young priest he was stationed at Valmanente near Pisa, Nicholas passed his whole life in the Marches.

Even when young, Nicholas was remarkable for his virtuous life, especially for the extent in which he fasted. When scarcely seven years old, on learning that his illustrious patron, St. Nicholas of Bari, had practiced much fasting, he began to fast on several days of the week, a practice which he retained for the rest of his life, usually taking nothing more than bread and water for his nourishment.

While still only a clerical student, Nicholas was made a canon of the Church of the Holy Savior in his home town of Sant' Angelo, and in the ordinary course of events he seemed destined for the secular clergy. However, one day he heard a sermon on the vanity of worldliness and the dangers of loving the world, and he was so moved by what he heard that he resolved to give up the world completely and not even become a secular priest. The preacher who so affected him was a member of the religious order known as the Hermits of St. Augustine, more commonly called the Augustinians. Nicholas, therefore, applied and was received into this order.

Having completed his novitiate and taken his vows as an Augustinian, Nicholas studied theology in the houses of his order at San Ginesio and Macerata, and was ordained a priest at Cingoli—all towns in the Marches. To his usual fasting he now added many other penances, but far from making him sad and disagreeable to others, this austere life of his kept him so united to God in prayer, and filled him with such holy joy, that he overflowed with charity, patience and meekness towards all with whom he lived. Since he was a perfect model to others in his exact observance of all the rules, he was appointed novice master in the Augustinian novitiate at Sant' Elpidio. However, after Nicholas had been in this office for a year, his superiors recognized

that he would do even greater good in the active ministry. Therefore, about the year 1275, he was transferred to the Augustinian
monastery at Tolentino, a town of the Marches situated on the
Chiente River.

Here he spent the last thirty years of his life devoting himself wholeheartedly to the spiritual and temporal welfare of the
people of this town and of the surrounding countryside. He
nourished their souls by his daily preaching, and he cared for
their bodily needs by his boundless charity. With a meek, guile-
less and simple spirit, he bore with heroic patience the various
ailments that afflicted him during the last years of his life, until
at length he found his repose in heaven on September 10, 1306.
His mortal remains are entombed at Tolentino where he is still
greatly venerated by the people. Even during his lifetime he is
reported to have worked many miracles, and since his death this
child of grace, who was born as an answer to prayer, has never
ceased to answer his devoted clients with heavenly favors.

Saint Nicholas of Tolentine was canonized by Pope Eugene IV
in 1446, and devotion to him has been spread by the Augustinians throughout the world. In art he is shown in the black habit
of the Hermits of St. Augustine, with a star above his head or
on his breast, and holding in his hand a lily or a crucifix wreath-
ed with lilies. Sometimes he is represented with a vessel containing bread or money—all symbols of purity, his love of the cross,
zeal as a preacher, and charity to the poor.

Saint Olga
Widow

9 7 0
(July 11)

T HE HISTORY OF Europe, especially in the twentieth century, would probably have been quite different if Russia had received the Latin form of Christianity from Rome instead of its Greek form from Constantinople. Yet it is the irony of fate that this great country, which spreads out over the frontier between Europe and Asia, just missed receiving Christianity from Rome. The one who almost succeeded in bringing Christianity in its Latin rite to Russia was the first Christian queen of this country, St. Olga.

When Princess Olga was born in about the year 890, the Russians were still pagans. The tradition which attributes the first introduction of Christianity at Moscow and Kiev to St. Methodius, about the year 880, is quite doubtful. Even if it is true, the work of this famous apostle of the Slavs had no permanent results here. During most of her life, Olga, like her husband Igor I, grand duke of Kiev, was a pagan.

After the death of her husband in 945, Olga ruled for ten years as regent for her young son, Sviatoslav. About the year 957 she went on a journey to Constantinople. The Byzantine emperor, Constantine Porphyrogenitus, thought so little of the Russians, who were then but a small barbaric nation in the distant hinterland, that he kept Olga waiting a long time before granting her an audience, and then only consented to see her on condition that she would become a Christian. Olga had no need to fear this condition; she had already become entranced with the beauty of Christianity from her first meeting with it at Constantinople. In 958 she was baptized here and took, in addition to her Russian name of Olga, the Christian name of Helen, after St. Helena, the wife of Constantine the Great and the first Christian empress.

Back in Russia soon after her conversion, Olga sent an embassy to Constantinople asking that Christian missionaries be sent to her country. But when the Byzantine emperor demanded that Russia should become a vassal state of his empire and pay him tribute, Olga refused his missionaries as well as his demands. Thereupon, about the year 960, she sent an embassy to the German emperor, Otto I, and petitioned for missionaries of the Latin rite. Otto was happy to grant her request, and appointed the monk Adalbert of Triers head of the Catholic mission to Russia. After being consecrated a bishop, Adalbert went to Kiev, which was then the capital of Russia. But he could stay here only about two years (961-962); the pagan reaction against the introduction of Christianity forced him to return to Germany.

Until she died in 969 or 970 Olga not only remained loyal to her faith in Christ; she bravely strove to keep the spark of Christianity alive among the few who had embraced the faith. The wooden church at Kiev, which she built and dedicated to St. Sophia or Holy Wisdom—named after the magnificent basilica at Constantinople was the first Christian edifice erected on the soil of "Holy Russia." Her son Sviatoslav, however, remained a pagan, and so also did his son Vladimir I during the first part of his reign (980-1015). However, in 988, when Vladimir married the Byzantine princess Anna (the sister of the emperor Basil II), he was baptized a Christian at Constantinople. Although he had previously persecuted the few Christians in his realm, this grandson of Olga now became the great Christianizer and civilizer of the Russians, so much so that he is venerated in the Russian Church as St. Vladimir. The form of the liturgy which he introduced into Russia was that of the Greek Church, but the language used was Russian, and this has ever since been the practice in the Russian Church. At the time of Olga and Vladimir the Greek Church was still in communion with the Latin Church, and therefore these early Russian Christians were completely Catholic. In fact, even for some time after 1054, when Michael Caerularius, the Patriarch of Constantinople, broke away in schism from Rome, the Russian Church remained in communion with the pope at Rome. Gradually and almost unconsciously the Russians followed the lead of their mother Church at Constantinople, so that without knowing how or why, they broke the bond that tied them to unity of the faith in the See of St. Peter's successors at Rome, and thus were they separated from the rest of Christian Europe, and the work of their first mother in Christ, St. Olga, was undone.

The feast of Saint Olga is celebrated on July 11 as a holyday of high rank by all Russian Christians, not only by the schismatics, but also by the Catholics of the Russian rite. Saint Olga, therefore, has every right to be regarded and venerated as a genuine Catholic saint.

Saint Pancratius

Martyr

c. 3 0 4

(May 12)

IN THE WESTERN wall of Rome that runs along the top of the Janiculum Hill lies the *Porta di San Pancrazio* or Gate of St. Pancratius. About a mile west of this gate out in the country on the *Via Aurelia* or Aurelian Road, lies the venerable old Church of Saint Pancratius. The original church on this site was built in the fourth century over the tomb of this martyr in the Catacombs of Calepodius. About the year 500, Pope Symmachus renovated this old church, and in the seventh century Pope Honorius (625-638) handsomely restored it, as known from an inscription that is still preserved there. The present church, despite some relatively recent restorations, dates essentially from that time. It is certain, therefore, that ever since the time of his death, Rome venerated Pancratius as one of its most famous martyrs.

Pope Saint Gregory the Great (590-604) was greatly devoted to this holy martyr. In a sermon (Homily 27) which he delivered on the feast of Saint Pancratius, he said, "We are present at the tomb of a martyr the nature of whose death, which brought him to the heavenly kingdom, we know. If we are not called upon to sacrifice our body for Christ, at least let us overcome our soul for His sake. God is pleased with such a sacrifice, and with the sentence of His generous judgment He will crown the victory of our peace. For He looks with kind regard on our struggle, and our Lord Jesus Christ, who later will reward those who conquer, now helps them as they fight." For the proper care of the Church of Saint Pancratius, this pope established a Benedictine abbey next to it.

The Benedictine monk, Saint Augustine of Canterbury, whom Saint Gregory sent to England to convert the Anglo-Saxons, brought with him to this country the cult of Saint Pancratius, and built several churches here in his honor. As a result, many churches in medieval Catholic England were dedicated to "Saint Pancras," as the English commonly called him.

Saint Gregory of Tours (538-594) refers to a strange custom, the origin of which is obscure. He calls Saint Pancratius "the great avenger of perjuries" and says that, when the veracity of a witness at Rome is doubted, this man is brought to the tomb of Saint Pancratius and, if he then swears falsely, God punishes him by striking him dead, or at least by letting him become possessed by a devil.

Unfortunately practically nothing is known for certain concerning the life and martyrdom of Saint Pancratius. His so-called "Acts" is a composition of the sixth century or later, and it is difficult to distinguish between fact and fable in this account. However, since it is relatively short and offers a good example of the nature of the spurious "Acts" of the martyrs, a translation of it is given here, made from the Latin text as edited in the *Acta Sanctorum*, Vol. 15, page 21.

At that time, under the wicked emperors, Diocletian and Maximinian, there was a cruel persecution of the Christians to make them sacrifice to the idols. Now, it happened that in the city of Synnada of the Province of Phrygia death took away Cleonius and Cyriaca, the parents of Pancratius, who were of noble descent. Since Pancratius was an only child, after the death of his mother his father confided him to the care of his uncle, Dionysius, making the latter swear by the almighty and great power of the gods that he would safeguard all the property which he possessed here and in the city of Rome and would not be led by hateful avarice to deprive Pancratius of any of it, but would, as a worthy brother of Pancratius' father, prove himself most devoted to him. Since Dionysius loved his brother dearly, he therefore bestowed love and affection on Pancratius also.

Three years later Dionysius and Pancratius went to Rome, and resided there in the region called Cuminana on the Coelian Hill where they had a large estate and many slaves. Now in those days, because there was a persecution of the Christians, a certain pope of Rome, called Caius, hid in a house on the street where Dionysius and Pancratius dwelt. Dionysius thus heard of all the good deeds that Pope Caius was doing and how he was inducing all the people to give up the worship of idols and was leading them on the true way to everlasting life. Wishing to know more about him, Dionysius went with his nephew Pancratius to the residence of Saint Caius, where they met Eusebius, the doorkeeper, a man of great sanctity, and they asked him to introduce them to the pope. Eusebius entered the house and said to Saint Caius, "Holy Father, there are certain noblemen outside who would like to meet Your Holiness." This filled Pope Saint Caius with great joy and, kneeling down in prayer, he said, "I thank Thee, Lord Jesus Christ, King of Kings and Lord of Lords, that Thou hast graciously chosen me, the last and least of Thy servants, to reveal to them Thy Holy Spirit." Then he at once gave orders to have them brought in. Casting themselves at the feet of Saint Caius, they began to beg him to teach them to worship the same Lord whom he worshipped. Having raised them up and embraced them, the saintly man began to teach them all the heavenly doctrine. Twenty days later he baptized them and made them Christians. Filled with the power of the Christian sacrament, they soon became so fervent in the fear of God that they offered themselves of their own accord to the persecutors.

It happened, however, that after a few days, Dionysius, dear to God and rich in heavenly merits, departed to the Lord. Such was the madness of the pagans against the Christians that they cried out with fury: "O most excellent emperors, purge this city of the cruel and sorcerous Christians who are deceiving all the world and overthrowing your whole empire." Thereupon Diocletian, full of wrath and indignation, issued an edict that whoever was found belonging to this religion should be punished without even a hearing. Among those who were then arrested was Pancratius. When the persecutors who had arrested him learned of his noble birth, they notified Emperor Diocletian of this. The latter ordered him to be brought at once to his palace.

When Diocletian saw Pancratius, he was astounded that such a mere boy should be holding out in his desire to die for Christ rather than worship the idols. "My boy," Diocletian said to him, "let me dissuade you from dying so evil a death. You do not look as much as fifteen years old, and you are of a noble family. Your father, Cleonius, was a good friend of mine. If you give up this madness of the Christians and return to your father's religion, I will give you even greater honors and riches, and you will never need to leave my court, where I will treat you as my own son. But if you despise my kind words, I will order you to be killed and your body to be burned up, so that the Christians may not come and honor you as a martyr." But Saint Pancratius answered him: "Do not be deceived, my lord Emperor. Though I am but a boy of fourteen, I am not lacking in wisdom and common sense. Our Lord Jesus Christ has bestowed such understanding on us Christians that all the terror of your magistrates and judges means no more to us than a mere picture. For your gods and goddesses, whom you ask us to worship, are deceitful demons who have not spared their own parents and who raped their own sisters. I marvel that you do not consider it a disgrace to worship such demons, and that you order your true servants to be killed with such unheard-of cruelty."

Then the emperor Diocletian gave orders to have Pancratius led out on the Aurelian Way and there be put to death because he felt disgraced to be overcome and reviled by such a mere boy. And thus Pancratius, the blessed athlete of Christ, was led out on the Aurelian Way and won the crown of martyrdom by being beheaded. In the dark of night the lady Octavilla secretly took away his body and, wrapping it in spices and a shroud, buried it on the twelfth of May.

Thus far the "Acts" of Saint Pancratius. It is to be noted, however, that on the same day, May 12, the Church commemorates the equally famous martyrs, Nereus and Achilles, who died in an earlier persecution and were buried in a different cemetery, the Catacombs of Domitilla on the Via Ardeatina, south of Rome. In the present Roman liturgy all these martyrs, together with Saint Domitilla, are commemorated together in a single liturgical prayer, though originally St. Pancratius had his separate Mass.

Saint Pantaleon

Martyr

3 0 4

(July 27)

A s with many others among the martyrs of the Roman persecutions, the only thing that can be said with certainty about Saint Pantaleon is that there really was a martyr by this name who gave his life for Christ. He was venerated as a martyr at too early a date for any doubts to be cast upon the fact of his existence. Moreover, it can be said with good probability that he died about the year 304 or 305 in the bloody persecutions inflicted on the Church by the Emperor Diocletian, and that the place of this martyrdom was the city of Nicomedia in northwestern Asia Minor. Beyond that, the story of his life and martyrdom must be put down as purely legendary.

According to the legend, which was composed a few centuries after his death, Pantaleon's father, Eustorgius, was a rich pagan of Nicomedia. His mother Eubula, however, was a devout Christian who saw to it that her son was raised a Christian. As a young man he studied medicine and eventually became the personal physician of the Emperor Galerius Maximinianus. A victim to the bad example around him, Pantaleon fell away for a time from the practice of his religion and even gave up the faith. However, through the efforts of a zealous priest, named Hermolaus, he repented of his sins and returned to the faith.

Having come into the possession of a large fortune at the death of his father, Pantaleon was denounced by his envious colleagues as a Christian when the edict of Diocletian against the Church was published at Nicomedia, even though he had already distributed his wealth among the poor. Together with Hermolaus and two others, he was arrested and hailed before the emperor. The latter, wishing to save the life of this valuable physician, urged him to give up Christianity, but Pantaleon boldly confessed his faith and refused to renounce Christ. To prove the truth of the Christian faith, he miraculously cured a paralytic in the presence of the emperor. This, however, had no effect on the unbelievers, and Pantaleon, together with his Christian companions, was condemned to death.

After suffering many torments, the others were beheaded, but Pantaleon's execution was postponed until the next day. Wonderful to say, the first five attempts to kill him—burning him with torches, plunging him into a cauldon of liquid lead, throwing him into the sea, exposing him to wild beasts, and binding him to a rolling wheel—all proved fruitless. Miraculously the torches were extinguished, the liquid lead became like cool water, the anchor to which he was tied floated on the sea, the wild beasts fawned on him, and the wheel broke. Even the sword which was then used to behead him bent harmlessly when it touched his neck. Praying to God to forgive his executioners (who eventually were converted and died as martyrs themselves), he finally permitted himself to be beheaded.

In the East, Saint Pantaleon has ever been honored as the "Great Martyr and Wonder-worker," and one of the "Holy Moneyless" physicians who treated the sick without remuneration. In the West, he became one of the "Fourteen Holy Helpers" and, with Saint Luke and Saints Cosmas and Damian, one of the patrons of doctors and midwives. His relics were venerated in various parts of the world.

The name of Pantaleon, which comes from the Greek word *panteleemon* (meaning "all-merciful") has, through a peculiar

course of events, given us some of our common words in modern
English. One of the places where Saint Pantaleon has long been
venerated as a principal patron is the city of Venice. In the late
Middle Ages so many men in Venice were named after him that
the Italian form of his name, Pantaleone, came to mean a Venetian. In an old Italian comedy that was very popular during the
Renaissance one of the characters, originally a rich old Venetian
merchant, was known as "Pantaleone." In a later form of this
pantomime comedy, Pantaleone became a foolish old man and
the object of the butts of the clown Harlequin. The peculiar kind
of long trousers worn by Pantaleone in the play were named
after him in the form of the Italian plural noun *pantaleoni*. This
comedy was also popular in 16th and 17th century England,
where the old man was called "Pantaloon," and his trousers "pan-
taloons." This has given us, in shortened form, the word "pants,"
and the diminutive "pantalets."

Saint Pascal Baylon

Confessor

1 5 9 2

(May 17)

GOD IS NOT bound by social status. He takes His saints from every walk in life. In the case of Saint Pascal Baylon He chose a child of a lowly peasant family that lived in the little hamlet of Torre Hermosa ("Beautiful Tower") in Aragon, northeastern Spain. The boy was born on May 24, 1540, which was Pentecost in that year, and since Pentecost is sometimes called in Spanish "Pascua del Espiritu Santo," "the Pasch of the Holy Spirit," he was given the name of Pascual, or Pascal, in baptism. His parents, Martin Baylon and Elizabeth Jubera, were unusually devout and they led their little son on the paths of holiness from his earliest years. He seems to have been disposed toward piety, and many stories were told of the religious practices in which he engaged even before he could walk or talk. One day, for instance, after his mother had previously taken him to Mass as a baby, he suddenly disappeared. Much frightened, she hunted for him everywhere. At last, going to church to pray for his safe return, she found him sprawled out on the steps of the altar rail, gazing at the tabernacle. Since he was not old enough to walk, he must have crawled there. A few years later, seeing one of his little boy friends whose mother had put a small Franciscan habit on him because of a vow, Pascal longed to become a Franciscan, and he never lost this holy desire.

From his seventh to his twenty-fourth year Pascal worked as a shepherd, at first for his father and later for other men. Never having had any formal schooling, he taught himself to read and write, and that in quite a novel way. He somehow obtained a little book containing the Office of the Blessed Virgin Mary. Asking any passer-by to read to him some sentence from it, he would memorize this sentence; then, analyzing the way in which it was printed, he would learn each letter and the sound it had to form words. Finally, by copying out with a piece of charcoal on a scrap of paper each sentence as he studied it, he gradually learned to write as well as to read.

Pascal's whole life was quite literally spent in the supernatural. The existence of God and of our Lady and the Saints was just as certain to him as was the material world and its creatures, and he was always as conscious of the one as of the other. He loved and talked with Christ in the Blessed Sacrament with no less effort than the Apostles had in conversing with the divine Master in Galilee. His devotion to the Holy Eucharist was, in fact, his outstanding characteristic through life. Living as he constantly did in this supernatural atmosphere, he seems to have taken miracles for granted. He never worked any miracles for his own benefit. No true saint ever would, just as Jesus in His life on earth voluntarily submitted to all the natural conditions of the human nature which His divine Person had taken on Himself without ever working a miracle to help Himself. Pascal never hesitated to ask his beloved Lord to work a miracle to help others, and the number of true miracles which he unquestionably performed before and after his death is simply astounding.

Like the little Poor Man of Assisi, whose Franciscan habit he was to wear for most of his life, Pascal was noted not only for his love of poverty and his holy simplicity, but also for his constant joy of spirit. Gloominess and true holiness are inconsistent. As a shepherd boy he learned to play the guitar, and he would accompany himself on this instrument as he sang popular hymns to Our Lady in his fine strong voice.

One of his shepherd companions, John Apparico, who lived to be a very old man, gave testimony many years later at the canonical process for Pascal's beatification. This man testified that when they were shepherds together, the angels used to come and show the Blessed Sacrament to Pascal who would then gaze at it in rapturous adoration. John himself could see nothing except the ecstatic look on his companion's face, but Pascal revealed to him the nature of his visions. John also said that Pascal once told him that he had a vision of a friar and a nun of the Franciscan order who invited him to leave the world and join them in religion. Although Pascal himself did not identify these visionary friends of his more precisely, his early biographers did not hesitate to say that they were Saint Francis of Assisi and Saint Clare.

When Pascal was eighteen years old he sought admittance in the monastery of Our Lady of Loretto at Monteforte in the region of Spain called Valencia, about two hundred miles south of his native village. This was one of the first monasteries founded by St. Peter of Alcantara who "reformed" or restored the Spanish Franciscans to their original fervor. This extremely austere saint was still living at the time when Pascal came to Valencia, but there is no evidence that they ever saw each other in life. The good friars at this monastery did not know what to make of this strange youth who came seeking admittance among them, and they put him off for the time being. Undaunted, Pascal continued his life as a shepherd, working for Martin Garcia, a wealthy landowner of Monteforte. Soon Senior Garcia and his wife took such a liking to this young shepherd that they, who had no children of their own, offered to adopt him as their son. Pascal's heart, however, was set on becoming a poor brother of the Poverello of Assissi, and he graciously but firmly refused their kind offer.

At length, when Pascal was twenty-three or twenty-four years old, he was finally received into the Franciscan monastery at Monteforte, and here on the Feast of our Lady's Purification,

February 2, 1565, he made his holy vows as a friar. In this monastery, and in various other ones of the Alcantarine Franciscans in Spain, he spent his holy life as a humble lay brother. Even to his fellow friars who tried to imitate the penitential life of their leader, St. Peter of Alcantara, this simple lay brother Pascal seemed a marvel of penance. Scarcely eating enough hard crusts of bread to keep his body and soul together and ever torturing his flesh with disciplines, Pascal never lost his joyous composure. Humble, modest, and patient, he honestly thought himself the last and least of all.

One of the sayings which he wrote in his little notebook was, "Whoever is intent on saving his soul must have three hearts in one: towards God the heart of a son, towards his neighbor the heart of a mother, towards himself the heart of a judge." That he acted like a rigorous judge toward himself can be seen from his austere life. That he was an utterly devoted son towards his heavenly Father is evident both from his longing to be in the chapel before the Blessed Sacrament as much as his busy labors would allow, and to serve as many Masses as possible.

That he truly had the heart of a tender mother towards his neighbor is abundantly proved by his unbounded charity to the poor. He really saw Christ in them, and he could never do enough for them. Having the office of "porter," or doorkeeper, most of his life, he had plenty of opportunity for helping the needy who knocked at the monastery gate for their daily meals. When the friars themselves had but little food on hand, Pascal did not hesitate to ask God to work a miracle. Once, another brother, on seeing him put a few little crusts of bread in a big cauldron of water, said to him, "Brother Pascal, that soup is not likely to interfere with your clients' digestion." "Don't worry about that," replied the saint, "that is God's business." Sure enough, this particular pot of soup, when brought out to the poor, proved to be very rich, tasty and nourishing.

Sometimes the friars thought that Pascal went too far in giving the poor everything he could lay his hands on. Being such holy men themselves, however, they did not have the heart to stop him. At the process of beatification the brother gardener, Pedro d'Aranda, told that, on mornings following the days when Pascal made extensive raids on the garden, the plants would be there again, just as if they had never been touched.

During the early years of his religious life Pascal was sent on an errand to the Franciscan monastery at Jeres de la Frontera, near Cadiz, in the extreme south of Spain. Here he met a fourteen-year-old boy who was devoted to the friars at this monastery. With his miraculous insight into souls, Pascal saw at once that he had found a treasure in this boy. He induced the boy's poor widowed mother to give up this only son of hers to God. The boy accompanied Pascal back to Valencia where he became an Alcantarine Franciscan. He was John Ximenes, one of the shining lights of his order who, at the time of Pascal's death was his Father Provincial, and who later became his first and most important biographer.

On another occasion Pascal was sent on a journey to deliver an important message to the Franciscan General in distant Paris. France was at that time a dangerous country for foreign Catholics to enter, especially for a Spanish friar like Pascal. The Protestant Hugenots did not take kindly to their presence. Yet alone, with no guide and no provisions, Pascal went north through Spain, crossed the Pyrenees, and entered France. Then his worst troubles began. "Down with the Papist! Death to the idolater!" the Hugenots screamed at him. He fearlessly argued with them on the truth of Christ's real presence in the Blessed Sacrament. On several occasions he was beaten and pelted with stones, one of which struck him hard on his left shoulder and broke the bone. He suffered from this injury for the rest of his life.

He would gladly have died a martyr, but in marvelous ways God protected him so that eventually he reached Spain again despite his many harrowing experiences. It was not only in France that Pascal showed he could speak learnedly on the Blessed

SAINT PETER CLAVER

The African slave trade was an outrage that cried to Heaven for vengeance. The only ray of light in this dark night of man's inhumanity to man was shed by the heroic labors of the Catholic missionaries in the New World. And the most outstanding of these was the Jesuit Father, Saint Peter Claver, whose astounding labors for the victims of the outrage won for him the title of *Apostle of the Negroes*.

SAINT MARY OF EGYPT

Ledoux

According to her legend, Saint Mary of Egypt spent the early years of her life in sin. Following this, she lived a solitary life of great holiness and severe penance for a period of almost forty years in the desert. The elaborate form of her legend was attributed to Saint Sophronius.

Eucharist and other points of Catholic doctrine. In Spain, also, he was interviewed by learned theologians who were amazed at his wisdom. Since his education never went beyond the rudiments of reading and writing, the knowledge which he showed of things divine can only be attributed to what is called supernaturally infused science. Father Emmanuel Rodriguez, one of the ablest theologians of the time, testified to this gift. He visited Pascal and spent several hours testing him, only to end up exhausted. "It is astounding," he said, "this brother undoubtedly has infused science. If I were a bishop, I would have no hesitation about ordaining him, so certain am I that the Holy Spirit speaks through his lips."

Pascal's gift of prophecy was likewise astonishing. He knew when God was about to call a soul from this life, or when a soul was about to be released from purgatory. It was rather embarrassing for people at times to find that Pascal could read their minds, revealing to them the thoughts that they were trying hard to conceal from others. Yet he himself never thought there was anything extraordinary in these marvelous gifts. In his own eyes he ever remained a poor ignorant shepherd, a sinful creature, in fact, who knew that he would fall into temptation unless he constantly held his body in subjection.

When Pascal was in his fifty-third year, it was revealed to him that he would soon die and that this would happen at the monastery of Our Lady of the Rosary in Villareal, Valencia, where he was then stationed. For a time he did not know the exact date, but when this was finally revealed to him he was filled with joy. Death came to him as a friend on May 15, 1592, which in that year was the feast of Pentecost. His birthday in heaven, therefore, was on the same feast as his birthday on earth. Just as he lay dying, Mass was being celebrated in the monastery church. At the consecration of the Holy Eucharist at this Mass he cried out, "Jesus, Jesus!"—and breathed his last.

The news of his death spread rapidly, and soon the monastery was filled with men who tried to strip his poor cell for relics.

When his body was laid out in the monastery church, crowds of people from far and wide flocked to see the marvelous sight of a corpse that resisted the natural laws of death. His flesh continued to retain its lifelike freshness and color, as if the blood still flowed in his veins. His limbs remained supple and flexible. A certain liquid, it is true, came like perspiration from his face. This had the fragrance of the richest perfume and, when applied to those with bodily ailments, effected marvelous cures. Even months later, when Pascal's tomb under the altar was opened, his body was found to be still free from corruption.

One of the most astonishing things connected with the tomb of Saint Pascal was the strange phenomenon known as "Saint Pascal's knocks," which continued for a couple of centuries. Peculiar sounds, as if someone were knocking on a door, would come from his tomb. The nature of these knockings varied on different occasions. Eventually it became clear that with a slow, gentle knocking St. Pascal was giving his approval of something; with rapid, loud knocks, his disapproval, or his warning of some calamity. Serious scholars, who first scoffed at the idea of the reality of these knocks, investigated the phenomenon and came away convinced of its truth. In fact, some of these doubting Thomases were frightened out of their wits when they heard Pascal's thunderous knockings in disapproval of their doubts. So, *los golpes di San Pascal*, "the knockings of St. Pascal," cannot be attributed solely to popular imagination.

Saint Pascal's innumerable miracles include even the raising of the dead to life. One of the oddest concerns, strange to say, not a man but a horse. A poor peddler had a horse with the remarkable name of Coco, on which he and his family depended for a livelihood. One day Coco took sick and died. Leaving him lying dead in the field, the peddler's wife went to the tomb of St. Pascal and begged him for the love that he always had for the poor to come to their aid now that their horse was dead. What was her surprise when, on coming back home, she saw Coco galloping about the field and eating heartily!

On account of the immense number of certified miracles wrought through Pascal's intercession, the Holy See dispensed with the law requiring a longer interval between the death and the beatification of a saint. Pascal was therefore beatified by Pope Paul V in 1618, even before the beatification of the great founder of his branch of the Franciscans, Saint Peter of Alcantara, who had died thirty years before Pascal. He was canonized by Pope Alexander VIII in 1690. Finally, in 1897, Pope Leo XIII solemnly declared Saint Pascal the heavenly patron of all Eucharistic Congresses, and of all Associations in honor of the Most Blessed Sacrament.

Saint Paul of the Cross
Confessor
1 7 7 5
(April 28)

CHRIST'S PASSION AND death, a central mystery of Christianity, should of course be the object of special devotion for all Christians. For St. Paul of the Cross, the Passion of Christ was quite literally, though in another sense of the word, the all-consuming passion of his soul. The story of the external events of his life is essentially a record of his activity to win men to God by preaching Christ crucified and by founding a religious order, commonly known as "the Passionists," for this same purpose. An account of his interior life would necessarily be a description of the growth of his soul in ever closer union with God through his contemplation of divine love as revealed in Christ's Passion and death on the cross.

He who was later to be known as Paul of the Cross was born on January 3, 1694, and baptized three days later as Paul Francis Daneo. His birthplace was the little town of Ovada in Italy that lies about halfway between Genoa on the south and Alessandria on the north. The neighboring region, while fairly mountainous, is not as high as the northern end of the Appennines to the east, or the coastal range of Liguria to the south, or the foothills of the Alps, called the Piedmont, to the west.

In one of the narrow streets of this town, Paul's father, Luke Daneo, earned his livelihood as proprietor of a small dry goods store. Though Luke's first wife had died after five years of childless marriage, his next marriage, with Anna Maria Massari, was blessed by God with no less than sixteen children. Their oldest child, a girl, died in infancy. Their next child was Paul Francis. Another son, John Baptist, was to be Paul's lifelong companion and his valiant assistant in founding the Passionists.

Within this family circle Paul received his first lessons in virtue and piety. His mother was an especially devout woman who taught her children not merely prayer formulas, but how to really talk with God in prayer in their own simple way. The bed-time stories she told her little ones were from the lives of the saints. Paul soon got to know these so well that eventually he took his mother's place in retelling them to his younger brothers and sisters. Like many another boy in a pious Catholic household, he built himself a little altar where he would imitate a priest saying Mass. There have not been many boys who, like him, got up two or three hours before the rest of the family to pray before such an altar. Anna Maria Daneo also knew how to give a very practical turn to her lessons in religion. If she could not help inflicting a little pain on Paul, as when the comb she used pulled his hair, she would put a small crucifix in his hand and say, "Look how Jesus suffered for you!" Thus at an early age Paul acquired his love of suffering—not as something abnormal, but as a means of showing Christ his love for Him. Later in life he used to say, "If I am saved, as I hope to be, I owe it all to my good mother's teachings."

No doubt Paul also owed something to the Carmelite Fathers who taught in the little school at Cremolino which he attended when the ever growing Daneo family moved to this nearby town. Luke Daneo still kept his store in Ovada, but the few rooms above it were no longer sufficient for his many children. An interesting story is told of Paul as happening during this period of his life. Once when he and his younger brother, John Baptist, were walking from their home in Cremolino to their father's store in Ovada, they fell into a stream called the Olba that ran swiftly

through the hills. No one heard Paul's cry of "Mama, help me!"
Yet suddenly a beautiful lady appeared and pulled both of the
boys out of the water. Paul never doubted that it was the Blessed Virgin Mary. Later in life he was to experience many similar
instances of supernatural protection.

In 1718, when Paul was twenty-two years old, the Daneo family finally settled in the town of Castellazzo which was only a
few miles south of the city of Alessandria. This was the birthplace of Luke Daneo, and here he now gave his roving family a
permanent home. Paul, however, had not always been with his
family during these various moves. There is some evidence that
as a poverty-stricken student he had made some higher studies
at Genoa. Also at this time, in 1715-1716, he had a strange inter-
lude at soldiering. When Pope Clement XI called for a new crusade against the Turks, Paul, thinking that this would be a good
opportunity to serve the Church and perhaps even gain the crown
of martyrdom, enlisted in the Venetian army. However, the
Christian forces never left Italy. Paul was soon disillusioned. Not
that he minded too much the long, tiring marches back and forth
over the plains of Lombardy; he was always a good walker, and
physical hardships did not distress him. It was the depraved
atmosphere among the rough soldiers with whom he was forced to associate that threatened to suffocate his soul. The time
came when he realized that he was called for a different kind of
combat in Christ's cause. He went to his commanding officer,
stated his case, and was released from the army.

Back with his family, Paul met with another trial. An uncle of
his, Father Christopher Daneo, offered to bequeath the young
man his estate if Paul married. Paul certainly had no intention
of ever marrying, yet he did not wish to appear ungrateful, and
he knew that his impoverished family could well use this financial
aid. His dilemma was solved by the sudden death of Father
Christopher who left him a good legacy with no matrimonial
strings attached to it. Paul, however, refused the legacy and accepted only his uncle's breviary as a memento of his kindness.

During the next few years Paul tried to live as a religious though still dwelling with his family. A certain sermon which he heard at this time made a deep impression on him, and he resolved to increase his corporal penances and give still more time to prayer. The experiment which he made of taking a vow to carry out with religious obedience whatever the members of his family asked him to do, and to request their permission for anything that he wished to eat or make use of was a failure. His sisters and brothers could not help taking this as a big joke, and he had to have the vow commuted.

In his spiritual education Paul was largely self-taught. He thoroughly learned St. Francis de Sales' *Treatise on the Love of God*, and he was acquainted with some of the mystical writings of St. John of the Cross, such as *The Ascent of Mount Carmel*. His efforts to obtain spiritual direction from his parish priest were unsuccessful. This good, but gruff old man had no patience with "mystics," and sometimes scolded Paul so loudly in the confessional that the people in the church must have thought some great sinner was seeking absolution. Paul rejected as a temptation of the devil the thought of looking for another director. "This confessor is good for me," he said to himself; "he makes me bow my head." The priest, however, finally advised him to look elsewhere for a spiritual director. Ultimately Paul found a much more understanding director in the Capuchin Father Columban, but when the latter was transferred from Castrolazzo in 1719, the young mystic had to go to Alessandria, a round trip of eight miles, for confession and spiritual guidance. Here Monsignor Cerutti, a canon at the Cathedral whom he had chosen for his new director, tried him at first in many ways, but in the end had to admit that Paul was indeed a chosen soul.

In the ordinary course of events Paul should have entered one of the well established religious orders, but deep in his heart he had a presentiment that God was calling him to a special vocation though as yet he had no clear idea what it would be. On the one hand he always had a strong inclination for the life of a hermit—a type of spiritual life still fairly common at that time in which a man dwelt alone in some solitary cave or hut, living a simple, austere life of prayer and manual labor far from the distractions of the world. On the other hand, he believed that God wished him to take an active part in making the divine goodness known to men. Eventually Paul would evolve both for himself and for his followers, the Passionists, an harmonious combination of these two forms of religious life. For the time being all he could do was to pray for and await the light of the Holy Spirit to show him the path he was to tread. Once while praying before the Blessed Sacrament, he heard an interior voice say to him, "My son, he who draws near me comes into thorns." On another occasion he heard our Lord warn him: "I wish to make you another Job." Or, again, he beheld a vision of an angel bringing him a golden cross and a scourge marked "Love," the lashes of which were made of golden chains. In this way he was given to understand that his way to Heaven was to be the royal road of suffering.

Finally God made His will much more clearly known to Paul. Toward the end of summer in the year 1720, as Paul was returning from Holy Communion rapt in spirit, he saw himself clothed in a long black tunic with a white cross on its breast. Below the cross in white lettering was the Holy Name of Jesus, and a voice said, "This is to show how pure and spotless that heart should be which is to bear this Holy Name." Shortly thereafter he had another vision in which he beheld the Blessed Virgin Mary wearing a similar black tunic, but on her breast there was a heart, outlined in white, surmounted by a white cross. Within the heart in white lettering were the words, *Jesu XRI Passio* (that is, *Jesu Christi Passio*, "Jesus Christ's Passion"), while at the base of the heart were three white nails. Mary explained to Paul that she was dressed in black as a sign of mourning for the death of her Son, and she then added: "You must found a religious congregation whose members shall be similarly clothed and shall thus join me in continual mourning for the Passion and death of my Son."

Now Paul was certain of what God wished him to do. How, when or where he was to do it was still a mystery. If for a moment he had doubted God's will, the whole thing would have seemed impossible to him. Here he was, a mere layman, with little formal education, starting out to found a new religious order of which he, himself, was still the only member! Yet God had willed it, he told himself, and therefore he must get busy at once. After all, he was already twenty-six years old and he did not know how much longer he had to live.

As soon as possible he laid the matter before Bishop Francis di Gattinara of Alessandria. The Bishop finally consented to clothe him in the black habit, but without the "Passion Sign." The simple ceremony took place on November 21, 1720. The founder of an order of which he was the sole member now changed his name to "Paul of the Cross." All he wore was the rough black tunic, reaching to his ankles and fastened with a rope at the waist. He had no cloak or mantle, no hat or shoes. For years he always went barefoot. Back at Castellazzo, he no longer lived at home, but in a small room attached to the sacristy of St. Charles' Church. Here, in the cold dampness, with no heat and little light, with bread and water his only nourishment, and with the floor for his bed, he made a retreat of forty days. While his body suffered, his soul soared. Strengthened by a vision of the holy founders of other religious orders, he began to write the Rule of his new order on the second of December. Five days later he finished it, convinced that it was practically dictated to him by God.

After his retreat Paul presented his Rule to the Bishop of Alessandria. The latter, however, advised him to have it examined by the Capuchin Father Columban who was now in Genoa. In the depth of winter with the roads covered with ice and snow, Paul walked barefoot over the Ligurian Mountains to Genoa. Had not a passing police patrol come to his rescue, he might well have died of hunger and exhaustion on the forty-mile journey. When he could later report to his bishop that Father Columban approved of his Rule, the bishop officially allowed Paul to live according to it as a hermit. An abandoned hermitage was found for him near the Church of St. Stephen outside of Castellazzo, but the bishop also told him to teach catechism at the Church of St. Charles in the town. Paul was delighted with his new life, and his joy increased when his brother, John Baptist, came to receive the black habit of Christ's Passion and join him in his hermit's life. At the bishop's request, Paul, though still a layman, preached a triduum in Castellazzo at carnival time, just before Lent, the good effects of which were truly marvelous.

This, however, was about as far as the bishop of Alessandria would allow Paul to go. Without authorization from the Holy See he would not let Paul establish a true monastery at Castellazzo. Bearing the manuscript of his Rule and a cordial letter of recommendation from his bishop, Paul sailed in September, 1721, from Genoa to Civitavecchia, Rome's chief port of entry at that time. As his ship slowly passed Monte Argentario, the Tuscan promontory that rises over two thousand feet above the sea (almost cut off like an island from the mainland), Paul recalled the words that he had once heard in prayer before a statue of our Lady: "Come to Monte Argentario, for I am there alone." On his return voyage he would, he hoped, be able to visit the seagirt mountain.

At Rome, Paul went hopefully to the papal palace on the Quirinal Hill. In his simplicity he walked up to one of the guards at the gate and said, "Please, I would like to see the Pope." The guard took just one look at him. To all appearances Paul was merely another of those troublesome tramps who haunt the gates of the nobility. With a few gruff words the guard closed the gate in Paul's face. The first attempt to get papal approval for the new Rule was a complete fiasco. Before leaving Rome, Paul knelt before the image of the Madonna in the Church of St. Mary Major and confided his future congregation to her care, vowing to propagate devotion to Christ crucified—the distinctive "fourth vow" of the Passionists to the present day.

Then Paul went to Monte Argentario. The quiet and natural beauty of the lofty promontory delighted him. For a few days he lived there in holy peace in the abandoned hermitage of the Annunciation, then suddenly he remembered his brother, John Baptist. When he had left Castellazzo for Rome, John had said to him, "Go, if you must, but you will not be happy without me." Yes, John must now join him on the holy mountain. Before going back home for John, Paul asked permission to settle as a hermit on Monte Argentario from Bishop Fulvio Salvi of Sovana, in whose diocese the mount was situated. The latter consented, provided Bishop di Gattinara of Alessandria agreed. These formalities were soon attended to, but there was still one limitation. Permission was granted for Paul to have only one companion. Naturally he chose his brother, John Baptist. The time for founding a true Passionist monastery had not yet come.

For over a year (1722-1723), Paul and John lived as hermits in prayer and penance on Monte Argentario. The holy founder was later to regard it as the happiest period of his life, for now he was raised to the highest degree of mystical contemplation. The two brothers differed greatly in temperament, but this, far from leading to disagreement and conflict between them, tended rather to complement each other's characters to their mutual benefit. Spiritually John knew that he needed the inspiration of his more gifted brother, but Paul also realized that he could not well dispense with John's steadying influence. John Baptist was well named, for his stern and austere nature resembled that of Christ's holy Precursor. Despite all the hardships that he imposed on himself, Paul was more gentle and amiable toward others. He was also at times inclined to be despondent over the many reverses he met with in establishing his order. Thus in his iron-willed brother he found a strong right arm to bear him up. John would hardly have thought himself a co-founder of the Passionists, yet due credit should be given to him, too. The first violinist may win all the applause, but his melody would be lacking in harmony unless another humbly played second fiddle.

At the neck of land that kept Monte Argentario from being an island there were two settlements, the little village, mostly of fisherfolk, called Portercole to the south, and the fair-sized town of Orbetello to the north. To one or the other of these places Paul and John went for Mass and confession, and later they were to exercise their ministry as priests in both places.

In the summer of 1723, the two brothers received an invitation to go to Gaeta, situated about a hundred and fifty miles to the southeast, halfway down the coast from Rome to Naples. Bishop Pignatelli of Gaeta was welcoming hermits to his diocese. An- thony Schiaffino, who had known Paul at Castrolazzo, was already among the hermits of Gaeta and he had recommended him to Bishop Pignatelli. Hoping that among the Gaeta hermits they might be able to get candidates for their new order, Paul and John left Monte Argentario with the permission of its bishop and settled as hermits at Gaeta. Though Bishop Pignatelli gave the two brothers opportunity to work in the active ministry in his diocese, even asking Paul (who was still a layman!) to preach the ordination retreat to his seminarians, the actual founding of the first Passionist monastery seemed as far away here as ever.

In the fall of the same year, Bishop Cavalieri, an uncle of St. Alphonsus Liguori, invited Paul to his diocese of Troia which lay some eighty miles northeast of Naples. Although Paul did not stay here very long, he won the warm friendship of this bishop who gave him good advice on how to proceed at Rome for obtaining permission to found a new order, and who also supplied him with valuable letters of introduction to various prelates at Rome.

In 1725, Paul and John went to the Eternal City to gain the indulgence of the Holy Year, and while there they happened to meet Monsignor Crescenzi who took such a lively interest in their cause that he introduced them to Cardinal Corradini. The Cardinal arranged for Paul to have an informal audience with Pope Benedict XIII (1724-1730), and to Paul's great joy the pope gave him permission to gather members for his congregation.

Back at Gaeta, however, Paul found that the hermits were not interested in his plans. Then, in 1726, he lost a good friend in the death of Bishop Cavalieri of Troia. With no hope now of establishing a monastery in these southern regions, Paul and John returned to Rome. Here they worked for a while as nurses in the Hospital of St. Gallicanus which Cardinal Corradini had recently founded. The Cardinal soon saw that the two brothers did better work with souls than with bodies and suggested that they should be ordained priests. John at first objected, but later agreed. After a concentrated course in theology under the Franciscan Father Dominic, they were raised to the priesthood on June 7, 1727 by Pope Benedict XIII.

Almost at the same time came word of their father's death. Having obtained permission for the journey, they returned home to settle his estate, and to give their new priestly blessing to the rest of their family. The long journey on foot took more than two months, and Paul was so exhausted that for a few weeks he was too ill even to say Mass. In December they took their final farewell, and it was indeed final, for they were never to return to Castellazzo.

Back in Rome, Paul and John found conditions had changed at the Hospital of St. Gallicanus. They were now expected to take a greater share in the medical treatment of the patients, even to assist at operations. Paul's gentle nature could not take it. For all his good will and desires to suffer in his own body, he could not bring himself to inflict physical pain on others. It literally made him sick. Now that he was a patient himself in a place full of contagious diseases, the authorities agreed that hospital work was not for him. The Cardinal understood and obtained permission from the Pope for Paul and John to return to Monte Argentario.

It was now seven years since Paul had been commissioned by Christ to found a religious order and write its Rule. Barefoot, he had travelled many weary miles, seeking authorization from four bishops, one cardinal, and even a pope. He and his brother had indeed been ordained priests, but beyond that, what had he achieved? Now that he was thirty-three years old he seemed as far as ever from his longed-for goal. Even at Monte Argentario a new disappointment awaited him. His former friend and fellow hermit, Anthony Schiaffino, who had now turned hostile toward him, was found in possession of his old hermitage of the Annunciation.

Nothing daunted, Paul and John set to work to repair another small hermitage on the mountain, that of St. Anthony, which was in a ruinous state. In the Lent of 1729, Bishop Christopher Palmieri (who had recently succeeded the deceased Bishop Salvi in the diocese of Sovana), came to visit the hermits on Monte Argentario and, since Paul and John were now priests, he gave them faculties to preach and hear confessions. The true missionary work of the first two Passionists could finally begin. Their preaching activity for the first year was limited to the towns of Portercole and Orbetello at the foot of Monte Argentario. In both places Paul and John instructed, exhorted and converted the spiritually abandoned people. In the following year, 1730, the first formal missions were given at several other towns in the vicinity.

After a Lenten mission preached at Orbetello, the people of this town offered Paul a site for a monastery and church on the site of Monte Argentario outside their town. Scarcely had the foundations been laid when it was discovered that the property belonged to the king of Naples. Paul walked all the way to Naples, but failed to obtain the royal consent. Making a still longer pilgrimage on foot to Loretto, he confided his troubles to Our Lady of Loretto, and Mary came to his aid.

After "the War of the Polish Succession" (1734-1735), between Spain and Austria, this corner of Italy was given to the victorious Spaniards, and the Spanish commander at Orbetello gave Paul permission to finish the construction of his monastery. However, there was still difficulty in obtaining authorization from Rome for the use of the new church that Paul and John were building there. Twice Paul had walked to Rome and back before all the obstacles were removed. Meanwhile half a dozen candidates, one of them already a priest, had asked to be admitted into Paul's missionary order. Finally, on September 14, 1737, the first Passionist monastery and church were solemnly blessed. Paul called this and all his later monasteries "retreats." This was called "the Retreat of the Presentation of Our Blessed Lady." Thus on his beloved Monte Argentario St. Paul of the Cross at last saw the beginning of his dream come true. It was now seventeen years since he had written the Passionist Rule, ten years since he was ordained. Although he was forty-three years old, he still had almost forty more years to live, years in which he would preach hundreds of missions, found eleven more Passionist monasteries, win (after long opposition) full ecclesiastical approval for his order, and bequeath his love for Christ Crucified to future generations of his spiritual sons who would wear his black habit and "Sign of the Passion."

Over and over again St. Paul of the Cross had to walk the long road to Rome to plead with cardinals and popes for his institute. In the opinion of the cardinals the Rule of the Passionists was too strict, their austerity simply impossible. Ultimately Pope Benedict XIV (1740-1758) agreed to approve the Rule provided some of its austerities were eased: the material for the habit was to be less coarse, sandals were to be worn, a hat and cloak could be used in winter, and so forth. When Paul humbly accepted these conditions, Pope Benedict XIV signed a rescript on May 15, 1741, approving of the amended Rule of "the Congregation of the Discalced Clerics of the Most Holy Cross and Passion of our Lord Jesus Christ"—to give the Passionists their full title. Paul brought the joyful news back to Monte Argentario. He and his community then made a special spiritual retreat, and on the 4th of June he placed on his own breast, and on the breasts of his community then made a special spiritual retreat, and on the become a reality.

For almost thirty years St. Paul of the Cross continued to preach one mission after another throughout the cities, towns and villages of the Papal States and the Duchy of Tuscany. At the same time that St. Alphonsus Liguori was giving missions and founding his missionary Congregation of the Most Holy Redeemer in the Kingdom of Naples (in southern Italy), St. Paul of the Cross was carrying on his similar activity in the central regions of Italy. Religion had reached a low ebb in the 18th century. The semi-paganism of the French court at Versailles (that was to be later wiped out by the French Revolution toward the end of that century), was imitated in every little royal court of Europe. The lesser nobility and even the clergy were contaminated by this decadent spirit. It needed zealous saints with the fiery zeal of St. Paul of the Cross, St. Alphonsus Liguori, the Franciscan St. Leonard of Port Maurice, and the uncanonized but holy companions of these ardent leaders to awaken the dormant faith of the people by proclaiming to them in ringing tones the eternal truths of salvation.

Paul of the Cross always made the dominant note of his missions the theme of Christ's holy Passion. When, with cross in hand and outstretched arms, he preached God's love as shown in the sufferings and death of the divine Savior, even the hardest hearts were moved to repentance. Afterwards, in the confessional, the saint would be a tender father toward his penitents, exhorting them to a sincere and persevering amendment of life.

Interesting stories are told of Paul's kindness toward sinners which won him the friendship of rather surprising characters. Because of his genial nature he held a strange sway over the many bandits and outlaws whom he met on his frequent journeys through the "Maremme," the wilderness of the swampy coastland to the north and south of Rome. Not one of these bandits ever thought of harming him. Once when a priest said to him in jest, "If I were pope, I'd make you patron of the bandits," Paul took it as a compliment. The only reason why these men would sometimes stop him was to ask him to hear their confessions. One bandit expressed his gratitude in an astounding way for the grace of conversion which Paul had brought him. "Father Paul," he

SAINT PASCAL BAYLON   C. Bosseron Chambers

Like the little Poor Man of Assisi, whose Franciscan habit he was to wear
for most of his life, Pascal was noted not only for his love of poverty and
holy simplicity, but also for his constant joy of spirit. Canonized in 1690,
less than 100 years following his death, Saint Pascal was declared the
patron of all Eucharistic Congresses by Pope Leo XIII in 1897.

SAINT OLGA

The history of twentieth-century Europe would probably have been different if Russia had received the Latin form of Christianity instead of the Greek form from Constantinople. One who almost succeeded in bringing the Latin rite to Russia was its first Christian queen. Saint Olga, who strove bravely throughout her life to keep the spark of Christianity alive in Russia. The above was reproduced from a nineteenth-century triptych.

said, "how can I ever repay you! If you have any enemy, just let me know, and I'll be glad to wipe him out of your way." The saint could appreciate at least the good will of the man, if not his offer. Moreover, while Paul was at Monte Argentario during the war of 1734-1735, he became a sort of unofficial military chaplain for both of the opposing forces, and the soldiers loved him so much that they let him pass freely from one army to the other, both sides holding their fire as he walked across no-man's land.

Now that Paul had won at least a simple form of papal approval for his order (and with the fame of the Passionists' mission spreading throughout the country), scores of earnest aspirants begged to be admitted into his austere institute, and more monasteries were needed to accommodate them. Hence, in the midst of his unceasing labors in giving missions, Paul was often engaged in negotiations for new foundations. In March of 1744, he opened two new Passionist houses, one at Soriano and the other at Vetralla, both north of Rome in the Papal States. In January of 1748, Ceccano (at the southern end of the Papal States) became the fourth Passionist monastery, and in March of the same year the house at Toscanella, halfway between Rome and Monte Argentario, opened as the fifth foundation. Thus the process continued with a new Passionist "retreat" or monastery being dedicated every few years.

Yet even these years were not free from new trials for the saint. In several places he and his missionaries met with opposition or outright hostility, not only from heretics, but at times from worldly secular priests and, sad to say, even from otherwise good religious. The older mendicant orders had a privilege from the Holy See that a new monastery was not to be built within four miles of any of their own houses. Almost all the new Passionist foundations were in towns where there was already an older mendicant monastery, and the result was endless litigations at Rome. Other enemies began a campaign of abuse against the Passionists, calling them wolves in sheep's clothing, disturbers of the peace, imposters preying on the people, preachers of novel and suspicious doctrines, and even outright heretics. Paul could write half-jokingly about it in a letter: "We are being treated as if we were worse than Luther, Calvin or Mohammed," but nevertheless he feared the harm that this whispering campaign could do.

Pope Benedict XIV appointed a commission of cardinals to carry out a sort of minor Inquisition on the Passionists who were to be examined in every accusation brought against them. Questionnaires were sent by the Holy See to every diocese where Paul and his companions had given missions. The reports from these bishops were so favorable to the Passionists that ultimately, on April 7, 1750, the cardinals issued a unanimous verdict fully vindicating Paul of the Cross and his followers.

So far the Passionists had taken only "simple" vows, not the more binding "solemn" vows of the older religious orders. When Paul now asked permission for solemn vows in his order, the cardinals told him that he would have to lessen some of the strictness of his Rule and drop some of its penitential practices before such a permission could be granted. The alleged reason for this was that members might find, after several years under vows, that the life was too hard for them and ask for a dispensation, and it would be much more difficult to dispense from solemn vows than from simple ones. Paul, however, would not agree to this condition and preferred to have his members without solemn vows, rather than to see any relaxation in the distinctive austerity of his congregation. In later years he believed that God had led him to stand firm on this point and he thanked Him for it since he thus had greater freedom in dismissing unworthy members. Therefore, at a latter occasion, when he could have obtained the right of taking solemn vows without any change in his austere Rule, he chose to retain the simple vows which the Passionists still have to this day.

After Paul had been preaching missions for thirty years, and was now seventy years old, he still tried hard to keep up his old pace, although it was proving too much for him. Sometimes he looked so worn on a mission that no one expected him to finish it. In addition, he was crippled with rheumatism and sciatica as a result of his miles and miles of barefoot travel through ice and snow. In March of 1758, he wrote: "I have completely given up the missions because I can no longer hold out on them." Yet four months later the old warrior was back again giving missions. It was not until 1763 that he broke down so completely on a mission that he finally had to be resigned to the inevitable.

In 1765, on a day in July when Paul was celebrating Mass at His favorite "retreat," the Passionist monastery at Vetralla, an interior voice warned him of a great grief that was in store for him. It proved to be the death of his dear brother, John Baptist, who fell very ill and passed away on August 30 of that year. Paul could not help recalling the long life of joys and sorrows they had spent in each other's company. Together they had tasted the pure bliss of mystical contemplation on Monte Argentario, and together they had tramped barefooted in winter's cold and summer's heat. Each had depended so much on the other, and now that John Boptist had gone home without him, Paul felt a strange loneliness and homesickness for Heaven.

Although he still had ten more years to live, when Paul of the Cross began a visitation of his houses in 1765, he knew it would be for the last time. He could no longer walk and had to be driven in a carriage, but his journey turned into a triumphal procession with the people crying out, to his consternation, "Come and see the saint!" This was simply beyond his comprehension, and he naively remarked: "I was never so confused and abashed in all my life." At last he could not take it and begged to be brought to his favorite "retreat" of Vetralla. Here he became very ill and suffered such agony that the last sacraments were administered to him. However, he recovered and lingered on, a semi-cripple for several more years.

During these last years of his life he was especially tormented by the devil. Several times in his earlier years he had been harassed by the infernal foe, but these final attacks were the worst of all. The horrible noise of banging doors, crashing furniture and unearthly screaming kept him from sleeping and, if he did doze off, he would be violently thrown from his bed. These frightening sounds were heard by others. Father Nicholas, who shared his room, even saw a gigantic figure and, full of fear, cried out to Paul: "Don't you see him?" "Be calm," answered the saint, "don't be afraid. He has not come for you."

In his last years on earth St. Paul of the Cross had the happiness of witnessing the complete realization of his lifelong dream. On November 15, 1769, Pope Clement XIV issued the Bull *Supremi Apostolatus* by which he confirmed the Passionist Rule and granted the institute all the spiritual favors and privileges that the Holy See had bestowed on the older religious orders. In 1773, the same pope gave the Passionists charge of the venerable church and monastery of Saints John and Paul on the Caelian Hill in Rome. This ancient sanctuary was dedicated to the two brothers, John and Paul, who had given their lives for Christ in the Roman persecutions, and the pope thought it fitting that it should now be the Roman headquarters of the religious order founded in honor of Christ Crucified by St. Paul of the Cross and his brother John Baptist Daneo. Finally, on September 15, 1775, just a little more than a month before the death of the holy founder, Pope Pius VI issued the Bull, *Praeclara virtutum exempla,* by which the Rule and the institute of the Passionists were again solemnly confirmed and approved.

Paul of the Cross had long desired to found an order of nuns whose cloistered lives of prayer and penance in honor of the Passion of Christ would win grace from Heaven on the missionary work of his Passionist Fathers. In 1771, four years before his death, he had the happiness of seeing this wish come true when the first convent of the Passionist Nuns, wearing the black habit of penance with the "Sign of the Passion" on its breast, was founded at Corneto, situated about forty miles southeast of Monte Argentario. Paul, himself, wrote the Rule for these nuns.

In March of 1770, the Holy Father, who wished Paul of the Cross to make Rome his headquarters, gave him permission to visit the Passionist monasteries north of Rome. The aged saint, however, could not get to all of these houses; he found it too great an ordeal. Once more on Monte Argentario, his eyes flowed with tears when he beheld two flourishing monasteries of his order, each filled with fervent religious, where he and his faithful brother John had for several years been the only Passionists in the world.

Paul would have preferred to die at his favorite retreat of Vetralla, but the pope wished him to pass his last years in Rome. The wish of the Holy Father was a command for Paul. In fact, it was apparently from obedience to the pope that Paul of the Cross survived for three additional years. In 1772, the saint felt that he was about to die, and so sent for the papal blessing in the hour of death. When the Holy Father sent back word that he did not wish him to die at present because he was still needed in Rome, contrary to all expectations the saint rallied and lingered on for three more years. He was more than eighty years old when his crucified Lord finally let him breathe his last on October 18, 1775.

Paul of the Cross was beatified by Pope Pius IX in 1852 and canonized by the same pope in 1867. His body lies in the Basilica of Saints John and Paul, the church in Rome given him by Pope Clement XIV.

Saint Peregrine Laziosi

Confessor

1 3 4 5

(April 30)

FROM THE TWELFTH to the fifteenth century Italy was torn between two main political factions, the Guelphs and Ghibellines. The Guelphs fought against the rule of the German emperors for the independence of the small Italian city states and represented, to a large degree, the Papal party in Italy, since the Popes were often at odds with the German emperors. The Ghibellines, on the other hand, harking back to the old ideal of a strongly united Roman Empire, were the "Emperor's men" in Italy. Individually the Ghibellines could be as staunchly Catholic in religion as any of the Guelphs. But when the Papacy was in conflict with the emperor, the Ghibellines would line up politically against the Pope as a temporal prince. In almost every Italian city state both parties were represented, with now one and now the other in the ascendancy. But medieval politics were seldom limited to peaceful balloting; widespread bloodshed was often the tragic outcome of these disputes.

All the religious orders that were founded in the thirteenth century, the so-called "Mendicant Orders," such as the Dominicans, the Franciscans, and the Carmelites, strove to establish peace between these warring factions. But the religious order that was especially devoted to this good work was the order of the Servites or, to give them their full title, the Servants of Mary. Originally a lay organization, founded at Florence in 1240 by "the Seven Holy Founders," the Servites had as their particular end the spread of devotion to Mary, especially as the Sorrowful Mother. But, as the conditions of the times required, one of the main objects of their preaching was the bringing about of peace between the political factions that were causing such bloody havoc in Italy.

In the year 1283 Pope Martin IV sent Saint Philip Benizi, Superior General of the Servites, to Forli, a city of the Romagna, northeast of Tuscany, to reconcile there the bitterly warring factions. One day, as Philip was engaged in preaching at Forli, he was insulted and beaten up by a certain young man who was the son of one of the Ghibelline leaders in this city. When Philip, however, bore this attack with heroic patience and meekness, the young man who struck him was so overcome with remorse for his sudden act of violence, that he threw himself down at the feet of the saint and begged his forgiveness.

This young man was Peregrine Laziosi. Born at Forli about the year 1265, he had always been basically good and pious and of an essentially generous nature. But his violent attack on St. Philip Benizi proved a turning point in his life. Not content with obtaining the saint's pardon, Peregrine decided then and there to become his follower. Resolving to devote the rest of his life to the cause of peace in God's service, he was received into the Servite order at Siena in Tuscany, where he began his life of heroic virtue. So great was his humility that he had to be commanded under holy obedience to be ordained a priest. Sent back by his superiors to his native city of Forli, he built the first Servite monastery and church in this city, and here he spent the rest of his life working by word and example in the cause of civic peace. His patience and humility was so remarkable, that the people used to call him a second Job.

One day, as he was praying before the crucifix, he was suddenly cured of a malignant ulcer of the leg from which he had suffered for a long time. His fame as a wonder worker soon spread far and wide among the people. Many miraculous cures, especially of ulcers of the leg and of other forms of cancerous growth, were attributed to his intercession both during his lifetime and after his holy death.

Saint Peregrine died on May 1, 1345. But when he was canonized by Pope Benedict XIII in 1726, his feastday was set on the 30th of April. His body, buried in the church which he had built at Forli, has remained wonderfully preserved from corruption during the centuries, and large pilgrimages to his tomb are still frequent. On account of the miraculous cure which God worked in favor of this His humble servant, St. Peregrine Laziosi is regarded as the special patron against diseases of the leg.

Saint Peter Canisius
Confessor, Doctor

1 5 9 7

(April 27)

P OPE LEO XIII called Saint Peter Canisius "the second apostle of Germany, after St. Boniface." This title is certainly
well merited, for probably no other individual did more than
Canisius to save southern Germany for the Catholic Church in
the tumultuous period of the sixteenth-century Protestant Reformation.

The year 1521 in which Peter Canisius was born was the same
year in which Martin Luther left the Catholic Church and began his revolt in Germany against papal authority that developed
into the so-called Reformation. In the same year Ignatius Loyola
in Spain gave up his military career to enlist in the service of
Christ. God seems thereby to have given a sign foretelling that
Peter Canisius, fighting as a Jesuit under the leadership of Ignatius Loyola, would be one of the most valiant champions of the
Church in its struggle against Martin Luther and his followers.

Although Canisius spent most of his life in Germany, by birth
he was a Dutchman, born in the city of Nijmegen in the Nether-
lands on May 8, 1521. His last name, Canisius, is the Latinized form of the Dutch name, Kanijs, and is not connected, as is
sometimes supposed, with the Latin word *canis*, "dog." His father, Jacob Kanijs, was a wealthy citizen of Nijmegen. Peter's
mother, Aegidia van Houwenigen, died shortly after his birth,

and some years later Jacob Kanijs took another wife. A son
born of this second marriage, Theodorich Canisius, later followed his older half-brother, Peter, in entering the Society of Jesus
and won for himself quite a name as a theologian and rector of
various Jesuit colleges, though his fame has been somewhat
eclipsed by that of his more brilliant half-brother.

In 1536, when fifteen years old, Peter Canisius was sent by his
father to the University of Cologne for higher studies in literature
and civil law. During the first few years of his stay at this city
on the Rhine, Canisius became acquainted with several pious
men who exercised a lasting influence on his life. Thus, among
his intimate friends here were the Carthusians, especially Justus
Landsberg (or Lanspergius, as he is more commonly known by
the Latinized form of his name), as well as Nicholas von Essche
and others of the "Devotio Moderna," the religious movement in
the Low Countries which a century before had produced the
Imitatio Christi ("The Following of Christ").

In 1540, after receiving his degree of Master of Arts at Cologne, Canisius decided, against his father's wishes, to go on to
the study of theology. His father also had plans for him to marry a certain rich young lady, but Peter put an end to them by
taking a vow of celibacy in this same year.

Even in these early years of his life Canisius realized the importance of publishing good Catholic books. Thus, in 1543, when
only twenty-two years old, he brought out an edition of the works
of the great Dominican mystic of the 14th century, John Tauler
—the first time that some of these works appeared in print. So
also, in 1543 Canisius published the works of St. Cyril of Alexandria and of St. Leo the Great. By 1544 he was already teaching at the University of Cologne.

Canisius' life, however, was not to be spent in merely scholastic
pursuits. In April of the year 1543 he made the "Spiritual Exercises," or retreat, at Mainz under the guidance of Blessed Peter
Faber, one of the first six companions of Ignatius Loyola. As
a result of this retreat Canisius decided to become a Jesuit him-

self, and on May 8, 1543, he was received into the Society of Jesus—the first German Jesuit. Later, with the help of Leonhard Kessel and a few others, he opened at Cologne the first Jesuit house in Germany. As early as 1545, when only twenty-four years old, he showed his ability in diplomacy, for which he would become famous in later life, by acting as representative for the Catholics of Cologne before the emperor Charles V in a successful protest against their archbishop, Hermann van Wied, who was trying to turn their city Protestant.

After Peter Canisius was ordained a priest in June 1546, his work for the preservation of the Catholic Church in Germany went on constantly increasing. In 1547 he took part in some of the deliberations of the Council of Trent as theological consultant for Cardinal Otto Truchsess, Bishop of Augsburg, just as later, in 1562, he was to be present again at this Council as papal theologian.

In 1548 Canisius was summoned to Italy by St. Ignatius Loyola. After spending a year at Messina (Sicily), where he preached in Italian as well as in Latin, he was called to Rome by the founder of the Jesuits and there admitted to solemn profession—the eighth Jesuit to receive this honor. However, in 1549, when Duke William IV Bavaria had requested Pope Paul III to send some Jesuits to teach at the University of Ingolstadt, Canisius was among those chosen by the General of the Jesuits, for Ignatius realized that the best field for Canisius' zeal lay in Germany. On his way north Canisius was given the degree of Doctor of Theology, then a rather rare degree, at the University of Bologna on October 4, 1549.

Space would be lacking here to give a detailed acount, mentioning all the dates and places, of St. Peter Canisius' untiring activity during the next three decades, when he played a decisive role in the preservation and restoration of the Catholic faith throughout southern Germany. Devoting himself entirely to this good cause, he taught, preached and wrote at Ingolstadt from 1549 to 1552, at Vienna from 1552 to 1554, at Prague from 1555 to 1556, at Augsburg from 1559 to 1566, and at Innsbruck and Munich from 1571 to 1577, not to mention the many other cities and towns that benefited from his apostolic zeal during these years. The effects of his energy were felt, in fact, over the whole German Empire, even in places where he did not appear personally. This he achieved, first through his work as Superior of the Upper German Province of the Society of Jesus; secondly, through the influence he exercised as a diplomat in the relations between Church and State in southern Germany; and thirdly, through his voluminous writings.

In 1556, shortly before St. Ignatius Loyola died, Peter Canisius was appointed Provinical Superior of the newly erected Upper (or southern) German Province of the Society of Jesus. With two short interruptions he held this important post till 1569. His Province included the regions of Swabia, Bavaria, Upper and Lower Austria, Hungary, and Bohemia. During the thirteen years that he was in this office, by his founding of several Jesuit colleges and his recruiting of new members of the Society of Jesus to staff them, he laid the foundation for the extremely valuable work which the German Jesuits did in the following centuries towards keeping these regions in the fold of the Catholic Church.

Even more important was the influence Canisius exerted and the power he wielded in the diplomatic relations between the papacy and the south German states. As the confidant of popes, emperors and kings, he went on innumerable diplomatic missions, to help preserve friendly relations between these secular princes and the Holy See. In an age when it was taken as axiomatic that the religion of the ruler determined the religion of his subjects, the importance of Canisius' work in this field can hardly be overestimated. He was a close friend of all the leading men of his time and the counsellor of papal legates and nuncios in Germany. He took part in all the principal meetings and councils which were held to settle the religious quarrels in Europe. Most of his proposals toward the renovation of the Catholic Church in Germany, such as the increase in the number of papal nunciatures and the founding of new seminaries there, as well as the extension of the Collegium Germanicum (the special seminary in Rome for training future priests to work in Germany) were accepted by the popes, particularly Pope Gregory XIII (1572-1585). His efforts, however, to abolish the privilege of nobility for Church prelates, which easily led to scandalous abuses, met with failure, because this custom was too firmly established to be done away with in so short a time.

Most important of all was Canisius' literary activity. The mere list of the titles of his published writings takes up thirty quarto pages in the bibliography of Jesuit authors. Saying that it was more important to write in defense of the Church in Europe than to convert Hindus, Canisius not only published so many books himself; he also urged others to write and he did his best to foster Catholic publishing houses, going so far as to request the Holy See to support them with financial subsidies. Besides his scholarly works in theology, Sacred Scripture and the Founding of the Church, he published many popular religious works, such as prayer books, the lives of the saints, and other devotional reading. His most influential publications, however, were his catechisms: for college and university (*Summa Doctrinae Christianae*: Vienna 1555), for children (*Catechismus Minimus*: Ingolstadt 1556), and for high school students (*Parvus Catechismus Catholicorum*: Cologne 1558), which were reissued in more than two hundred editions in his lifetime and in the following centuries, so that the term "Canisi" was till recently used in Germany as a synonym for "Catechism." In this special field, which seems to be quite simple yet requires great skill, Canisius was a pioneer who was seldom equalled and never surpassed.

All this feverish activity would not have been as richly fruitful as it was if St. Peter Canisius had not been activated by deeply religious motives. As can be seen in his "Confessions" (1570) and his "Testament" (1596)—writings which reveal a good deal of his inner life, all of Canisius' labors were inspired by his constant union with God, which sprang from his consciousness of the call given him in a vision at St. Peter's in Rome on September 2, 1549. On this day, as he was about to leave Rome to begin his great work in Germany, he received a clear call from God to devote himself entirely to the good of the Catholic Church in that country. In keeping with the "Devotio Moderna" which he had learned in his early life, his piety was marked by a cultured Christian humanism as well as by a wide knowledge of the Sacred Scriptures and the writings of the Fathers of the Church. At the same time it was not without its mystical gifts, as can be seen in his revelation of the Sacred Heart of Jesus granted him on the day of His profession as a Jesuit.

With all his fervent zeal as a defender of the revealed truths of the Catholic faith, there was nothing of the fanatic in Peter Canisius. His approach to the religious problems raised by the Protestant Reformers was always irenic and, when possible, conciliatory. In controversy he never descended to personal invectives. The names of Luther and Calvin are not even mentioned in his catechisms. It would have gotten him nowhere with the Protestants, had he claimed there were no moral abuses in some of the members, high and low, in the Catholic Church. The sad fact of these abuses was only too obvious. What he did do, however, was to show that the Protestants were not really "reforming" these evils in the Church, but were destroying the Church itself. Canisius and his fellow workers, especially among the Jesuits, went about it in the right way to achieve true reform *within* the Church. It is rather unfortunate that their noble work is usually called, even by Catholics, "the Counter-Reformation," as if the only thing it consisted in was counteracting the efforts of the Protestants at reform. On the contrary, they were primarily concerned with true reform in the Church. It was a positive, not a negative thing which they did.

While Canisius was always unshakably faithful to the Holy See, as he was ever unswervingly loyal to the Society of Jesus, he did not confuse the accidental with the essential. Thus, in the question of allowing the laity to receive Holy Communion "under the two species," that is, to partake of the consecrated wine as well as the consecrated bread, Canisius was in favor of allowing this where the people wanted it, provided they held the teaching of the Church that both the Body and the Blood of Christ are truly received under either "species" alone just as much as under both together. He sensibly argued that it would be a pity for the Catholic Church to lose a large part of northern Europe merely over such a matter that did not touch the essence of Christian Doctrine. However, in 1563, when Father James Laynez, the successor of Ignatius Loyola as General of the Jesuits, expressed himself as bitterly opposed to the granting of this concession to the laity, Canisius, good Jesuit that he was, went along with his superior in this matter.

So also in regard to the demands of many Germans for the Mass in German in their country, Canisius would no doubt have willingly granted this point also, though there is no evidence that he advocated it, since he foresaw that such a concession would certainly not be granted at that time. His own attitude, however, can be seen in his zeal for the spread of non-liturgical prayers and hymns in German. Canisius had a deep love for the people of Germany and he understood their spiritual needs far better than his Spanish and Italian confreres did. While we admire his profound humility which caused him to relinquish all too readily what he considered merely his own personal opinions and desires, one cannot help regretting that he was not firmer in opposing the attempts of Italian and Spanish ecclesiastics to enforce Latin-Renaissance religious practices on the people of Germany, who were still greatly attached to their old practices of medieval piety, which was to a large degree a Germanic creation.

For a decade after Peter Canisius was relieved in 1569, by his own request, of the office of Provincial Superior of the Upper German Province of the Society of Jesus, he continued to preach in the various cities of southern Germany. But in 1580 certain differences of opinion over questions of practical reform between him and his successor as Provincial, Father Hoffaeus, led to his transfer to the city of Fribourg (Freiburg) in Switzerland. Here, at the University of Fribourg, Canisius founded the Jesuit college of St. Michael, and for the next decade he made this city, which lies near the borderline between the French and the German-speaking Swiss, the center of his apostolic zeal. He also preached in German-speaking cities of Switzerland, as at Luzern in 1584, when he passed through on a pilgrimage to Our Lady's shrine at Einsiedeln. But after St. Nicholas, the patron of Fribourg appeared to him in a vision and asked him not to abandon this city, he stayed here for the rest of his life. It was only in 1590, when Canisius was nearly seventy years old, that age and infirmity forced him to limit his incessant preaching. Yet even after this, during the last seven years of his life, he continued his apostolate of the pen.

Peter Canisius died at Fribourg on December 21, 1597. Here his sacred remains were first buried in the city's principal Church of St. Nicholas, but in 1625 they were removed to the neighboring Jesuit Church of St. Michael, where they still repose. Although he was venerated by the people as a saint ever since his death, it was not till 1864 that Peter Canisius was beatified by Pope Pius IX. One of the reasons for this unfortunate delay was no doubt the fact that Canisius had been so conciliatory to the Protestants—whom his Christlike charity brought back to the Church by the thousands. One of his published works had in fact been temporarily placed on the Church's "Index of Forbidden Books." It was left for the great pontiff Pope Pius XI in 1925 to give to St. Peter Canisius his just dues, not only by adding his name to the Church's list of canonized saints and extending his feast (on April 17) to the universal Church, but also by declaring him in the same year a Doctor of the Church.

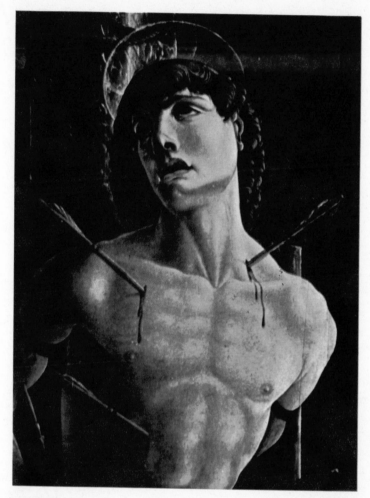

SAINT SEBASTIAN   Cosimo Tura

The numerous Renaissance paintings of Saint Sebastian portray him as
tied to a stake and pierced by arrows. And since the sudden, devastating
blow of pestilence was likened to a fast-flying arrow, this Saint became
the patron invoked in times of plague. Among the more recent occurrences
when cities were delivered from pestilence through Sebastian's intercession
were those of Milan in 1575, and Lisbon in 1599.

SAINT NICHOLAS OF TOLENTINE

After taking his vows as an Augustinian, Nicholas was ordained at Cingoli, Italy. Shortly thereafter, in 1275, he was transferred to the Augustinian monastery at Tolentino and here he devoted the last thirty years of his life attending the spiritual and temporal welfare of the people of this town and the surrounding countryside. He nourished their souls by his daily preaching, and cared for their bodily needs by his boundless charity.

Note: On the following pages appear an illustration and a literal translation of a letter by Peter Canisius contained in the Vatican Apostolic Library. The letter is addressed to Cardinal John Morone and concerns Canisius' *Opus Marianum*. It is the original letter with the text apparently in a secretary's hand, but with the signature in the hand of Peter Canisius. It is a magnificent example of the pure Ciceronian Latin that was used in the sixteenth century Renaissance.

Only the closing words, "Servus in Christo Jesu, Petrus Canisius," are in the handwriting of the saint. The rest is almost certainly written by a professional scribe. All you have to do is to compare the "Christo" and the "Jesu" of this signature with the "Christi" (first line) and the "Jesus" (sixth line from the bottom of the letter itself) to be convinced of this.

Pax Christi nobis aeterna Reuerendiss.
et Illustriss. Dñe patrone.

Meminit haud dubie Amplitudo tua Illustriss. me superiore anno cum
Ratisbonæ uersaremur, aliquod Marianj operis nostri monstrasse specimen,
et quasi primum dedisse gustum. Nunc quoniam Dij gratia liber toty absolutus
in lucem prodijt, facere non potui, quin hunc partum ampliss. celsitudini tuæ
mitterem, ac summo Patrono quicqd hoc est muneris, reuerenter offerendum
demandandum curarem. Scio enim quantum Societas hæc nostra uniuers. in Germania
spertim, summo Cardinali ac sacri huiq ordinis Decan. debeat: scio quanta beneuolentia
& beneficentia illeipse me sibi tot iam annis deuinctum teneat: scio denique, quam
rara & eximia liberalitate Collegium nostrum Dilinganum perget prosequi, et
spehora plurimorum studia, quæ illic admirabiliter florent, hac etiam ratione ad tot.
Germaniæ pfectum conseruet ac prouehat. Agnoscimq sane ac merito
ædicamq hanc tantam optimi Mecenatis gratiam, summumq Deum ex animo
pcamur, ut non modo spiritualib., sed æternis etiam pmijs hanc uere paternam
erga nos inopes charitatem abunde compenset. Cæterum hunc nostrum
laborem, quem studio sanctiss. Virginis ac augustissiæ Dominæ nostræ aduersus
hæreticos uindicando suscepim, ita Illustriss. celsitudini tuæ comendamq, ut
maxime possumq, nimirum ut si opus fuerit, sua etiam autoritate huic tanquam
pupillo istic exulanti fidissime patrocinetur. Dominus Jesus celsitudinis
tuæ conaty ad sui nominis gloriam, sanctæq Ecclesiæ utilitatem
usq prosperet. Canonicy est Bombergensis & Augustanq. qui
hoc munq eorum porriget. eandem Illustriss. celsitudinj tuæ
in his quæ petet, de meliore nota cupins esse comendatum.
Ingolstadij. 26 Nouembris an. 1577.

Seruus in Christo Jesu
petrus Canisius

PAX CHRISTI NOBIS AETERNA REVERENDISSIME ET ILLUSTRISSIME DOMINE PATRONE.

*M*EMINIT *haud dubie Amplitudo tua Illustrissima, me superiore anno cum Ratisbonae versaremur, aliquod Mariani operis nostri monstrasse specimen, et quasi primum dedisse gustum. Nunc quoniam Dei gratia liber totus absolutus in lucem prodiit, facere non potui, quin hunc partum amplissimae celsitudini tuae mitterem, ac summo Patrono quicquid hoc est muneris, reverenter offerendum donandumque curarem. Scio enim quantum Societas haec nostra universa, in Germania praesertim, summo Cardinali ac sacri huius ordinis Decano debeat; scio quanta benevolentia et beneficentia ille ipse me sibi tot iam annis devinctum teneat; scio denique, quam rara et eximia liberalitate collegium nostrum Dilinganum pergat prosequi, ut praeclara plurimorum studia, quae illic admirabiliter forent, hac etiam ratione ad totius Germanie profectum conservet ac provehat. Agnoscimus sane ac merito praedicamus hanc tantam optimi Maecentis gratiam, summumque Deum ex animo praecamur, ut non modo spiritualibus, sed aeternis etiam praemiis hanc vere paternam erga nos inopes charitatem abunde compenset. Caeterum hunc nostrum laborem, quem studio sanctissimae Virginis ac augustissimae Dominae nostrae adversus haereticos vindicandae suscepimus, ita Illustrissimae celsitudini tuae commendamus, ut maxime possumus, nimirum ut si opus fuerit, sua etiam autoritate huic tanquam pupillo isthic exulanti fidissime patrocinetur. Dominus Jesus celsitudinis tuae conatus ad sui nominis gloriam, sanctaeque Ecclesiae utilitatem usque prosperet. Canonicus est Bambergensis et Augustanus, qui hoc munus coram porriget; eundem Illustrissime celsitudini tuae in his quae petet, de meliore nota cupimus esse commendatum. Ingolstadii. 26 Novembris, anno 1577.*

Servus in Christo Jesu

Petrus Canisius

MAY THE PEACE OF CHRIST BE EVER UNTO US, MOST REVEREND AND ILLUSTRIOUS, LORD PATRON

*N*O doubt Your Eminence remembers that, when we met last year in Ratisbon (Regensburg), I showed you a sample and gave you, as it were, a foretaste of our work on Mary. Now that the work, thanks be to God, is completed and has seen the light of day, I cannot but send a copy of it to Your Eminence and humbly offer it as a gift to you, our esteemed patron. I know how much this Society of ours (the Society of Jesus), in every place but especially in Germany, owes to you, most eminent of Cardinals and Dean of their sacred college; I know how your great goodness and kindness these many years have made me your debtor; and I know with what exceptional and extraordinary generosity you have continually favored our college at Dilligen, whereby you have fostered and encouraged to the advantage of all Germany the excellent studies that are there so admirably pursued by so many students. We gladly acknowledge and rightfully praise these great benefits we have received from you, our gracious Maecenas, and we wholeheartedly pray God almighty to repay abundantly with both spiritual and everlasting rewards this truly fatherly charity towards us, your needy children. This work, then, of ours, which we have undertaken for the sake of defending our august Lady, the most holy Virgin, against the attacks of the heretics, we commend as earnestly as we can to Your Eminence, so that, if need be, you may with your authority protect it most faithfully as your ward here in exile. May the Lord Jesus prosper all your endeavors unto the glory of His name and the benefit of His holy Church. The bearer of this gift to you is a canon of Bamberg and Augsburg. We would like to commend him for his good qualities to Your Eminence in any petition that he may make. Ingolstadt. The 26th of November, 1577.

Your servant in Christ Jesus,

Peter Canisius

Saint Peter Claver
Confessor

1 6 5 4
(September 9)

S LAVERY, THE INHUMAN practice of owning men and women
and forcing them to work without just return to themselves
for their labors, is as old as sinful mankind. There is still much
slavery in the world, though now it is the state rather than the
private individual who makes use of slave labor. Christianity
could not at once do away with the ancient pagan custom of
slavery, but its influence was so strong that within a few centuries this barbarous practice disappeared from Christendom.
However, with the coming of the neo-paganism of the Renaissance and the so-called Protestant Reformation, the old institution of slavery was revived to exploit with cheap labor the vast
wealth of the New World. Slavery in itself was bad enough, but
the African slave trade, the kidnapping of innocent Negroes from
western Africa and shipping them like cattle to America which
was begun by the Portuguese in the 16th and 17th centuries (and
continued by the English and their North American colonists in
the 18th century), was an outrage that cried to Heaven for
vengeance.

The only ray of light in this dark night of man's inhumanity
to man was shed by the heroic labors of the Catholic missionaries
in the New World. Though these great men could not abolish
slavery itself or the slave trade, they strove with might and main

to lessen the sufferings of the poor captives and to win the far greater boom of heavenly salvation for these unfortunate victims who had been robbed of their freedom and happiness on earth. The most outstanding of these Catholic missionaries was the Jesuit Father, Saint Peter Claver, whose astounding labors for these victims of the African slave trade won for him the title of the "Apostle of the Negroes."

Peter Claver was born about the year 1581 of pious farmer folk in the little village of Verdu in the province of Catalonia in northeastern Spain. Since he displayed a keen mind and a devout soul at an early age, his good parents managed to procure for him a better-than-ordinary education in the hope that he might someday become a priest. At the age of twenty, when he had received his first degree at the Jesuit college in Barcelona, he decided after some hesitation to enter the Society of Jesus, though in his humility he would have preferred to be a lay-brother rather than a priest. His shy and retiring nature would have inclined him more to the contemplative life than to that of an active missionary had he not been encouraged by another saint, Alphonsus Rodriguez, to undertake the arduous work of the foreign missions.

After completing his Jesuit novitiate at Tarragona, and a year in the study of the humanities in the Jesuit college at Gerona, he was sent in 1605 for his philosophy course to the Jesuit house of Montesion at Palma on the island of Majorca. Here he met St. Alphonsus Rodriguez, a man of kindred spirit, who exercised a far-reaching influence on his life. Rodriguez was remarkable in many ways. He had been a married business man, but after losing his wife and children in death, in 1571, at the age of forty-four he became a Jesuit laybrother. For the following forty-six years he lived a life holy simplicity as a humble Brother Porter at the college of Montesion. He was already an old man when Peter Claver came there.

Rodriguez soon saw that Claver was destined for great things in God's service, and he often spoke with him of the need of zealous missionaries in the Indies (as the New World was then called), and he assured him that God was calling him to such a self-sacrificing life. When Claver finished his course in philosophy at Montesion, he volunteered at Rodriguez' fervent urging for missionary work in America. His superiors, however, thought that it was still too early to act on this, and therefore sent him to study theology at the Jesuit college in Barcelona. However, he had finished only two years in his theology course here when they decided that his repeated requests could be granted and he was thereupon sent to America for the rest of his studies in preparation for his ordination to the priesthood.

With tears of joy Peter welcomed this letter appointing him to the South American missions. On the way to Seville, where he was to take ship, he passed within a few miles of his old home. For a moment he thought of turning aside to say good-bye to his dear father and mother, but then he remembered the words of his divine Master: "He who looks back after putting his hand to the plough is not fit for the kingdom of God." Kneeling in prayer on the road, he offered God the sacrifice: without going home he continued on his journey to Seville, to the New World, and to a life-long martyrdom.

In April of 1610 Peter Claver sailed from Spain, never more to return. After a long and tiring voyage his ship landed at Cartagena in what is now the northwestern part of the Republic of Colombia. This port city, the center at that time of the African slave trade, was to be the scene of his tremendous labors for almost forty years. First, however, he was sent to finish his study of theology at the Jesuit college in Santa Fe, though his two years in this house (which was still poorly staffed and equipped) seem to have been spent more in fulfilling the offices of porter, sacristan and cook, than in study. He then passed another year of "tertianship" novitiate at Tunja, a town near Bogota (the capital of modern Colombia), and here he took his final vows as a solemnly professed Jesuit. Finally, in 1615, he went back to Cartagena where he was ordained a priest, and where he celebrated his First Mass — the first Jesuit to do so in this city. Under the guidance of the veteran missionary, Father Alphonsus de Sandoval, Peter Claver began his heroic labors for the Negro slaves. Sandoval had, himself, spent forty years in this work, and in Claver he knew that he had found a worthy successor. After one year of priestly work in Cartagena, with full knowledge of what it would cost, Peter Claver took a vow dedicating himself as "the slave of the Negroes forever." Until death gave him his eternal freedom, thirty-eight years later, he literally remained the slave of the Negro slaves, helping and comforting, nursing and instructing, saving and loving them.

To understand the heroism of Claver's life it is necessary to know something of the appalling conditions of the slave trade. About ten thousand slaves were landed each year at Cartagena. The poor creatures, if still alive when the slavers' ship arrived, came in a state of utter misery and agony, dread and despair. Men, women and children — they had been snatched away from their primitive surroundings in the bush and jungle of inner Africa and driven in bonds under the lash to the slave marts on its western coast. The whites had no need to hunt for slaves; the Negro chiefs on the coast did the hunting for them and sold their prey to the slavers at about two dollars a head. The slavers got as much as two hundred dollars apiece for their slaves at Cartagena. After all, the slaves had to be given a minimum of food and water to keep them alive during the long sea voyage, and then, too, the loss was very high. Often about one third of the human cargo died on the way. To carry as many slaves as possible the ships had several decks just high enough to creep around in. Between these decks the slaves were crowded in, row after row, all stark naked, the men chained down to keep them from violence. Portholes were kept to a minimum, to prevent the ship from taking in too much water in a storm. Fresh air scarcely penetrated the noisome decks, and heat in the tropical sun was almost unbearable. Nearly all the poor wretches suffered from seasickness and dysentery. Their wounds festered as they lay day and night in the unspeakable filth. The stench was so overpowering that strong white men sometimes fainted when they had to enter these cramped quarters.

Yet Father Peter Claver made it a matter of principle to be the first to go aboard every slave ship and visit all its miserable victims as soon as it anchored in the harbor of Cartagena. One reason why he boarded every vessel as soon as possible was that the slaves who were likely to die before they were sold were put to death in the harbor, for the slavers had to pay custom duties on every live slave that they brought ashore! Claver could not stop this barbarous slaughter, but at least he could baptize the victims before they died.

Although he had previously shown himself so timid and different, the Apostle of the Negroes now threw himself into his work with vigor and enthusiasm, and soon he developed a well-conceived plan for helping his poor spiritual charges. New slave ships arrived on the average of one or two a week. Between arrivals Claver would go about the city begging for food and medical supplies. He enlisted the services of others, though few dared to go to the extremes that he himself went in helping the slaves. Certain Christian Negroes of Cartagena who spoke one or more of the various languages used by the newly arrived slaves were particularly useful to him as interpreters, since it was impossible for him to learn the many languages and dialects spoken in the different parts of Africa where the captives had once lived.

As soon as he received news of a ship's arrival, he and a few of his Negro assistants rowed out to board it where it rode at anchor. The people of the new cargo would first be filled with terror at the sight of him. Every white man they had known had been their enemy, but his evident love for them, even though they might not understand a word he spoke, soon calmed their fears. His very presence in these holes of stench and filth soothed them and comforted their grief. The biscuits, lemons, tobacco and brandy that he offered them quickly sealed the new friendship. "We must speak to them first with our hands," he used to say, "before we try to speak to them with our lips." He also knew that he could achieve but little for the salvation of their souls unless at the same time he did all he could to cure their bodily woes. Besides the more healthy slaves who were now brought up into the open on the top deck, there were always scores who still lay sick and dying below deck. The interpreters could seldom bear to go down into the hold on account of the overwhelming stench, but Father Claver never hesitated to go anywhere on a ship where there might be souls to save. Somehow he could make the dying understand him, and they gladly let him pour the waters of baptism on them before their souls left their wretched bodies.

It is said that Father Claver was often surrounded with "rays of glory" as he entered these dismal pits of death. Is it hard to believe that these poor wretches below deck also saw this radiance that took all fear from their eyes and made them forget for a moment their tortured bodies? Out of the horrid darkness a tender face bent down to theirs and gentle hands ministered to them. True love is a universal language that all can understand. Small wonder, then, that when he came the next time they greeted him with childlike cries of joy.

As soon as the slavers cleared their papers with the port authorities, they brought their human cargo ashore and the new slaves were kept in sheds awaiting the middlemen who bought them for inland planters and miners. During these days Father Claver would be among his new slaves as much as possible, bringing them more food and drink, washing the filth from their bodies, healing their wounds, and nursing the sick among them. Many of these slaves were kept for quite a while in Cartagena. These he prepared more thoroughly for baptism. He taught them mostly by means of big, brightly colored pictures — scenes of Christ's Passion, and of happy Negroes being baptized. He even succeeded in impressing on these simple minds that, despite the unspeakable sufferings they had undergone on their recent voyage and despite the years of hard slavery that lay before them.

they should still thank God for having let all this happen to them for otherwise they would never have come to know Christ and share in His redemption. From the wickedness of the men who had enslaved them God knew how to bring spiritual blessings for the souls of His poor dark-skinned children.

Nor did Father Claver stop at baptism. He strove to turn the Negro slaves into real, comprehending Christians. His spiritual labors, therefore, did not end in Cartagena. When the slaves were sold and taken elsewhere, he went as far as he could over mountains and across steaming swamps and jungles to keep in touch with his new converts. His reunion with those whom he had previously cared for when they landed was a touching sight to see. He had won them by love, and their love for him held them in the only tender bondage that they knew.

Father Claver had other priestly duties in the Jesuit church at Cartagena. His holiness and spiritual wisdom made him a much sought-for confessor even among the Spaniards, but his dear slaves always held first place in his time as well as in his affections. When certain fine Spanish ladies complained of the stench in the church after the Negroes had come to his Mass at daybreak, and when they asked how they could be expected to go into a confessional where slaves had preceded them, he answered: "You should go to some other confessor. I am not the proper confessor for fine ladies. Besides, my confessional is not built for ladies of quality. It is too narrow for their gowns and suited only for poor Negresses."

When these Spanish ladies would still not be put off, he meekly consented to hear their confessions. "But," he added, "I am afraid you will have to wait until all my Negresses are absolved." It is said that in one year he heard five thousand confessions, and it is estimated that in his whole life he baptized about three hundred thousand slaves.

Even though the Negroes always came first in his zeal, he could not bear to see any one in spiritual need without trying to come to his aid. He made valiant efforts to convert the Moham-

medans who had come to Cartagena, and in some cases succeeded in winning to the faith these notoriously stubborn infidels.
Among the Protestants, too, who were in Cartagena as seamen
or traders, he made converts to Catholicism. A most surprising
case in this regard was that of the Anglican Archdeacon of London who had been brought to this port as a prisoner of war
from an English ship which the Spanish had captured. When this
dignitary lay dying in a hospital at Cartagena, he embraced the
Catholic faith through the efforts of this tireless priest. Claver,
in fact, made it a regular practice to visit all the patients in the
two hospitals of Cartagena as often as he could.

One of his special activities was to prepare for death the many
men in this wild port city who were condemned to death for
some crime or other. An interesting story is told in this regard
about a certain Spanish captain who was to be burned for coun-
terfeiting, but was first allowed to be strangled. Claver had visited him in his cell, heard his confession, and got the poor man
ready to meet God. During the hanging the rope broke, and
Claver steadied the half-dead man until the rope was readjusted.
Some pedant nearby cried out that he had incurred canonical
"irregularity" for taking part in the execution of capital punishment. "Well, so be it," said the saint, "if at this price I can save
a soul." He knew that the man was talking nonsense, and he
told him so to his face. Later the prayer book of the executed
captain was found in his cell. In it were written these words:
"This book belongs to the happiest man in the world."

Many miracles were told, of course, as wrought by this amazing saint. His cloak which he often used as a cover for men covered with ulcers, as a pillow for the sick, and as a pall for the
dead, became so filthy with dirt and blood that it constantly
had to have a thorough cleaning. Yet men struggled to touch it,
that it might cure them of their ills. It was finally torn to
shreds even during his lifetime for the sake of relics.

Peter Claver had a miraculous power of reading minds which
sometimes proved embarrassing to others. He seemed to sense

where trouble would be, and he would hurry to the scene, often remote, and thus frequently saved many lives. Suffice it to refer here to one miracle that is inspirational enough to be cited. A master who remembered (when his slave woman was dying) that he had promised her baptism, sent in haste for Father Claver. The saint knelt down by the dying woman who seemed already lifeless, and spoke her name. She opened her eyes. "Please give me a sign," he said, "if you wish to be baptized." "I do with all my heart," she answered. No sooner was she baptized than she grew better. She forthwith got up and thanked God Who had cured her. Then they took some of the baptismal water and poured it over a dying plant. The next day the plant was in full bloom.

It seems a miracle in itself that Peter Claver found the time to do all that he did, or that he had the physical strength to bear up under such killing labors. He hardly simplified matters by adding to the psysical exertion of his work a rigorous regime of mortification, and by spending a good part of each night in prayer. Yet no doubt the secret of his astonishing strength lay precisely here — in the power that he received from God as an answer to his prayers and penances. Often, especially during Lent, he rose at three o'clock in the morning to hear his Negroes' confessions for eight hours on end. For thirty-eight years he averaged about three hours sleep each night, and he never slept in the day. His regular food consisted merely of a few pieces of bread and some fried potatoes.

When we read of the utter horrors amidst which Father Claver worked without flinching, we marvel that he withstood w h a t nauseated and repulsed other men. He half-jokingly tried to explain his seeming indifference in handling loathesome diseases to a lack of sensibility. When he heard himself spoken of as a saint, he laughingly said, "If being a saint consists in having a strong stomach and no sense of taste, I admit that I may be one." Yet the fact is that, if he had listened to his natural likes and dislikes, he would have been as sensitive to these disgusting things as anyone else. When at times he could not help becoming sick in the stomach, he grew angry with himself and bestowed still more care and attention on the most loathsome cases to atone for his weakness. His poor Negro slaves were treated as animals by others, but Claver's sense of the dignity of every human being (who is made in God's image) induced him to do all he could to restore a sense of self-respect even in these poor creatures. He truly believed in God's love for every individual soul, and his own life was a miracle of love.

In 1650, when Father Claver was nearly seventy years old, the plague struck Cartagena and he fell a victim to it. After receiving the last sacraments, he partially recovered and lingered on for four more years. However, he remained a helpless invalid, unable to do any more work for his beloved Negroes, unable even to say Mass. He was placed in the care of a certain young Negro who, forgetting all that he owed this great man, treated him with neglect, insults and cruelty. No doubt the other Jesuits, who were taxed beyond their strength in the care of the plague-stricken victims in the city, must have thought that the Negro was caring for him. Since they heard no complaint from Claver, they seldom even came to visit him. Perhaps they recalled his great love for solitude, and so thought they were doing right in not disturbing him. In any case, he was badly neglected, often not even served the food which the Negro was supposed to bring him. No word of complaint ever escaped his lips. He was grateful even for this last opportunity to unite his sufferings with those of his divine Savior Whom he had always loved so well and served so faithfully.

On September the 6th, after hearing Mass and receiving holy Communion, he told Brother Nicholas Gonzalez who had long been his faithful helper, "I am soon to die." That evening he fell into a coma. News of his approaching death quickly s p r e a d throughout the city. The forgotten man was remembered. All Cartagena realized at last that Father Peter Claver had been their great Apostle. Nobles and commoners, whites and Negroes, came in droves to his poor little cell to kiss his toil-worn hands for the last time, and to take what relics they could from the almost empty room. The only thing they left with him was a picture of his old friend from his Palma days, Brother Alphonsus Rodriguez. They knew that this was the only earthly thing he prized.

On the Birthday of his Heavenly Queen, September 8, 1654, he answered his Master's call: "Come, blessed of My Father! . . . Inasmuch as you did it for these, the least of My brethren, you did it for Me." The forgotten days of Peter Claver were now over. The fame of his heroic life was heard throughout the world. Miracles continued to be wrought through his intercession. Pope Pius IX beatified him in 1850, and Pope Leo XIII canonized him — together with his friend, Saint Alphonsus Rodriguez—in 1888. The same Pope, Leo XIII, in 1896, solemnly declared him the heavenly patron of all missionary enterprises for Negroes throughout the world.

Saint Raphael
Archangel

(October 24)

SINCE ANGELS HAVE never had a mortal life, one cannot, strictly speaking, write the "life" of an angel. They live beyond the realm of human biographers. In their regard we can merely recount what Scripture and tradition say of them. All that we know with certainty about Saint Raphael is to be found in the Book of Tobias.

In this Book, Raphael first appears in the guise of a man who calls himself "Azarias, the son of the great Ananias" (5,18). The elderly Tobias, or Tobit, who had gone blind, sent his son, the young Tobias, on a long and dangerous journey to collect a large sum of money that a friend had borrowed from him. Not knowing at first that Azarias, who volunteered to travel with him, was an angel, young Tobias made the journey successfully with the help of his angelic traveling companion. As they were crossing the River Tigris on their way, a large fish threatened the life of young Tobias. With the help of the angel the young man caught the fish. Not only did its flesh serve them as food, but the angel said, "Take out the entrails of this fish, and lay up its heart and gall and liver for yourself; for these are necessary for useful medicines" (6,5). Actually, after the debt had been collected and the travelers arrived safely back home, the gall of this fish was rubbed on the blind eyes of old Tobias, "and a white skin began to come off his eyes, like the skin of an egg. And Tobias took hold of it and drew it from his eyes, and immediately he recovered his

SAINT SCHOLASTICA

The lightning in the background is indicative of an event in the Saint's life wherein she wished to speak with her brother, Saint Benedict, of the joys of heaven. He, however, insisted he had to return to his monastic cell whereupon the heavens opened, a violent storm raged, and he had no choice but to remain. As a result of this incident, Saint Scholastica has subsequently been invoked against storms.

SAINT RAPHAEL THE ARCHANGEL

All that we know with certainty about Raphael is to be found in the
Book of Tobias wherein the Saint appears in the guise of a man calling
himself Azarius. Crossing the Tigris River with young Tobias, the archangel saves the young man from a large fish. Not only did this fish then
provide the travellers with food, but its gall, when rubbed into the eyes
of old Tobias, restored the elderly man's sight.

sight. And they glorified God, both he and his wife and all that knew him" (11,14-16).

The angel not only helped the family of Tobias; he also brought health and happiness to a certain young woman called Sara, the daughter of Raguel, a kinsman of Tobias. This Sara was afflicted by the evil spirit Asmodeus, who killed every husband of hers on his wedding night. Seven young men had thus been brought to an untimely end, and Sara was losing hope of ever having a happy marriage. Now, it so happened that both she and old Tobias were praying at the same time for God's help. "At that time the prayers of them both were heard in the sight of the glory of the most high God, and the angel of the Lord, Raphael, was sent to heal them both" (3,24-25). Young Tobias stopped at Sara's house to visit his kinsman Raguel on his journey with the angel, and he fell in love with her and asked her hand in marriage. Raguel and his wife feared the worst, and even had a grave dug in preparation for this new victim of Asmodeus. But the angel had said to the young man, "Hear me, and I will show you who they are over whom the devil can prevail. For they who in such manner receive matrimony as to shut out God from themselves and from their mind and give themselves to lust as the horse and the mule, which have no understanding, over them the devil has power. But when you take her, go into the chamber and for three days keep yourself continent from her, and give yourself to nothing else but to prayers with her. And that night lay the liver of the fish on the fire, and the devil shall be driven away" (6,16-19). "Tobias, remembering the angel's words, took out of the bag part of the liver and laid it upon burning coals. Then the angel Raphael took the devil and bound him in the desert of upper Egypt" (8,2-3). Thus, with the help of God's angel, Tobias and Sara entered a happy marriage, and the grave which Raguel had secretly prepared for the young man was just as quietly filled in again without its intended occupant.

When young Tobias came back to his father with both the money from the debt and a lovely bride in the bargain, the old man wished to give a handsome reward to Azarias, his son's wonderful traveling companion. The latter, however, thereupon revealed his identity: "It is good to hide the secret of a king, but honorable to reveal and confess the works of God . . . When you prayed with tears . . . I offered your prayer to the Lord . . . And now the Lord has sent me to heal you and to deliver Sara, your son's wife, from the devil. For I am Raphael, one of the seven who stand before the Lord" (12,7-15). And with that, the angel "was taken from their sight, and they could see him no more" (12,21).

As the angel whose special function is to heal the ills of God's servants, Raphael is well named; for in Hebrew, *el* means "God" and *rapha* means "he has healed"; so his name "Rapha-el" signifies "God has healed." Raphael speaks of himself as "one of the seven who stand before the Lord," that is, who are special assistants at the throne of God. For this reason these seven angels are also called "archangels" or chief angels. The other two of the seven are presumably St. Michael and St. Gabriel. Jewish tradition has supplied various names for the remaining four; thus, in the apocryphal Book of Henoch they are called Uriel, Raguel, Sariel and Jerahmiel.

In connection with the account in St. John's Gospel of Christ's cure of the crippled man at the pool by the Sheepgate in Jerusalem (chapter 5), some manuscripts add this verse (4), which however is of doubtful authenticity: "An angel of the Lord used to come down at certain times into the pool, and the water was troubled. And the first to go into the pool after the troubling of the water was cured of whatever infirmity he had." Whether this verse belongs to the original Gospel of St. John or not, at least it represents a very old tradition, and popular devotion has rightly identified this angel with St. Raphael, the great "health-bringing" angel of the Old Testament.

Besides being invoked by the sick, St. Raphael is also one of the special patrons of travelers, especially of those who must leave their own country to journey into foreign lands. He is thus the principal patron of the "Raphael-Verein" or Society of St. Raphael, a German Catholic organization interested in the spiritual and temporal welfare of emigrants from Germany.

Although St. Raphael has been invoked in the Litany of the Saints and honored in other ways since the early Middle Ages, it was only in 1922 that the Saint's feastday was extended by Pope Benedict XV to the universal Church.

In addition to being one of the special patrons of travelers, and the principal patron of the Society of Saint Raphael, this Saint is also the principal patron of the Archdiocese of Dubuque, in the state of Iowa.

Saint Robert Bellarmine
Bishop, Confessor, Doctor

1 6 2 1

(May 13)

THE SOCIETY OF Jesus was providentially established by God in the 16th century as the main bulwark of the Church in its defence of its ancient Christian faith against the attacks of the so-called reformers of the Protestant Reformation, and one of the leading members of the Society of Jesus (or of the Jesuits, as they are more commonly called) in this work of the Counter-Reformation was St. Robert Bellarmine.

If Robert Bellarmine had wished to pursue a career in the world or if he had directly desired to hold high office in the Church, he would no doubt have been eminently successful in either of these endeavors; for his father, Vincent, was a descendant of the noble house of the Bellarmini, while his mother, Cinthia Cervini, was the sister of Marcello Cardinal Cervini, who later became Pope under the name of Marcellus II (1555). But Bellarmine sought for neither of these things, and high honors in the Church eventually came to him only in an indirect way and against his wishes.

Robert Francis Romulus Bellarmine—to give him his full name —was born on October 4, 1542 at Montepulciano, a town in Tuscany, about twenty-five miles southeast of Siena. Raised in a devout household, Robert was sent for his schooling to the Jesuit college which had been recently established in his home town. The teachings and good example of his instructors enkindled in him the desire to follow their way of life. Therefore, he applied for admission into the Society of Jesus and became a Jesuit at Rome on September 20, 1560, when not quite eighteen years old.

While leading a religious life in which he was a shining example of all the virtues, he made his philosophical studies for three years (1560-1563) at the Roman College of the Society of Jesus. According to the custom of the Jesuits, he then taught, as a "scholastic," first at Florence and then at Mondovi (the latter city in the Piedmont region of northwest Italy). In 1566 he began his theological studies at Padua, but his superiors later sent him to Louvain in Belgium, in order that, by finishing his theological course in this city which was near the Protestant countries, he might get a better, first-hand acquaintance with the theological errors of the Protestants.

Even before Bellarmine was ordained a priest in 1570 by the eminent Biblical scholar, Cornelius Jansenius, Bishop of Ghent, he was authorizied to preach. Soon he was recognized as one of the most powerful preachers against the errors of Protestantism. After his ordination he was appointed professor of theology at the University of Louvain, the first Jesuit, in fact, to be commissioned by this university to give lectures on the *Summa Theologica* of St. Thomas Aquinas. Soon acknowledged as one of Europe's leading theologians, Bellarmine succeeded in winning back to the Catholic Church many Protestants through his lectures and sermons.

Although St. Charles Borromeo, Archbishop of Milan, and several other bishops sought Bellarmine's services for their own dioceses, he continued to teach and preach at Louvain till 1576. In this year, however, Pope Gregory XIII had the Superior General of the Jesuits transfer him to Rome, that he might take over the newly established "Chair of Controversial Theology" at the Roman College of the Jesuits. This post Bellarmine occupied with great distinction for the next twelve years, from 1576 to 1588. The lectures which he gave during these years were incorporated in a three-volume work, *De Controversiis*, published in 1586-1593. This is unquestionably Bellarmine's masterpiece and, though some of its historical assumptions are no longer held, it is still of great value as a defence of Catholic doctrine against the classical tenets of Protestantism. So strong and convincing were the arguments of the learned Jesuit in this work that ordinary Protestants were forbidden by their pastors to read it, and special courses to combat it were given in Protestant seminaries and colleges.

Bellarmine was now appointed to several important posts in the Society of Jesus. From 1588 to 1591 he was Spiritual Director of the Jesuit students at the Roman College; from 1592 to 1594 he was Rector of this institution; and from 1594 to 1597 he was Provincial Superior of the Neapolitan Province of the Jesuits. Among the Jesuits scholastics under his spiritual care at the Roman College was Aloysius Gonzaga (who died there in 1591), and Bellarmine later on was one of the promoters of the cause for the beatification of this saintly youth.

At the request of Pope Clement VIII (1592-1605) Bellarmine returned from Naples to Rome, where he was made papal theologian and consultor of the Holy Office. Thus, from 1597 to 1602 Bellarmine again resided at Rome and, with his vast theological learning and keen sense of prudence and justice, he rendered invaluable service to the Holy See. During this period he also wrote several works treating particularly of dogmatic and moral questions which at that time were matters of lively dispute between Catholic and Protestant theologians. All of these learned works were, of course, written in Latin. But probably the most important, and certainly the most popular of the works which he composed at this time were written in Italian; these were his "Little Catechism," published in 1597, and his "Larger Catechism," published in 1598. Bellarmine's "Little Catechism" proved to be a phenomenal success, reissued about 400 times in the course of the centuries and translated into 56 different languages and dialects, especially for use on the foreign missions.

Pope Clement VIII thought so highly of Bellarmine that in 1599 he made him a Cardinal. When the humble Jesuit begged the Pope to be spared the necessity of accepting this dignity, the Pontiff insisted, saying that "the Church of God has not his equal in learning." But in 1602 there was a falling out between the two. There had been for some years a lively dispute between two schools of Catholic theologians, the Thomists and the Molinists, concerning the difficult problem of harmonizing the seemingly contradictory dogmas of Catholic teaching—that, on the one hand, man has free will in accepting or rejecting God's grace, and, on the other hand, God's grace is infallibly efficacious and must necessarily achieve its end. Clement wanted to have this question settled once and for all, whereas Bellarmine advocated still further delay in order to allow the theologians more time to find a satisfactory solution to the problem. Since this opposition from his chief theological consultant seemed embarrassing to the Pope, Clement thought it best to remove Bellarmine from his position in Rome. In order to show, however, that there was not the least personal animosity involved in this, the Pope appointed Bellarmine, again against his earnest protests, archbishop of Capua, an important see near Naples, and he himself bestowed the episcopal consecration on his erstwhile theologian.

For three years (1602-1605) Bellarmine lived at Capua, full of holy zeal in the exercise of his new office. As previously in Rome, so now also at Capua this leading theologian of his age did not disdain to teach the catechism to the children and ignorant adults of his diocese. As much as the dignity of his state would allow, he continued to live in simplicity and poverty, generously bestowing almost all his revenues on the poor. Particularly worthy of note are the social reforms which Bellarmine inaugurated in his diocese by bringing about a division of several large landed estates into smaller farms for the use of the peasants, as well as the creation of various industries for the unemployed in his territory.

Bellarmine was proved right in his contention that the disputed question of harmonizing man's free will with God's efficacious

grace should not be settled at this time; actually no official decision of the Church was given on this point during the pontificate of Clement VIII or during that of any succeeding Pope.
After Clement's death in 1605 and the short reign of Leo XI (27
days in 1605), Pope Paul V (1605-1621) recalled Bellarmine to
Rome and again appointed him a member of the Holy Office and
of various other pontifical committees. The Pope told him that
he could retain his see of Capua and rule it by a vicar, but the
saintly Cardinal insisted that the Pope should accept his resignation from this see, and Paul V ultimately agreed.

As head of the Holy Office or Roman "Inquisition," as it was
commonly called, Bellarmine had the disagreeable task of warning Galileo Galilei to be more prudent in advocating the Co-
pernican system of astronomy, since at the time it seemed to
contradict the teachings of Sacred Scripture. Bellarmine had always taken a keen interest in the discoveries of this great Italian
scientist, and it was primarily for the purpose of not scandalizing
the simple faithful that he now counseled Galilei to be more re-
served in proposing new theories which were not yet fully established by adequate proof. He did not live to see the unfortunate
outcome of this well-known episode, when Galilei was formally
condemned in 1623 for his persistence in championing these
theories.

One of the controversies in which Bellarmine became involved
was the thorny question of the relations between Church and
State. Holding to a middle course, he defended the view that the
Pope, as head of all Christendom, had *indirect* authority over
Christian rulers even in temporal matters. This moderate view
caused him to be denounced as a "regalist" by those in the
Church who thought he gave too much independent power to the
State, and as a "papalist" by those who claimed that he was violating the so-called "divine right of kings." This controversy took
quite a practical and acute form in the dispute over the oath of
allegiance which King James I of England, who had been baptized as a Catholic, demanded of all his subjects. This oath in-

cluded a repudiation of the Pope's claim to the right of deposing heretical kings, and consequently Catholics in England were not sure whether they could take it with a good conscience. Bellarmine wrote in defence of this Papal claim, and James I published a rebuttal attacking Bellarmine's doctrine. It is interesting to note that the writings of the learned Jesuit Cardinal on the limited powers of royal rulers had a considerable, though probably only indirect influence on Thomas Jefferson in his composition of the American Declaration of Independence.

Another difficult task that fell to the lot of Bellarmine was the writing of the Introduction to the Church's official edition of the Latin Vulgate Bible as issued by Pope Clement VIII in 1592. Bellarmine had been a member of the committee appointed by Pope Sixtus V to prepare the text of this Bible. The committee had done its work very well, consulting the oldest and best Latin manuscripts then available and producing quite a creditable work. But before Sixtus V gave it his approval, he took it on himself to make a rather thorough revision of the committee's work, often in an unfortunate way. This edition of 1590, containing the ill-advised changes of Sixtus and full of printing mistakes as it was rushed through the press, was prefaced with a letter of this Pope himself declaring this the official Latin Vulgate as the Council of Trent decreed it should be issued. But scarcely were the first copies of this edition available for distribution when Sixtus died and Bellarmine's committee induced the new Pope to stop its sale. A much better edition, restoring in almost all places the readings adopted originally by the committee was issued in 1592 by Pope Clement VIII. This edition still called it "the Sixtine Bible," though in later editions it was called "the Clementine Bible" and it is still the official Latin Bible of the Church. Now, to safeguard the good name of the deceased Pontiff, Bellarmine stated in his Introduction that it had been the wish of Sixtus V to have this corrected edition of his Bible published. He has often been accused of insincerity in making this statement. But actually there is good evidence to show that Sixtus really did intend to have a corrected edition of his Bible published, at least as far as the typographical errors of his original edition were concerned. In any case there is no good reason to believe that Bellarmine was not subjectively convinced that he was honestly carrying out the wishes of the deceased Pope in publishing a much better Latin Vulgate Bible than the edition of 1590 had been.

Less well known is the fact that Bellarmine was also the head of a committee which prepared a critical text of the Greek New Testament during the years 1615 to 1621, that was intended to be issued as the official Greek New Testament of the Church. This work was indeed completed shortly before Bellarmine's death, but for some unknown reason Paul V failed to give it his approval and it was never published. Another work on the Bible which the Cardinal produced at this time was a commentary on the Psalms, published in 1611. Towards the end of his life he also composed several interesting ascetical works, such as "The Sighing Dove" and "The Art of Dying Well."

Full of merits and good works, Robert Cardinal Bellarmine died at Rome on September 17, 1621. Even apart from the extremely valuable services which he had rendered to the Church, he well merited the Church's highest honors because of his saintly life of unselfishness and charity, purity and humility, mortification and the spirit of prayer. No one ever doubted his heroic sanctity; miracles were wrought through his intercession; and it was taken for granted that soon after his death he would be canonized. Yet the process of his beatification, which was introduced in 1627 and which gave him the right to be called "Venerable," dragged on and on, from one century to the next. The main difficulty alleged against it was that he was such a vigorous defender of the rights of the Holy See, that an official approval of his life and works by the Church would have been taken as an offence by the temporal rulers of the so-called Christian states of Europe. It was therefore primarily for reasons of political expediency, that is, to avoid arousing undue anomosity against the Church, that the cause of his beatification suffered this long delay.

Pope Pius XI, however, at last decided that in the 20th century these reasons were no longer valid. Therefore, on May 13, 1923 (the day now set as his annual feastday) this great Pontiff finally declared Robert Bellarmine "Blessed"; on June 29, 1930, he solemnly canonized him a Saint; and in 1931 he issued a decree proclaiming him a Doctor of the Church.

The mortal remains of St. Robert Bellarmine were first buried in the Jesuit Church of the Gesu at Rome, but in 1931 they were transferred to the nearby Jesuit Church of St. Ignatius Loyola, to repose next to the relics of his beloved spiritual son, Saint Aloysius Gonzaga.

Note: On the following pages appear an illustration and a translation of an autograph letter of Robert Cardinal Bellarmine to Alesandro Ansidei, custodian of the Vatican Library, contained in the Vatican Apostolic Library.

The abbreviation in the second line stands perhaps for "Maestro." The word which occurs after the name "Gio Gioseffo" is unintelligible. It is either a title or a term designating the place where this man came from. The translation is intentionally literal throughout to point up the slightly archaic grammar of the seventeenth century Italian.

Molto Ill.re et m.to R.do Signor, il portatore di
questa è il S.r Gio. Gioseffo Scaliolo, medico, et dottissimo in lingua hebrea, più che altri, che sia in
Roma, del quale parlai a V.S. la vigilia di S. Pietro. Questi si offerisce di far'un indice di
tutti li libri, che sono nella biblioteca vaticana,
in lingua hebraica, il che sar molto necessario
per sapere che cosa habbiamo: farà ancora il
catalogo de libri chaldei scritti co caratteri hebraici. et tutto questo si offerisce tutto gratis,
et presto. spererei, che lei quando sarà conosciuto
l'eminenza della sua scienza, di allor' adoperato
in altre cose ed qualche servitio. No altro
questa per altro, me li raccomando, et preggoli
da Dio ogni prosperità. di casa li 28. di
Giugno 1614.

Di V.S. m.to Ill.re et m.to R.do

come fratello

il Card. Bellarmino.

Molto illustrissimo et molto riverendo signor,
Il portatore di questa, Giovanni Gioseffo, rasoldo, medico,
et dottissimo in lingua hebrea, piu che altri, che sia in Roma,
del quale parlai a V.S. la vigilia di S. Pietro. Questi si offer-
isce di far' un indice di tutti li libri, che sono nella bibliotheca
vaticana in lingua hebraica, il che par molto necessario per
sapere che cosa habbiamo. Fara ancora il catalogo de libri
Chaldei scritti con caratteri hebraici, et tutto questo si offer-
isce farlo gratis, et presto, sperando, che poi quando sara con-
osciuta l'eminenza della sua scienza, di esser' adoperato in
altre cose con qualche sussidio. No essendo questa per altro,
me li raccomando, et pregogli da Dio ogni prosperita. Di casa
li 28 di Giugno 1614.

> *Di V.S. molto illustrissima et molto riverendo,*
> *Como fratello,*
> *il Card. Bellarmino.*

Most Illustrious and most Reverend Sir,
The bearer of this letter is Mr. (?) Giovanni Gioseffo, physi-
cian and very learned in the Hebrew language, more than
anyone else in Rome, about whom I spoke to your Lordship
on the Vigil of the Feast of St. Peter. This man is willing to
make an index of all the books of the Vatican Library that
are written in Hebrew, and it seems that this would be very
useful for us to know what we have there. He will also make
a catalogue of the Chaldaean books written in Hebrew letters.
And he offers to do all this gratis and quickly, in the hope
that, when the excellence of his knowledge is recognized, he
will be hired for other things with some pay. Since this is
the only purpose of this letter, I now recommend myself to
your prayers, and for you I beg all happiness from God. At
home, the 28th of June 1614.

> *Of your most Illustrious and most Reverend Lordship,*
> *Like a Brother,*
> *Cardinal Bellarmino.*

Saint Scholastica
Virgin
5 4 3
(February 10)

S AINT SCHOLASTICA WAS doubly fortunate in having a saint, Benedict, for a brother, and another saint, Pope Gregory the Great, for her biographer. Not that Gregory wrote a complete "Life" of Saint Scholastica; it is only in connection with his account of St. Benedict that he tells us of just one incident in her life, and this an event that happened a few days before her death.

From the scant information that we have from elsewhere about Scholastica we know that under her brother's guidance she was abbess of a monastery of nuns. Just as he (the Father of Monasticism in the West) was the founder of the Benedictine monks, she in turn can rightly be regarded as the foundress of the Benedictine nuns. The last monastery over which she presided as abbess was situated about five miles south of Benedict's famous abbey at Monte Cassino (midway on the old inland road from Naples to Rome) which everyone heard of in World War II. This high hill with the great monastery on its crest was a strategic strongpoint and took a terrific shelling during the hostilities of the Italian campaign.

Saint Gregory's story of Scholastica's last days is so quaint and touching in its original simplicity that it should be read just as he wrote it in Latin, or at least in a faithful translation. This account occurs in Chapters 33 and 34 of the second Book of his work called *The Dialogue.* Here, after recounting many miracles that Saint Benedict wrought by the power of prayer, Gregory discloses that the prayers of even the saints sometimes seem to go unanswered.

"What man in the world," he asks, "was raised to greater heights of holiness than Paul (the Apostle)? Yet even he, when he twice begged the Lord to free him from 'the thorn in his flesh,' was not able to obtain his request (I Cor. 12, 7-9). So also it would be well to tell of the time when our venerable father Benedict was not able to obtain his request either. His sister Scholastica, who had been dedicated to the almighty Lord from her very childhood, used to visit him once a year. The man of God would come down to see her in a place belonging to the monastery and not far from its gate.

"Once, when she came according to her custom, and her venerable brother, together with some of his disciples, went down to meet her, they spent the whole day in speaking of the goodness of God and of other holy things. Then as evening drew near, they partook of a meal together. While they were still seated at the table and the time was slipping by in their holy conversation, this devout woman said to her brother, 'Please do not leave me tonight, that we may speak till dawn of the joys of heaven.' 'What are you saying?' he answered, 'It is quite impossible for me to remain out of my cell.'

"Then the holy woman, on hearing her brother's refusal, folded her hands on the table and bowed her head down to her hands, to pray to the almighty Lord. Now the weather had been so good that not a cloud could be seen in the sky. But scarcely had she raised her head from the table when there was such an outbreak of thunder and lightning and a downpour of rain that neither the venerable Benedict nor the brethren, who had come with him to the place where they were sitting outside the monastery enclosure, dared to move from the spot. It was evidently the action of the holy woman in bowing her head on her hands and pouring forth a flood of tears that had drawn the torrent of rain from the clear skies. For it was not as if some little time passed between her prayer and the downpour, but there was such a connection between the two, that she seemed to raise both the thunder and her head at the same time; as her head went up from her hands, the rain came down.

"Then the man of God, seeing that it was impossible for him to go back to his monastery through the thunder and lightning and cloudburst, began to grumble sadly: 'May almighty God forgive you, sister! Why have you done this?' 'Look,' she answered, 'I asked you, and you would not listen to me; I asked my Lord, and He answered my request. Go out now, if you can, to leave me and return to your monastery!' So he, since he could not leave the shelter, had to stay unwillingly where he had not been willing to stay of his accord. And thus it came to pass that they kept vigil the whole night through and found mutual satisfaction in holy conversation on the spiritual life.

"That is why I said that there was something that he wished for but was not able to obtain. For if we look into the mind of the venerable man, we shall see that he surely wished for a continuance of the clear weather in which he had come down from his monastery; but against his wishes almighty God worked a miracle at the prayer of His handmaid. Nor is it surprising that the woman who desired to see her brother for a longer time was at the same time more powerful than he was; for, since John says, 'God is love' (I John 4,16), it was eminently just that she could do the more who loved the more.

"On the following day the venerable woman returned to her convent, and the man of God went back to his monastery, Three days later, while he was in his cell, he raised his eyes to the sky, and behold, he saw his sister's soul, that had left her body, flying like a dove into the depths of heaven! Full of joy that such glory was hers, he broke forth in hymns of praise and thanks to God almighty. Then he told the brethren of her death and sent some of them to bring her body to his monastery and lay it in

SAINT VALENTINE   Jacopo Bassano

It is fitting that Saint Valentine, who as priest and physician did so much good for the souls and bodies of his fellowmen out of love for Jesus, should have become the patron of chaste Christian courtship. This reproduction portrays the Saint baptizing Saint Lucilla, a subsequent martyr.

SAINT URSULA Ledoux

One of several conflicting legends portrays Saint Ursula as fleeing from England with 11,000 virgins to escape the invading Saxons, only to be massacred by the Huns upon landing at the mouth of the Rhine River. A more plausible version is that the Saint suffered martyrdom with ten companions in the Cologne territory at the end of the third century.

the tomb he had prepared for himself. Thus it happened that these two, whose hearts and minds had always been one in God, should not be separated from each other in body by the tomb."

Although, as Saint Gregory says here, Saint Scholastica was buried in the same tomb in which her brother, Saint Benedict, was interred at Monte Cassino, it seems probable that the relics of this holy virgin were removed to Fleury-sur-Loire in France about the year 653, when the Benedictine monastery at Monte Cassino was destroyed by the Lombards.

Saint Sebastian

Martyr

c. 3 0 4

(January 20)

THAT SAINT SEBASTIAN was one of the great heroes of Rome who gave their lives in defense of the Christian faith is a fact that can be established as certain from the early date of his cult. The Roman catalogue of feastdays that was drawn up in the year 354, just a half century after his death, lists Saints Fabian and Sebastian as having the anniversary of their martyrdom on January 20 and mentions the Cemetery of Saint Callistus on the Appian Way as the burial place of both these martyrs. These two saints, however, did not die in the same year; for, while Pope Fabian suffered martyrdom in the year 253 during the persecution of the emperor Decius, Sebastian died as a martyr, according to all the evidence, during the persecution of the emperor Diocletian (284-305). In the year 367 a basilica was built over the tomb of St. Sebastian on the Appian Way and dedicated in his honor. This Church of St. Sebastian has always been considered one of the seven principal churches of Rome. Cardinal Scipio Borghese had a new edifice erected on the site of this ancient church. This basilica, completed in 1611, is well known to all the pilgrims who visit Rome because it is situated near the entrance to the most famous of all the Roman catacombs, that is, the underground cemetery which was named after Pope Saint Callistus (219-224), and which is not to be confused with the Catacombs of Saint Sebastian.

In the second half of the 4th century St. Ambrose, archbishop of Milan, speaks of Saint Sebastian as having been a native of this city and testifies to the fact that this Roman martyr was greatly venerated at this time in Milan. However, the city of Narbonne in southern France has always claimed that Saint Sebastian was born in Narbonne. The Roman Breviary harmonizes this discrepancy by saying that Sebastian's father was a Narbonnese and his mother a Milanese.

The oldest known picture of Saint Sebastian, probably dating from the 4th century, is found in the crypt of St. Cecilia in the same Catacombs of St. Callistus. It shows him as dressed in tunic and pallium, the ordinary dress of that time. A mosaic dating from the year 682 in the Church of St. Peter in Chains at Rome portrays the saint as a bearded man, wearing Byzantine court dress. In neither of these two early pictures is there any sign of arrows. On the other hand, the numerous Renaissance paintings of St. Sebastian portray him as a young man, stripped almost naked, tied to a tree or stake, and pierced by arrows.

This latter type of picture is based on the account of the martyrdom of Saint Sebastian as given in his so-called "Acts." Unfortunately, this composition, which dates from the beginning of the 5th century, is without historical value. Apart from the nature and style of this story which show it to be pious fiction, there are inaccuracies here which prevent it from being taken at face value. Thus, for instance, it implies that Sebastian suffered martyrdom during the pontificate of Pope Cajus and in the persecution of Diocletian. While it is true that the pontificate of St. Cajus coincided in part with the reign of Diocletian, the former being pope from 283 to 296 and the latter being emperor from 284 to 305, it is practically certain that Diocletian did not persecute Christians until the last three years of his reign, that is, at the time of Pope Marcellinus (296-304) and Pope Marcello I (304-309). However, since these "Acts of St. Sebastian" may be based on some earlier tradition and thus contain some elements of historical truth, a short summary of this pious legend would not be out of place.

This account presents Sebastian as an officer in the imperial bodyguard of Diocletian and a favorite of this emperor because of his bravery and other good qualities. Though Sebastian is a Christian, he cannot make an open profession of his faith on account of his position in the army and at the court. He does, however, gladly assist his fellow Christians who are suffering for the faith, by consoling them in their afflictions and encouraging them to return true to Christ in their imprisonment and tortures.

One such occasion is the arrest of the two brothers, Mark and Marcellian. When their parents, Tranquillian and Marcia, who are pagans, urge them to save their lives by renouncing Christ, Sebastian preaches a long sermon to them on the great merit of martyrdom. Since they are imprisoned in the house of Nicostratus, the latter's wife Zoe, though deaf and dumb, miraculously hears this sermon. She therefore falls at the feet of Sebastian and professes her faith in Christ. When at the prayers of Sebastian she is permanently cured of her affliction, her husband Nicostratus also proclaims his desire to become a Christian. The sight of Zoe's miraculous cure likewise induces Tranquillian and Marcia to embrace the Christian faith of their sons. Pope Cajus thereupon baptizes all these new converts whom Sebastian has won for Christ.

When they are all brought before the judge Chromacius and accused of being Christians, Sebastian speaks up in their defense and presents the Christian truth in so persuasive a way that this judge himself is converted to Christianity and dismisses the case against the Christians. A new trial, however, is then held before the prefect Fabian, who condemns them all to death.

Diocletian, hearing of these happenings, summons Sebastian and asks him if he too is a Christian. This brave soldier now boldly confesses his faith in Christ. Having tried in vain by alluring promises as well as dire threats to induce Sebastian to deny Christ, the emperor orders his Numidian archers to tie the Christian officer to a stake and shoot him to death with arrows. The sentence is carried out, and Sebastian is left for dead. But that night a Christian woman caled Irene, whose husband Castulus had died as a martyr, comes to take away the body of Sebastian for burial, and is surprised to find that there is still some life in him. After loosening him from the stake and drawing the arrows from his body, she carries him to her home and treats his wounds. With God's help he recovers.

Scarcely is Sebastian restored to health when he goes to confront Diocletian and rebuke him for his cruelty against the Christians. The emperor, on recovering from his astonishment at seeing his former officer still alive, is so enraged by Sebastian's words that he commands his lictors to beat him with rods till he expires. The dead body of the martyr is then thrown into the "cloaca" or main sewer of Rome, to prevent it from becoming an object of veneration for the Christians. The sacred corpse, however, is not carried through the sewer to the Tiber, but gets caught in an underground obstruction. At night Sebastian appears in a vision to the saintly woman Lucina and, telling her where his body is to be found, asks her to have it buried in the Catacombs of St. Callistus on the Appian Way. St. Lucina carries out this order and places the body of St. Sebastian in a tomb in this cemetery near the bodies of various other holy martyrs. Thus far the "Acts of St. Sebastian."

Since the sudden and devasting blow of pestilence was often likened to a fast-flying arrow, Sebastian, who had been pierced by arrows according to the account of his "Acts," became the special patron to be invoked in times of pestilence. Thus, in the pestilence that struck Rome in 680, public prayers offered to St. Sebastian brought this plague to a miraculous stop. Among more recent occurrences when cities were delivered from pestilence through the intercession of St. Sebastian are those of Milan in 1575 and Lisbon in 1599.

Saint Stanislaus Kostka
Confessor
1 5 6 8
(November 13)

I N HIS VERY fine book on St. Stanislaus, *Portrait of a Champion,* Joseph E. Kerns, S.J., writes that while the boy was studying at the Jesuit College in Vienna, his classmates liked him and yet were puzzled at him. "Strange the impression he made. They didn't know how to describe it. There was something so fresh and alive and clean about him. As one of them remarked, 'when you look at him, it makes you feel ashamed of yourself.'"

Stanislaus was born in the castle of Rostkovo, Poland, in 1550, the second son of Lord John Kostka, a Polish Senator. His mother, Margaret Kryska, was the sister of another Polish nobleman, the Duke Palatine of Masovia. Although his parents were devout Catholics, they lived a rich and elegant life, proud of their noble descent. Family honor came first with Lord John. Stanislaus, however, even as a little boy, was deeply religious. He was not long at the Jesuit college in Vienna, which he entered as a student at the age of fourteen, when he felt the stirrings of a vocation to the religious life. He wanted to be a Jesuit. No matter how hard he strove against the idea, he always came face to face with this fact. Yet, knowing so well what his family's reaction would be, he was filled with grave misgivings. Although he rightly feared that his father would never grant him permission, and wrongly worried that he himself was unworthy to enter the religious life, he still ardently longed to be a member of that dedicated group of men who taught him. That he was confused and troubled is not to be wondered at.

His older brother Paul, whom he loved and admired, was with him at the college, but that young man threw himself into the merry roistering of the city and was bitter toward his younger brother whose only joy was in prayer and virtue. Later, when they had to leave their quarters at the college, they moved into the home of Senator Kimberger, a Lutheran. Here Stanislaus suffered much unhappiness. He withdrew more and more into his life of prayer and made long visits in the church. Paul greatly resented this, and he, as well as many of their fellow students, looked upon Stanislaus' way of life as a rebuke to themselves. Finally one day Paul struck him. When his younger brother did not strike back, Paul's anger turned into constant bullying. This was hard for Stanislaus to bear, especially since he was the stronger of the two and could have given the bullier a good thrashing. At last he threatened: "This will end in my running away and not coming back. Then you will have to explain it to father and mother."

Although at first Stanislaus found his studies rather difficult, he worked hard and forged ahead till at last he had very little trouble in mastering his lessons. He was very much alone since he avoided the parties the others frequented. Paul urged him to learn to dance, declaring that this was a necessary part of his social education, but Stanislaus, who unwillingly agreed, felt that this was a frivolous waste of precious time.

Then Stanislaus was stricken with a sudden illness so severe that he thought he was about to die. He pleaded for a priest that he might receive the last sacraments, but Paul and the others, knowing that Kimberger would not let a priest come into his house, refused to grant the poor young man's request. Desperate, he remembered that St. Barbara was said to be able to obtain for those devoted to her the grace of receiving holy Communion when it would otherwise be impossible for them. So he earnestly begged this favor of her. It is said that one day the Holy Eucharist was brought to him by angels and that he had a vision of Mary with the Child Jesus. She even placed her divine Child on his bed, where Stanislaus embraced Him. Before she left, she told him that he would not die of this illness, but would recover and eventually join the Society of Jesus. To the astonishment of all who lived with him, he was soon completely cured. The doctors had a difficult time trying to give a natural explanation for the marvelous recovery.

Stanislaus went to his confessor and told him of his ardent desires to become a Jesuit, but Father Magius, the Provincial of the Jesuits in Austria, when he learned of Stanislaus' application, withheld his approval fearing what Lord John Kostka might do in retaliation against the Jesuits. They were having a troublesome time holding on, as it was. Stanislaus went courageously from one to another, but all he ever got was a rather hopeless, "Pray over it." He soon realized that only by running away from Vienna and going to the Jesuits in another part of Europe could he ever hope to attain his heart's desire. With much persistence he was able to obtain letters of introduction and recommendation from influential men in Vienna. Finally he tried to slip quietly and quickly out of Vienna, but his brother soon set out in hot pursuit. According to one of the stories, Paul actually caught up with Stanislaus, but did not recognize him in his rough pilgrim's habit and passed him by.

In any case, after a long, tiresome journey Stanislaus eventually reached Augsburg in Swabia (southern Germany) and finally the nearby town of Dillingen on the upper Danube. Here he met Father Peter Canisius, Provincial of the Jesuit province of Upper Germany, to whom he presented his petition and letters of recommendation. The great Canisius, later to become a canonized saint himself, thought it well to test the young man's virtue by having him work as "house boy," to wait at table and clean the rooms. Stanislaus fulfilled his lowly tasks with such constant cheerfulness and humility that he won the hearts of all. Canisius, too, was much pleased with the determined youth who clearly showed he had a true vocation to the religious life. After three weeks he let Stanislaus accompany two Jesuits who were on their way to Rome—a journey over the Alps which in those days took about a month to complete.

His two companions on this journey were amazed at his patience and gentleness, his humility and piety, and his manly strength of character. He not only won their respect and affection; he filled them with a sense of awe when they seemed to see a supernatural light that shone at times about his face and person. That a youth of seventeen could accomplish all that he did under every possible trying circumstance would in itself have been proof that he was under a special guidance and providence of God.

At Rome, Stanislaus was kindly received by Francis Borgia, the Father General of the Society of Jesus, and himself another of the early Jesuits who would eventually be a canonized saint. Admitted at once into the Jesuit novitiate at Rome, Stanislaus received the religious habit on October 28th, the feast of the holy Apostles Simon and Jude, in 1567. His happiness now knew no bounds. Even the harsh and threatening letter that he received a few days later from his father, who by now had found out where he was, could not shatter it. Visitors from Poland told him how his father had sworn that if he had the chance of laying hands on his young son, he would put him in chains for the disgrace he had brought on his family's name.

All this, however, failed to ruffle the joyful serenity of Stanislaus' days in the novitiate. In the midst of other holy men he was outstanding for his obvious sanctity, although in his deep humility he did his best to hide his virtues from others. His whole life now was one of continual prayer. The ardent longing of his soul for the most intimate union with God was soon to find its fulfillment.

Stanislaus again fell ill, and a premonition of death gave him assurance that his departure for heaven would not long be delayed. On August 15th (the feast of Our Lady of the Snow), while talking with Father Emmanuel de Sa about Our Lady's Assumption into heaven, he said, "How happy a day for all the saints was that on which the Blessed Virgin was taken up into heaven! No doubt all the blessed in heaven celebrate its anniversary with special joy, as we do here on earth. I hope that I, too, will be there to celebrate its next occurrence with them." His love for Mary was one of the outstanding characteristics of his life. He had had it ever since he was a little boy, when he thought she must be a stately, loving, beautiful woman, much like his own mother. In his dark hours he had always gone to Mary, beseeching her help. Once Father de Sa asked him why he loved her so much? He was silent for a moment, and then said simply, "After all, she is my Mother." Could there be a more convincing reply?

According to the custom in the Jesuit novitiate, on the first day of every month Stanislaus and his fellow novices each drew the name of one of the saints of that month for a special patron. At the beginning of July, Stanislaus drew the name of St. Laurence whose feast falls on the 10th of August. For the following days he was especially devoted to this young martyred deacon of Rome. Then on the feast day of this monthly patron, he fell gravely ill and knew in his heart that his time had come. Though every care was given him and he seemed to rally, this time his recovery did not last. No one could understand his steady decline since the Father who had the care of the sick diagnosed his case as merely one of mild malaria. Before the end came the superior told him that he would be permitted to pronounce at once his first vows as a member of the Society of Jesus. The making of these vows overwhelmed him with utter joy. Those at his bedside saw the color come back into his face and thought that he was getting better. Yet this was not the natural glow of health; it was rather a supernatural radiance from heaven. Again he was favored with a vision of Mary, and then he lay so still that those about him thought he was sleeping. He had been dead almost an hour before they realized it. The day was the

15th of August in 1568. His prayer had been heard: his heavenly Mother let him celebrate the feast of her Assumption with her in heaven.

A month later his brother Paul arrived in Rome. The news of Stanislaus' death came as a terrible shock to him. Recalling with shame and horror the cruel things he had done to Stanislaus, he now realized that despite his brutality he had always loved his younger brother. From that time there came a great change into Paul's life. He turned to prayer and penance; he performed many acts of charity, among them the founding of several houses for the Jesuits. At the age of sixty he asked that he himself might be received into the Society of Jesus. Claude Aquaviva, who had known and loved Stanislaus and who was now the Father General of the Jesuits, approved of his reception. However, Paul became ill and died of fever just as he was about to leave Rome. Previously, however, he had had the happiness of being present in Rome at his brother's beatification.

Stanislaus was beatified in 1605, the first of the many Jesuits to receive this honor. Many miracles had been wrought through his intercession and all Rome was already calling him a saint. Two years after his death, when his body (which had not been embalmed) was removed to the new novitiate church in Rome, it was found to be quite free from decay or corruption. On the date of this transference of his relics, the 13th of November, his feast day is now celebrated. Pope Clement VIII, who beatified him, would also have canonized him at once had not the Jesuits wished that their founder, Ignatius Loyola, should be the first of their number to receive this higher honor. Meanwhile the Poles made Stanislaus, jointly with St. Casimir, the chief patron of their country. Yet it was not until 1726 that Pope Benedict XIII solemnly declared him a saint. Except for the recently canonized Dominic Savio and the boy martyrs of the Church, the seventeen-year-old Stanislaus Kostka is the youngest saint in the calendar. "Having become perfect in a short while, he reached the fullness of a long career" (Wisdom 4,13).

Saint Tarsicius

Martyr

Third or Fourth Century
(August 15)

POPE SAINT DAMASUS I (366-384) was greatly devoted to the holy martyrs of Rome. In their honor he composed some thirty short Latin poems, mostly in the classical hexameter form. These "epigrams," as they were called in the original sense of "inscriptions," were carved in beautiful lettering and placed in the churches and catacombs over the tombs of the respective martyrs. Most of them are still well preserved to this day and are a source of valuable history for the early Church.

One of these inscriptions was placed in the Catacomb of Saint Callistus over the tomb of Saint Tarsicius. Rendered into English prose, this poetic inscription reads as follows. "Let the reader know the equal merits of the two men in whose honor Pope Damasus erects this inscription. Stephen, though stoned by the Jews when he urged them on to better things, snatched the trophy from the enemy, and thus this faithful Levite was the first to win the crown of martyrdom. Saint Tarsicius, while carrying the sacrament of Christ, was met with a mad demand to hand it over to profane men; but he preferred to lay down his own life under their blows rather than surrender the heavenly Body to these rabid dogs."

This inscription makes it certain that in the second half of the fourth century Saint Tarsicius was a well-known Roman martyr and that he gave his life in defense of the Blessed Sacrament. By comparing him with Saint Stephen, the famous deacon of the early Church in Jerusalem, Pope Damasus seems to imply that Tarsicius also was a deacon. It is common knowledge that in the early Church the distribution of Holy Communion was one of the regular functions of the deacons. When killed by the pagan mob in Rome, Tarsicius was probably bringing the Blessed Eucharist to the sick or to the Christians who were in prison waiting martyrdom. It is also possible that he was engaged in carrying what was known in the early Church at Rome as the *fermentum*, that is, a portion of the bread which was consecrated at the pope's Mass and distributed to the pastors of the various parish churches in the city as a sign of the union existing between the chief shepherd and his flock and as a symbol of the unity of the holy Sacrifice, which, though offered up in different places, is one and the same Sacrifice of Christ. In time of need, as during the persecutions, the task of carrying the Blessed Sacrament for any of these reasons was at that period entrusted not only to deacons, but to the lesser officials in the Church and even to laymen.

In the sixth century these strictly historical facts about St. Tarsicius were embellished with legendary material in the writing known as his "Acts." Here the saint is said to have been, not a deacon, but an acolyte. In the early Church an "acolyte" was not an "altar boy," but, as the Greek word *akolouthos* signifies, a "follower," an attendant or assistant, to a bishop. The "acolytes" of the early Church were mostly married men, not mere boys. The acolyteship is the highest of the four Minor Orders, which are no longer functional in the Church but merely stepping stones to the Major Orders.

This sixth-century legend of St. Tarsicius has the saint carrying the Blessed Sacrament as Holy Communion to the Christians who were in prison during the persecution of Valerian, therefore around the middle of the third century. It is possible, however, that Tarsicius was killed in the persecution of Diocletian at the beginning of the fourth century.

The Roman Martyrology for August 15th, after mentioning that on this day the feast of our Lady's Assumption into heaven is celebrated and that this day is the anniversary of the death of St. Hyacinth of Poland and of St. Stephen, king of Hungary, gives a summary of the martyrdom of St. Tarsicius, as taken from his sixth-century "Acts," in these words. "(On this day the martyrdom) at Rome, on the Appian Way, of Tarsicius, the Acolyte. When the pagans met him as he was carrying the Sacrament of the Body of Christ, they began to ask him what he had with him. But since he considered it a shameful thing to throw away pearls to the swine, he was attacked by them with clubs and stones for so long a time that he finally breathed forth his soul. When the sacrilegious assailants had turned over his dead body, they could not find a trace of Christ's Sacrament either in his hands or in his garments. The Christians then took up the body of the martyr and buried it with honor in the Cemetery of Callistus."

Since St. Tarsicius has, rightly or wrongly, been long regarded as a young acolyte, he is one of the patrons of altar boys. This martyr of the Holy Eucharist is also one of the patrons of the Fathers of the Blessed Sacrament.

Saint Valentine
Martyr

c. 2 6 9

(February 14)

MOST AMERICANS KNOW the 14th of February is Saint Valentine's Day. They also believe that, for some unknown reason, Cupid is especially active on this day, flying around on little wings and shooting his arrow of love to the tune of "Hearts and Flowers."

Actually no one knows much about Saint Valentine, except that there was a genuine Roman martyr by this name who gave his life for Christ on February 14th in or about the year 269, and was buried in a Christian cemetery on the Flaminian Road situated a short distance outside the northern gate of Rome. To complicate matters, the Roman Martyrology for February 14th mentions two saints by this name: "At Rome, on the Via Flaminia, the heavenly birthday of Saint Valentine, priest and martyr, who, after a life famous for his teaching and wonderful cures, was beaten with clubs and beheaded in the reign of Emperor Claudius . . . At Interamnae, (the heavenly birthday) of Saint Valentine, bishop and martyr, who, having been scourged for a long time and then thrown into prison, could not be overcome, but was finally brought out of prison in the silence of midnight and beheaded by order of Placidus, the prefect of the City."

It is quite possible that there were really two different martyrs called Valentine; the name itself was very common among both pagans and Christians at this time. One of them would have been a priest at Rome and possibly also a physician. The other would have been a bishop at Interamna, modern Terni, a city on the Flaminian Road some fifty miles north of Rome. Apparently the latter also suffered martydom at Rome. Now, the Emperor Claudius, of whom the Martyrology speaks, is certainly Claudius II, also known as "Claudius the Goth," who reigned 268-270, and not Claudius I who was Nero's predecessor. The Roman priest Valentine, therefore, was martyred about the year 269. On the other hand, Placidus, the prefect of Rome, by whose orders Bishop Valentine of Interamna was put to death, is certainly the same as Furius Placidus who was consul of Rome in 273, since the "Acts" of this St. Valentine calls this prefect "Furiosus Placidus." It is most unlikely that two different saints of the same name should have suffered martyrdom at Rome on the same day of the same year. If originally the two martyrs were distinct, later tradition must have confused one with the other.

In any case, the veneration of Saint Valentine outside the Flaminian Gate at Rome is very ancient. In the 4th century a church dedicated to him was built over his grave in this catacomb on the Flaminian Road. In the 7th century his relics were taken from the subterranean grave in which they had first been laid and placed in this church itself. From the 9th to the 14th century the Benedictines had a monastery beside this church, but when the church and monastery fell into ruins in the 14th century, the relics of St. Valentine were removed to the Church of St. Prassede in the heart of the city, where they still repose. During the Middle Ages the ancient Porta Flaminia (Flaminian Gate) at the north of Rome, which is now called the Porta del Popolo (Gate of the People), was commonly known as the Porta di San Valentino (Gate of St. Valentine).

It would be of interest to find in the late and largely unhistorical "Acts" of Valentine some incident that could have given

SAINT VITUS

This boy martyr suffered under the persecution of the Emperor Diocletian
c. 300. After he had driven the devil out of the Emperor's son, Diocletian
attributed the cure to sorcery and had Vitus tortured. The saint succumbed only after repeated tortures. The artist has portrayed him with both
the red cross, emblematic of martrydom; and the palm branch, symbol of
victory for all holy martyrs.

SAINT ROBERT BELLARMINE

The *Society of Jesus* was established providentially in the sixteenth century as the main bulwark of the Church against the attacks of the so-called reformers of the Protestant Reformation. One of the leading Jesuits of this period was Saint Robert Bellarmine. Born of the aristocracy (the family coat of arms can be seen on the backrest of his chair), he was canonized in 1930.

rise to the modern custom of sending "valentines" on his feast day. But one would look in vain through either form of these "Acts," whether of St. Valentine of Rome or of St. Valentine of Terni, for any such incident. Sad to say, the custom of lovers calling each other their "Valentine" on St. Valentine's Day has apparently nothing at all to do with the saint himself.

This custom seems to have arisen in the Middle Ages and was especially popular in England, though also known in France, and it was based on the strange belief that on the 14th or middle day of February birds picked their mates for nesting in the coming spring. Thus, the poet Chaucer (1340-1400) wrote in his "Parliament of Fowls" (the spelling is here modernized):

For this was on Saint Valentine's Day,
When every fowl cometh there to choose his mate.

Some interesting letters from 15th century England have come down to us in which a young lady, writing to her fiance on St. Valentine's Day addresses him as "my Valentine." In those hearty days a young lady did not hesitate to take the first move towards a proposal of marriage. She simply wrote to her beloved shortly before St. Valentine's Day, "Won't you be my Valentine?" — which meant no more or less than "Won't you marry me?"

When the English colonists came to America in the 17th and 18th centuries, they brought this old custom with them. Strange to say, while the sending of greetings for St. Valentine's Day has now almost completely died out in England, as it had earlier disappeared from France, it is still quite in vogue in America even though the original meaning of the custom has become rather obscure. Good Saint Valentine, who gave his life blood for Christ in 3rd-century Rome, may never have dreamed that his name would some day be connected with the sending of greetings between young lovers. Yet it is fitting that he who as priest and physician did so much good for the souls and bodies of his fellow men out of love for Christ should have become the patron of chaste Christian courtship.

Saint Veronica Giuliani
Virgin

1 7 2 7

(July 9)

ONE DAY IN the year 1664 a young mother gathered her children about her deathbed to give them her last blessing. She had already seen two of her little ones precede her in death, and she wished to confide her five remaining children to God before she left them orphans. Spiritually she gave to each one of the five a refuge in one of the Five Wounds of Christ. Her youngest, a four-year-old daughter, she entrusted to the wound in the side of Christ, praying that this one might always be close to the pierced Heart of Jesus. This dramatic scene must have left a lasting impression on the mind of this little girl. All her life she remained united to the wounded heart of her crucified Savior, so deeply devoted to His sacred Passion that, through her supernatural gift of the "stigmata" or wounds of Christ, she literally shared in His sufferings.

This girl, who in later life often added the term, "Daughter of the Cross," to her signature, we now call Saint Veronica Giuliani. Veronica, however, was her name "in religion." When she was born on December 27, 1660, she was given the baptismal name of Ursula. Her parents, Francesco Giuliani and Bendetta Mancini, both belonging to families of the lesser nobility, lived in Mercatello, a town in the province of Pesaro in the Duchy of Urbino, then part of the Papal States, when she was born. Here

998

Ursula spent the first eight years of her life. But her father moved with his children to Piacenza in Lombardy (northern Italy) in 1668, when he was made superintendent of finance in this city.

At a very early age Ursula Giuliani gave proof of her ardent desire to make sacrifices for love of Christ and thus be united with Him in His atoning sufferings. Even as a child she used to fast every week on Wednesday, Friday, and Saturday, the ancient, traditional fastdays of the Church. Her favorite saints were Catherine of Siena and Rose of Lima, and as far as she was able, she endeavored to imitate their prayerful, penitential lives. Once when her little hand was accidentally caught in a door and painfully crushed, she bravely fought to hold back her tears, as she offered up this suffering for love of her Savior.

During these early years too she loved to practice charity to the poor and to give them all she could. Touching stories are told of her in this regard. She had built a small altar which, in addition to her beloved crucifix, had a statue of the Madonna holding the Divine Child, and here, where she was accustomed in her simple way to commune in prayer with God, she used to place the food which she denied to herself in order to give it to the poor. Once as she set such food on this altar, she saw the Madonna come down from her pedestal and let her Divine Child bless and taste of Ursula's offering. On another occasion, when Ursula had given away her pair of shoes to a poor barefoot child, she was surprised to find the shoes back on her altar, but now covered with precious jewels.

On February 2, 1670, when Ursula was ten years old, she made her First Communion at Piacenza. On returning home from church, she told her older sisters that she had a painful feeling in her heart as if it were on fire, and thinking that everyone who received our Lord in Holy Communion had this feeling, she innocently asked them how long it would last.

Ursula, however, was a normal girl, and from her own admission, made in later life, we know that she had her little faults to contend with. Thus, she confesses, she was inclined to be somewhat dictatorial and chided others for not leading as pious and strict a life as she did. Once, in a fit of temper, she went so far as to give a slap in the face to one of the servants of her household. After her father moved to Piacenza and lived in better quarters than she had known at Mercatello, she took a natural but, to her way of thinking, inordinate pleasure in these more refined surroundings. At the age of sixteen, however, she had a vision in which Christ chided her for her cold "heart of steel." Overwhelmed with shame and contrition, she resolved to be more meek and humble and to do penance for these sins. During the rest of her life, whenever she performed her frequent and frightful penances in atonement for the offenses that sinners offer to Christ, she included herself with all sincerity within this same class of sinners.

Despite these little faults, Ursula never gave up her longings to become a nun; for she rightly felt that only in a convent could she fully satisfy her desires to offer herself completely as a sacrificial victim to God. Her father, however, good man though he was, had other plans for her; there was a certain wealthy young nobleman to whom he would give her hand in marriage and thus strengthen the family ties. But Ursula remained resolute; nothing could change her determination to become a nun. Signor Giuliani then sent her to relatives in Florence, so that in this brilliant capital of Tuscany she might see more of the world and thereby give up her notion of entering the convent. But this device also proved futile. Ursula merely prayed and mortified herself all the more, in order to obtain the grace of remaining undefiled by contact with worldly pleasures. Then on her return home she fell ill with a mysterious malady. Fearing that this was a punishment from God for his opposition, Ursula's father finally relented and promised God that, if his daughter's life was spared, he would give her his permission to follow the call she had received from on high. Shortly after this she recovered her health, and her father, true to his word, let her go to the convent.

On July 17, 1677, when she was seventeen years old, Ursula entered the convent of the Capuchin Poor Clares at Citta di Castello, a city on the upper Tiber in the province of Perugia. Here on October 23 of the same year she received the holy habit and began her novitiate. On account of her great devotion to the Passion of Christ she was given the name of Veronica, the traditional name of the holy woman who wiped the blood-stained face of our Lord with a towel as He carried His cross to Calvary. At the close of her reception ceremony the presiding bishop said prophetically to the Mother Abbess of the convent, "I commend this new daughter to your care. She will some day be a great saint."

Sister Veronica Giuliani had chosen this particular religious order because its very austere rule offered her the best opportunity to live a life of poverty, prayer and penance. Though the penitential practices in this convent might have proved hard on the other novices, Veronica found them easy, since she had long In fact, as far as she could obtain permission, she used additional since accustomed herself to rigorous fasting and bodily austerities. means, over and beyond the rigors of the rule, in chastising her body.

The most exact observance of even the smallest rule was a joy to her, as she strove to make herself a true daughter of Saint Francis of Assisi. All the nuns of the community were edified by her spirit of humility, joyfulness and courage. Toward both her superiors and her spiritual director she made her soul an open book. This habit of complete candor regarding her spiritual life, which she kept up till her death, proved to be her best safeguard against the attacks that Satan raised up against her. Despite all her fervor and love of the religious life, the devil tempted her severely, urging her to leave the convent and return to the world. He even tried certain tricks against her which, if they had not been recognized as his work, would have resulted in her dismissal from the convent. But in all her trials and humiliations and in all the dryness of spirit which she sometimes experienced at prayer, her constant stay and support was the thought of Christ hanging on the cross, abandoned by all.

Veronica's persevering efforts were rewarded on November 1, 1678, when she was permitted to pronounce her solemn, perpetual vows that bound her forever to her crucified Lord. Every year thereafter she celebrated the Feast of All Saints (November first) with special joy as the anniversary of this her utter dedication to God to suffer with Him in atonement for the sins of the world.

As a professed nun, Veronica accepted with equal joy every office in the community that obedience assigned to her. In turn she was cook, infirmarian, sacristan and portress, besides carrying on all the regular labors of the convent. In all her relations with her fellow Sisters she was ever a model of kindness and charity. Whenever she noticed in herself a natural repugnance towards someone or something, she strove heroically to overcome it. "Whoever wishes to live unto God," she used to say, "must die to self." Some of the means she took to conquer her natural sense of repugnance may seem to us poor mortals rather excessive. Thus, as cook, she once felt a moment's repugnance at some strong-smelling fish in the kitchen. To punish herself for this weakness, she obtained permission to keep a putrid fish in her cell for some days and she would frequently put it to her nose and breath deeply of its odor as if it were the most exquisite perfume. It is to be hoped that, for the sake of the other nuns, she meanwhile kept her cell heremetically sealed.

Shortly after her profession she had a vision which struck the keynote of her whole religious life. We know of this from the account of it which she wrote at the command of her spiritual director. "I seemed to see," she modestly said, "our Lord carrying His cross and inviting me to bear this precious burden with Him. As I was filled with an ardent desire to share in His sufferings, He seemed to impress His cross on my heart, while at the same time He made me understand that this would be more precious to me than all the treasures of the world. . . . When I came to myself, I felt a violent pain in my heart, which has since then never left me. Yet the desire which I then conceived of suffering for Christ's sweet sake was so intense that I would have gladly borne every imaginable torment to satisfy it. . . . Sufferings and the cross are the only true treasures, pure joys." It was from this time on that the saint used to sign her name as "Veronica, daughter of the cross."

Though it may seem to us rather gruesome, the fact is that after her death a sort of autopsy was performed on the chest of St. Veronica by a competent surgeon in the presence of the bishop and several other reliable witnesses, and all of these testified that there were found on her heart clear markings, not only of the cross, but also of other instruments of Christ's Passion.

In several other, later periods of her life Veronica had similar visions. Thus, she once beheld our Lady present her with a chalice and invite her to drink deeply of this chalice of her divine Son's sufferings. Or again, on April 4, 1694, our Lord came to her in a vision and took the crown of thorns from his own head and laid it on hers. From that day forward she suffered headaches which were so excruciating that she herself admitted she had never before experienced such terrible pain. This pain never left her, but on Fridays and during Lent, especially in Holy Week, it grew still more intense. Nor was this without its external manifestation. A circle of protrudences surrounded her head as if caused by the piercing of thorns beneath the skin. When she revealed this, like everything else, to her confessor, he wished to discover if it was something truly supernatural or merely some natural affliction. Therefore he ordered her to have it treated by a physician. The latter's "treatment" only added to her pains. He tried to remove the swellings by cauterizing them with a hot bodkin or even by cutting them off. This torture was so frightful that none of the nuns had the courage to watch it. Yet Veronica not only bore it unflinchingly; she even assisted the physician in applying his instruments. All these efforts, however, proved useless; the marks of the crown of thorns could not be removed but remained on her head all her life.

In the following year, on March 5, 1695, Christ appeared again in a vision to Veronica and asked her to fast for three years on nothing but bread and water. Obediently she asked permission from her director and superior to do this. When the permission was quite understandably refused, Veronica told her divine Lord that she could not carry out His request, since her first obligation was to obey her superiors. Christ merely smiled knowingly at her. Surprisingly enough, the permission was soon granted.

There now began for her the most severe period of her sufferings in soul as well as in body. Every Friday she experienced the various torments which Christ suffered in His Passion, particularly the torture that He bore in His scourging. This became especially intense during Lent and reached a climax on Good Friday. On this Good Friday,, April 5, 1697, our Lord appeared to her in a vision as He hung on the cross, and bright rays came from His five wounds and burned similar wounds in her own hands and feet, while she was racked with pain as if she herself hung on the cross. There is no reason to doubt that this was a genuine case of the supernatural phenomenon known as the "stigmata," a spiritual gift which Veronica's father in Christ, St. Francis of Assisi, was the first to receive.

Some of the nuns in the convent were imprudent enough to tell outsiders about what was happening to Sister Veronica, and soon the news spread not only in the town of Citta del Castello, but in other parts of Italy. Before long Msgr. Luc' Antonio Eustachi, the bishop of this city, was ordered by the Holy Office at Rome to investigate this matter and send in a report on it. Bishop Eustachi knew that the surest way to test the genuineness of Sister Veronica's supernatural favors was to put her moral virtues to the test. If she proved humble and obedient in all things and if there were no signs of conscious deceit or unconscious delusion, he would have to admit that these extraordinary manifestations came from God.

Bishop Eustachi, therefore, gave orders that Veronica should be deposed from the office of Mistress of Novices, a position which she had held for some time, and isolated completely from the community. She was thus confined to a cell in the infirmary and subjected to the constant supervision of a lay Sister, who was obliged to report on everything that the mystic did. Various learned men were then commissioned to subject Veronica to a severe inquisition. When accused by these men of being a heretic and a sorcerer and when threatened by them with life imprisonment in some dungeon unless she admitted deceit or hallucination, the poor nun could only reply meekly that her sole longing had always been to do nothing but God's will and that she had never in any way desired or sought for these strange things which were happening to her; if it was God's will, she would gladly spend the rest of her life imprisoned in a dungeon. This inquisition went on for months and months, and during all this time she was faithful to Christ's command to partake of nothing but a little bread and water, while she continued to endure all the sufferings of His sacred Passion in which He let her share. Yet for her the hardest penance of all was the fact that throughout this period she was never allowed to receive Holy Communion and was permitted to hear Masses only on Sundays and holydays.

At the end Bishop Eustachi was convinced of the genuineness of both the virtues and supernatural gifts of Veronica. In the report which he sent to Rome on September 26, 1679, he wrote: "Sister Veronica always lives in the practice of exact obedience, deep humility and remarkable abstinence, without ever showing any sign of sadness. On the contrary she always appears with an unspeakable peace and tranquility. She is the object of the admiration of her companions, who, however, cannot keep secret the feelings she inspires in them, so that they talk to seculars about her. I have tried my best to stop this. In order to prevent curiosity and talk among the people from increasing, I have threatened the Sisters with punishment if they do not stop their talk."

When this trial was finally over, Veronica was restored to her place in the community and lovingly welcomed back by all her

Sisters in the convent. Again she took up her office as Mistress of Novices, a position which she fulfilled with marvelous success for many years.

The wonderful supernatural gifts which God bestowed on St. Veronica were combined with great natural gifts of practical wisdom and common sense. As Mistress of Novices she knew how to lead her young charges to the heights of sublime sanctity through the traditional method of ascetical training. Since she had never sought mystical favors for herself, she would not let her novices aspire to them for themselves either. The conscious desire for such things, she well knew, could easily lead to vanity, hallucinations and a hidden form of self-love. Therefore, she would not let them read books treating of mystical theology, but made them confine their reading to ascetical works dealing with the ordinary virtues of the religious life. As the Infant Jesus Himself had taught her to do in a vision which He granted her one Christmas, so also she taught her novices to walk in the way of humility and simplicity, unless it is abundantly clear that the Holy Spirit would lead them on some other way. However, in her lectures explaining to them the catechism, the rules and ceremonial of their Order, she knew how to make these simple lessons serve as a source of inspiration for growing in the love of God. "Do not neglect these little things," she used to tell them, "for in God's eyes they are not what they seem to be in the eyes of men."

In 1716 Veronica was unanimously elected Mother Abbess of her community, and she remained in this office till her death eleven years later. In this important post she again showed how richly God had endowed her with common sense and good judgment. She never expected her Sisters to follow the life of extremely rigorous penance that she led. All she asked of them was the conscientious fulfillment of the Rule for love of God, which, she said, would be penance enough for them. In fact, her heart was always so full of tender sympathy for the sufferings of others, that she dreaded the thought of seeing any of her spiritual daughters bearing the pains that she had to endure, unless God clearly wished it of them, as He had of her. Whenever any of the Sisters were sorely tried and afflicted in body or soul, she would gently console them and offer to take their crosses on her own shoulders. Though she always insisted on the strict observance of true Franciscan poverty, she sensibly realized that the Sisters required a minimum, not of creature comforts, but of creature necessities. Therefore, besides several other material improvements which she made in the house, she had a new dormitory built and a certain amount of plumbing installed in the convent, which till then had been without running water.

These external activities did not in any way interfere with Veronica's interior life of prayer and suffering. With the years she continued to grow in mystical union with her crucified Savior, till she reached that most sublime intimacy with the divinity which is called by the rather unsatisfactory name of the soul's "mystical marriage" with Christ. This is nothing more or less than the highest possible degree of contemplative knowledge of God through love that a soul is able to enjoy here below without having the beatific vision itself which the blessed have in heaven.

When the time came for Veronica to offer up her final sacrifice for love of God and fall asleep forever in the Lord on July 9, 1727, her soul, that had so long borne the cross with Christ, rose triumphantly with Him, to behold Him, now no longer in a mysterious vision, but face to face in glory.

St. Veronica Giuliani was canonized by Pope Gregory XVI in 1839. She is usually represented in art as crowned with thorns and embracing the cross.

Saint Vitus

Martyr

c. 3 0 0

(June 15)

THE SO-CALLED "Martyrology of Saint Jerome," a compendium of the martyrs, compiled from earlier sources and wrongly attributed to this saint, makes it certain that there was an historical martyr by the name of Vitus whose feast was celebrated then, as now, on the fifteenth of June. This martyrology gives little more than the names of the martyrs and the place of their martyrdom, under the day of their death. Here, under June 15th, Vitus is mentioned twice: first in connection with Saints Modestus and Crescentia as having suffered martyrdom in Sicily, and then at the head of eight other martyrs as having died for Christ in Lucania—the Roman province in southern Italy which could be called the "instep," if the whole Italian peninsula is regarded, from its appearance on a map, as a "boot."

It seems fairly certain that the same Saint Vitus is involved in both these entries. Perhaps Saints Modestus and Crescentia were not originally connected with his martyrdom, though the Roman Martyrology mentions these three saints together for June 15th as having first been tortured under the Emperor Diocletian in Lucania, and then having died from later tortures in Sicily. What this probably means is that their cult spread at an early date from Lucania to the neighboring island of Sicily.

As the fame of these martyrs spread in the Church, popular devotion was not content with the bald fact of their martyrdom. In the sixth or seventh century, therefore, a purely legendary account of their "Acts" was composed.

Vitus, according to this legend, was a mere boy when he gave his life for Christ; one version makes him seven, another version twelve years old. His father Hylas was a rich pagan senator of Sicily, who entrusted the rearing of his son to two of his slaves, the married couple, Modestus and Crescentia. The latter, however, were Christians, and they soon had Vitus secretly baptized and raised in their faith. Young Vitus was endowed with the gift of curing people who were afflicted with various kinds of nervous diseases, believed at that time to be caused by diabolical possession. The fame of his many miracles and of the conversions to Christianity which he made soon reached his father's ears. Since the persecution of Diocletian was then raging, Vitus' father handed him over to Valerian, the governor of Sicily. But neither the blandishments which Valerian and Hylas lavished upon him nor the sound whippings which they gave him could induce the brave boy to deny Christ. Inspired by God, Vitus fled with Modestus and Crescentia in a boat, miraculously guided by an angel, to Lucania. Here they preached the gospel of Christ, and Vitus continued to work his miraculous cures. Hearing of Vitus' marvelous power, the Emperor Diocletian ordered him to come to Rome and cure his own son, who was possessed by the devil. Accompanied by his two faithful foster parents, Vitus went to Rome and drove the devil out of the emperor's son. Far from being grateful for this favor, Diocletian attributed the cure to sorcery, and had the three Christians tortured for refusing to sacrifice to the gods. When thrown into a cauldron filled with molten lead and boiling pitch and resin, the three remained unharmed and sung the praises of God like the three youths in Nabuchodonosor's fiery furnace. No more effective against them was the ferocious lion to which they were exposed; it meekly licked their feet. Whereupon they were stretched on a rack where they were scourged and har-

rowed with iron rakes. Then a mighty storm arose which over-
threw the pagan temples and killed the idolatrous worshippers,
and an angel came down from heaven, rescued the holy martyrs,
and brought them back to Lucania where they peacefully died
from the effects of their tortures.

This legend was very popular in the Middle Ages, and the cult
of these three martyrs spread from Italy into northern Europe.
In Germany, Saint Vitus became one of the "Fourteen Holy Helpers." Prague in Bohemia made him one of its principal patrons.
He was invoked against attacks by wild animals, against storms,
and, remarkably enough, against oversleeping. His help was invoked by those who suffered from epilepsy and other nervous
diseases. In fact, the nervous disease technically known as chorea
which is characterized by spasmatic twitchings, is still popularly
called "St. Vitus' dance." Moreover, if he could keep people from
abnormal dancing, he could also help people in their normal dancing, and thus he also became one of the patrons of professional
dancers and actors.

In art Saint Vitus is generally pictured as standing in or beside
a large cauldron, but sometimes as having a lion lying quietly at
his feet.

Calendar of Saints

A

Aaron, June 21, July 1
Abachum, Jan. 19
Abban, Oct. 27
Abdas, May 16
Abdjesus, May 16
Abdon, July 30
Abraames, Feb. 14
Abraamius, Feb. 5
Abraham, Mar. 15, Nov. 30
Acasius, Mar. 31
Acepsimas, Mar. 14
Achard, Sept. 15
Achates, Mar. 31
Acheolus, May 1
Achilleus, May 12
Acius, May 1
Adalbert, Apr. 23, Dec. 13, Dec. 16
Adamnan of Ireland, Sept. 23
Adauctus, Aug. 30
Adelaide, Feb. 5
Adelard, Jan. 2
Adelbert, June 25
Adelemus, Jan. 30
Adelhard, Jan. 2
Adjuntr, Apr. 30
Ado, Dec. 16
Adrian, Jan. 9, Mar. 4, Mar. 5, Sept. 8
Adulph, June 17
Aed, Aug. 15
Aedar, Aug. 31
Aedicius, Apr. 8
Aelred, Jan. 12, Mar. 3
Aemiliana, Jan. 5
Aemilius, May 22
Aengus, Mar. 11
Afra, Aug. 5
Agape, Apr. 3
Agapetus, Aug. 18, Sept. 20
Agapius, Aug. 19
Agatha, Feb. 5
Agathangelus, Jan. 23
Agatho, Jan. 10
Agilbert, June 25
Agilus, Aug. 30
Agnan, Nov. 17
Agnes, Jan. 21
Agnes of Monte Pulciano, Apr. 20
Agoard, June 25
Agrecius, Jan. 13
Agricola, Nov. 4
Aibert, Apr. 7
Aicard, Sept. 15
Aid, Apr. 11
Aidan, Aug. 31, Oct. 20
Aidanus, Jan. 31
Aile, Aug. 30
Aithilahas, Mar. 14
Ajutre, Apr. 30
Alban, June 22
Albert, Jan. 8
Albeus, Sept. 12
Albinus, Mar. 1
Alemund, Mar. 19, Sept. 7
Aldegund, Jan. 30
Aldhelm, May 25
Aldric, Jan. 7
Alexander, Feb. 26, Mar. 18, Mar. 28, Apr. 22, May 3, May 29, Dec. 12

Alexander Akimetes, Jan. 15
Alexis, July 17
Alexius, July 17
Alfrida, Aug. 2
Alice, Feb. 5, Dec. 16
Alipius, Aug. 15
Almachius, Jan. 1
Alnoth, Feb. 27
Alosia, Oct. 22
Aloysius, June 21
Alphaeus, Nov. 18
Alphonsus Mary de Liguori, Aug. 2
Alphonsus Rodriguez, Oct. 30
Alphonsus Turibius, Mar. 23
Alto of Ireland, Sept. 5
Amand, June 18
Amandus, Feb. 6
Amatus, Sept. 13
Ambrose, Dec. 7
Ambrosimus, Nov. 10
Ame, Sept. 13
Ammon, Oct. 4
Ammonarium, Dec. 12
Amphilochius, Nov. 23
Anacletus, July 13
Ananias, Apr. 25
Anastasia, Apr. 15
Anastasius, Jan. 22, Apr. 21, Apr. 27
Andeolus, May 1
Andrew, May 15, Aug. 22, Nov. 30
Andrew Avellino, Nov. 10
Andrew Corsini, Feb. 4
Andrew of Crete, Oct. 17
Andronicus, Oct. 11
Angela Merici, May 31
Angelus, May 5
Anian, Nov. 17
Anicetus, Apr. 17
Anne, July 26
Anno, Dec. 4
Ansbert, Feb. 9
Anscharius, Feb. 3
Anselm, Mar. 18, Apr. 21
Anstru, Oct. 17
Anstrudis, Oct. 17
Anthelm, June 26
Antherus, Jan. 3
Anthimus, Apr. 27
Anthony, Apr. 14
Anthony Cauleas, Feb. 12
Anthony Grassi, Dec. 13
Anthony Mary Zaccaria, July 5
Antipas, Apr. 11
Antoninus, May 10
Antony, Jan. 17
Antony of Egypt, Jan. 7
Antony of Padua, June 13
Apeleius, Oct. 7
Aper, Sept. 15
Aphrates, Apr. 7
Apian, Apr. 2
Apollinaris, Jan. 8, July 23
Apollinaris Sidonius, Aug. 23
Apollo, Jan. 25
Apollonia, Feb. 9
Apollonius, Mar. 8
Apollonius the Apologist, Apr. 18
Appia, Nov. 22
Arbogastus, July 21
Arcadius, Jan. 12

Archinimus, Mar. 29
Ard, Aug. 15
Armogastes, Mar. 29
Arnoul, July 18, Aug. 15
Arnulphus, Aug. 15
Arontius, Sept. 1
Arsenius, July 19
Artemas, Jan. 25
Artemius, Oct. 20
Arthemius, Jan. 24
Asaph, May 1
Asclas, Jan. 23
Aspasius, Jan. 2
Asterius, Mar. 3, Aug. 23, Oct. 30
Athanasius, May 2
Attalus, June 2
Atticus, Jan. 8
Attracta, Feb. 9
Aubert, Dec. 13
Audifax, Jan. 19
Audoen, Aug. 24
Audry, June 23
Augulus, Feb. 7
Augustine, May 28, Aug. 28
Aunaire, Sept. 25
Aurea, Oct. 4
Aurelian, June 16
Aurelius, July 20
Austremonius, Nov. ?
Auxentius, Feb. 14
Avertin, May 5
Avitis, Feb. 5
Avitus, June 17
Avoice, Oct. 17
Avy, June 17
Azades, Apr. 22

B

Babolen, June 26
Babylas, Jan. 23
Bacchus, Oct. 7
Bademus, Apr. 10
Bain, June 20
Balaam, Nov. 19
Baldechilde, Jan. 30
Baldrede, Mar. 6
Baldwin, Jan. 8
Barachisius, Mar. 29
Baradat, Feb. 22
Barbara, Dec. 4
Barbas, Feb. 19
Barbashemin, Jan. 14
Barbasymas, Jan. 14
Barbatus, Feb. 19
Barhedbesciabus, July 21
Barnabas, June 11
Barnard, Jan. 23
Barr, Sept. 25
Barsabias, Oct. 20
Barsamja, Jan. 30
Barsanuphius, Feb. 6
Barsimaeus, Jan. 30
Bartholomew, June 24, Aug. 24
Barulus, Nov. 18
Basil of Ancyra, Mar. 22
Basil The Great, June 14
Basilides, June 12, June 28
Basiliscus, May 22
Basilissa, Jan. 9, Apr. 15
Bathildes, Jan. 30
Bavo, Oct. 1
Bean, Oct. 26

Beanus, Dec. 16
Beatrice, July 29
Becan, Apr. 5
Beccelin, Sept. 9
Bede, May 27, Oct. 29
Bees, Sept. 6
Bega, Sept. 6
Begga, Dec. 17
Benedict, Mar. 21, May 7
Benedict XI, July 7
Benedict Biscop, Jan. 12
Benedict Joseph Labre, Apr. 16
Benedict of Anian, Feb. 12
Benen, Nov. 9
Benezet, Apr. 14
Benignus, Nov. 1, Nov. 9
Benjamin, Mar. 31
Bennet, Jan. 1
Bernadette Soubirous, Feb. 11
Bernadine of Fossa, Mar. 26
Bernard, Aug. 20
Bernard Ptolemy, Aug. 21
Bernard, Nov. 20
Bernardinè of Siena, May 20
Bertha, July 4
Bertilia, Jan. 3
Bertille, Nov. 5
Bertin, Sept. 5
Bertran, July 3
Besas, Feb. 27
Bettelin, Sept. 9
Beuno, Apr. 21
Bibiana, Dec. 2
Birinus, Dec. 3
Blaan, Aug. 10
Blaesilla, Jan. 22
Blaise, Feb. 3
Blandina, June 2
Babo, May 22
Boisil, Feb. 23
Bolcan, July 4
Bona, Apr. 24
Bonaventure, July 14
Boniface, Mar. 14, May 14,
     June 5, June 19, Oct. 25
Bonitus, Jan. 15
Bonosus, Aug. 21
Botolph, June 17
Braulio, Mar. 26
Breaca, June 4
Brendan the Elder, May 16
Brice, Nov. 13
Bridget, Feb. 1, Oct. 8
Brieuc, May 1
Brihtwald, Jan. 9
Brihtwold, Jan. 22
Brinstan, Nov. 4
Bronacha, Apr. 2
Bruno, July 18, Oct. 6
Brynoth, May 9
Burckard, Oct. 14
Bwian, June 4

C

Cadoc, Jan. 23
Cadocus, Jan. 23
Cadroe, Mar. 6
Caesaria, Jan. 12
Caesarius, Aug. 27, Nov. 1
Caesarius of Nazianius, Feb. 25
Caius, Apr. 22
Cajetan of Thienna, Aug. 7
Calais, July 1
Calixtus, Oct. 14
Callistus, Oct. 14
Camillus De Lellis, July 14
Cammin, Mar. 25
Canice, Oct. 11
Canicus, Oct. 11
Cantianilla, May 31
Cantianus, May 31
Cantius, May 31
Canute, Jan. 7
Canutus, Jan. 19

Caprais, June 1
Caradoc, Apr. 13
Caraunus, May 28
Caro, May 28
Carpus, Apr. 14
Carthage the Younger, May 14
Casimir, Mar. 4
Cassian, Aug. 13
Castus, May 22
Cathan, May 17
Catharine De Ricci, Feb. 13
Catharine of Sweden, Mar. 22
Catherine, Nov. 25
Catherine of Bologna, Mar. 9
Catherine of Genoa, Sept. 14
Catherine of Siena, Apr. 30
Catuldus, May 10
Ceada, Mar. 2
Ceanan, Nov. 24
Cecilia, Nov. 22
Cecilius, June 2
Cecily, Nov. 22
Cedd, Jan. 7
Celestine, Apr. 6
Celsus, Apr. 6, July 28
Ceolfrid, Sept. 25
Ceolwulf, Jan. 15
Cerealus, June 10
Ceslas, July 20
Chad, Mar. 2
Charity, Aug. 1
Charles, Mar. 2
Charles Borromeo, Nov. 4
Chef, Oct. 29
Chelidonius, Mar. 3
Chillen, Nov. 13
Chionia, Apr. 3
Christina, July 24
Christopher, July 25
Chrodegang, Mar. 6
Chromatius, Aug. 11
Chronion, Feb. 27
Chrysanthus, Oct. 25
Chrysogonus, Nov. 24
Chuniald, Sept. 24
Clare, Aug. 12
Clare of Montefalco, Aug. 18
Clarus, Jan. 1, Nov. 4
Claude, June 6
Claudius, Aug. 23
Clement, Nov. 23
Clement Hofbauer, Mar. 15
Clement of Ancyra, Jan. 23
Cletus, Apr. 26
Clodulphus, June 8
Clotilda, June 2
Clotildis, June 2
Clou, June 8
Cloud, Sept. 7
Coeingen, June 3
Colentin, Dec. 12
Colette, Mar. 6
Colman, Feb. 18, June 7,
     Oct. 13, Oct. 29, Dec. 12
Colman Elo, Sept. 26
Columb, Dec. 12
Columba, June 9, Sept. 17,
     Dec. 12, Dec. 31
Columban of Ireland, Nov. 21
Columkille, June 9
Comgall, May 10
Comgan, Oct. 13
Comman, Dec. 26
Conald of Ireland, Sept. 24
Conall, May 22
Conan, Jan. 26
Concordius, Jan. 1
Congall, July 27,
Conon, May 29
Conrad, Nov. 26
Conran, Feb. 14
Constant, Nov. 13
Constantin, July 27
Constantine, Mar. 11
Corbinian, Sept. 8

Corentin, Dec. 12
Cormac, Sept. 14, Dec. 12
Cornelius, Sept. 16
Cosmas, Sept. 27
Cougat, July 25
Crescentia, June 15
Crispin, Oct. 25
Crispinian, Oct. 25
Cronan, Apr. 28
Cucufas, July 25
Cumin, Aug. 19
Cunegundes, Mar. 3, July 24
Cungar, Nov. 27
Cuthbert, Mar. 20
Cuthburge, Aug. 31
Cuthman, Feb. 8
Cybar, July 1
Cyprian, Sept. 16, Sept. 26
Cyriacus, Aug. 8
Cyril, Jan. 28, Mar. 18,
     May 29, July 7, Dec. 22
Cyrus, Jan. 31

D

Dabius, July 22
Dairchilla, June 17
Damasus, Dec. 11
Damhnade, June 13
Damian, Sept. 27
Daniel, Feb. 16, Feb. 21, Nov. 23
Daniel the Stylite, Dec. 11
Darias, Oct. 25
Datius, Jan. 14
Dativa, Dec. 6
Dativus, Feb. 11
David, Mar. 1, July 24, Aug. 9
Darius, July 22
Deicolus, Jan. 18
Delphina, Sept. 27
Denis, Oct. 9
Deodatus, June 19
Deogratias, Mar. 22
Desiderius, May 23
Deusdedit, Aug. 10
Didacus, Nov. 13, Dec. 1
Didymus, Apr. 28
Die, June 19
Diego, Nov. 13
Dionysia, Dec. 6, Dec. 12
Dionysius, July 27, Oct. 9
Dionysius of Corinth, Apr. 8
Dionysius the Areopagite, Oct. 3
Dionysius the Great, Nov. 17
Diser, Sept. 8
Disibode, Sept. 8
Dismas, Mar. 26
Docmael, June 14
Docunus, Nov. 27
Doda, Apr. 24
Domina, Aug. 23
Dominic, Aug. 14
Dominic Loricatus, Oct. 14
Dominic of Sora, Jan. 22
Dominic Savio, Mar. 9
Dominic of Ossory, Feb. 13
Domninus, Oct. 9
Donatian, Feb. 24, Mary 24,
     Oct. 14
Donatus, Aug. 1, Oct. 22
Dorotheus, Sept. 9
Dorotheus of Tyre, June 5
Dorotheus the Theban, June 5
Dorothy, Feb. 6
Dotto, Apr. 9
Droatan, July 11
Droctovaeus, Mar. 10
Drugo, Apr. 16
Druon, Apr. 16
Dubricius, Nov. 14
Dumhade of Ireland, May 25
Dunstan, May 19
Duthak, Mar. 8
Dympna, May 15

E

Eadbert, May 6
Eadburghe, Dec. 12
Eadgith, Sept. 16
Eanswide, Sept. 12
Ebba, Apr. 2, Aug. 25
Edana, July 5
Edaena, July 5
Edberge, June 20
Elburge, Dec. 21
Edelbirge, Oct. 11
Edelburga, July 7
Edelward, Mar. 23
Editha, Sept. 16
Edmund, Nov. 16, Nov. 20
Edward, Mar. 18, Oct. 13
Edwin, Oct. 4
Egbert, Apr. 27
Egbin, Oct. 19
Egwin, Jan. 11
Eingan, Apr. 21
Elesbaan, Oct. 27
Eleusippus, Jan. 17
Eleutherius, Feb. 20, Sept. 6
Elias, Feb. 16
Elier, July 16
Eligius, Dec. 1
Elizabeth, June 18, July 8,
  Nov. 5
Elizabeth of Hungary, Nov. 19
Eloy, Dec. 1
Elphege, Apr. 19
Elutharius, May 26
Elzear, Sept. 27
Emebert, Jan. 15
Emeterius, Mar. 3
Emiliana, Dec. 24
Emma, June 29
Emmeran, Sept. 22
Eneratis, Apr. 16
Engratia, Apr. 16
Enna, Mar. 21
Ennodus, July 17
Ephraim the Syrian, June 18
Ephrem of Edessa, July 9
Ephysius, Jan. 15
Epimachus, Dec. 12
Epiphanius, Jan. 21, May 12
Epipodius, Apr. 22
Equitius, Aug. 11
Erasmus, June 2
Erasmus of Elme, Nov. 25
Erconwald, Apr. 30, Nov. 14,
  Dec. 10
Erementiana, Jan. 23
Erhard, Jan. 8, Feb. 9
Eric, May 18
Erluph, Feb. 10
Erminold, Jan. 6
Erthad, Aug. 24
Eskill, June 12
Ethbin, Oct. 19
Ethelbert, Feb. 24, Feb. 26,
  May 20
Ethelburge, Oct. 11
Etheldreda, June 23
Etheldritha, Aug. 2
Ethelwolf, Aug. 1
Euatachius, Apr. 14
Eubulus, Mar. 5
Eucherius, Feb. 20, Nov. 16
Eugendus, Jan. 1
Eugenia, Dec. 25
Eugenius, July 13, Aug. 23,
  Nov. 15
Eulalia, Feb. 12
Eulogius, Sept. 13
Eulogius of Cordova, Mar. 11
Eunan, Sept. 7
Euphemia, Sept. 16
Euphrasia, Mar. 13
Euplius, Aug. 12
Eupsychius, Apr. 9
Eusebius, Jan. 23, Jan. 31,

June 21, Aug. 14, Sept. 8,
  Sept. 26, Dec. 15
Eustaches, Sept. 20
Eustasius, Mar. 29
Eustathius, July 16
Eustochium, Sept. 28
Eustochius, Sept. 19
Euthymius, Jan. 20
Eutropius, Jan. 12
Eutychius, Oct. 5
Euxuperius, Sept. 28
Evaristus, Oct. 26
Everilidis, July 9
Evre, Sept. 15
Evroul, Dec. 29
Evurtius, Sept. 7
Ewald, Oct. 3

F

Fabian, Jan. 20
Faith, Aug. 1, Oct. 6
Fanchea, Jan. 1
Fara, Dec. 7
Faro, Oct. 28
Faustinus, Feb. 15, July 29
Faustus, Oct. 13
Fechin, Jan. 20
Fedlimid, Aug. 9
Felan, Jan. 9
Felician, Jan. 23
Felicianus, June 9
Felicitas, Mar. 7, July 10
Felimy, Aug. 9
Felix, Mar. 8, July 7, July 12,
  July 29, Aug. 30, Sept. 1,
  Sept. 10, Oct. 24
Felix I, May 30
Felix of Bourges, Jan. 1
Felix of Cantalicia, May 21
Felix of Nola, Jan. 14
Felix of Valois, Dec. 9
Ferdinand III, May 30
Ferreol, Sept. 18
Ferreolus, June 16
Ferriolus, Jan. 4, Jan. 16
Ferrutius, June 16
Fiachna, Apr. 29
Fiacra, Sept. 1
Fiaker, Aug. 30
Fidelis of Sigmaringen, Apr. 24
Fides, Oct. 6
Fidharleus of Ireland, Oct. 1
Finbar, July 4
Finbarr, Sept. 25
Fingar, Dec. 14
Finian, Mar. 16, Apr. 7,
  Sept. 10, Dec. 2, Dec. 12
Finnan, Feb. 17
Fintan, Feb. 17
Fintan Munno, Oct. 21
Firman, Sept. 25
Firbinus, Sept. 1
Flan, Dec. 15
Flannan, Dec. 16
Flavia Domitilla, May 12
Flavian, Feb. 17, Feb. 24
Flora, Nov. 24
Florence, Dec. 15
Florentius, Jan. 3
Flour, Nov. 3
Foillan, Oct. 31
Fortunatus, Sept. 1, Nov. 1
Frances of Rome, Mar. 9
Frances Xavier Cabrini, Dec. 22
Francis Borgia, Oct. 10
Francis Caracciolo, June 4
Francis de Sales, Jan. 29
Francis Geronimo, May 26
Francis of Assisi, Oct. 4
Francis of Paula, Apr. 2
Francis Solano, July 24
Francis Xavier, Dec. 3
Frederick, July 18
Frideswide, Oct. 19

Fridian, Mar. 18
Fridolin, Mar. 6
Frobert, Jan. 8
Frodobertus, Jan. 8
Fructuosis, Jan. 21, Apr. 16
Frumentius, Oct. 27
Fulgentius, Jan. 1
Fursey, Jan. 16
Fuscian, Dec. 11

G

Gabinus, Feb. 19
Gabriel Possenti, Feb. 27
Gabriel the Archangel, Mar. 24
Gal, July 1
Galdin, Apr. 18
Gall, Oct. 16
Galla, Oct. 5
Galmier, Feb. 27
Gamaliel, Aug. 3
Garibaldus, Jan. 8
Garthagh, May 14
Gaspar del Bufalo, Dec. 28
Gatian, Dec. 18
Gaucher, Apr. 9
Gaudentius of Brescia, Oct. 25
Gaugericus, Aug. 11
Gelasinus, Aug. 26
Gelasius, Nov. 21
Gemtian, Dec. 11
Genebern, May 15
Genebrard, May 15
Genevieve, Jan. 3
Genesius, June 3, Aug. 26
Genou, Jan. 17
Genovefa, Jan. 3
Genulfus, Jan. 17
George, Apr. 23
Georges, Feb. 19
Gerald, Mar. 13, Apr. 5, Oct. 13
Gerard, Apr. 23, Sept. 24,
  Oct. 3
Gerard Majela, Oct. 16
Geremar, Sept. 24
Gerlac, Jan. 5
Germaine Cousin, June 15
German, Feb. 21
Germana, Sept. 7
Germanicus, Jan. 19
Germanus, May 12, May 28,
  July 26, Oct. 30
Germer, Sept. 24
Germianus, Sept. 16
Germinianus, Jan. 31
Gertrude, Mar. 17, Nov. 15
Gervasius, June 19
Gery, Aug. 11
Getulius, June 10
Gilbert, Feb. 4, Feb. 14,
  Apr. 1
Giles, Sept. 1
Gildard, June 8
Gildas, Jan. 29
Goar, July 6
Gobain of Ireland, June 20
Gobrian, May 8
Godard, May 4, June 8
Godeschalc, June 7
Godfrey, Nov. 8
Godrick, May 21
Gomer, Oct. 11
Gontran, Mar. 28
Gordian, May 10
Gordius, Jan. 3
Gorgonius, Sept. 9
Gregory, Jan. 4, Feb. 16,
  Aug. 25, Sept. 30
Gregory II, Feb. 13
Gregory VII, May 25
Gregory Nazianzen, May 9
Gregory of Nyssa, Mar. 9
Gregory of Tours, Nov. 17
Gregory Thaumaturgus, Nov.
  17

Lewis Gonzaga, June 21
Liafwin, Nov. 12
Liberatus, Aug. 17
Liborius, July 23
Licinius, Feb. 13
Lifard, June 3
Limneus, Feb. 22
Linus, Sept. 23
Lioba, Sept. 28
Livin, Nov. 12
Lo, Sept. 22
Lollianus, Dec. 9
Loman, Feb. 17
Lomer, Jan. 19
Louis, Aug. 25
Louis Marie Grignion, Apr. 28
Luan, June 25
Luanus, Aug. 4
Lucia, Sept. 16
Lucian, Jan. 7, Jan. 8, Oct. 26
Lucius, Feb. 24, Mar. 4, Sept. 10, Oct. 19, Dec. 3
Lucy, Sept. 19, Dec. 13
Ludger, Mar. 26
Lufthild, Jan. 23
Lugid, Aug. 4
Luican, July 27
Luke the Evangelist, Oct. 18
Lullon, Oct. 16
Lullus, Oct. 16
Luman, Feb. 17
Lupus, July 24
Lupus of Leu, Sept. 1

M

Macanisius, Sept. 10
Macarius of Alexandria, Jan. 2
Macarius, The Elder, Jan. 16
Maccai, Apr. 11
Mac-cartin, Aug. 15
Macculindus, Sept. 6
Macedonius, Jan. 24
Machrina, July 19
Mackessoge, Mar. 10
Maclou, Nov. 15
Macnisius, Sept. 3
Macrina the Elder, Jan. 14
Macull, Apr. 25
Madelberte, Sept. 7
Madeleine Sophie Barat, May 25
Madelgisilus, May 30
Maden, May 17
Madern, May 17
Magliore, Oct. 24
Magnus, Apr. 16
Maguil, May 30
Mahanes, Nov. 30
Maharsapor, Nov. 27
Maieul, May 11
Maimbod, Jan. 23
Majolus, May 11
Malachy, Nov. 3
Malard, Jan. 15
Malchus, Mar. 28, July 27
Malo, Nov. 15
Malrubius, Apr. 21, Aug. 27
Mamas, Aug. 17
Mammertus, May 11
Mans, Apr. 16
Mansuet, Sept. 3
Mansuetus, Feb. 19
Marcella, Jan. 31
Marcellianus, June 18
Marcellina, July 17
Marcellinus, Apr. 26, June 2
Marcellus, Jan. 16, Sept. 4, Oct. 7, Nov. 1, Dec. 29
Marcellus the Centurion, Oct. 30
Marcian, Jan. 10, June 17, Oct. 4, Oct. 26, Nov. 2
Marciana, Jan. 9
Marcou, May 1

Marculfus, May 1
Marcus, June 18, Oct. 4
Margaret, Feb. 3, June 10, July 20
Margaret Mary Alacoque, Oct. 17
Margaret of Cortona, Feb. 22
Maria Crocifissa di Rosa, Dec. 15
Marian, Apr. 30
Mariana, June 18
Marina, June 18
Marinus, Mar. 3
Marius, Jan. 19, Jan. 27
Mark, Mar. 29, Apr. 25, Oct. 7, Oct. 22
Marman, Mar. 2
Maro, Feb. 14
Martha, Jan. 19, July 29
Martial, June 30
Martialis, Oct. 13
Martin, Nov. 11, Nov. 12
Martina, Jan. 30
Martinian, July 2, July 27
Martinianus, Feb. 13
Martyrius, May 29
Mary, Mar. 15, Nov. 1, Nov. 24
Mary Magdalen of Pazzi, May 25
Mary Magdalene, July 22
Mary Magdalen Postel, May 24
Mary of Egypt, Apr. 9
Mary of Oignies, June 23
Matthias, Feb. 24
Mathildis, Mar. 14
Mathurin, Nov. 9
Matthew, Sept. 21
Maud, Mar. 14
Maura, Sept. 21
Maurice, Sept. 22
Maurilius, Sept. 13
Mauront, May 5
Maurus, Jan. 15
Maw, May 17
Maxentia of Ireland, Nov. 20
Maxentius, June 26
Maximian, July 27
Maximilian, Mar. 12, Aug. 21
Maximinus, Jan. 25, June 8
Maximus, Apr. 14, Apr. 30, May 25, May 29, June 25, Nov. 27, Dec. 30
Medard, June 8
Medericus, Aug. 29
Meen, June 21
Meinrad, Jan. 21
Melania, Dec. 31
Melanius, Jan. 6
Melchiades, Dec. 10
Meletius, Feb. 12
Meleusippus, Jan. 17
Melito, Apr. 1
Mellitus, Apr. 24
Mello, Oct. 22
Memmius, Aug. 5
Mennas, Nov. 11
Mercutia, Dec. 12
Meriadec, June 7
Merri, Aug. 29
Methodius, July 7, Sept. 18, Dec. 22
Meuris, Dec. 19
Michael, May 14
Michael the Archangel, Sept. 29
Mida, Jan. 15
Milburge, Feb. 23
Mildgytha, Jan. 17
Mildred, Feb. 20
Milles, Nov. 10
Miltiades, Dec. 10
Mineve, July 22
Mitrius, Nov. 13
Mochemomoc, Mar. 13
Mochteus, Aug. 19

Modan, Feb. 4
Modestus, June 15
Modomnoc, Feb. 13
Modwena, July 5
Molingus, June 17
Moloc, June 25
Mommolin, Oct. 16
Monan, Mar. 1
Monegondes, July 2
Monica, May 4
Moninna of Mount Cullen, July 6
Monon, Oct. 18
Montanus, Feb. 24
Mummelin, Oct. 16
Munchin, Jan. 2
Munde, Apr. 15
Mungho, Jan. 13
Muredach, Aug. 12

N

Nabor, June 12, July 12
Narcissius, Dec. 14
Narcissus, Oct. 29
Narses, Nov. 30
Nathalan, Jan. 19
Nathy, Aug. 9
Nazarius, June 12, July 28
Nehemias of Ireland, June 14
Nemecianus, Sept. 10
Nemesion, Dec. 19
Nennoca, June 4
Nennus, June 14
Nenook, June 4
Neon, Aug. 23
Neot, Oct. 28,
Nereus, May 12
Nessan, Dec. 1
Nestor, Feb. 27, Sept. 8
Nestorius, Sept. 8
Nicander, June 17
Nicephorus, Feb. 9, Mar. 13
Nicetas, Apr. 3, Sept. 15
Nicetius, Apr. 2, Dec. 4
Nicholas, May 9, Dec. 6
Nicholas of Tolentine, Sept. 10
Nicodemus, Aug. 3
Nicomedes, Sept. 15
Nicon Metanoite, Nov. 26
Nilus, Nov. 12
Nilus the Younger, Sept. 26
Ninian, Sept. 16
Nissen, July 25
Norbert, June 6
Nunilo, Oct. 22
Nympha, Nov. 10
Nynias, Sept. 16

O

Odilo, Jan. 1
Odo, July 4, Nov. 18
Odrian, May 8
Odulph, July 18
Oduvald, May 26
Olaus, July 29
Olon, Jan. 1
Olympias, Dec. 17
Omer, June 20, Sept. 9
Onesimus, Feb. 16
Onuphrius, June 12
Opportuna, Apr. 22
Optatus, Apr. 16, June 4
Osith, Oct. 7
Osmanna, Sept. 9
Osmund, Dec. 4
Oswald, Feb. 29, Aug. 5
Oswin, Aug. 20
Othilia, Dec. 13
Otho, July 2
Otteran, Oct. 27
Oudoceus, July 2
Ouen, Aug. 24

P

Pachomius, May 14
Pacian, Mar. 9
Palaemon, Jan. 11
Palladius, July 6
Pambo of Nitria, Sept. 6
Pammarchus, Aug. 30
Pamphilus, Feb. 16, June 1
Pancras, May 12
Pantaenus, July 7
Pantaleon, July 27
Paphnutius, Sept. 11
Papoul, Nov. 3
Papulus, Nov. 3
Paragrus, Dec. 9
Paregorius, Feb. 18
Paschal Baylon, May 17
Pascharius Radbert, Apr. 26
Paschasia, Jan. 9
Pastor, Aug. 6, Aug. 27
Pa-termuthes, Sept. 19
Paternus, Apr. 15
Patiens, Jan. 8, Sept. 11
Patricius, Apr. 28
Patrick, Mar. 17
Patroclus, Jan. 21
Paul, Feb. 8, Mar. 7, Mar. 12,
　　Mar. 22, June 7, June 26,
　　June 30, July 25, Dec. 20
Paul of the Cross, Apr. 28
Paul, the first hermit, Jan. 15
Paula, Jan. 26
Paulinus, Jan. 28, Oct. 10
Paulinus of Nola, June 22
Pega, Jan. 8
Pelagia, June 9, Oct. 8
Peleus, Sept. 19
Pellegrini, Aug. 1
Peregrinus, Aug. 1
Perpetua, Mar. 7
Peter, Apr. 29, May 8, May 15,
　　June 2, June 29, Nov. 26
Peter Arbues, Sept. 17
Peter Balsam, Jan. 3
Peter Canisius, Apr. 26
Peter Celestine, May 19
Peter Chanel, Apr. 28
Peter Chrysogonus, Dec. 4
Peter Claver, Sept. 9
Peter Fourier, Dec. 9
Peter Gonzales, Apr. 15
Peter Nolasco, Jan. 31
Peter of Alcantara, Oct. 19
Peter of Luxemburg, July 5
Peter of Pisa, June 1
Peter of Sebaste, Jan. 9
Peter Paschal, Dec. 6
Peter Regalati, May 13
Peter Thomas, Jan. 6
Peter Urseolus, Jan. 10
Petroc, June 4
Petronilla, May 31
Phaebadius, Apr. 25
Pharaildis, Jan. 4
Philastrius, July 18
Phileas, Feb. 4
Philemon, Mar. 8, Nov. 22
Philibert, Aug. 22
Philip, May 1, June 6, Oct. 22
Philip Beniti, Aug. 23
Philip Neri, May 26
Philip of Jesus, Feb. 5, Mar. 5
Philogonius, Dec. 20
Philoromus, Feb. 4
Philothea, Dec. 9
Phocas, July 3
Piat, Oct. 1
Pionius, Feb. 1
Pius I, July 11
Pius V, May 5
Pius X, Aug. 20
Placidus, Oct. 5
Plato, Apr. 4
Plechelm, July 15

Plutarch, June 28
Poemen, Aug. 27
Pollio, Apr. 28
Polycarp, Jan. 26
Polyeuctus, Feb. 13
Pontian, Nov. 19
Pontius, May 14
Poppo, Jan. 25
Porpherius, Feb. 16
Porphyrius, Feb. 26
Possidius, May 17
Potamon, May 18
Pothinus, June 2
Potitus, Jan. 13
Potomiana, June 28
Praejectus, Jan. 25
Praxedes, July 21
Pretextatus, Feb. 24
Primolus, Feb. 24
Primus, June 9
Prior, June 17
Prisca, Jan. 18
Priscilla, Jan. 16
Priscus, Mar. 28
Prix, Feb. 24
Probus, Oct. 11
Processus, July 2
Proclus, Oct. 24
Procopius, July 8
Prosdecimus, Nov. 7
Prosper of Aquitain, June 25
Protasius, June 19
Proterius, Feb. 28
Protus, Sept. 11
Prudentius, Apr. 6
Psalmod, Mar. 8
Psalmodius of Ireland, June 14
Ptolomy, Oct. 19
Publius, Jan. 25
Pudentiana, May 19
Pulcheria, Sept. 10
Pulcherius, Mar. 13

Q

Quadratus, May 26
Quintin, Oct. 31
Quiricus, June 16
Quirinus, June 4, June 12

R

Radbod, Nov. 29
Radegundes, Aug. 13
Ralph, June 21
Randaut, Feb. 21
Raymond Nonnatus, Aug. 31
Raymund of Pennafort, Jan. 23
Regimus, Jan. 19
Regina, Sept. 7
Regulus, Mar. 30
Reine, Sept. 7
Reinold, Jan. 7
Remaclus, Sept. 3
Rembert, Feb. 4
Remigius, Oct. 1
Repositus, Sept. 1
Respicius, Nov. 10
Rhenus, Feb. 24
Richard, Feb. 7, Apr. 3, June 9,
　　Aug. 21
Richarius, Apr. 26
Richimirus, Jan. 17
Rictrudes, May 12
Rieul, Mar. 30
Rigobert, Jan. 4
Rita, May 22
Robert, Jan. 4, Mar. 27, Apr. 29,
　　June 7
Robert Bellarmine, May 13
Roch, Aug. 16
Rogatian, May 24
Roger, Mar. 5
Romaric, Dec. 8
Romuald, Feb. 7

Rosa of Viterbo, Sept. 4
Rosalia, Sept. 4
Rose of Lima, Aug. 30
Rose of Viterbo, Mar. 8
Rotiri, Sept. 24
Rouen, Sept. 17
Romanus, Feb. 28, July 24,
　　Aug. 9, Oct. 23, Nov. 18,
　　Dec. 9
Ruadhan, Apr. 15
Ruffin, July 24
Rufina, July 10, July 20
Rufinus, June 14
Rufus, Apr. 22, Dec. 18
Rumold, July 1
Rumwald, Nov. 3
Rupert, Mar. 27
Rusticus, Sept. 24

S

Sabas, Jan. 14, Dec. 4
Sabas the Goth, Apr. 12
Sabina, Aug. 29
Sabinas, Jan. 17
Sabinianus, Jan. 29, Sept. 1
Sabinus, Dec. 30
Sabrinianus, Sept. 1
Sadoth, Feb. 20
Saethryth, Jan. 10
Salvinus, Oct. 12
Salvius, Jan. 11, Sept. 10
Sampson, July 28
Samuel, Feb. 16
Sanctus, June 2
Sapor, Nov. 30
Saturas, Mar. 29
Saturninus, Feb. 11, Nov. 29
Satyrus, Sept. 1
Sauve, Jan. 11
Scholastica, Feb. 10
Seachnal, Nov. 27
Sebastian, Jan. 20
Sebba, Aug. 29
Sebbi, Aug. 29
Secunda, July 10
Secundin, Nov. 27
Seine, Sept. 19
Senan, Mar. 8
Sennen, July 30
Septimeus, Sept. 1
Sequanes, Sept. 19
Serapion, Mar. 21
Serapion, July 27
Serenus, Feb. 23
Serf, Apr. 20
Sergius, Oct. 7
Servatius, May 13
Servulus, Dec. 23
Sethrida, Jan. 10
Severianus, Feb. 21
Severin, Oct. 23
Severinus, Feb. 11
Severnus, Jan. 8
Sexburgh, July 6
Sidronius, Sept. 8
Sigebert, Feb. 1
Sigefride, Feb. 15
Sigfrid, Feb. 15
Sigismund, May 1
Silan, May 17
Silvae, May 17
Silverius, June 20
Silvin of Auchy, Feb. 17
Simeon, Feb. 18, Apr. 17,
　　Nov. 30
Simeon Salus, July 1
Simeon Stylites, Jan. 5
Simeon Stylites the Younger,
　　Sept. 3
Simon, Mar. 24
Simon Stock, May 16
Simon of Zealot, Oct. 28
Simplicius, Mar. 2, July 29
Sina, Nov. 10

Index

(Book One & Book Two)